Funeral Rites Reformation for Any African Ethnic Community Based on the Proposed New Funeral Practices for the Agikuyu

Funeral Rites Reformation for Any African Ethnic Community Based on the Proposed New Funeral Practices for the Agikuyu

Johnson Nganga Mbugua

Foreword by Mary N. Getui

RESOURCE *Publications* · Eugene, Oregon

FUNERAL RITES REFORMATION FOR ANY AFRICAN ETHNIC COMMUNITY BASED ON THE PROPOSED NEW FUNERAL PRACTICES FOR THE AGIKUYU

Copyright © 2016 Johnson Nganga Mbugua. All rights reserved. Except for brief quotations in critical publications or reviews, no part of this book may be reproduced in any manner without prior written permission from the publisher. Write: Permissions, Wipf and Stock Publishers, 199 W. 8th Ave., Suite 3, Eugene, OR 97401.

Resource Publications
An Imprint of Wipf and Stock Publishers
199 W. 8th Ave., Suite 3
Eugene, OR 97401

www.wipfandstock.com

PAPERBACK ISBN: 978-1-4982-9090-6
HARDCOVER ISBN: 978-1-4982-9092-0
EBOOK ISBN: 978-1-4982-9091-3

Manufactured in the U.S.A.

To all Africans including the Agikuyu living and dead who are the subject of this book.

Also to all Christians the world over who might find this study helpful in coping with the death of their loved ones.

Finally to theologians, scholars, students, researchers, pastors, academic institutions and other readers who might find this study useful.

May the Almighty God shower His blessings on you all.

SYNOPSIS

THIS BOOK HAS BEEN written on the premise that the mode of coping with death of virtually all African ethnic communities have taken proportions and turns that are neither cultural, scriptural nor necessary. Current rites are complicated, time consuming, expensive and are leaving most families and their neighbors improvised. They have been extremely commercialised and a large number of African families simply do not have land and resources sufficient to bury their dead the "modern" way. Were the Agikuyu (read Africans) to curb numerous funeral demands which they deem necessary and "customary", when in actual fact they are not, funerals for them would become cheaper, faster, simpler and at the same time would be decent enough for the dead. Additionally, it would take care of those left behind, would be environmentally friendly and would bring glory to God. The issue of how African diaspora away from their ancestral homeland should cope with death is also addressed. Additionally the issue of cremation or the destruction of the human body by any other means e.g. being eaten by wild beasts or at worst cannibalism has been addressed and analysed. It is shown in the book that none of these will hinder the all powerful God at the resurrection according to us new "spiritual" i.e. "immortal" bodies which it should be noted will have no bearing whatsoever with the material substance of our earthly (mortal) body; whether one is cremated or not God will give us spiritual bodies.

I trust that this book will be of immense benefit to the Academia, Researchers, the Clergy, the Laity, the African Diaspora as well as to all Christians the world over.

Dr Johnson N. Mbugua

MTh cum laude, PhD (Theology) SATS.
KIKUYU TOWN, KENYA.

CONTENTS

LIST OF FIGURES | xv

LIST OF TABLES | xvi

FOREWORD BY MARY N. GETUI | xvii

ACKNOWLEDGMENTS | xix

LIST OF ABBREVIATIONS | xxi

CHAPTER 1: INTRODUCTION | 1

Burial and Accompanying Funeral Rites · 1

Purpose of the study · 6

Problem Statement · 6

Objectives of the study · 6

Research Questions · 7

Significance of the Study · 8

Scope of the Study · 9

Limitations and Delimitations · 9

The Current State of Scholarship · 9

Methodology · 12

CHAPTER 2: TRADITIONAL FUNERAL PRACTICES OF THE AGIKUYU INCLUDING A FEW OTHER AFRICAN TRIBES AND SOME RELIGIOUS FAITH | 15

The Agikuyu · 17

Origin of the Agikuyu · 18

Agikuyu Society and Culture · 19

Relationship of the Agikuyu with their Neighbors especially the Maasai · 25

The Kikuyu Traditional Religion · 28

The Agikuyu Ancestral Spirits (Ngoma) · 32

Agikuyu Traditional Burial Rites · 36

Death Ceremonies—Members of the Agikuyu Guild · 38

Death Ceremonies of an Elder—Agikuyu Guild · 38

Extramarital Sex, Sex Taboos and Some Other Aspects Of Agikuyu Sex Life That Were Observed in the Past but not Presently · 48

Disposal of the Dead—Agikuyu Guild—Others · 51

Disposal—Abnormal Deaths of Kikuyu Guild Members · 52

The Ukabi (Maasai) Guild Burials and Accompanying Rites · 53

Summary of the Kikuyu Rites Concerning Death · 55

Traditional Funeral Rites of Selected African Tribes · 57

Akamba View of Death and Their Burial Rites · 58

Kenya—Gusii Tribe · 58

Tanzania—Sukuma People · 60

Ghana—The Ga-Adangbe People · 62

Nigeria—The Urhobo People · 63

English Funeral Rites · 64

Some Examples of Bizarre Funeral Rites and Practices · 67

Zoroastrians of Persia and India Funeral Practices · 67

Funeral Rites—The Poor of the Philippines · 70

Funeral Rites of Other Religions · 71

Judaism Funeral Rites · 71

Islamic (Muslim) Funeral Rites · 73

Hindu Funeral Rites · 74

Buddhist Funerals · 76

Humanist Funeral Ceremonies · 77

Economy of Burial Grounds · 78

The City of Paris · 78

Italy · 79

West Germany · 79

Mexico · 79

Final Observation about Future Cemetery Space · 80

CHAPTER 3: PRESENT-DAY BURIAL RITES OF THE AGIKUYU CHRISTIANS | 82

Introduction · 82

Changes that have Taken Place over the Last 120 Years to the Agikuyu Methods of Disposing of the Dead · 82

Noticeable Development of Agikuyu Funeral Rites since Independence (1963) · 96

Present-day Agikuyu Funeral Rites · 97

Recent Development Touching on Modern Agikuyu Christian Funeral Rites · 107

CHAPTER 4: BURIAL IN THE BIBLICAL PERIOD | 109

Introduction and Methodology · 109

Burial in the Biblical Period · 116

Burial of Patriarchs and Matriarchs—Old Testament · 116

Burial of other Biblical Patriarchs and Matriarchs · 119

Burial During the Period of the Exodus and Conquest Generations · 121

Burial During the Period of the Judges · 122

Burial During the Monarchic Period · 122

The Pentateuchal Legislation on Burial and Mourning · 126

Burial Practices—Israel in Palestine · 126

Burial Practices in the New Testament · 127

Summary of the Biblical Rites of Burial and Burial Customs · 132

Conclusion · 135

CHAPTER 5: BURIAL RITES FOR THE EARLY CHRISTIANS FROM 33 AD TO 600 AD, AND ALSO DURING THE MIDDLE AGES | 137

Introduction · 137

Synopsis of Early Christianity · 138

Early Christian Burial Rites · 145

Introduction · 145

Acts Performed Before Death—Early Christianity · 147

Acts Performed Soon After Death · 149

Clothing of the Dead · 151

Crowning the Dead and Significance of Crowns
in Early Christianity · 153

The Wake Held Over the Dead · 155

The Funeral Procession · 159

The Singing of Psalms during the Christian Procession · 162

Interment and Why the Early Christians Were Against
Various Pagan Practices · 163

The Christian Vale · 166

Place and Mode of Burial · 167

Christian Burial From the Middle Ages · 172

Conclusion · 173

CHAPTER 6: THE ISSUES OF THE RESURRECTION AND OF THE RESURRECTED BODY | 175

Introduction · 175

The Concept of Resurrection and its Development among
the Jews and Christians · 176

Resurrection—the Biblical Teaching · 180

Centrality of Resurrection in the New Testament · 185

Denials of Resurrection · 187

The Resurrection of Believers and the Resurrected Body · 188

Conclusion · 192

CHAPTER 7: CRITICAL CORRELATION OF THE STUDY | 195

A Table Offering a Visual Summary and Correlation of the Funeral
Practices of the Various Traditions Discussed in this Study · 196

Regarding this Chapter · 202

How the Idea of Burial Arose · 203

Actions Performed Before Death · 205

Actions Done Soon After Death · 209

Clothing of the Dead · 211

Crowning the Dead · 213

The Wake Held Over the Dead · 214

Mourning · 216

Funeral Procession and Time of Burial · 218

Interment · 220

Place of Burial · 224

Rituals Performed After Burial · 227

Life After Death · 231

Economy of Burial Grounds and Spaces · 233

The Chapter that Follows · 233

CHAPTER 8: RECOMMENDATIONS, CONCLUSION, AREAS OF FURTHER RESEARCH AND CONTRIBUTION TO THE FIELD OF PRACTICAL THEOLOGY | 234

Introduction · 234

Recommendation Towards Formulating A Model For Agikuyu Christians' and other African ethnic communities Funeral Rites That Integrates Relevant Cultural, Scriptural and Practical Norms · 236

Range of Recommendations · 242

Legal Aspect · 242

Acts to be performed before death including leaving a will, and similar · 242

Indicating how and where one wishes to be buried · 243

Fear of death · 243

Respect to the Body · 244

Acts to be performed soon after death · 245

Same day as death funeral or an immediate funeral · 246

Planning of Burial if it will take place a few days or weeks after death · 249

Planning for the burial of those who die far from home, especially outside the country · 251

Simplifying Funeral Procedures, Reducing Costs and Adopting Alternative Funeral Practices · 253

Simplicity · 254

Mortuary · 254

Delaying Burial · 255

Announcements · 255

Clothing the dead · 256

Funeral procession · 257

Funeral photographs and Videos · 257

Taking the body to Church · 258

Cost · 259

Graves · 262

Tombstones · 264

Flowers · 265

Feeding mourners · 265

Giving to the poor · 265

Cremation · 265

Unveiling the Cross · 267

Conclusion · 268

Areas of Further Research · 269

Similarity between the traditional funeral practices for the Wa Sukuma of Tanzania and the Agikuyu of Kenya · 269

The issue of widows succumbing to tradition · 269

Before the current High God (Ngai or Mwene Nyagah) of the Agikuyu which was their Deity? · 270

Resurgence of diseases from entombed corpses · 271

How This Study Contributes to the Field of Practical Theology · 271

APPENDIX I: Saturday Nation—National News: October 10, 2009, Page 9 | 1

APPENDIX II: Respondents Interviewed Regarding The Kikuyu Culture, Tradition, Religion and Traditional Funeral Rites | 275

WORKS CITED | 279

FIGURES

Figure 1: The layout of a traditional Agikuyu homestead of a man with four wives | 94

Figure 2: The layout of a traditional Agikuyu homestead of a man with four wives, a widowed mother and three married sons | 95

TABLES

Table 1: Death Announcement charges by a leading newspaper in Kenya | 106

Table 2: Charges of Announcement of appreciation and memorials on death by the same leading Kenya newspaper. | 106

FOREWORD

I am grateful to Dr. Johnson N. Mbugua, PhD, for asking me to write the preface to this book. It is an opportunity to gain new insights on a sensitive and albeit, controversial subject—death, with particular reference to funeral rites.

Mbugua's approach is commendable in that he has focused on a specific African community, namely the Agikuyu. To enlarge the horizon he has incorporated selected communities from across Africa and also from other religious traditions. While this is not a comparative study, the insights outside the Agikuyu go to show that beliefs regarding death and the accompanying rites are not unique to the Agikuyu but are a universal concern.

Mbugua has also provided a detailed account on burial as covered in the Bible, the burial rites in early Christianity and also during the Middle Ages. This serves him well as reference points when it comes to providing his own insights on what ought to prevail for the contemporary Agikuyu. Mbugua highlights the changes and challenges on the Agikuyu indigenous practices by indicating the contemporary and prevailing funeral rites as carried out by Agikuyu Christians. Going by the quantity and quality of references, there is no doubt that he has read widely on death and funeral rites. The voices of opinion leaders are included.

The model Mbugua is recommending on how and why the Agikuyu Christians should conduct funerals is revolutionary, justified, common sense and practical. Indeed, there are new dimensions on how Christian funerals are conducted in Africa which have no cultural or Christian basis. For example, there is a commercial angle that is determined by the deceased or bereaved social, religious or political standing. Could this be a wave that cannot be stopped because of the dynamics of cultural change? It should also be borne in mind that the contemporary Agikuyu Christians may be performing certain funeral rites as therapeutic mechanisms of coping with death, or simply following the crowd because in moments of bereavement the chief mourners could have minimal or limited say or control.

While many of the ideas raised in this book apply to the Agikuyu Christians, the principles put forth by Mbugua are of relevance in other parts of Africa where the encounter between culture and Christianity and the globalization realities necessitates the need for searching for a common and friendly ground where the fullness of life can be realized.

Prof Mary N. Getui, Ph.D

Professor, Religious Studies Department
The Catholic University of Eastern Africa
Nairobi, Kenya
March 2016

ACKNOWLEDGMENTS

To God Almighty who gave me life and the ability to accomplish this task.

To MY PhD DISSERTATION supervisor at SATS (The South African Theological Seminary) Dr Kevin Gary Smith (DLitt; PhD) whose guidance was invaluable in the accomplishment of my PhD study. To the assistance and understanding I received during my MTh and PhD programmes at SATS, from the Principal Dr. Reuben David van Rensburg PhD, who authorized a partial scholarship for me when my studies almost came to a halt due to a cash flow problem I was facing near the completion of my doctoral programme. Also my thanks and appreciation goes to the Faculty and Staff at SATS who were there when needed and they never stepped back.

My darling wife Dr Naomi W Mbugua PhD and our children Waithera, Nyokabi, Dr Njeri and Njoki who gave me love, support and encouragement during my MTh and PhD studies at SATS and during the time of preparing this book for publication. To my sons-in-law for their moral support.

My gratitude and appreciation goes to the Chief Librarians and Staff of Tangaza College, Nairobi; The Catholic University of Eastern Africa (CUEA), Nairobi; Africa International University (NEGST), Nairobi; Saint Paul's University, Limuru and Daystar University, Nairobi. Also to the personnel of Kenya National Archives, Nairobi, Kenya.

My sincere thanks to my respondents and to all those who gave me assistance and their views on numerous issues that were required in the completion of my PhD dissertation culminating in the writing of this book.

To numerous academic and pastoral giants whose input is invaluable in the emergence of this book, including Professor M N Getui PhD, Professor, Department of Religious Studies and Director, Quality Assurance, The Catholic University of Eastern Africa, Nairobi, Kenya, (who has written the preface to this book). Others whose endorsements appears on the back cover of this book, are Professor JJ Kritzinger DD, Emeritus, Pretoria University and Research Fellow Free State University, South Africa; Professor Christopher Byaruhanga, ThD, Professor of Historical and Systematic Theology and

Dean of the School of Research and Postgraduate Studies, Uganda Christian University; Dr. Kevin Gary Smith (DLitt; PhD), Vice Principal and Academic Head, South African Theological Seminary (SATS); The Right Rev Peter Karioki Njenga, Retired Provost, ACK All Saints Cathedral, Nairobi & as Bishop ACK Diocese of Mount Kenya South; Professor Faith Nguru PhD, Deputy Vice Chancellor(Academic), Riara University, Nairobi Kenya. Finally but not least to my Publishers WIPF & STOCK, Eugene, Oregon, USA who made it possible to make my dream of becoming a published author a reality. By applying professional coaching and guidance, WIPF & STOCK ensured that I produced a publishable book.

Dr. Johnson N. Mbugua.

MTh cum laude; PhD (SATS).
Kikuyu Town
KENYA.
March, 2016.

ABBREVIATIONS

ACC&S	African Christian Churches & Schools
ACK	Anglican Church of Kenya
AICs	African Instituted (or Independent or Initiated) Churches
AIM	African Inland Mission
AIPCA	Africa Independent Pentecostal Church of Africa
CCM	Consolata Catholic Mission
CMS	Church Missionary Society
CPK	Church of the Province of Kenya
CSM	Church of Scotland Mission
DC	District Commissioner
FAM	Friends Africa Mission
GMS	Gospel Missionary Society
Ksh	Kenya Shilling
LMS	London Missionary Society
PCEA	Presbyterian Church of East Africa
RC	Roman Catholic Church
SDA	Seventh Day Adventists
SMS	Short Message Service
St	Saint
TV	Television
UMM	United Methodist Mission
VAT	Value Added Tax

CHAPTER 1

INTRODUCTION

Burial and Accompanying Funeral Rites

BURIAL IS THE INTERMENT of a corpse including the accompanying ceremonies (Tenney 1973:77-78). Tenney observes that burial of the dead has been practised for longer than history has been recorded. He advises that the oldest memorials of human culture, some dating back to prehistory are graves. With few exceptions, he notes, evidence points to a degree of ceremony attending burial.

White (1990:161) expresses similar views and advises that from prehistoric times, burial and the disposal of the dead was a matter of duty, reflecting religious worldviews and ideas about life, purity and social obligation. Louis-Vincent Thomas (1989:31) indicates that death is not only a biological occurrence leaving the corpse as a residue that must be dealt with; it is also, and more importantly, a socio-cultural fundamental, because of the beliefs and representation it gives rise to and the attitudes and rituals it brings about.

Numerous scholars have attempted, over the ages, to write on the known history of interment of human remains. A good example is Long (2009:3) who advises that "in the 1960s, an anthropologist exploring a cave in northern Iraq came across the graves of several Neanderthal men, tombs believed to be nearly 50,000 years old and among the oldest human burial sites ever found". Long further advises that "Thousands of miles away, at Sungir near Moscow, was found a cluster of Cro-Magnon graves, thirty millennia old, in which lie the remains of what appears to be a family". Long observes and gives evidence of ceremonies accompanying these ancient burials. He is of the view that the flowers, the beads, the rings and the other artefacts near to and surrounding those human remains bear witness that from the earliest times, human beings have cared tenderly for their dead.

Disposal of the dead has not always been done the same way. Reforming the rites of burial has occurred periodically in almost all countries, religions and cultures. Various religions the world over and numerous Christian denominations, amongst them the Roman Catholic Church, have addressed the issue of reforming funeral rites. For example, the Constitution on the Sacred Liturgy of Vatican Council II (Rennings 1968:1-4) demanded a reform of the present burial rite. Another religious denomination that addresses similar issues is the Church of England (the Anglican Church), which has an association for addressing reformation of matters affecting the lives of its followers. This contention is supported by Wakeford (1890:4) where he indicates that when writing his book he was "mainly indebted to the publications of the Church of England, Burial, Funeral and Mourning Reform Association and of the Cremation Society of England".

The Agikuyu Christians have not escaped the periodic reformation of coping with death. The Agikuyu have over the last 100 years adopted new methods of conducting funerals. This has, as discussed in Chapter 3 of this study, been necessitated by demands and influences of other religions and cultures, which have interacted with the Agikuyu during that period.

To the Agikuyu in modern times, as well as to almost all races, tribes and religions worldwide, burial is an important event and taken very seriously. For the Agikuyu, this statement is supported and exemplified by an article in the Kenya's *Saturday Daily Nation* (October 10, 2009 page 9). Citing "Villagers Force Family to Bury Man in Coffin", the article narrates the ordeal of a family in Nyeri County of Kenya, whose bid to bury an octogenarian in a low-cost ceremony was thwarted, after villagers demanded that the deceased must be accorded a proper burial (see Appendix 1).

When one analyzes this incident; one is bound to ask numerous questions, most of which demand answers. A few of the questions one may ask include: what is the cultural manner of burying dead people, and in this case, an elderly Agikuyu man? Why would the sons of that man not bury their father privately? Why should they be forced by the villagers to bury him in a coffin and not in a sack? Why should the family be compelled to hire a vehicle and transport the body to the mortuary; be forced to hold a public burial and be forced to invite people? These are just a few of the questions that come to mind. These, and numerous issues touching on the Agikuyu Christians' mode of coping with death is the essence of this study.

The study additionally attempted to establish what is expected of an Agikuyu Christian in burying the dead. Should this be according to traditional cultural Agikuyu doctrine (procedure), which very few Agikuyu living today know about, let alone follow? Or should it follow the funeral practice of the contempary Agikuyu Christians, which they refer to as "Christian funerals" or "Christian burial"? It is worthy of note that contemporary Agikuyu Christians' funeral practice should not be construed, as most of the Agikuyu Christians do, to mean that such practice emanated from scripture or was ordered by the early Christian fathers. This is so, as neither the Bible nor the early Christian fathers mandated or directed a specific or normative manner of how Christians ought to cope with death. This contention is supported by Decker (2007:9) in regard to the biblical aspect, who asserts that "there are biblical absolutes in terms of what we believe about life and death, but how we handle the death of a loved one is not specified." The funeral practice that is observed by the contemporary Agikuyu Christians, as shown in this study, is one that has evolved over the last one hundred years or so. It is an adaptation of funeral rites and practices from various religions, cultures and races.

Regarding usage of the term "Christian Funeral" a good number of theologians feel, as I do, that there is no definite funeral practice that can correctly be referred to or defined as the pure form of Christian funeral. What is generally referred to as a Christian funeral is, as shown in this study, a funeral that is guided by Christian principles and teachings, but often incorporates acceptable cultural practices that do not contravene Christian teachings and practices. This contention is supported by Long (2009:15), who is of the view which is similar to mine, that "the variety of Christian funeral practice stems partly from historical, ethnic, cultural and denominational differences, but there is also no one pure form of Christian funeral because there is no one pure form of Christian." Long goes on to advise "Christians do not live or die in abstract. They are real people who live real lives and they die real and very different deaths."

As shown in this study, the Agikuyu Christians use the term "Christian funeral" to refer to their kind of funeral and also to differentiate their funerals from the funerals of atheists, Jews, Muslims, Hindus, Humanists, traditionalists and others who might not be practising Christians. The Agikuyu Christians, it should be noted, use the term "Christian funeral" in that context, and this does not in any way imply that their funeral practice is the pure form of Christian funeral: neither that their practice was mandated by early Christian fathers, nor is it a biblically normative funeral practice.

Long (2009:8) feels that there is a need to define what can be referred to as Christian funerals. In this regard Long asserts:

> "...in sum I believe amid the swirling changes and uncertainties of American death pattern, it not only makes sense but is in fact an urgent task to describe, nurture and practise what can be called 'the Christian funeral"

Long further advises that what gives unity to the individual bits and particularities of a Christian funeral is the fact that,

> "In a Christian funeral, the community of faith is invited once more, and in dramatic fashion to recognise that Christian life

is shaped in the pattern of Christ's own life and death. We have been, as Paul says in Romans, baptized into Jesus' death and baptized into Jesus' life: do you not know that all of us who have been baptized into Christ Jesus were baptized into his death? Therefore we have been buried with him by baptism into death, so that, just as Christ was raised from the dead by glory of the father, so we too might walk in newness of life. For if we have been united with him in death, like his, we will certainly be united with him in a resurrection like his (Rom 6:3-5)."

The issue of the reformation of funeral practices has been addressed by a number of scholars and theologians. They include among them proponents of the discipline of Practical Theology such as me. The input of Practical Theologians is relevant on this issue, as their key task is to assist and where necessary and possible to carry out research and give guidance based on scriptural teachings and principles to their fellow Christians on how best they can solve problems that affect their lives and faith. This, of course, includes how they should be coping with death. A question also tackled by Practical Theologians is how various populations and religions cope with death, leading to an analysis of the reforms that have been proposed and instituted.

Reformation of funeral practices as indicated earlier has taken place over the ages, and has involved numerous populations as well as religions. A number of scholars and theologians have researched and written on the reformation of funeral rites. Those who have done so, include the ones who have addressed the reformation of funeral practices of the British and the American populations respectively. For example, Wakeford (1890) called for reformation of the British ways of coping with death. He dwelt on numerous aspects that he felt required reforming, especially the need for the "simplification" of how the British bury their dead. The Americans on the other hand have produced a number of theologians and other academics including Long (2009) whose thoughts have already been mentioned earlier. Another American theologian is Decker (2007:17) who advises:

> ". . . I am proposing that Christians ought to re-think some of the traditional trappings of American funerals and make choices that better reflect a Christian view of the person and of the death . . ."

Still another American author is Mitford (1963:20-23) who called on Americans to reform their funeral practices. Her book produced a tremendous response and might have contributed immensely to the way Americans cope with death. It is worthy of note that Mitford's book was revised in 1978 and further reprinted in 1998 under the title *The American Way of Death Revisited*.

The above illustrations show that reforming funeral practices is not limited only to the Agikuyu Christians. They further show that it is a problem that has affected, and continues to affect, numerous other populations around the globe. Additionally, they show that it is a problem that has been addressed by a number of academicians and theologians, as it is a social as well as a theological problem. It therefore requires scholars, theologians, Christians, secular leaders and others to formulate an acceptable basis for funeral praxis.

A good illustration that confirms the contention made earlier that the modern Agikuyu do not know how traditionally the Agikuyu coped with death is best exemplified by a statement by a Kikuyu respondent reported in Kirwen(ed.) (2008:232), where the Kikuyu respondent is said to have indicated in response to the question posed to all respondents on page 223 which reads:

> "Describe dying and death of a person in your ethnic group. What is said to explain the death? What are the major rituals? Is there a difference in the rituals and the rites if it is a man, woman or child? How is the grave dug? What is said at the gravesite? Is there a memorial feast at some later date? How is dying and death related to the themes of CREATOR GOD, LINEAGE IDEOLOGY and THE WITCH?"

In answer to these questions, the Agikuyu respondent said (page 232):

> "More often, death is associated to something. Frankly speaking, I am ignorant about the dying rites and rituals in my culture. The people join Creator God in spirit form when they die."

Note should be taken that the respondents in Professor Kirwen's book were mostly African students undertaking Master of Arts (MA) in African studies and Master of African Studies (MAS) at Tangaza College, a constituent college of the Catholic University of Eastern Africa. Tangaza College is also affiliated to Saint Mary's University—USA. Additionally, Tangaza College offers a joint Tangaza College/Saint Mary's University Certificate in African Studies and a Tangaza College Diploma in African Studies. One would expect such students to have a fair knowledge of how traditionally their ancestors coped with death. Their not being aware is a good indication that a large proportion of the contemporary Agikuyu do not know what the funeral practices of their ancestors were.

One of the major problems of this study is that there does not seem to be any work that has been undertaken on how to reform Agikuyu Christian funeral rites. As far as can be ascertained, no work on reforming the funeral rites of any African ethnic community has so far been undertaken.

Globally though, as indicated earlier, there have been a number of works on the reformation of funeral rites. Those few works on reformation, however, address other populations outside the African Continent, especially the Americans and the British. Others concentrate only on the church minister's role in the funeral ceremony, and do not extend their coverage to other aspects of funeral practices such as the cultural demands of funerals.

There have been numerous books and articles, and much research done, on death and how burials were conducted, or how they are conducted, but as again indicated above very few on how burial customs can be reformed. Most of those works dwell on what burials are/or were like, but not how burials should be.

Purpose of the study

The purpose of this book is to propose reformation of Agikuyu burial rites such that the resultant reformation would be practical and would bring the Agikuyu burial rites into greater harmony with truly Christian and cultural norms.

Problem Statement

The main aim of the study is to formulate a model for Agikuyu Christian funeral rites that would integrate relevant cultural, scriptural and practical norms.

Objectives of the study

Specifically, the book aims at achieving the following objectives:

1. To establish how the Agikuyu treated death before coming into contact with Christianity and other cultures. Additionally, to analyze traditional burial rites of a few selected African tribes, as well as the burial rites of some other world religions.
2. To show and analyze the present-day burial rites of Agikuyu Christians.
3. To analyze what the Scriptures have to say about funeral rites.

4. To analyze how the early Christians were buried.

5. To analyze what scripture and the works of various theologians have to say about the resurrected body. To establish whether or not this issue has any bearing on the present-day Agikuyu funeral rites. Additionally, to establish whether the aversion to cremation felt by a considerable number of Agikuyu Christians and even Christians in other African countries has any relevance to resurrection, and so on. To come up with an acceptable explanation that would enable these Christians to get rid of such aversion.

6. To recommend how today's Agikuyu Christians' funeral rites can be simplified and become less expensive, while still relating to the Agikuyu and other Africans culture and Christian ethos.

Should the recommendations given in this book be adopted by Agikuyu Christians and other Africans, it will have solved a social problem that should have been addressed many years ago, before funeral rites of the Agikuyu and of numerous other African communities got out of hand. It will also give other people in Africa as well as in the rest of the world an insight into how they can reform their funeral practices. Further, how funeral rites can be simplified and still be dignified, and at the same time retain some acceptable cultural, scriptural and Christian norms.

Research Questions

The book will be guided by the following research questions:

1. How did the Agikuyu treat death before interacting with and embracing Christianity and other cultures? Additionally, what were the traditional burial rites of some other African tribes, and also what are the burial rites of some selected other world religions?

2. What is the structure of present-day Agikuyu Christian funeral rites?

3. What does Scripture, in this case the Old and New Testament of the Holy Bible say about funeral rites?

4. How were the early Christians buried during the first six centuries up to AD 600?

5. What does the Scripture (the Bible) and various theologians say about the resurrected body? To establish whether or not this issue has any bearing on the present-day Agikuyu and other African Christian funeral rites.

6. How can the present trend of Agikuyu Christian burial and funeral rites be modified, and if possible simplified and become less expensive?

Significance of the Study

The study is significant in several ways, such as uncovering what the traditional funeral rites of the Agikuyu were before making contact with the Europeans? This knowledge, the author has ascertained, is unknown to the majority of the present-day Agikuyu generation. The study will also bring to light what Scripture teaches about burial. Also, how the early Christians were buried. The correct Christian funeral rites, as stated above, have as yet to be defined, as currently there are no specific or universally accepted practices which are deemed the genuine "Christian funeral practice" that should be adopted by all Christians. It is worthy of note that a Christian funeral is not necessarily, as some of the Agikuyu and other African Christians might think, the funeral rites and practices that were accorded to the very early Christians including Jesus himself, the apostles and those Christians who were buried in the first to the sixth centuries AD. This was before and soon after Emperor Constantine (AD 313) embraced Christianity and by so doing enabled Christianity to be adopted by the Romans and soon thereafter to acquire a lot of characteristics especially from the Greek and Roman cultures. A lot of Agikuyu and other African Christians are not aware of this, and most assume that Christian funeral rites as they know them today are Christian, while in fact they are more European than Christian.

The study will also establish the influence that other cultures and religions have had on the Agikuyu and other Africans burial and funeral rites.

The study will, it is hoped, be of significance, as it will investigate ways of integrating what is good as far as burial is concerned in Agikuyu and other Africans traditional beliefs and practices with scriptural teachings and early Christian practices. This might enable the Christian faithful to "feel comfortable" at the manner in which modern African including the Agikuyu Christians should be buried. The findings obtained and recommendations proposed will, it is hoped, fill the gap that has been missing as to what the funeral rites of the Agikuyu and other African Christians of today should be and why? It is to be hoped that this will heal the uncertainty among Agikuyu and other African Christians caused by the divergent beliefs and practices from numerous origins.

Scope of the Study

The study will be limited to Kikuyu District of Kiambu County (before the new boundaries were enacted recently). Kikuyu District was represented in the Kenya Parliament by the Member of Parliament for Kabete, but lately has been split into two constituencies namely Kikuyu and Kabete. It is now represented in Parliament by two Members of Parliament—one for Kikuyu and the other for Kabete. The district comprises seven divisions namely Kabete, Nyathuna, Muguga, Kinoo, Kikuyu, Karai and Nachu. The researcher is confident that enough data on Agikuyu past and present funeral practices will be obtained from this area. This is so because the area is currently semi-rural and semi-cosmopolitan and, except for very minor exceptions and variations, all the Gikuyu culture is represented in this district. Additionally, Agikuyu from all the Agikuyu districts are represented in Kikuyu District including people from Embu and Meru. Equally, burial and funeral rites from other cultures can easily be obtained, as the district is home to national and international citizens.

Limitations and Delimitations

The study is delimited to all Agikuyu Christians living today especially those residing within the universe of this research mainly those residing in the Kikuyu District of Kiambu County, Kenya, better described as those living in the current Kikuyu and Kabete Constituencies of Kenya.

The Current State of Scholarship

A number of scholars have undertaken research in the area of reformation of funeral rites. However, as far as I have been able to ascertain, none has been undertaken on how to reform the funeral rites of any African ethnic community. Those that attempt to achieve the same objective as the one of this study are geared to reforming funeral rites of peoples outside the African continent, especially the British and the American population. These, however, have been very helpful as shown below.

Long (2009) gives invaluable information on how we ought to cope with death by dealing with our dead. He indicated that his book is to enable his audience to 'rethink basic assumptions about what makes for "a good funeral"'. His excellent book goes beyond the scope of my study, as he also analyzes and gives views on how the clergy and others ought to cope with death. Although the book is for the American population, numerous suggestions by Long can, as reflected in Chapter 8, be applicable to the Agikuyu situation in relation to the theme of this study. Rev. William Wakeford (1890) book although written more than a century ago, and although principally addressed to the British population, was extremely relevant to this study. This is so as what he proposed to the British population at that time might, in my opinion, be relevant not only to current British nationals, but also to Christians worldwide including the Agikuyu Christians. One is bound to ask, however, whether the British have heeded the advice of Wakeford, judging from the pomp and cost relating to the recent funerals of some leading British nationals, such as the recent funeral of Baroness Margaret Thatcher. Decker (2007), *Is it Better to Bury or to Burn?* although meant for the American population was very helpful in this study.

His article on cremation deals in depth with the history of cremation in the Western World, and gives invaluable insight on the theological issues involved in cremation. Decker (2007), *If you meet the Undertaker before you meet the 'Uppertaker'* gives a Christian view of death, dying and funerals. This article although written for the American population was of immense value in this study. It captures extremely well the ways that funerals can be simplified and yet retain their dignity. Jones (2010:335-347) wrote for the American population. In the author's words, the article is to "provide the reader with the material needed in order to develop an informed Ethic of Cremation . . . etc." His article has also been of benefit to this study. He covers similar areas to those of Decker (2007) and even makes reference to Decker's article. Mitford (1963) although written for the American population was helpful in numerous areas especially on page 246, where the author indicates that the body need not be present at the funeral service. This idea is recommended in Chapter 8 of this book. McCane (1990) was extremely helpful on the issue of "secondary burial". Van't Spijker's (2005) is a well researched article on the behaviour and characteristics of a particular African people namely the people of Rwanda, Africa. In this research, it is most gratifying to observe on page 160 that Van't Spijker makes an observation that has escaped most students of African culture, religion, and so on. He stresses that "funeral rites are not the same everywhere in Africa", and goes on to assert, which I fully endorse, that "every people or region has its own set of rituals and customs". Van't Spijker makes reference to two funerals that took place in Kenya, where in addition to Christian funeral rites being observed, additional traditional rituals were performed. I wish to stress that those two incidences, and most likely similar incidences anywhere in Africa and the world at large, have no bearing on, and bear no resemblance to the contemporary Agikuyu funeral practice. The Agikuyu, as shown in this study, have over the last fifty years or thereabouts abandoned all their traditional funeral practices. Chapter 3 of this book demonstrates that their contemporary funeral rites have absolutely nothing to do with tradition.

Equally, Kwame (1994) has no bearing or relevance to this study. The Agikuyu traditionally did not observe almost all the rituals observed by the Akan people of Ghana. The social structure of the Agikuyu was such that they did not have, for example, chiefs, as in the case of the Akan. The Agikuyu did not believe in minor deities, and so on. Kwame's article seems to be covering various eras of the history of the Akan people, namely the precolonial and postcolonial, for example, where he indicates that "rum" used to be poured down the throat of the corpse. Rum, it should be noted, is not an African brew. The social and political structure of the Akan was very different from that of the Agikuyu: the Akan are a matrilineal society while the Agikuyu are patrilineal. The article is not on the reforming of Akan funeral rites but rather as Kwame advices on page one of his article "the intention is to show the economic implications of the rites" and also "the relationship of the increasing expenditure on funeral rites to today's economy". Kwame's article although excellently written was of no relevance or assistance to this study, as it scarcely indicates how the Akan's funeral rites can be reformed.

Touching on authors and researchers who generalize about African customs, rites, religions, a good example of such is an article by William A Brown (1983:5-16). Brown refers to and lumps together numerous religions of various African tribes under the one term African Religion. It is noteworthy that Brown wrote his article in 1983 and indicated that the Agikuyu practice traditional African religion. As one of his sources, he uses Kenyatta (1938). By 1983, it should be noted, hardly any Agikuyu observed, practiced or indeed had any knowledge of the traditional Agikuyu religion. It was correctly asserted by Van't Spijker (2005) that "every people or region has its own sets of rituals and customs". To this I would add that "and has its own traditional religion". It is important to note that the traditional religion of almost all the 2000 or thereabouts African tribes is to a large measure unique to each tribe. One should therefore take care not to apply the singular form/term "African Religion" when referring to all or a group of African traditional religions.

The traditional religion of every African tribe should be referred to as the traditional religion of such and such a tribe, but not termed African religion as there is no such thing or one religion.

Numerous articles were obtained from the internet, covering numerous aspects of reforming funerals. They dwelt and touched on various issues and gave views as to how funeral rites can be reformed. The areas covered by these articles include, but are not limited to, how to plan funerals, where to purchase items connected to funerals, how to reduce the costs of funerals and many aspects touching on funerals. Most of these articles are addressed to the American population. These articles include: *Don't Get Buried in Debt* (Funeral Consumers Alliance, 2007); Funeral Arrangement Planning (Tsavo Media Canada, 2014). The latter source covers literally all aspects of reforming funerals for the American population.

Other sources on reforming funeral rites especially for the American population, can be obtained from the internet.

Methodology

Because of the diversity of this study, Cowan's (2000) LIM model (Loyola Institute Model) of theological research was applied (cf. Tucker 2014: 238-242). Cowan (2000) asserts that Practical Theology stresses the correlational, hermeneutical, critical and transformative character of doing theology. Cowan advises that the LIM model for theological research is a "correlational method because it works by holding two things in reciprocal relationship—the vision and values of our religious traditions ("the world as it should be") and the state of the actual world in which we live ("the world as it is")." Cowan further advises that "it is a hermeneutical method because it recognises and highlights the role of interpretation in reading our world and our traditions". Cowan further asserts that "it is a critical method because its constant concern is to bring the real world into greater harmony with the Creator's intentions".

The LIM model shows that the major steps to be undertaken in a study such as this are to articulate, and identify issues which in this study will be burial rites. Secondly, to interpret the world as it is, which in this case is the present Agikuyu burial rites. Thirdly, interpreting the world as it should be, which in this case is selected scriptural text on burial, also theological classic and church teachings on burial rites. Fourthly, interpreting our contemporary obligation, and considering what would be the ideal method of Agikuyu Christian burial rites.

For the LIM to be fully applied it is necessary to articulate and identify relevant issues. This will be effected in Chapter 2, which will bring to light the traditional Agikuyu methods of coping with death. Chapter 1 dwells on various issues including defining the research problem and formulating research questions. The second step of the LIM model is to interpret the world as it is, which in this study is to survey and analyze the current Agikuyu funeral rites. This is fully covered in Chapter 3. In Chapter 4 of this book scriptural and biblical texts are analyzed and critiqued, as well as works of numerous scholars and theologians, in order to establish whether the scriptures contain specifically a directed or normative manner as to how Christians ought to cope with death This is as stipulated by the LIM model, which indicates that the third step required is to interpret the world as it should be, which is contained in Chapter 4 by a selection of selected scriptural texts on burial, and an examination of theological classic and church teachings on burial rites. To this have been added chapters 5 and 6, which analyze burial rites for early Christians, and the issue of the resurrection and the resurrected body respectively. The fourth and final step of the LIM model is interpreting contemporary obligation, and considering what would be the ideal method of Agikuyu Christian burial based on acceptable traditional practices, together with scriptural principles, teachings of the early Christian fathers, as well as views from Agikuyu Christians, pastors, laity and what has been discovered in this study. This is covered and dealt with in Chapters 7 and 8 of this book.

This book consists of eight chapters as follows:

Chapter 1 Introduction. The introduction will present the background to the research, research problem and methodology.

Chapter 2 The Agikuyu, their culture and traditional religion. Their burial rites before embracing Christianity—data on this will be obtained from a literature review and oral interviews with elders. For comparative purposes burial rites of selected other world religions, and a few traditional burial rites of other African tribes will be analyzed. Data for this will be generated from a literature review.

Chapter 3 Present-day burial rites of Agikuyu Christians. Data on this will be from own experience and observations, interviews, document analyzes, funeral programmes, newspaper articles and funeral advertisements, and similar material.

Chapter 4 Analyzes of burial rites in both the Old and New Testament. This will be a synchronic survey of biblical passages.

Chapter 5 Burial rites for the early Christian—from AD 33 to AD 600. This will involve an in-depth literature review of works done on this period.

Chapter 6	The issues of the resurrection and of the resurrected body. Again this will be scriptural and a literature review on this issue. Chapter 6 is deemed necessary as both the early Christians, as shown in this book, and a good number of Africans are averse to cremation, due to a belief that once a body is cremated it cannot be resurrected. An attempt to arrive at an acceptable explanation and persuasion which would enable them overcome this aversion.
Chapter 7	Critical correlation of the study in order to combine the findings of all the aspects of the study in an attempt to move towards the proposed reforms.
Chapter 8	Conclusion, recommendations, areas of further research and contribution in the area of Practical Theology.

Works Cited

Tables

Appendices

Figures

CHAPTER 2

TRADITIONAL FUNERAL PRACTICES OF THE AGIKUYU INCLUDING A FEW OTHER AFRICAN TRIBES AND SOME RELIGIOUS FAITH

EVERY SOCIETY IS INFLUENCED by its history, beliefs, and values (Kunhiyop 2008:3). In this chapter it is therefore necessary to establish who the Agikuyu are, how they migrated from West Africa to their present ancestral land of Central Kenya (Bantu Migration). In addition it is important to understand their culture, customs and traditional religion. The study will also further examine other aspects of the pre-colonial Kikuyu society, including how the Agikuyu coped with death before interacting with and embracing Christianity, other foreign religions and cultures. This is in accordance with the LIM model whose initial step to be undertaken in a study/research of this nature is to analyze and bring to light, in this case, the traditional Agikuyu manner of coping with death.

Relevant information on all those issues will be obtained from a literature review of the few works that have been produced. To confirm the written literature on pre-colonial Agikuyu, I deemed it necessary to carry out an oral interview of 22 elders who during their youth observed and experienced all the aspects of the pre-colonial Agikuyu society. Those elders were all born and brought up in Kikuyu District of Kiambu County. This is the scope of this study. All of them were over 75 years old at the time of the study. The oral interviews took place in the months of October and November 2011. They were interviewed at their homes individually, not as a group, and the interviews were conducted orally by me in the Kikuyu language.

The other reason for interviewing those elders was that there are very few authors who have written extensively on all the aspects of the pre-colonial Kikuyu people and society. This was confirmed by S G Kibicho in his 1972 PhD dissertation (Preface) where he indicates that due to lack of adequate written sources of the Kikuyus before colonization, he had to resort, just as I have done for this chapter, to personally obtaining the relevant information from the respondents. The respondents whom I interviewed are reasonably aged as indicated in the schedule of respondents (Appendix II) at the end of this book. However, they were old enough in the first few decades of the twentieth century to have experienced the traditional Kikuyu way of life. Those were the years when the Agikuyu were starting to embrace Christianity and the practices of other cultures, but the majority were still observing and practising traditional religion and way of life.

I asked all my respondents a number of similar questions. To start with they were requested to state as precisely as possible what they recalled about the history (folklore) of the Agikuyu, the traditional religion, about the Agikuyu ancestors, culture, family life, governance, the relationship of the Agikuyu with their neighbors, especially the Maasai; their recollection of how the Agikuyu coped with death, and how the Agikuyu viewed the afterlife. The elders gave very clear and detailed comments on all the aspects of pre-colonial Kikuyu. The information they gave matched exactly, word for word, with the works of Kenyatta (1938), Leakey (1977) and Muriuki (1974). These three writers are the ones I view as having written authoritatively about the pre-colonial Agikuyu.

Two of my respondents confirmed that Leakey, although of European ancestry, was a Mugikuyu in the true sense, especially having been circumcised following Agikuyu traditions. He belonged to the Agikuyu *riika* (age-group) called *Kimiri*. Leakey lived with the Agikuyu and knew the Kikuyu language and their customs intimately. Muriuki (1981:120) reviewing Leakey's book (*The Southern Kikuyu Before 1903*) states that Louis Leakey was qualified to write about the Kikuyu. Son of a missionary, he was born and brought up in their midst, thereby gaining a unique opportunity to study their language and customs. Much of the material for Leakey's book was checked or supplemented at meetings of Kikuyu arranged by Chief Koinange in 1937-8. Leakey's expertise in this field became widely acknowledged by both scholars and the British Government officials alike.

Muriuki further indicates that it was only after Leakey's death that the means to finance the publication of his vast ethnography were obtained through the Leakey Foundation. Only after the publication of his work can we now join Leakey in a tour of the Kiambu countryside, and share his expert observations on almost every facet of Kikuyu life, social organization, land tenure, agriculture, food and drinks, crafts, warfare, law, history, religion, funeral practices, among other subjects.

This chapter also contains comparative funeral rites of selected African tribes and a few races especially the British. Inclusion of the latter is deemed important, as the British colonized the Agikuyu (Kenya) between 1890 and 1963 and during that period impacted heavily on Agikuyu customs, worldview and religion, not forgetting the Agikuyu mode of coping with death.

Funeral rites of a few other races and countries have been considered as well as examining how they are coping with inadequate burial space: and in addition, how they are trying to curb extravagance along with exorbitant funeral expenses and other excesses. A few bizarre (weird) funeral rites and burial practices have also been addressed in this chapter. Also for comparative purposes funeral rites of a number of other world religions, including those of Judaism, Islam, Buddhist, Hinduism and Humanists have been analyzed and considered.

The Agikuyu

Kenya's 2009 population official census reflected that Agikuyu numbered 6,622,576 out of the country's total population of 38,610,097. According to that census, the Agikuyu were the largest Kenya tribe out of the 42 indigenous tribes of Kenya. The Agikuyu are followed by the Luhya numbering 5,338,666, Kalenjin numbering 4,967,440, and the Kambas numbering 3,893,157 (*The Standard Newspaper* pg 1, dated 1-09-2010). Adams and Mburugu (1994:159-66) indicate that the Kikuyu people are a large powerful society of Central Kenya (cf. Fay 1999: 1082-9).

Traditionally, the Agikuyu inhabited the former Central Province of Kenya before the boundaries were altered by the Kenya's new constitution adopted through a referendum in 2010. Their traditional homeland was the previous administration districts, namely, at the centre Muranga, which is traditionally considered as their ancestral home, while to the north and the south are Nyeri and Kiambu Districts (now counties) respectively.

In addition to the Agikuyu who traditionally inhabited the three counties indicated above, there were the Agikuyu very close cousins living on the eastern, southern and northern slopes of Mount Kenya. These Kikuyu cousins are all related in physical characteristics, culture and language. They include the Aameru, Embu, Aambere, the Ndia Kikuyu and Gichugu Kikuyu. The Ndia and the Gichugu are referred to as Kikuyu although they have slight cultural differences (Middleton 1953:11).

Meru County is occupied by several distant cousins of the Agikuyu. The Meru tribal groups include the Tigania, Igembe, Imenti, Miutini, Igonji, Mwimbi, Muthambi, Tharaka, Nithi, and Chuka, all of which, with the exception of Tharaka and Chuka, are traditionally part of the so-called *Meru*, perhaps a territorial rather than a tribal name (ibid.,11-2). Adams and Mburugu (1994:159-66) observe that within the larger Kikuyu ethnic group, some individuals may define themselves as Kikuyu for some purposes and as not Kikuyu for other purposes. They assert that this is true of the Wameru and other sub-societies around Mount Kenya.

The above are the traditional homelands of the Agikuyu, but since the arrival of the Europeans in Central Kenya around 1890 AD a considerable number of the Agikuyu have migrated to areas outside their ancestral homeland, especially to urban centres like Thika, Nairobi, Nakuru, and Mombasa among other towns. They have also settled in distant rural areas, especially in the Rift Valley. Additionally, the Agikuyu have settled in many countries in the world, even outside the African continent.

Origin of the Agikuyu

Agikuyu mythology has it that Gikuyu, the father of the Agikuyu tribe, was shown what was to be the Kikuyu ancestral land by *Ngai* (God) at the top of Mount Kenya with his wife Mumbi. Gikuyu descended from Mount Kenya and settled at a place called Mukurwe wa Nyagathanga in the present-day Murang'a County. As noted by Cagnolo the place is currently gazetted by the Kenya government as a historical site and a tourist destination. At this place the legend of origin of the Agikuyu is very clearly depicted with a rich illustration of folklore (Cagnolo 2006:16).

According to Muriuki (1974), and Cagnolo (2006), historical studies (Bantu migratory patterns), archaeological discoveries and linguistic evidence show that the root Bantu language to which group the Agikuyu language falls emerged in what is now Nigeria and Cameroon around 2000 BC. By 1000 BC in a series of migrations Bantu speakers had spread south to the savannah lands of Angola and east to the Lake Victoria region. Over the next 1000 years they scattered throughout Central and Southern Africa interacting with and absorbing, mostly by intermarrying, the indigenous population as they spread. Cagnolo and Muriuki further observe that the group that entered the present-day Tanzania mainland, spread through central Tanzania leaving some groups like the Wanyamwezi before splitting into two groups (Cagnolo 2006:16; Muriuki 1974:37-82).

Cagnolo (2006:15) particularly indicates that one such group headed south towards the present-day South Africa (the Nguni or Ngoni) while the other group headed east towards the East Coast of Africa. Some of the groups that were left near or at the East Africa Coast are the Chaaga, Mijikenda, and other Bantu of East Coast of Africa. Over the following hundred years, migration continued westwards from present-day Kenya coast, to leave behind the Wataita (Wadavida) near Voi. Those who continued westwards left the Akamba in present-day Ukambani area of Kenya as they proceeded towards Mount Kenya. On the eastern slopes of Mount Kenya, they left the Aameru and the Ambeere, before ultimately crossing the mountain to settle on the south-western slopes (Muranga) as the Agikuyu, leaving behind in the present-day Kirinyaga County, the Gichugu and Ndia Kikuyu. I concur with Cagnolo's views where he indicates that this historical version agrees in total with the Agikuyu legend. According to the legend noted earlier the Agikuyu descended from Mount Kenya. According to the historical facts they crossed Mount Kenya to get to their ancestral home in Muranga County (ibid., 16).

It is interesting to note that in the Aameru traditional legend of origin they indicate that they came from *Mpua* (The Great Ocean). This shows that this group came from the coast, as there are no seas or oceans in or near the area currently occupied by the Aameru. The Agikuyu arrived in their present ancestral homeland, namely the Central Province of Kenya, in the fifteenth century, that is about 700 years ago. The Agikuyu did not however reach the southern parts of Kiambu district which is bordered by the Nairobi River and Ondiri swamp until the middle of the nineteenth century (Cagnolo 2006:16; Muriuki 1974:37-61; Middleton 1953:11-15). This contention is confirmed by ACK (2001:2) where it is indicated that the migration of the Kikuyu was a continuous affair and by the time the Europeans arrived in Kikuyuland around AD 1890 the Southern Kikuyu had migrated to the south as far as Nairobi River and Ondiri swamp which is a walking distance from Ngong Hills. Ngong Hills were, and are still today, on the border of Maasai and Kikuyu territory (ibid.,1-2).

It should be noted that this study is based on the Agikuyu who settled in the area of Kikuyu District of Kiambu County popularly known as Kabete. This area is the southernmost part of Kiambu County and Kikuyu traditional homeland.

Agikuyu Society and Culture

Kikuyu society was largely moulded by two factors, namely the mode of their migration and the subsequent pattern of settlement (Muriuki 1974:37-61; Muriuki, in Ogot 1976:125). After migration to the Kikuyu plateau, the pioneers often settled on separate ridges, usually demarcated from each other by rivers, valleys or deep ravines. This is in tune with the physical configuration of the Kikuyu plateau. Muriuki indicates that from the onset each pioneering group formed an independent and self-contained unit that often competed with the other units in exploiting the vast natural resources of the new homeland. Muriuki further advises that the life of the pioneers was admittedly a difficult one. With time the pioneers became legendary folk heroes and were held in high esteem. They became founders of the *Mbari* (sub clan). The land on which the sub-clan settled was held jointly by all members of the *Mbari*. After the founder (pioneer) died or became too old, each Mbari selected the most able member to be a *Muramati* (trustee of the family matters especially land). The *Muramati* was usually the most senior member of the *Mbari*. After about seven generations or so, the *Mbari* land often became overpopulated. This forced numerous members of the *Mbari* to migrate to other unoccupied lands in search of fresh farming and grazing land (ibid., 126). In respect of conduct within the *Mbari*, it should be noted that all circumcised and married male members of the *Mbari* formed a council, which under the *muramati* leadership regulated *Mbari* affairs. Besides being the basic social and economic unit the *Mbari* was also the basic religious unit.

By the end of the nineteenth century the Kikuyu society was patriarchal, uncentralized and highly egalitarian (Muriuki 1974:110). The Kikuyu society and social organization was based on three important factors namely the family, the clan, (*Muhiriga*) and age grouping (*Rika*). The family (*Nyumba*) brought together all those who were related by blood, namely a man, his wife or wives, children, grand- and great-grandchildren. The family was supreme over all individual interests and included everyone within one homestead including orphans (Middleton 1953:26-30; Muriuki 1974:123-5). The clan (*Muhiriga*) joined in one group several *Mbari* units which had the same clan name, for example, A-ambui or A-acera or A-anjiru among others; these are believed to have descended from one family group in the remote past (Kenyatta 1938:1). These clan names originated from the names of the daughters of Gikuyu and Mumbi, the founders of the Agikuyu tribe.

It is obvious that due to the then existing polygamous practice of the Agikuyu, a family or *Mbari* unit increased rapidly and in one generation it was possible for a *Mbari* to have had a hundred members or more. Thus, in a few generations the number increased to hundreds and at times to thousands of family members. On such occasions numerous units of the same *Mbari* would migrate to distant lands in search of fresh agricultural and grazing lands.

When this happened Kenyatta (1938:1) notes the bond that is left between a group which was once united by close blood relation is the *Muhiriga* (Clan) identity. This knitted together distant relatives and facilitated the feeling of rendering mutual support in all important matters in the interest and welfare of the muhiriga. Kenyatta further observes that in perpetuation of this feeling of clanism (*Muhiriga*), representatives of a *Muhiriga* met occasionally on the occasion of big events such as marriage ceremonies, initiation or circumcision (ibid., 1).

However, with time almost all traditions were done away with. Today there are never such gatherings of members of the same clan. An effort to organize such a gathering would be impossible, as members of one clan of the Agikuyu would turn into hundreds of thousands. Today *Muhiriga* or *Mbari* refers to the whole of the Kikuyu tribe, usually referred to as *Muhiriga wa Agikuyu* (Tribe of the Kikuyu) or *Nyumba ya Mumbi* (Family of Mumbi). As indicated earlier Mumbi was the mother of the Kikuyu tribe. She was the wife of Gikuyu who founded the Kikuyu tribe.

Muriuki, in (Ogot 1976:124- 36) observes that the wider community of *Mbari ya Mumbi* was of little practical importance in the day-to-day life. Its importance was only relevant when it was desirable to foster solidarity and unity within the Kikuyu community as a whole. Surprisingly, this occurred during periods of deep internal crisis or when faced by external threats such as the period of *Mau Mau* and the emergency (Muriuki, in Ogot 1976:124-36). Another factor is the system of age grading (*Riika* whose plural is *Mariika*). It is observed that there are four types of *Mariika*. The most conspicuous and distinctive features of the age-grouping was the *ituika*. This was the handing-over process held every thirty to forty years, during which one generation handed over to the successor the authority of power to conduct the political, judiciary and religious functions. Other scholars who have written on this important aspect of Agikuyu, namely on the *ituika* include Kabetu (1947:89-91); Kenyatta (1938:105,180-9); Leakey (1977:1281); and Peterson (2004:3-4). Secondly, there was the *riika* which in its restricted sense meant an initiation set which comprised boys and girls who had undergone initiation in a given year (Muriuki, in (Ogot 1976:126-8); cf Kenyatta 1938:125-56; Middleton 1953:61-4; Cagnolo 2006:92-102; Sandgren 1962:197-200). The same authors additionally explain that such initiation sets were grouped together to form an army contingent, and for this purpose they were given an all-embracing name. Unlike the boys, girls were initiated every year, as they did not undergo a closed period, *muhingo*. Thus, there were occasions when an initiation set was exclusively female in composition. Such an exclusively female initiation set was also called a *riika* and given an individual name which distinguished it from others. Initiation, in the form of circumcision, was of momentous significance in Kikuyu society. Its importance was underscored by the fact that it was the basic prerequisite for the attainment of full adult social status. Moreover the initiation rites dramatized the transition of an individual from childhood. It was also at this juncture that the neophytes were instructed in the traditional role; equally, the new initiates qualified for the allocation of important roles, responsibilities and privileges in the social system. For example, the male initiates could now become members of the warrior group whose primary duty was the defence of the country. Military services apart, the warrior corps formed a reservoir of able-bodied manpower for performing other public functions. They acted as executive officers to the elders, being entrusted with such activities as policing duties in the markets and during festivals, the arrest of habitual criminals and the arranging of public gatherings during which rules and prohibitions were promulgated or important announcements made. Other warrior duties included the clearing of virgin land, herding livestock, planting specified crops such as bananas and yams, providing building materials, and building houses and cattle kraals, as well as performing any other arduous tasks. Otherwise, the warriors were a privileged elite, which to a casual observer did nothing else except gorge enormous amounts of food and meat. When warriors became of age they were expected to terminate their active military service, and in due course to marry and thereby qualify for admission to the next stage of their life, which is the council of elders or *Kiama*. Like the warrior group, elders were divided into junior and senior elders and according to territorial divisions.

Numerous scholars have written on the Kikuyu traditional culture especially on the role and duties of various members of the Kikuyu community including Bottignole (1984:30-3); Leakey (1977:128-505); Kenyatta (1938:52-94); Kabetu (1947:87-9); Cagnolo (2006:28-30); and Muriuki (1974:111-34). These authors and comments from my respondents (Appendix II, interviewed in the months of October and November, 2011) indicate that the family was the basic unit on which the traditional social system hinged. Kikuyu society, as mentioned earlier, was a strictly patrilineal system, where the man was considered the head of the family without question, and he could, according to his financial resources, take as many wives as he wished. Moreover, he was the master of the land on which his family lived. The woman, after the wedding contract, became part of the family of the husband, made her home in the residence of his family and cultivated part of the land allotted to her. The sons born of such a union, carried on working on that land, and in this way maintained the link between it and the ancestors, after whom they were named, while the daughters settled in the new homes on their husband's land.

The relationship and setup among the members of a family formed in such a way, was characterized not only by very strict and strong links with the closest members of the family, but also by heavy duties towards all other members. Of course, these duties were transformed into rights when one of the members found himself in a condition of need. In fact, when a member of the clan is in need, all the clan members participate in helping. On the other hand, this member is expected to act in the same way when any other member of the clan is in need. It was always within the family that the children learnt their duties and rights towards their parents, grandparents, relatives and members of their clan. Grandparents and parents were the natural teachers of their children. The former taught them the legends and tribal traditions transmitted orally from generation to generation, and tried to develop their memory. In addition, because of the clear-cut division of labour between the sexes, the mother became the natural teacher of the daughters and the father of the sons. Daughters and sons were, quite soon, trained to help their parents in their domestic activity, field work and cattle breeding.

As so well indicated by Kunhiyop (2008:21), John Mbiti was probably the first to articulate the African concept of community when he (Mbiti 1969:108-9) wrote that in the traditional life, the individual does not and cannot exist alone, only corporately. The individual owes his existence to other people, including past generations and his contemporaries. He notes that the individual is part of the whole. The community must therefore make, create or produce the individual; for the individual depends on the corporate group. Only in terms of other people does the individual become conscious of his own being, his duties, his privileges and responsibilities towards himself and towards other people. Mbiti notes that when an individual suffers, he does not suffer alone but with the corporate group, and when he rejoices he rejoices not alone but with his kinsmen, his neighbours and his relatives whether living or dead. When he gets married he is not alone, neither does his wife "belong" to him alone. This also happens with the children, they belong to the corporate body of kinsmen, even if they bear only their father's name. Whatever happens to the individual happens to the group and whatever happens to the group happens to the individual. Therefore Mbiti notes the individual can only say, "I am because we are, and since we are therefore, I am." Kunhiyop (2008:21) feels that another way of saying this is, 'I am because we are related." Similar views are expressed by Gehman (1989:51) where he indicates, "The deep sense of kinship, with all it implies has been one of the strongest forces in traditional life."

The same authors and respondents state that circumcision was a very important education stage, and the cornerstone of tribal life. Through that ceremony the youth, boys and girls, proved their courage and were considered adults. In fact, after having been extensively informed about their new status, their duties as adults and the secrets of the tribal life, they could marry and have children. The men could possess land, cattle and engage in political activities. All the youth circumcised in the same year became automatically members of the same "age grade". The age-grade mates had very strong links to each other. They were expected to help each other as much as blood-brothers, if not more, and to act in a united manner in the major decisions concerning the welfare of the tribe.

Agricultural activity constituted the pivot of the economic traditional system. To own land was, therefore, of vital importance. A series of very precise rules, linked to this fact, had been established (1) to regulate the acquisition of the properties (at the beginning, through simple deforestation); (2) the property descent (usually inherited by the sons at their father's death); (3) the land purchase (that proved necessary because of the huge growth of the tribe) and (4) the borders' delimitation. Also, the main reason for the clear-cut division of labour between the sexes was because of the agricultural activity including cattle-breeding. According to such a division, men had precise duties to deforest and to break the soil, to plant specified crops, to provide sticks for bananas and cassavas, to manage the irrigation systems and to look after the domestic animals. Moreover, they were in charge of building the hut frame, of defending their family and homestead, of hunting and of iron processing. Women, for their part, were responsibe for preparing the soil for sowing, for planting maize, beans, and sweet potatoes, and for taking care of the fields and the crops. In addition they were supposed to take care of the running of their home This started with supplying wood and water and ended with the cooking of food and the care of the husband, children and any guests; they had also to deal with the manufacturing of leather clothes, potteries, and baskets and, lastly, they completed the building of new houses by thatching the walls and roof. Both men and women were involved in trading, very often through barter. Usually women bartered cereals and vegetables, while men exchanged cows, goats, and sheep. The exchange of such animals was very important, because to own domestic animals was not only a sign of wealth, but in some cases (such as sacrifice and wedding festivities) it became an absolute necessity. In fact, to allow their daughters to marry, the parents were supposed to receive a certain number of goats or some cows (bride wealth).

The same authors and respondents additionally contend that even if great respect was awarded to the woman, especially in her role of mother and educator, the traditional society did not allow her to have a say in public life; in fact, the political activity was exclusively exercised by men representing their family group. The Kikuyu tribe did not have a king or chiefs, instead it was ruled by an egalitarian political system; therefore every male adult (circumcised, married and well settled in the administration of his wealth) had the same opportunity of participating in political life. To belong to a certain "age group" determined his position in the various tribal groups; if under 30 years of age, he was in the warrior group, and after warriorhood he joined the elders. The tribe was ruled by the latter group which, democratically, every thirty years was supposed to hand over power to the following generation, even if the members of the previous group still retained great authority and a consultative function. The ceremony of handing over power from one generation to the next was called *ituika*.

The political activity started at family level and extended to the village, district and tribe level. The head of the family was, in this way, responsible for all the decisions taken within his family group and he represented it at the councils at village level, which were chaired by the oldest and more respected member. Thus one, in turn, represented the whole village at district level. The district council was chaired in rotation by elders. In line with the then Agikuyu egalitarian mode of governance, no particular elder could be elected to hold the post of chairman permanently. The councils, formed in such a way, discussed in long debates the most important legislative questions, established priorities of the various activities of the government, made the laws effective in punishing the trespassers, and in guarding the peace and respect of tradition within the tribe. The Kikuyu traditional culture hinges, therefore, on the great respect bestowed upon the elders (also *Ngai*, in the legend, had the attribute of Great Elder); on the sacredness of the land, on the tangible link between generations, perpetuated by sons and daughters, who are considered real blessings, and in the ancestral spirits of those members of the community who have died and their souls (*ngoma*) departed to the spiritual world of the ancestors (*Kwa-ngoma*) as well as by the relationship shown and upheld among the members of an extended family and by the traditional political structure.

Relationship of the Agikuyu with their Neighbors especially the Maasai

Various authors, and Muriuki (1974) in particular, give a very interesting version of the Kikuyu relationship with their neighbors especially the Maasai. Holmes (1976:926) reviewing Muriuki's work notes that Muriuki has made an effort to dispel a number of tenacious misconceptions about Kikuyu relations with their neighbors. A few years earlier, Hammond (1974) when also reviewing Muriuki's book (*A History of the Kikuyu 1500-1900*) gives a similar view. Hammond and Holmes contend, as I do, that the Maasai and Kikuyu were not traditional enemies. Muriuki (1974), Hammond (1974), and Holmes (1976) assert that the popularly-held version which was portrayed by ill-informed missionaries and colonialists is erroneous, especially where they painted the Maasai as having for long been "the terror and scourge of all their neighbors" (cf. Fay 1999:1085). Muriuki (1974:83-109) stresses, and I fully agree with him, that the view often portrayed that the Maasai were a terror to their neighbors, or that they were constantly at war with them, needs drastic qualification as far as the southern Kikuyu/Maasai relationship was concerned. Giving reasons for feeling that way, Muriuki concedes that admittedly considerable raiding expeditions took place between the Maasai and the Kikuyu. He feels, however, that this state of affairs was mitigated by other extraneous factors which were conducive to their mutual understanding. He further asserts that the Maasai, being pastoralists, needed some agricultural produce in the same way that the agriculturalists required some animal products. In this, he notes that the Maasai, up to the present were particularly vulnerable to famine.

During the times of famine the Maasai heavily relied on their agriculturist neighbors. At times they had to seek refuge in order to avoid starvation. Peaceful coexistence was recognized as being of prime importance to the wellbeing of the two communities. Muriuki notes, for example, that during various disasters that overtook the Maasai in the nineteenth century there was a large scale influx of Maasai refugees to the Kikuyu land while others settled among the Taveta, Chaaga and Arusha communities (Muriuki 1974:83-109).

Trade activity continued even during periods of tension. Muriuki observes that this stimulated peaceful coexistence. As stated earlier, the Maasai needed from the agriculturists most of their daily requirements, such as gourds for milk and tobacco, while the agriculturists needed hides, skins, leather cloaks, livestock, and salt from the Maasai (Muriuki 1974:83-109). This is also supported by Leakey who additionally asserts that even at times of intense hostilities between the Maasai and the Kikuyu, women from both sides used to cross the borders unmolested (Leakey 1977:1035-73).

Muriuki further asserts that the bloodthirsty or wanton killing of women or children was strictly forbidden, and it was taboo for both Maasai and Kikuyu warriors to rape or seduce women prisoners during a raid. It was the accepted practice that prisoners could be ransomed, failing which they remained in the country of their captors and became full members of the family of their captors (Muriuki 1974:125). I fully confirm this contention, as my own paternal grandfather, who was a fierce Kikuyu warrior from Kabete had, out of his nine wives, two Maasai women who had been captured that way. Even at the time of their death, after being married to my grandfather for over forty years they had not fully mastered the Kikuyu language.

The relationship between the Maasai and the Agikuyu is very important in this dissertation mainly because the Agikuyu Maasai contact had far-reaching consequences. Muriuki observes that some Agikuyu *Mbari* trace their origin to Maasai ancestors, while even larger numbers have absorbed Maasai blood. The reverse is also true: the majority of Maasai have blood from their agriculturist neighbors, in this case the Agikuyu and vice versa. Consequently Muriuki observes that there has been deep and extensive cultural fusion particularly along the northern and southern frontiers of Kikuyuland.

Muriuki further observes that the Agikuyu and the Maasai warriors had the same insignia such as hair style and shield decoration. Secondly, the Kikuyu language although mainly Bantu is heavily indebted to the Maasai language, from which it has borrowed nearly all the descriptive words relating to cattle. The name of God in Kikuyu *Ngai* is believed to be from the Maasai word for God "*EN-KAI*." However, it is not clear whether it is the Maasai who borrowed that name from the Agikuyu or vice versa.

Another important aspect was that those Agikuyu who had Maasai or non- Kikuyu descendance were grouped into a Maasai "guild" for ritual or initiation purposes. The Kikuyu word for Maasai tribe is *Ukabi*. So, in Kikuyu that guild is known as Ukabi Guild. Their children were initiated according to Maasai (*Ukabi*) rites which, it should be noted, were slightly different from those practised by the Kikuyu Guild. Moreover, the ceremonies were less elaborate and less expensive than their counterparts in the Kikuyu Guild (Karanja 1999:31-2; Leakey 1977:626-65, 687, 938, 967, 975; Muriuki 1974:135; Middleton 1953:64-6).

The above is important in this dissertation as the religion of the southern Kikuyu, the manner in which they treat affairs of their ancestors as well as the manner of disposing dead bodies is to a large measure governed by the practice of the Kikuyu Guild. This is so as by far the larger number of the Agikuyu of Kikuyu District of Kiambu County, which is the scope of this study, are descendants of members of the Kikuyu Guild. However, there are a reasonable number of families who descended from the Ukabi (Maasai) Guild (Muriuki 1974:135; Leakey 1977:988; Middleton 1953:65-6). In this regard I am a living testimony of this contention that a considerable number of Kikuyu have blood from their neighboring tribes. My maternal great-great-great-grandfather was a pure Maasai called Mung'e Ole Jung'ei. Over 250 years ago there was a great famine in Maasai land. My said ancestor who at that time was living in Kilgoris area of Narok County migrated using the route of Narok, Magadi, Kitengela and ultimately settled under the Ol Ndonyo Sabuk hill near Thika Town. In the course of time he married additional women in addition to his Maasai wives. The new wives were from both the Agikuyu and Akamba tribes. One of the wives, a Mkamba, had a daughter who married a Kikuyu man. This couple had a daughter who married a Kikuyu man. That couple had a daughter who married a Kikuyu man.

They were blessed by a daughter who they named Nyokabi (meaning from *Ukabi*) literally meaning from Maasai. That daughter, Nyokabi, who was my maternal grandmother married a Kikuyu man who happened to be my maternal grandfather. This implies that I have a mixture of three bloods namely Kikuyu, Akamba and Maasai. It is out of this lineage and Kikuyu custom that one of my own daughters is named Nyokabi. Because Kikuyu District has Kikuyu from both guilds, this study will consider traditional burial rites and practices of both the Ukabi (Maasai) Guilds and Kikuyu Guilds.

The Kikuyu Traditional Religion

A few authors give a fairly good coverage of Agikuyu traditional religion. They include Macpherson (1970), ACK (2001), Karanja (1999), Middelton (1953), Cagnolo (2006), Kenyatta (1938) and Mbiti (1969). Mbiti gives a sound overview of numerous Africa religions and philosophy. The most thorough and comprehensive coverage of the Agikuyu traditional religion is, however, obtained from Leakey (1977) and Kenyatta (1938). Evans-Pritchard (1965:27) asserts that traditional religion is seen in all aspects of traditional African life. Therefore, it influences all areas of the African life. He feels that African traditional religions have been largely responsible for shaping the characters and culture of African peoples throughout the centuries. Even if it has no written literature, Evans-Pritchard feels that it is written everywhere in the life of the people. He notes that Africans are notoriously religious, and that in each African society, religion is embedded in the local language, so that to understand the religious life of the people properly one needs to know their language.

As indicated above, Evans-Pritchard (1965), just like Mbiti (1969), advises that Africans are extremely religious. Both scholars note that religion permeated all departments of life so freely that it was not easy or possible to isolate it. Mbiti further observes that religion was the strongest element in traditional background, and exerted probably the greatest influence upon the thinking and living of the people concerned. This contention is in every respect similar to the attitude of the Agikuyu towards their traditional religion. Mbiti further advises that because traditional religion permeated all the departments of life, there was no formal distinction between the sacred and the secular, between religious and non-religious, between the spiritual and the material areas of life. He further asserts that wherever the African was, there was his religion. He observes that the African carried religion to the fields when sowing seeds or harvesting crops. He took it with him to the beer party and even when attending funeral ceremonies, and if he is educated he takes it to the examination room at school or the university. If he is a politician he takes it to the houses of Parliament (Ibid.,1-2). Dickson (1984:54-5) expresses similar views by indicating that Africans have deep respect for God. God is held in very high esteem in the thinking of the African. He is the one on whom you lean and do not fall; he is He who responds when called: the one who has always been there, the old, old one. Kenyatta (1938) as far as the Kikuyu tribe is concerned had indicated earlier that many African languages (including Kikuyu) do not have a word for religion. Mbiti (1969:2) confirms this contention and asserts that partly due to this lack of a definite term for religion the missionaries in East Africa borrowed the Arabic derived Swahili term *Dini* to translate the English term religion in the various African languages. They note that religion accompanies the individual from the day he is born to long after his physical death, as will be expounded later in this book (Mbiti 1969:2; Kenyatta 1938:231-42).

Mbiti further observes, and I support his views which are similar to those of Kenyatta, that traditional religion is not for an individual but for the community of which he is part. In traditional society there were no unreligious people. A person could not detach himself from the religion of his group, for to do so was to be severed from his roots, his foundation, his context of security, his kinship and the entire group of those who make him aware of his existence (Kenyatta 1938:231-68; Mbiti 1969:2). Mbiti further notes that to be without religion amounted to self- excommunication from the entire life of the society, and African peoples did not know how to exist without religion (Mbiti 1969:2).Other commentators on the traditional religiosity of Africans include among others, Odak (1995:41-9); Kunhiyop (2008:15-8); Ray (2000:4-13); Brown (1983:5-15); Turaki Yusuf (2006:54-9).

Leakey expresses similar views and advises that Kikuyu religious beliefs and practices were so interwoven with the social organization of the tribe and the life of each family that they cannot be completely isolated. Leakey further advises that Kikuyu religion was an essential part of social organization. Religion was necessary for the maintenance of family life, so much so that a Kikuyu who did not believe in Kikuyu religion did not really count as a Kikuyu at all (Leakey 1977:1074).

Leakey further notes that religion to the Kikuyu was not an individual matter; it was not something to be accepted or rejected at will, but rather a family matter and through the family a tribal concern. Religion to the entire Kikuyu was extremely important. If a member of a family rejected the religion of the tribe and family, he did not only affect his own life, but he seriously interfered with the life of his family, for many family religious rites were not complete unless all members of the family participated in them (Ibid.,1074).

Leakey stresses that if any member of the family disbelieved and denounced the religion of his people, the only way to avoid serious disturbance to the life of the rest of the family was to disown and disinherit the disbeliever, and so make the family once more an undivided unit (Ibid., 1074). In confirming this, ACK (2001:1) advises that lives of the Kikuyu revolved around religion. It observes that God's consciousness to Kikuyu was a life vein. Nothing was done, said, observed or done without an element of God or Spirits being evoked.

Kenyatta advises that in Kikuyu religion there was no provision of official priesthood nor was there any religious preaching. He notes that this was due to the fact that religion is interwoven with the traditions and social custom of the Agikuyu. He asserts that all members of the tribe acquired automatically during their childhood teachings and upbringing all that was necessary to know about religion and custom. He advises that the duty of imparting this knowledge was customarily entrusted to the parents, who were looked upon as the official ministers of both religious and social customs. Kenyatta notes that Kikuyu religion could be defined as the belief in a Supreme God (*Ngai*), and on constant communion with nature. To Kenyatta, religion and state (community or tribe) were one (Kenyatta 1938:241).

Giving more insight on this matter, Bottignole (1984:37) asserts that the Kikuyu society was regulated even in the smallest details by traditional religion, with which it was fully identified. Bottignole feels that the sense of sacredness permeates every act of the traditional life. This is exactly the view expressed by Mbiti, Leakey and Kenyatta. Bottignole further indicates that from childhood the Kikuyu grew up in an environment that helped them to learn the basic beliefs and values of their tribe. This happened especially through the teachings of legends and proverbs, and sometimes through participation in sacred rituals. This is similar to the views that are expressed by Kenyatta. The ideological knowledge acquired as such was transformed automatically into beliefs, because the adults acted within a complex of social structures, which conformed literally to these beliefs, as religion is interwoven with traditions and social customs of the people. Thus, all members of the community are automatically considered to have acquired, during their childhood teachings, all that it is necessary to know about religion and custom. The duty of imparting this knowledge to the children was entrusted to parents, who were looked upon as the official ministers of both religious ethics and social customs (Kenyatta 1938:46).

ACK (2001:3-5); Karanja (1999); Leakey (1977:1075-102) and Kenyatta (1938:46) assert that among the Kikuyu the highest God was said to be without form. This is why the Agikuyu would say that *Ngai ndari nduiri* (God has no form). Though without form and unknowable, *Ngai* to the

Kikuyu was active and some of His manifestations of His presence included thunderstorms, strong winds, lightning, prosperity of the community and calamities in the community. ACK (2001) further notes that the Kikuyu beliefs may be classified into two separate but related areas. The first was belief in *Ngai* (High God) who was regarded as omnipotent and omniscient. He was the only creator and sustainer of all things. *Ngai's* dwelling place was generally thought to be in the sky, but His presence was associated with Mount Kenya (*Kirinyaga*) and to a lesser extent with the three other landmasses along the perimeter of Kikuyuland. These were *Kirima kia Mbiruiru* (Ngong Hills), *Kia Njahi* (Donyo Sabuk) and *Kia Nyandarua* (Aberdare Ridges). *Ngai* was a distant being with little interest in individuals in their daily lives. He was only called upon in the major crisis of people's lives. Secondly, Kikuyu believed that the ancestors, though dead, continued to exercise their influence over the living through their *ngoma* (ancestral spirits) (ACK 2001; Leakey 1977:1103- 4). The Kikuyu as ACK (2001), and Leakey (1977:1103- 4) note identified three types of spirits. First, there was the spirit of the immediate forebears to whom the living family made offerings of food and drinks as tokens of fellowship. Secondly, there were the spirits of the clan, whose concern was the welfare of the entire clan. Thirdly, there were the age-group spirits whose concern was the wellbeing of the whole society, and who had to be approached by the appropriate leaders of the living age group. The spirit world was considered to be co-terminous with the physical one, but separated from it by having to conform to a different order of being.

ACK (2001); Leakey (1977:1075-102); Karanja (1999) and Cagnolo (2006:189) further note that the Kikuyu were God-conscious people who had ways of relating to *Ngai* and the spirit world. It is said that God-consciousness was like a life vein of the Kikuyu. Nothing was done, said or observed without an element of God or spirit being evoked. In relating with *Ngai*, sacrifices were offered under a *Mugumo* tree. The *Mugumo* tree acted as a sacred shrine for the Kikuyu. Being sacred these Mugumo trees were not to be used for firewood. The manner and steps followed in sacrificing to *Ngai* under the *Mugumo* tree is described in detail by Kenyatta (1938:222-59); Leakey (1977:1084-9) and more recently by Brown (1983:9-11).

Sacrifices were the most solemn form of worship. Their chief function was to maintain a healthy relationship between God and man, the departed and the living. When this relationship was disturbed, it was believed people experienced misfortunes and suffering. Hence, they offered a sacrifice to appease the supernatural powers. Sacrifices also served to make and renew contact between the spiritual and physical worlds. Only good people of good social standing officiated at a sacrificial ceremony (ACK 2001; Leakey

1977:1106-113; Karanja 1999:16-24; Cagnolo 2006:159-74). Many tribes in Africa used to make libations to the spirits, and this contention is confirmed by Ganusah (2001:282- 3) where it is indicated that libations are made in other parts of the African Continent such as Ghana. Ganusah further indicates that even in the Bible libation or drink offering is found in Genesis 35:14, Exodus 25:28, Numbers 29; 1 Samuel 7:16 and Hosea 9:4. Allusions to libations are also found in the New Testament in Philippians 2:17 and Hebrews 9:9-12. Ganusah feels however that the words of Hebrew 9:9-12 seems to eliminate the necessity of libation due to the words,

> "According to this arrangement, gifts and sacrifices are offered which cannot perfect the conscience of the worshipper, but deal only with food and drink and various ablutions. . . . .But when "Christ appeared as a high priest of the good things that have come, then through the greater and more perfect tent. . . he entered once for all into the Holy Place, taking not the blood of goats and calves but his own blood, thus securing an eternal redemption" (Ibid., 283)"

In their mode of sacrifices the Kikuyu sacrificed both to *Ngai* and Ngoma. However, their approach to *Ngai* was different from their regard for and approach to the ancestral spirits, who were subordinate to *Ngai*. While *Ngai* was only approached during times of major crises after all other ritual avenues had been exhausted, ancestral spirits could be approached at any time. Moreover, while the phrase used to sacrifice to *Ngai* was *guthathaiya Ngai* (to beseech God) that for sacrifice to the ancestors was *guitangira ngoma njohi* (to pour out beer for the spirits) or *guthinjira na guitangira ngoma njohi* (to slaughter a goat and to pour out beer for the spirits). ACK (2001) further clarifies that sacrifices and rituals marked the life of an individual and the community from childhood to adulthood and even after death (Leakey 1977:1075-102; Gathogo 2008:43-70; my respondents).

The Agikuyu Ancestral Spirits (Ngoma)

The use of the word *Ngoma* for Satan or devil needs to be qualified and to be critically addressed by theologians and the Christian church in Kikuyuland, as it is a terrible distortion of the meaning of the word and a great disservice to the ancestral spirits (*ngoma*) of the Agikuyu ancestors.

As expounded at great length by Kamuyu wa Kangethe (1988) in his excellent article, the Agikuyu traditional religion had two major components of beliefs, namely belief in one God (*Ngai—Mwene-Nyaga*) and belief in the spirits of the ancestors (*ngoma*). This contention is supported by Kenyatta (1938:241 and Leakey (1977:1074).

Kamuyu (1988) mentions a third force which he names Vital Power (*Hinya*). I do not agree with the existence of this third force. For me the existence of such a third force is debatable, as *Hinya* in Kikuyu means strength or power. In this case it refers to the Supernatural power of God. Therefore I will settle on the two components and not regard *Hinya* (Vital Power) as another component, since to the Agikuyu God (*Ngai*) was and is still all powerful among His other numerous attributes. The Agikuyu believed that God (*Ngai*) distributes His power and benevolence freely and evenly to every living organism. Kamuyu, Kenyatta and Leakey note that the belief in the ancestral spirits (*Ngoma*) was very strong among the Kikuyu. I do not agree with Kamuyu that such a belief is still strong, nor do I agree with some of his views, especially where he indicates that Agikuyu could be described as vitalist by faith.

However, I agree with Kamuyu when he indicates that the word *Ngoma* comes from the verb *Gukoma* (to sleep). *Gukoma* in the Kikuyu language refers to sleep. The Agikuyu referred to the ancestors as *Ngoma*. They believed that people do not die as such. They only sleep. When they do not wake up and take a long sleep, they go to join other people who are otherwise asleep (dead). Those who have thus died become *Ngoma* (ancestral spirits). The word *Ngoma* is used in both singular and plural forms.

Kamuyu (1988) observes that Agikuyu believe that the ancestors are ontologically higher in rank and therefore deserve to be respected and revered. Rituals and ceremonies were performed to appease them and to seek their protection from evil and misfortunes. This strong belief in the ancestors as noted by Kamuyu among the Agikuyu, led the missionaries to believe that the Agikuyu did not worship *Ngai*; rather, they worshiped the ancestors. As noted by Kamuyu, Rev. Barlow, a CSM missionary, concluded that: "*Ngoma* monopolizes attention of Agikuyu rather than God. Such worship of *Ngoma* is unnecessary, wrong and insulting to God."

Kamuyu notes that although the Agikuyu did not worship *Ngoma*, the missionaries could not be convinced otherwise. They believed that *ngoma* meant evil spirits(s). They therefore equated it with the English word devil. When the Bible was translated into the Agikuyu language in 1926, the word devil was translated as *Ngoma,* and the word "hell" was translated as *kwangoma.* The Agikuyu Christians subsequently believed that when a person died he became an evil person (a devil) and went to live in hell (*kwangoma*). This, as noted by Kamuyu, created an almost pathological fear of death which was non-existent traditionally. The missionaries view as elaborated by Kamuyu, that the Agikuyu worshipped the devil, led them to conclude that the Agikuyu had no conception of God, and, if they did, it was vague. He quotes an article by Mrs. E. Scott of the CSM describing the Agikuyu's conception of God as that "nebulous being called *Ngai* . . . who needs to be propitiated by sacrifice and his place is a bad place where it is cold and uncomfortable" (Kamuyu 1988:23-44).

Hobley, a colonial administrator wrote in 1922: "the belief of the tribes of Kikuyu and Ukamba generally consists of a rudimentary conception of a high god . . . This idea is naturally very vague . . . The belief in ancestral spirits . . . is the predominating spiritual factor in the minds of (these) people" (Hobley 1967:22; Kamuyu 1988:30).

Although some missionaries accepted the fact that the Agikuyu had a conception of a monotheistic deity, as noted by Kamuyu, they were apprehensive in accepting the fact that the Agikuyu *Ngai* was the same Christian God. As recently as 1953, Bewes, a CMS missionary, observed that although the missionaries used the term *Ngai* in the Bible translation, they only adopted the term, but the content had to be different (Bewes 1953:317). Kamuyu notes that this misconception and negative attitude toward Agikuyu religion led the missionaries also to have an even more negative attitude toward Agikuyu culture. This, he notes, was inevitable because Agikuyu culture and religion were inseparable. He asserts that it is difficult to talk about Agikuyu culture without talking about Agikuyu religion and social organization. Traditionally, the Agikuyu social organization was based on two basic units, namely the kinship and age-grade units. The kinship unit embraced all the individuals who were related by blood. Land ownership was associated with kinship unit. Land was considered sacred, because it is on that land that the ancestors slept and it is on the same land that the kinsmen got sustenance for their families and livestock. The alienation of land by the missionaries and the Europeans was therefore, a violation of the Agikuyu sacred value and belief.

Kamuyu (1988:23-44) asserts that the missionaries, confronted with culture and religion which was supposedly incompatible with Christianity, devised new techniques and theories of conversion in order to convert the Agikuyu from "heathenism" to Christianity. Kamuyu (1988:29-32) notes that, as pointed out by Beidelman, in Britain, conversion meant a rebirth of someone who was already a Christian but had grown lax. But in Africa conversion was essentially a rite of passage between the so called "pagan" African culture and Christianity. Beidelman (1982:105), as further noted by Kamuyu, goes on to observe the fact that missionizing in Africa particularly in the nineteenth century and the early part of the twentieth century made sense only if one had a negative evolutionary view of a culture one was trying to change. On this, Kamuyu adds that as long as the missionaries held the view that Africans had nothing to lose in their religion and culture other than magic, witchcraft, and misery, they had everything to gain in Christianity. The missionaries could therefore justify their work of evangelism. They felt that any form of syncretism should be totally rejected.

Kamuyu (1988:32) goes on to indicate that in general, anthropologists and psychologists consider conversion as a social change and alteration of personality. He notes that no theory on conversion has been done for Africa. Anthropologists have tended to concentrate on structural, functional, and procession changes in African culture. Kamuyu (Ibid., 32) observes that Beidelman has argued that "missionary views about the process of conversion ultimately amount to a theory of social change." Kamuyu sees Beidelman's argument as valid from the negative attitude missionaries had towards Agikuyu culture and religion. Such attitudes inevitably led the missionaries to demand radical social and cultural change among their converts and such a change was what was considered as "conversion". In order to convert the Agikuyu, the missionaries demanded that people make a total break from their traditional religion and culture. It was a heresy for these people to practise the traditional rites. Such practices came to be known as things of the devil (*maundu ma ngoma*) as opposed to things of God (*maundu ma Ngai*) (Ibid., 23-44). As indicated by Mbugua (2011:102) to the missionaries conversion was the act of turning from other religions (or no religion) to Christ (1 Thess 1:9; see also Young 1984: 150).

The above indicates that the missionaries misunderstood and distorted the Agikuyu view and standing of the concept of their ancestral spirits as well as the importance of their traditional religion.

Contrary to what the missionaries felt, the Agikuyu did not worship the ancestral spirits. This contention is supported by Kenyatta (1938: 235) who states:

> "... We can now proceed to discuss what is generally called "ancestor worship". In this account I shall not use that term, because from my practical experience I do not believe that the Gikuyu worship their ancestors. They hold communion with them but their attitude towards them is not at all to be compared with their attitude to the deity (God—Mwene Nyaga) who is truly worshiped..."

Confirming that the Agikuyu were Godly and sincerely believed in God and his benevolence, Kenyatta refers to an occasion when as a young boy he states:

> "In the case of the ceremony in which I took part (praying to God for rain under the sacred tree- Mugumo) I well remember

that our prayers were quickly answered for even before the sacred fires had ceased to burn torrential rain came upon us. We were soaked and it will not be easy for me to forget the walk home in the downpour (Kenyatta 1938: 244)."

Idowu (1973:182) contends that as observed by Parrinder, "Ancestral spirits are not worshiped. Swazi address them in much the same way as they speak to the living, and the word *tsetisa* (to scold) is frequently used to describe the manner of approach."

The above illustrates, as indicated by Kenyatta (1938:250), that the Agikuyu had a "vital communion with the High God (*Ngai*) of the tribe". In this regard and from observations referred to above, my view is that it is unfair and unjustified for anyone to condemn those early Agikuyu as un-godly. They were so godly that when they prayed to Him He promptly answered their prayers. To condemn the spirits (souls) of such people to the devil (*Kwa Ngoma*) is unfair and unwarranted. My feeling and wish is that the Agikuyu should cease referring to Satan as *Ngoma*: Satan should be called *caitani* and hell called "*gwa caitani*" or "*korokoro*". The word *Ngoma* should revert back to the spirits of the Agikuyu ancestors and the abode of their ancestral spirits to be referred to as *Kwa Ngoma*.

It is my view that full understanding about the ancestral spirits will be of value to the current Kikuyu generation, as they have no conception of Agikuyu ancestral spirits. As taught to their grandparents and parents by the early missionaries, the current Kikuyu generation view ancestral spirits as evil spirits and best ignored or not known at all. This issue of ancestor spirit is important to this study as before Christianity and colonization, the Agikuyu had no concept of heaven or hell. When one died, their soul (spirit) (*ngoma*) went to the world of the ancestors (*Kwa Ngoma*). To them that place was perfect in every way, as it was the place inhabited by their ancestors. A Mugikuyu longed to join them without fear or any doubt. This study, as reflected in the next section, will consider, among other things, the traditional manner of coping with death. The issue of where the spirit of the dead went to after death, which to the Agikuyu was the culmination of human existence, is of vital importance. As indicated earlier when life in this world ceased, the Agikuyu believed that was not the end, but a transition to a better place—the land of the ancestors (*Kwa Ngoma*).

Agikuyu Traditional Burial Rites

Githiga (1981:52-9) feels that the study of how Agikuyu traditionally dealt with death and how they carried out the resultant funeral rites has to some extent been studied by numerous scholars including Gathigira (1933); Macpherson (1970); Cagnolo (2006); Middleton (1953); Kabetu (1947) and Leakey (1977:957-91). However, from my findings, the most comprehensive study is that of Leakey.

Leakey (1977) and all my respondents observe that death coming as it does to all in due course, was viewed by the Agikuyu with a considerable degree of fatalism. They indicate that though death was never in ordinary circumstances welcomed, the Agikuyu did not have the haunting fear of death which grips the people of other civilizations. The fear of death of most civilizations was immortalized by Shakespeare in *Julius Caesar* where Julius Caesar tells Calpurnia (his wife) "Cowards die many times before their deaths; The valiant never taste of death but once. Of all the wonders that I yet have heard, It seems to me most strange that men should fear; Seeing that death, a necessary end, will come when it will come" (Shakespeare 1995:823).

Giving reasons for the Agikuyu's apparent lack of daunting fears when death was certain, Leakey and my respondents indicate that when a Kikuyu knew that his end was near, he usually faced the fact calmly and with equanimity. This can be accounted for, as indicated earlier, by the fact that in large measure they believed that all departed spirits were reunited in a single spirit world of the ancestors (*Kwa Ngoma*). Leakey and my respondents observe that the Kikuyu religious beliefs did not countenance the idea of a heaven and a hell, and when about to die a man was not tormented by the fear that after all he might be destined for the wrong place.

Additionally, the dying person was certain that as a departed spirit his life would not be unpleasant, for his needs would be taken care of by those members of his family who remained on earth and by their descendants, and eventually his spirit would be reincarnated and take its place once more among the living. The departed members of the community were reinstated by the birth of a child within the family who was named after the deceased. Leakey goes on to advise that to the Agikuyu, death took place because (*Ikundo ria mundu ucio niriathenga*). This according to Leakey means that "the knot of that man has been removed" (Leakey 1977:937-91). This is because when a Mugikuyu made an appointment so many days in the future, he would tie knots in a piece of string for each day until the appointed day. So the concept of death was that the appointed day of death of the individual had arrived, and there was therefore no need for worrying, as the day of death had come. The Agikuyu believed that the day of death was fixed at birth, and when a man's "days had run" death had to intervene, as nothing could alter that; there was therefore no need for worrying. It would be my wish that Christians adopt such an attitude towards death. I find the Christians' attitude towards death strange; most Christians fear death, while at the same time they realize that they cannot go to heaven unless they die. The reason for that fear might be the uncertainty most Christians have as to whether when they die they will go to heaven or to hell. Agikuyu did not have that problem. To them when one died one went without exception to the spirit world of their ancestors (*Kwa Ngoma*) where all are welcomed by those of their relatives who had died before.

This philosophical attitude towards death also meant that the relatives and friends of a dead person did not mourn unduly. Although they felt sorrow and loss of a dear one, they nonetheless were comforted by their sincere conviction that the dead person's spirit (*Ngoma*) would always be at hand. As death was inevitable there were no regrets that perhaps something should have been done to save the departed (Leakey 1977:938). It is not, however, clear why although death was not to be feared, yet a dead body was regarded as an unclean thing, and if anyone touched a dead body they had to be purified at once, as the Agikuyu believed that if this was not done, then the contagion of death would be transferred to another person (Ibid., 938; my respondents).

All of the above information regarding death and attitude to death by the Agikuyu was confirmed in total by the respondents who I interviewed orally in Kikuyu language during the months of October and November 2011. See their names and ages in the Schedule of Respondents Appendix II.

Death Ceremonies—Members of the Agikuyu Guild

As indicated earlier, the Kikuyu tribe consists of the members of the Agikuyu and Ukabi Guild. The Kikuyu Guild members' cultural practices differed considerably from the Ukabi (Maasai) Guild. Note should be taken here that the Ukabi (Maasai) Guild had nothing to do with the Maasai tribe (Leakey 1977: 1364).

I will first analyze the death ceremonies of the members of the Agikuyu Guild and later on analyze the death ceremonies of members of the Ukabi Guild.

Death Ceremonies of an Elder—Agikuyu Guild

In the Agikuyu Guild, the term "normal death" applied to deaths due to sickness or disease other than smallpox. Also deaths due to old age. Deaths due to violence, suicide or accident or deaths that took place away from home did not rank as normal deaths and were treated differently (Leakey 1977:938; my respondents).

When an Agikuyu man who was a polygamist, had a family which included grandchildren, and was also a responsible man, on finding himself at the point of death called his relatives around his death bed to express to them his last will (Cagnolo 2006:151). In the case of an elder who wanted to give and pass on the secret(s) of the ruling generation, he would summon one or more trustworthy elders of the same class. Cagnolo indicates that in such circumstances relatives took great care not to offend the dying in any way, as a complaint, or worse still a curse from his lips, would be the beginning of an endless trail of troubles. The dying man would then proceed to divide his fields and family property (Ibid., 153). Cagnolo further notes that the property of an average Kikuyu man amounted to very little, but there were a few who were wealthy, who owned large flocks of livestock and consequently a considerable number of wives (Ibid., 152). My paternal grandfather was such a person. He had large tracts of land, livestock and had nine legitimate wives. His brother was equally endowed with livestock and ten legitimate wives. On the other hand, my maternal grandfather had three legitimate wives. Cagnolo notes that the will was made verbally, but in the presence of numerous witnesses. He stresses that no one would ever think of challenging the will, because of the belief that the spirit of the dead maintained his interest in the affairs of the family and would visit with heavy penalties anyone who transgressed his will. A considerable number of Kikuyu even today fear the curse (*Kirumi*) of a dying person (Ibid., 152).

Leakey, Cagnolo and my respondents observe that as soon as an elder died and his death was pronounced, messages were sent to all his sons asking them to come home at once. Leakey explains that "an elder" does not mean any elderly or married man, but a married man who was of the standing of an elder, was a polygamist and had sons of his own who were circumcised and therefore old enough to take part in a burial ceremony. It is worthy of note that in Nyeri and Laikipia counties of Kenya and possibly in other areas where the Agikuyu reside, such elders were accorded and addressed respectfully as *muhomori* (singular) and *ahomori* (plural). That title and status was hardly known or applied by the Agikuyu of Kabete, Kikuyu District, Kiambu County, which as indicated earlier is the scope of this study. The body of an elder could not be disposed of until all his sons were present, but in practice it was held to be sufficient if the eldest son of each wife was present, and as many as possible of the others (Leakey 1977:940; my respondents).

As a preliminary to the burial of an elder who had died a normal death, a meeting of the elders was called immediately after the death of the elder. Cagnolo states that as there were no written rites, the elders endeavoured to piece together from their traditions all their recollection of the customs and rites to be performed on such occasions (Cagnolo 2006:152). It is worth noting, as Leakey asserts, that "*this was not an easy matter as most of the elders were only acquainted with the ritual from hearsay, (and this is emphasized) since the ceremony of burying anybody was performed very rarely*". The elders, who had been called and had arrived, told the senior son of the deceased how to put his father's body in the correct position for burial. This was necessary as the dead man had to be laid on his right side in "the sleeping position" that is to say, with his legs slightly flexed and with his right hand under his cheek and his left hand by his breast. What then followed? A lot of ritual and procedures, but briefly, the elders gave orders that the fires in every hut in the homestead had to be tended carefully day and night, and that in no circumstances was any fire to be allowed to go out until the *hukura* (to be explained later) ceremonies which concluded the death rites had been carried out. The elders ensured that the goat and cow bells of every animal in the homestead were removed, and that all he-goats that were mature enough to serve the females were to be castrated at once; additionally that all rams (which were never castrated) were to be taken away from the flock and shut up by themselves. Similarly all bulls were to be isolated from the cows (Leakey 1977:940; my respondents).

If death took place at night or early in the day, and if all sons were available, burial would take place on that day. All the flocks and herds had to be kept inside the homestead and fed with fodder, and all members of the family including the women and children had to remain within the homestead and not draw water or work in the fields. However, should the burial be delayed for a day or more owing to the absence of a son, the flocks could go to pasture and the women to the fields, but on the day chosen for burial no person or animal might leave the homestead until the body had been buried (Leakey 1977:940). It should be noted that the elders, where possible, ensured that the elder was buried the same day of death, so that the sun did not set before the burial (*Athikwo riua ritanathūa*).

When all the preliminary arrangements had been made, and where possible all the sons were present, the elders chose the site for the grave. The grave site had to be near to or on the far side of the rubbish midden *Kiaraini* (place where ashes from all the huts are deposited). This is unless the deceased had chosen a spot himself and marked it with a peg. The digging of the grave was started by the senior unmarried son of the deceased, and if there was no unmarried son, the senior unmarried nephew of the deceased would take up the task. Married sons had to be present, and the son who started the digging was later assisted by some of his junior brothers and nephews. The grave was an oval small pit about 6 feet long and 2 feet wide and 2 feet deep.

The Agikuyu used to dig with sharpened sticks (*Mīiro* or *Mīnyago*) made from hardwood (Cagnolo 2006:35). These sticks were the ones used to dig the grave. The earth had to be scooped out by hand. This in a way explains why the grave was not very deep. When the grave had been dug the gravediggers were instructed by the elders how to prepare the body. All the ornaments that the deceased was wearing had to be removed. The ornaments would then later be buried with him, but were never to be left on him. The body was then carefully wrapped in the skin garment of the deceased, after this had been knotted at the corners. His skin sleeping mat was also folded around him and then the whole bundle was tied up like a parcel with bark and roots of the plant called *Muoha akuu* (One that ties dead bodies). Care was taken not to cover the face of the dead man, which had to be allowed to peep out of the bundle. This was to allow the dead man to see what was going on (Leakey 1977:941; my respondents; Gathigira 1933:85, 86).

The body was then taken to the grave. Cagnolo (2006:156) notes that the procession was led by a medicine man carrying a burning torch The senior unmarried son took his father's head, with the other sons who had helped in digging the grave taking the feet and supporting the back. A body was not to be carried like an ordinary load, it was carried in the position in which it had lain immediately after death, with all the carriers on the same side of the bundle, by the man's back. The deceased's feet were carried first through the door of the hut in which he had died, and similarly through the main entrance (*thome*) of the homestead (Leakey 1974:941 and respondents interviewed). The funeral was not attended by close family members including wives or even friends. Agikuyu feared and avoided burials. Only the sons participating in the actual burial were present, his agemates, the officiating elders and the medicine man.

The body was carefully laid in the grave so that it was on its right side facing the homestead. The ornaments that the deceased was wearing when he died were all laid in the grave near his stomach. Then the wet skin (*Mūgūgūta*) of the goat or ox that had been slaughtered earlier in the day was laid over the bundle containing the body, care being taken not to cover the face and the eyes. The grave was then filled with earth and stones. Every son from the eldest to the youngest child that had been "born a second time" had to bring a branch of the *Mugaa* (Acacia thorn tree) and lay it over the pile of stones to represent their share of the burying ceremony. The young men who had dug the grave and carried the body had then to be purified from the contagion of death before they could eat anything. A small virgin ewe was slaughtered, and its stomach content (*tatha*) was used when mixed with water by the young men to bathe themselves all over the body with the mixture. The meat and skin of the slaughtered ewe was thrown away for the wild animals to eat, all except a small portion, which the elders had to eat, so that *mburi ndigateo ta mundu* (the ewe not to be thrown away like a person). This is unbelievable, as it means that the Agikuyu valued mutton or goat meat more than a human being. As shown later, the Agikuyu could throw away a dead person in the bush to be eaten by hyenas, but would not contemplate nor agree to mutton, beef or goat meat being thrown away to be eaten by wild animals, as they did the bodies of human beings. This more than anything else shows that the Agikuyu apparently had no regard for a dead body. Once someone died, that was the end of his earthly body, but not his spirit (*ngoma*), as the latter went immediately after death to join his ancestors.

When the body had been buried, and the meat from the animal from which the wet skin (*Mūgūgūta*) had been obtained earlier, had been eaten, any married sons of the deceased went back to their homes, but until the concluding *hukura* ceremony had been performed, they took care not to have sexual intercourse with their wives or with any other woman. They slept in their own huts and not in the hut of any wife (Leakey 1977:941; also respondents interviewed).

The very detailed account of the *hukura* ceremony was obtained from Leakey, my respondents as well as numerous authors and scholars. These scholars include, Gathigira (1933), Leakey (1977), Kabetu (1947) and Cagnolo (2006) among others. They observe that every single death involved the performance of a ceremony of *kuhukura* (the purification ceremony to free the home from the blight of death), which was considerably more complicated in the case of an elder than it was otherwise.

The object of the ceremony of *kuhukura*, as Leakey observes, was to remove the contagion of death and so enable all members of the family to resume normal life once more. As Leakey observes, the ceremony for an elder was divided into a number of stages and continued over a period of eight days, so that it might be brought to a close on the ninth day. In this respect it followed closely the customs connected with initiation. Similarly, too, the stages of the *hukura* ceremony were marked by ceremonial sexual acts on alternate days. The *kuhukura* ceremony was intended as a final rite of passage, marking the transformation of a living person to a departed ancestor. Leakey advises that the word *kuhukura* (to unbury) and *kuhuka* (to bury), are from the obsolete term –*huka*, which survives in such words as the noun *huko*, meaning mole rat, an animal notorious for burying objects. The body of the deceased was not, of course, literally unburied, but the ceremony was connected with the release of the soul and its transference to "the place of the spirits" (*Kwa-ngoma*) (Leakey 1977:943-5; my respondents).

The process of the *kuhukura* ceremony commenced when the moon reached the approximate stage it had been in when death occurred. The senior members of the deceased man's family arranged for some beer to be brewed by the deceased's widows. This beer was set to ferment in the hut of the senior widow, round which the ceremony would centre. When the beer was ready, they invited the council elders who had come to advise at the actual burial to come and drink the beer, which was called *njohi ya kuhukura* (beer for the traditional customs). Leakey advises that before the elders drank the beer they consulted the sons of the dead man about fixing a day for the ceremonies to begin, and they gave them instructions for the preliminary arrangements they had to make. Firstly, they had to make arrangements for an old woman who was accustomed to performing the ceremony of shaving the heads at *hukura* ceremonies to be present on the first day of the rites. Secondly, men had to be found who were willing to perform, for a fee, the services of ceremonial sexual intercourse with the widows during the course of the ceremonies. There had to be at least one of these men called *endia ruhiu* for each of the widows other than the senior widow. The latter was to perform this ceremonial act with a younger brother or patrilineal cousin of her deceased husband, not with the *mwendia ruhiu* (*ruhiu*) (a person who sells his sword (*ruhiu*) for a fee: his sword being the penis). Thirdly, they had to find certain number of *athuri matari kiene* (old men who had no social status), who would be needed in connection with the ceremonies. Fourthly, the arrangements had to be made for a few elderly widows of long standing to be present. Fifth, on the evening before the *hukura* ceremonies were due to start a fat ram of a single colour had to be tied to the bedpost of the senior widow so as to associate it with her and through her with the co-wives. This ram had to be slaughtered on the following day. The sixth arrangement was to take care to inform all the children of the deceased elder when the *hukura* ceremonies were to start so that all those who had to attend would be present. The seventh arrangement was that every widow of the deceased had to spend the days before the *hukura* started preparing quantities of cold cooked foods with the help of her daughters, because for the duration of the ceremonies no foods of any kind might be cooked (Leakey 1977:944; my respondents).

When all these arrangements had been completed, then the actual ceremony of *kuhukura* took place. On the first day early in the morning the first ram was brought out in the courtyard, where it was slaughtered by one or two male relatives of the deceased other than his children. After the animal had been cut up, one of the senior council elders who was acting as an advisor and counsellor, took the right foreleg, the right *ikengeto* (half-saddle joint) and another elder took a firebrand. These two elders were then joined by all the widows of the deceased and all the men who had come to perform the ceremonial sex acts with the widows. Leakey and my respondents assert that a younger brother of the deceased, or younger male patrineal cousin if there was no younger brother, also went with the procession. This was the man who would be the partner of the senior widow of the deceased in the sex rites. The procession was accompanied by a few senior members of the family—brothers or male cousins who were older than the deceased. They accompanied the others in order to witness the first stage of the *hukura* ceremonies, and to give advice as to the names of the deceased's dead relatives, who had to be called upon by name in the communion with the spirits that was about to take place. The widows of the deceased each carried bits of potsherd and broken gourds.

The whole procession, led by the council of elders made its way into the uncleared bush near the homestead. Having arrived at a secluded spot, the elders stopped and lit a small fire with the fire brands they had brought with them from the hut of the senior widow. When the fire had been lit and the meat had been grilled, the elders proceeded to cut most of the meat into small portions, placing these upon the bits of gourd and the potsherds that had been brought for the purpose. Leakey continues by indicating that they also cut off one large chunk of meat, which was laid aside. When all the meat had been cut up, each widow of the deceased, and each of the men who were to perform the ceremonial sex acts with them, tasted a little bit. Then the senior widow took a potsherd with meat in it, and while everybody else stood in silence she held it in the palms of her hands and called out the name of her deceased husband, saying, "*Uka riu nguhe rwiga ruaku, noureke igongona ciothe iirike wega*" (Come now that I may give you your portion, and may you allow all the sacrifices to be completed satisfactorily). The "sacrifices" referred to in these prayers were the ceremonial sex acts which each widow was to perform.

After the senior widow had thus called upon her dead husband and offered him his portion of the meat, the other widows, the younger brother of the deceased, and the men who were to *hukura*, each in turn called upon some deceased relative of the man for whom this ceremony was being performed. When the list of names of married deceased relatives of the same generation as the dead person had been exhausted, more pieces of meat were offered to the spirits that were called *thaka*. These were the spirits of dead members of the deceased's generation who had died before they were married and who would therefore never be reincarnated, since they had no descendants. Such spirits were never mentioned or called upon by name, but were addressed as *thaka* (Ibid., 945; my respondents).

Finally the large piece of meat that had been laid aside was held up by the senior widow and offered to *aria mariganiire* (those who have been forgotten). They were invited to come and share this large piece of meat among themselves. All the potsherds and pieces of gourd were then laid upon the ground in a little group at the foot of the *muthakwa* tree, with the offerings in them. This concluded the ceremonial communion with the spirits. The spirit of the dead elder had now formally joined the other departed spirits, and had been communicated with for the first time by those whom he had left behind (Ibid.,945; my respondents).

The whole party then returned to the homestead for the next rite; that of putting on *ngoka* for the departed spirits. The *ngoka* were rings made by one of the officiating elders by twisting a long tendril of the creeping grass known as *igoka*. As he made each one and laid it down finished, he called out the name of the dead man for whom the *hukura* ceremony was taking place. The ngoka rings were won above the elbow by each member of the family of the deceased, during the duration of the *hukura* ceremony.

Then each widow went to her hut accompanied by the man who was to perform the ceremonial sex act with her. Outside in the courtyard was the council of elders who were in charge of the proceedings and the old widows of long standing who had been called in. The senior widow accompanied by the younger brother or male cousin of her dead husband, now proceeded to have full ceremonial sexual intercourse once and once only. As soon as they had done so, the man was to clear his throat loudly. When the elders and widows out in the courtyard heard this sound they signalled the second senior widow, and she and the man who was with her had ceremonial sexual intercourse. When this man gave the same signal to show that they had performed the "sacrifice", the elders told the next widow to proceed, and so on until each widow had performed the ceremonial sex act. All her unmarried children and all the stock that belonged to her hut must be present so that they might participate in the ceremony. This ceremonial sex act on the first day of the ceremonies was called *gutheca gikuu* (to pierce death, namely, have intercourse with death) (Leakey 1977:947; respondents interviewed).

It should be noted that it was absolutely essential that every unmarried child of each widow be present in her hut while she was performing the ceremony of sexual sacrifice, for she was performing it not only for herself, but on behalf of all her unmarried children, including warriors and initiated girls. If any children were absent they would never be able to marry for they would not have been "purified from the contagion of death" and would infect whoever they married with this contagion of death as soon as they had sexual intercourse.

When all the ceremonial sex acts had been performed, the occupants of each hut went to sleep, but not before they had banked up the fires in each hut. If the fires were to go out on this night or any night while the ceremony of *kuhukura* was proceeding, it would be an even more serious matter than if they went out between the day of death and the start of the *hukura* ceremonies (Leakey 1977:943-8; my respondents).

All this, as observed, happened on the first day. The second day was called a *mutiro* day (or a day for suspending normal activities) and all that those who were engaged in the ceremonies did was eat, sit in the courtyard, and sleep. That night each widow slept in her hut, as did all her unmarried children, and the man who had performed the ceremonial sex act with her. But in no circumstance was sexual intercourse allowed on this night; it was a day and night of resting.

On the third day, each widow, with all her unmarried children and her stock present in the hut, again had ceremonial sexual intercourse once with her partner, in the order of seniority as on the evening of the first day and in the same way. This was called *gutheca tuura* (to have sexual intercourse with *tuura*). The meaning and significance of the word *tuura* is obscure and no longer known by the Kikuyu; it was handed down from the distant past with this custom (Leakey 1977:949; my respondents).

On the fourth day like the second day, this was a day of *mutiro*, when everyone rested and did nothing but eat, sleep and sit about. The proceedings opened on the morning of the fifth day with the slaughter of a he-goat known as *thenge ya gutiira* (the goat of propping up). Some of the meat of this animal was boiled in the hut of the various widows, and some of it was roasted; it was eaten by the elders officiating the ceremony, also by all the members of the family and by the men who were partners of the widows.

Apart from this meat eating, there was no special ceremony until nightfall, when everyone went to their huts. Then each widow and her partner had ceremonial sexual intercourse twice. There was no longer any need to observe any special order of seniority, and no longer any need to give signal when the sex had taken place. Nothing mattered so long as the pairs had intercourse twice between darkness and dawn next morning. On the sixth day, all the widows and their partners set to work to prepare sugar cane beer, which was called *njohi ya guthambia moko* (beer for washing the hands). In the afternoon, after the beer had been prepared, all the widows and their partner were ceremonially shaved a second time by the professional head-shaver. She then received her fee and went home. On this night, the night after the sixth day of the ceremonies, every person slept in the hut he or she had been sleeping in throughout the ceremony, but no sexual intercourse was allowed. This was a *mutiro* day, or day of resting (Leakey 1977:950; respondents interviewed).

The seventh day an elder uterine brother of the deceased came to the homestead bringing with him a stall-fattened ram (*ngoima*) and some beer. The ram was slaughtered and eaten by the family as a whole including the descendants of the dead man, as well as the man who had brought it, and any other near relatives who were available. This feast was called *kurianira ngoima* (to eat the stall-fed ram together). Its significance was that it once more reunited the members of the family as a whole with the immediate family of the deceased who, for the past five weeks, had been in isolation owing to the contamination. When the meat had been eaten, all members of the family who were old enough partook of the beer brought by the brother, and the beer brewed on the previous day by the widows and their partners (Leakey 1977:950; respondents interviewed).

On the evening of the seventh day, as the number seven was considered unlucky by the Agikuyu, all members of the family had to sleep in the huts and the women had to be with their partners, but there was no sexual contact. On the eighth day a ram or a virgin ewe was slaughtered and a medicine man was called in to carry out the ceremony of *gutahikia* (to purify) the widows and their partners. Each widow and the man who had performed the ceremonial sexual intercourse with her was purified in strict order of seniority, just outside the doorways of the respective widows' huts (Leakey 1977:951; respondents interviewed).

That night the widows and their partners once again slept together and had sexual intercourse twice. This completed the proceedings, and on the following day life returned to normal, and the men who had been partners of the widows (*endia-ruhiu*) received their fees and went home. The fee consisted of a sheep or a goat, and it was for this fee that the man "sold his sword" *ruhiu* (penis).

If, during the course of the eight days of the *hukura* ceremony, any of the men who had been partners of the widows should have formed a special friendship with his partner, then that man might, from this time on, claim a special right to come and have sexual intercourse with her and even beget children by her. Such children, it should be noted, did not rank as the children of their physical father but as children of the deceased man. Although the responsibility for looking after, feeding, and clothing the widow, was inherited by one of the relatives of the deceased, she could not be prevented from having her partner from the *hukura* ceremonies as her lover if she wished it (Leakey 1977:942-52; respondents interviewed).

At the start of the *kuhukura* ceremony for an elder, all those who were taking part helped each day to pull out a few of the wall planks (*mihirigo*) and roof supports of *thingira*, the hut in which death had taken place, so that by the eighth day of the ceremonies the roof collapsed inwards on the ruins of the hut, and the *murari* (soot on the inside thatch) fell to the ground inside. The poles and planks that were taken from the hut each day during the *kuhukura* ceremonies were used to keep a fire burning in the centre of the courtyard. Any timber planks left over after the ceremonies had been completed might be used as firewood for fires lit in the courtyard or in the entrance area, but not for fires inside any hut. On no account might any wood from a hut in which a man had died be used for building any other hut, nor might it ever be used for cooking purposes.

Leakey notes that, a short time after the *hukura* ceremony had been completed, arrangements had to be made by the sons or by junior brothers or nephews of the deceased to move the whole homestead to a new site. This was called *guthamira gikuu* (to move away from death). This move was only a ceremonial one and the homestead did not need to be moved more than a 100 ft, but every hut had to be moved except the one that had been pulled down and destroyed. The most important consideration was that the whole move had to be completed in a single day for the whole homestead to start a new life (Leakey 1977:965 and my respondents).

Extramarital Sex, Sex Taboos and Some Other Aspects Of Agikuyu Sex Life That Were Observed in the Past but not Presently

The issue of *mwendia ruhiu* (seller of his penis) might seem strange, but Middleton comments about it, although he does not mention the seller in the context of funeral rites (*kuhukura*). Nonetheless, he mentions the seller of the sword in connection with the sexual life of the senior widow, whereby Middleton indicates, 'the senior wife (Nyakiambi) may not remarry but she is inherited by the husband's brother or may live with a mate (*mwendia ruhiu*)' (Middleton 1953:51; my respondents).

The contemporary Kikuyu might regard extramarital sex as abhorrent, but it was part and parcel of the Agikuyu before colonization by the British and for a considerable period even after colonization up to around 1950, a few years before the state of emergence in Kenya due to the Mau Mau struggle (1952-1960). For example, Kabetu gives numerous Kikuyu taboos (*migiro*), some touching on extra-marital sex and abnormal sex which include:

- For a man to have sex with a sheep was taboo, and that sheep had to be killed.

- For anyone to practise homosexuality was taboo; those found doing so had to undergo a duel of death until one dies.

- When a wife loses a child by death, her husband could not have sexual intercourse with her until she had had intercourse with another man (Kabetu 1947:105-8)

Other sources that give strange angles of the sex life of the pre-Christianity Kikuyu include Kenyatta, who notes that after circumcision and before marriage premarital sex (*nguiko*) was allowed, but that it was strictly controlled. A girl and a boy would sleep together, but under no circumstance would the boy penetrate the girl. The Kikuyu girl had to marry when she was still a virgin (Kenyatta 1938:157-62).

Kenyatta goes on to indicate that agemates could exchange partners after marriage. When one went to visit an agemate, he could plant a spear (*Kuhanda itimu*) at the door of one wife and spend the night with that wife and have sexual intercourse with her. This is irrespective of whether the husband was in the same homestead or not. However, this privilege was strictly controlled, as none would dare plant a spear in front of the hut of a woman who was not of the same age group as her husband. A fierce fight would arise if such a thing happened; at times the adulterer was killed or seriously injured. Additionally, he had to compensate the offended husband with a goat or a ram (Kenyatta 1938:180-3). Non-Agikuyu scholars and missionaries have condemned the practice of wife-sharing. One of them in particular, Peterson (2004:3), advises that his respondents told him that at times of *ituika*, once the necessary goat had been paid, men of the rising generation were permitted to commit adultery with other men's wives. To me this view has been expressed from the missionary point of view, but has not taken into consideration the long-standing and time-honoured practice of wife-sharing by Agikuyu agemates which started, as explained earlier, soon after initiation, when agemates were allowed to have *nguiko*, during which period agemates could swap girls. It is worth noting that the practice of wife-sharing was common in numerous African tribes. An example is that of the Kikuyu's nearest neighbors, the Maasai, who are known to have continued with the practice long after it was abandoned by the Kikuyu.

According to Leakey (1977:1275), a woman who had given birth in any unnatural way, that is, whose baby had been born feet first or who had had twins or had had a child with six fingers or other unnatural feature, was required to have sexual intercourse with some man other than her husband before she could again resume normal relations with him. The underlying idea was that through the sexual act, the *thahu* (taboo) of the abnormal birth would be transferred from the wife to the other man, and would therefore not affect the husband. By this act the *thahu* (taboo) would be sterilized.

Kimani (2004:412) notes that marital sex takes place only inside the woman's hut and on her bed, never open in the bush. The marriage bed has to remain undefiled. No warrior was allowed to visit a married woman in her hut. This acted as a control valve against creating an opportunity for adultery between friends. The woman's hut functioned as a venue for significant family affairs such as sex for procreation. This took place at night at the woman's hut when all other unmarried family members were asleep in the same hut. This meant that the members of the family were part of the process of procreation. Extending the family through acquiring new members.

Middleton notes, as indicated earlier, that the senior wife (*nyakiambi*) may not remarry. She is inherited by the husband's younger brother or by his sons. Note should be taken that a man may not inherit the wife of his deceased son nor the widow of a younger brother, because he stands in the relation of father to her. Middleton indicates that if a widow has no brother-in-law, a stepson could inherit her, if not she was passed to a man of her own clan (Middleton 1953:51).

This custom by the Agikuyu has some similarity with the Levirate marriage practised by the Hebrews. Killen (1975:1083), and Hirsch (1939:526), advise that this was the marriage of a childless widow to her husband's brother, which was an ancient custom practiced at the time of the Patriarchs (Gen 38:8), and later incorporated into the law of Moses (Deut 25:5-10). It should be noted that since Levirate could take place only after the death of the first husband, it does not contradict the purpose of Lev 18:16; 20:21. These passages forbade marriage to a brother's wife as a general rule, but this was to be annulled when the first husband had died childless, in order that his family name might be maintained by another of his family. Either a brother or the nearest male kin was required to raise up seed in the name of the deceased. If the obligation was repudiated, the widow was to put him to open shame. Put in another way, while the law limited the matrimonial duty to the brother, and permitted him to decline to marry the widow, such a course was accompanied by public disgrace (Deut 25:5). Finally by the law of Numbers 27:8, daughters were given the right to inherit, in order that the family estate might be preserved, and the Levirate became limited to cases where the deceased had left no children at all (Killen 1975:1083) (cf. Unger 1988:821; Young 1984:359; Browning 2009:235).

Disposal of the Dead—Agikuyu Guild—Others

Other than the burial of a prominent elder as described above all the other people had their bodies disposed of as briefly described here. This was different for the body of an elderly married woman and very young children.

In the case of a young married man who had died a normal death and had no grown-up sons, he was not buried. The entrance of his hut was closed with a wooden plank or woven door together with large stones. Then some planks at the back of the hut were removed to make a gap. The body was left alone at night to enable wild animals to come through the gap and remove the body and take it away to devour.

When a man who had no grown-up sons able to bury him was taken seriously ill, he instructed his young sons to ask for help from some of his close relatives and others. When the brothers, cousins, agemates and others came he was carried out alive to the *kibirira* (an area in the bush set aside in that village, or ridge for the disposal of the dead). Here they lit a fire for him and made a temporary shelter. The sons took turns watching over their dying father. They removed all his ornaments from him when he was still alive, and laid them besides him. When he died the sons left the body there in the bush to be eaten by wild animals. Often, as wild animals did not come immediately; the body would rot, infesting the surroundings with its stench. Many times at night, the relatives would hear from their huts the sound of hyenas, jackals and leopards crunching the bones of the departed. They would huddle silently around the fire with their heads on their knees and sigh "*uhoro ni muthiru*" meaning all is over. If several days elapsed before the corpse was devoured this was taken as an evil omen (Cagnolo, 2006:152).

The mode of disposing the dead thus varied depending on the status, age and gender of the deceased. A very simplified version of burial rites that resembled those of an elderly man were those of an elderly married woman from a polygamist marriage, who was buried by the husband. In the case of an elderly widow, she was buried in a simple manner, but not by her sons but by her grandsons. An elderly married woman who had no co-wives was never buried, but taken to the *kibirira* to die there, and when dead to be devoured by wild animals. This shows how important polygamy was to the Agikuyu. A young married woman was never buried, but taken to the *kibirira* to die and be devoured by wild animals.

In the case of a young widow, she was inherited by one of the younger brothers of her late husband or by one of his sons. The widow and her children went to live in his homestead, and he inherited all the expenses or duties of the widow, although he did not take her as his physical wife unless she wished. The widow would in cases where she did not become the physical wife of the brother who inherited her, take lovers and even have children with them. Children from such union(s) belonged to the deceased and not her lover(s) and would be looked after by the brother who had inherited the widow. The disposal of her body, should she die, was the responsibility of the brother who had inherited her and not her lover. For the unmarried, uninitiated girl, her body was dragged and left at the *kibirira* to be eaten by wild beasts. This was also the case of an uninitiated boy or a young child. The latter was taken to the *kibirira* by the mother not by the father (Ibid., 152). The above shows that very few Agikuyu were buried as such. The majority were left to be eaten by wild beasts.

Disposal—Abnormal Deaths of Kikuyu Guild Members

According to Leakey, deaths caused by the following were regarded as violent deaths: deaths caused by spears, arrows, teeth, claws or horns of wild animals, falling branches of trees that were being felled, game pits, rock or earth falls, fire and death by lightning. A person whose immediate death was caused by any of these things was never touched nor his ornaments removed, but was left where he was, so that at night wild animals might come and devour him (Leakey 1977:940).

Death by drowning was a special case. Ultimately, when the body was retrieved from the river it was laid on the bank and left there to be eaten by wild animals. Death by suicide was usually by hanging. In such an occurrence, when the body was discovered, the normal custom was to cut the body down. No ornament was removed. Should suicide might have occurred indoors the doorway of the hut was blocked with thorns and stones and a hole made in the wall of the hut so that wild animals could enter it at night and devour the body (Leakey 1977:940 and respondents). Should suicide have occurred in the open, such as hanging on a tree, the body was cut down and left there untouched to be devoured by wild animals.

Death due to famine was common, as when there was prolonged drought, scarcity of food followed and a large number of people died. In such circumstances, as was the case when an epidemic of small pox was raging, normal ceremonies were suspended. The main reason was that no one was strong enough for the task of burial or carrying bodies out to the *kibirira* (Ibid., 940; and my respondents). Consequently the bodies were left where they lay, to rot or be eaten by wild animals.

The Ukabi (Maasai) Guild Burials and Accompanying Rites

Leakey (1977:940) and the respondents observed that the ceremonies, purification and accompanying rites connected with death and disposal of the dead were simpler among members of the *Ukabi* (Maasai) Guild. The major difference was that in respect of the burial of an *Ukabi* (Maasai) guild elder, immediately death occurs, all council elders of his generation age-group who lived in the vicinity were notified. On arrival at the deceased homestead, an ox (or for those not so rich, a big he-goat) was slaughtered and eaten by the elders. This was called *ndegwa ya kugaya gitonga* (meaning the ox for diving up (the property of) the rich man). A second animal (ox or a big ram for those not so rich) was killed and eaten by the family. This was called *ndegwa ya guthika muthuri* (the ox for burying the elder) (Ibid., 975 and respondents). When the elders had finished eating the first ox or he-goat they gave instructions for the digging of the grave, the wrapping of the body and so forth, details of these matters were the same as those of burial of a Kikuyu guild elder (Ibid., 975 and my respondents).

Burial took place the same day when death occurred. When the body had been laid inside the grave, the grave was then filled with earth and thorns. Observance of no sex either by animals or the family of the deceased until after *kuhukura* ceremony was also strictly observed. During the first day of the *kuhukura* ceremony, a ram was slaughtered. After being strangled and partially skinned, its blood was drawn off, mixed with fresh milk and put into a large gourd. This *ngibutu* (milk mixed with fresh blood) would be used in the evening for a "sacrifice."

Heads of all those who were to participate in the *hukura* ceremony, namely the younger brother or patrilineal male cousin of the deceased, and of the widows, were shaved. All the furniture and moveable property of the deceased were anointed with some of the ram's fat. Then each widow and each son who was present took one of these objects, so as to identify themselves during the *hukura* ceremony with the deceased.

In the evening of the first day, the senior widow handed her gourd of blood and milk to the leader of the ceremonies, the two of them sitting together on her bed. He drank some of it and gave the gourd back to her to drink. This was the Ukabi Guild equivalent of the ceremonial sex act of the Kikuyu Guild. In the other huts each widow drank from the gourd with her senior unmarried son. There was no activity on the second day except eating and lying about. On the third day all those participating in the ceremony went to the river and washed themselves. They then anointed their bodies with red ochre mixed with water. The rest of the day was spent in idleness and in eating, and no work was done.

According to the rules of the Ukabi initiation guild, the *hukura* ceremony came to an end on the fourth day. All the friends and relatives came to visit the family, bringing with them presents of beer, rams, he-goats and food of all kinds. The family and visitors participated in a great feast to celebrate the end of the mourning and the *hukura* ceremonies. One more month had to elapse before anyone was allowed to have sexual intercourse. When the next moon was reached, the younger brother or male cousin of the deceased who was the leader of the ceremonies went to the widow with whom he had drunk the blood and milk and had ceremonial sexual intercourse with her twice in one night. After an interval of a day or two, men of the Ukabi Guild who were personal friends and agemates of the deceased were invited to come and have ceremonial sexual intercourse with the other widows. This was done in strict order of precedence and with an interval of a day or two between each ceremony (Ibid., 979-80 and my respondents).

The final act of *kuhukura* was called the ceremony of *Gutindika Muthuri* (literally to push the elder). The essence of this ceremony was that the leader of the *kuhukura* ceremony together with some elders and their wives and all the widows and sons of the deceased proceeded a distance from the homestead in a procession. They made sure that the doors of all the huts were left open and a fire was burning brightly. They then slaughtered a young ram, half of which was roasted and eaten. At the same time they called the spirits of the departed, who were in the bush, to come and partake in the feast.

At least half of the roasted meat was wrapped in the animal skin and left at the foot of the bush. The breast (*githuri*) of the ram was hung up in the bush. The beer and the food were also laid at the foot of the tree. Then the elders invoked his spirit (the spirit of the deceased) and those of other dead members of the family to come and share these offerings. At the same time, they begged them to stay in peace and not come back to the homestead to bother those who were still alive. After a short interval the whole homestead was moved, including the hut in which the elder had died. The new homestead was erected at a distance from or near to the abandoned homestead.

Other deaths of the Ukabi Guild members were handled differently. In the Ukabi Guild not all elders were buried. Many of them, like junior married men in the Kikuyu Guild, were taken to the *kibirira* and left there for wild animals to devour. Elderly senior married women who had grown-up sons were buried lying on the left side behind her hut. If the widow of an elder had taken up residence in the homestead of one of her grown-up sons, when she died, she was buried not by her sons but by her grandsons.

For young unmarried men and women and uninitiated boys and girls when they became seriously ill they were carried out to a shelter in the *kibirira* area. The sick person was watched and carefully tended until he or she died. All ornaments on them were taken off before death and laid beside the body. Upon death the body was left there for wild animals to devour.

Should death have taken place suddenly, the body was wrapped up and carried out through a gap in the fence of the homestead to the *kibirira* and left there for the wild animals. A child's body was disposed off by the mother at the *kibirira* for wild animals to devour.

The body of those whose death was of a violent nature, and these included deaths from suicide, death due to smallpox or famine, or the death of a complete stranger, was left where it was or dragged to the *kibirira* for wild animals to devour. No ornaments were removed from these bodies. Anyone who had touched the bodies of any dead person had to be cleansed (Ibid., 979-80; and my respondents).

Summary of the Kikuyu Rites Concerning Death

The contents of this summary rely heavily on the works of Leakey (1977:988, 991). His accuracy to detail and thoroughness were in every respect similar to the information obtained from all my respondents interviewed orally in Kikuyu District during the months of October and November, 2011. From the above-mentioned observations a sharp distinction is drawn—in both the Kikuyu Guild and Ukabi Guild customs—between the deaths of people who were married and those of people who died before they were married.

It should be noted that where marriage payments were not transferred from one family to another it was not considered a binding marriage. For a marriage to be recognized, the dowry or a portion thereof had to have been paid. The woman in such a union still belonged to her family (clan). On her death, it would be her family who would dispose of her body. Should her husband die before her, then his clan would have to settle the full customary dowry to the clan of the woman. Failure to do so would oblige the woman to return to her clan and be married afresh to another man. A young married woman who had not yet had a child counted as a *thaka* and was grouped with the unmarried. The really important distinction between the two groups was the question of children. All those who had children, even if the children were all dead, were treated in a special way, which included the performance of a full *hukura* ceremony and the sacrifice of a special ram or ewe for the spirit of the deceased. The spirits of those who had not married or who had not yet borne children did not have a ram or ewe sacrificed to them. If a *hukura* ceremony was performed for them, it was only a very modified and insignificant variation of the full rite. From these facts it can be seen why every Kikuyu was so anxious to have children; it meant, among other things, that the spirit achieved a status which it would not have otherwise achieved. It is also noted that as much importance was attached to the spirit of senior married women as to those of senior married men, as it was believed that either was as capable as the other of doing good or evil to those who survived them.

A third fact which emerges is that especially among members of the Kikuyu Guild (which has a far bigger following in south Kikuyu than the Ukabi Guild), it was believed that there was some very definite connection between sex acts and death. In the rites and ceremonies of the Kikuyu Guild, for example, certain ceremonial sex acts punctuated the whole *hukura* ceremony. For the Ukabi Guild the only ceremonial sex acts were at the conclusion of *hukura* ceremony and before absolute normal life was resumed.

In both guilds no person closely connected with a dead person might have normal sexual intercourse before the *hukura* ceremonies were over, and the rule even applied to the cattle and stock of the deceased, if the deceased was a married man with more than one wife (i.e. if he was a polygamist). As women did not ordinarily own stock, this prohibition did not affect the stock of a homestead if a married woman died.

It is important to note that for married people who had children, death was marked by the *hukura* ceremonies. That fact that the *hukura* ceremonies were either omitted or much modified in connection with the death of unmarried people suggests that their deaths were considered premature, and had taken place before they were really qualified to move into the last stage of life. The very close similarity in both the Ukabi Guild and Kikuyu Guild rites between the stages of the *hukura* ceremony and the stages of initiation into adult status cannot fail to impress (Ibid., 979-80 and my respondents).

Leakey comments on the much criticized custom of "throwing bodies to the hyenas." He notes that this idea was by no means as callous or casual as many writers, Christians and foreigners (especially those outside the African continent) have made it appear. He notes that,

> "Apart from the body of a complete stranger which was dragged rather hastily to the bush, the Kikuyu, custom of taking dead bodies out to the kibirira was a carefully planned one. In every case the body had to be carefully wrapped up with hands and the legs in sleeping position, and placed in the kibirira facing the homestead. The fact that the body was allowed to be eaten by the wild animals instead of being buried was not at all upsetting to the Kikuyu, who considered the European practice of

incinerating (cremation) as an alternative to burial, an utterly revolting and horrible idea. It is all a question of one's point of view" (Leakey 1977:980).

Peterson (2004:3) is of the view that the Agikuyu as late as 1919 used to leave the dead to be devoured by hyenas, he states that "...some 14,293 young men from the Gikuyu District were conscripted during the First World War and served as carrier corps and suffered a 20 percent casualty rate. Nor were those at home spared. Famine and influenza decimated Gikuyu communities in 1918...Nyeri was especially hard hit. Some 10 percent of the districts population perished, so many that overfed hyenas left human bodies to rot in the open." Commenting on the abolition, during the British colonial era, of the mode of disposal by the Agikuyu of throwing the body in the bush Gathigira (1933) indicates that,

" No riu gutiri kiimba gitathikagwo, gwata kia mwana kana kia mundu mukuru kana mukia, tondu kiama kia Local Native Council nikiarutire watho ati gutiri kiimba gigacoka guteo o uguo githaka-ini, no muhaka ciothe ithikagwo, na mundu ukurega gwika uguo niarirutithagio thinjo kana akohwo. "

This means that the Local Native Council gave a directive (by-law) that all corpses, be they of a child or an old man or woman or a poor person, had to be buried. Failure to comply with this by-law could result in one being fined or jailed. The passing of these by-laws by the Local Native Councils of the then Kikuyu Districts appears to have happened in all districts according to Gathigira, who does not indicate when the by-laws were passed. His book was, however, published in 1933, and so it can be assumed that the by-laws were enacted before that date. From what has been revealed above in this book and as will be elaborated further in the following chapter, it is right to deduce that the influence of the Christian missionaries and the decree by the colonial British Administration contributed immensely to the Agikuyu ceasing to throw corpses of their dead to be devoured by wild animals. As indicated earlier, this occurred during the first half of the last century and long before Kenya attained independence from Britain in 1963.

Traditional Funeral Rites of Selected African Tribes

Africa has more than 2000 different tribes. Each tribe has its own dialect and distinct culture, as well as its traditional religion. As can be expected the traditional methods of disposing of the dead and belief in the after life differs from tribe to tribe. Scholars who have produced reasonable works on this matter include Odak (1996:41-53); Blakery et al. (1994:309-411); Olupona (1991:55-7); King (1970:74-83).

Akamba View of Death and Their Burial Rites

Gehman (1989:62-3) advises that the Akamba used to have funeral ceremonies after death, which were mostly centred around the death of a married man, especially the older ones. An unmarried man was considered as not fully human and failed to attain immortality, and hence could not be accorded similar funeral rites to those of a married man. The more powerful a person was before death the more elaborate the ceremonies were for him after death. Mourning began immediately after death and intensified during the time of burial. The mourning was shorter for the death of women and children and longer for fathers and grandfathers. Burial customs were very important. The body was covered by skins or blankets, and could not be seen by unauthorized persons. Only approved individuals who were old men, sexually inactive, could handle the body. A young man could never touch a dead person for fear that he might pass death on to the family through sexual activities. The Agikuyu beliefs about death and on the relationship between death and sex have a lot of resemblance to this.

Gehman (1989:62-3) asserts further that traditionally the corpses were disposed of by tossing the body into the bush far from home, so that wild animals would devour them. Gradually this custom changed as, regulations by the colonial government (British) were issued indicating where and how a corpse would be buried. After the burial a sacrifice was made to the ancestral spirits. After disposing of the body, purification was necessary in order to remove death. This was a ritual sexual intercourse to render death harmless. The bereaved person had to have ceremonial coition (sexual intercourse) before any other member of the family was permitted to engage in sex. The widow would perform this with the man inheriting her, the widower with another wife or with another woman. Anyone who had touched the corpse had to be cleansed by a medicine man. From this account of the funeral customs of the Akamba one notices some identical or similar practices to those of the Akambas immediate neighbors to the west—the Agikuyu.

Kenya—Gusii Tribe

Among the Gusii (a tribe in western Kenya), in the event of a husband being sick or seriously ill he was moved to his senior wife's hut. It was a custom that a man dies in the house of his first wife (Kingoina 1999:70). When the man died, the elders were alerted by the screaming, mostly of women at that home. The first thing the elders did was to establish whether the deceased had left a will. It was customary that when a man wanted to leave a will, he requested reliable elders, who included his son(s) if he had any, to come and listen to his will and last wishes. He would then verbally tell them of his wishes (Ibid., 70).

If there was no verbal will, a funeral committee which included elders, uncles, brothers, sons, would consider the fate of the widow and heirs of the deceased. All the assets of the deceased including land, livestock, and so on, were discussed, as well as all his debtors (Kingoina, 1999:70-72; Kamau 2009:54-62). Widows were to mourn their husbands by turning their clothes inside out. Early in the morning of the day following death, the eldest son marked the grave with a hoe at a site he was shown by the brother of the deceased. If the deceased had grandsons, it was the oldest grandson who marked the grave site. The burial site was to be on the right-hand side of the first wife's house as one goes out from the main door (Kingoina 1999:73; Kamau 2009:54-62).

A son who was not the biological son of the deceased could not mark the grave, as according to the Agusii, a man had to be buried by his sons, his own blood, "his own spear", a son born inside the marriage, not brought by the mother from another man. The "spear" here refers to the man's penis. This is also similar to the Agikuyu, who refer to the penis as sword; in other words, an instrument for piercing. After marking the grave, the grave was then dug by able-bodied men of the clan. The only exception was a man who had a wife who was pregnant; if this was the case, the Gusii believed that evil spirits would affect both the mother and the unborn baby.

If a husband died without having paid a dowry for his wife or wives, the clan first legalized the marriage or marriages by payment of dowry before the wife could bury the husband. As noted earlier in this study, payment of dowry was also of utmost importance in the Agikuyu community, as payment of dowry decided whether the dead woman was legally married, and therefore entitled to be buried by her husband or entitled to participate in the burial of her husband.

After burial, a he-goat was slaughtered in the first wifes' house. On the second day after burial a second goat was strangled and skinned as a sign of widowhood. The third goat was slaughtered on the third day after burial. This marked when members of the family could resume their normal work. The widows, their children and relatives, had their hair shaved after eating this goat. It was at this point that the widow(s) stopped putting their clothes inside out (Kingoina 1999:76; Kamau 2009:54-62).

The final ceremony was done two weeks later with the slaughtering of a mother goat. The purpose of the goat was to cleanse the whole family from all kinds of evil. It was also to appease the spirits of the dead (Kingoina 1999:76). Another point to be noted regarding the Gusii mode of coping with death is that the widows had to be looked after by the next of kin. The elders gave the widow three men from whom she would chose one as her new husband. The widows who were allowed to do so were young widows of child-bearing age. Senior brothers of the deceased did not take widows of the deceased. Neither did deceased juniors. Inheritance was only among same age groups. Of great interest is that the new husband was to provide seed to the woman. Any children born belonged to the deceased. If the child born was a boy he was named after the deceased father. The man gave guardianship and protection to the family of the deceased. The children born from that man did not, however, inherit anything from him. Any ceremonial rites touching on the woman and her children had to be done by the brothers or nephews of the deceased (Kingoina 1999:77-8; Kamau 2009:54-62).

Finally the elders' role was to help the widow solve the issue of debts that the deceased had. The debtors were summoned, and an open court was convened where each debtor gave an account of what he was owed. Thus, the issue of debts was settled, with those who owed the deceased being made to pay to the widow, while arrangements were made by friends of the deceased and the clan on how those owed by the deceased before he died would be paid (Kingoina 1999:82; Kamau 2009:54-62).

Tanzania—Sukuma People

In his thesis, Brown (1980) analyzes the funeral rites of African tribes in Tanzania, East Africa, but omits to indicate which particular tribe he is writing about. He indicates, " . . . Observation of the Sukuma, Tita, Kesewe and Zinsa tribes. . ."

He then talks of *Kilio* (Kiswahili word for crying or weeping), but which he refers to as a death ritual. However, what he analyzes is interesting, as it seems to have been obtained from personal observations, and has a lot of similarities to traditional Kikuyu funeral rites and customs.

In the first place, when the death of an elder (of whichever tribe of the four above-mentioned tribes Brown (1980) is describing) occurs, relatives remove the body from the house to a temporary hut built a few metres (yards) away from the house. Brown (1980) advises that burial rites take place the same day as the death happens. The *Mwesi*, the oldest brother of the deceased directs the funeral. Initially he uses a short-handled hoe and scrapes two parallel lines on the ground. Family and friends then help to dig the grave with hoes of normal length. A cow is then killed and skinned to the leg joints, leaving the bone in the skin below the joints. The cow's hide is cut into two, one piece placed under and the other over the body. The corpse is placed in the grave on the light side, facing the rising sun.

Brown (1980) further advises that after the grave is filled, the *Mwesi* throws the short hoe in the forest and then bathes in the river. The men in the burial party also bathe followed by the widow. The widow bathes only below the waist as well as other women. It should be noted that throughout the *kilio*, bathing will be permitted only when the group bathes communally (Ibid., 1980).

Death to that community as to most African communities was associated with pollution. Pollution caused by death is often believed to be removed through the ritual sex act—a prescribed indecent activity for a special occasion. Brown (1980) continues and says that in order to remove the pollution of death, brought about by the death of the elder, the relatives of the deceased fetch a *Mwesha* (sanctifier) from a remote tribe to sleep with the widow. The official mourning starts the day after burial and continues for five to eight days. On the first morning the *Mwesha* comes out of the widow's hut holding his throat as if he is choking. The significance of this is that the *Mwesha* is symbolizing a picture of the sacrificial goat killed by suffocation. Suffocation keeps the now polluted breath of life inside from escaping to the outside. The pollution has been contained by the *Mwesha* who now carries it away for the first time (Ibid., 1980).

After *Mwesha* leaves, on the first morning, the widow remains seated inside the house, with head bowed and eyes looking at the floor. She is not allowed to talk with anyone except the widows who are serving her. Late on the fifth day the *Mwesha* returns. That night he shaves the head of the widow and all her sons and then sleeps with the widow again. He leaves the following morning. The significance of the second sexual contact is that the *Mwesha* takes the rest of the widow's pollution to the distant, unknown outside world. She, but she alone, is clean (Ibid., 1980).

The *Mwesha* then tells the widow to bathe her whole body in the river in order to rid herself of her husband's sweat. She returns to the house and once again bows her head as the *Mwesha* declares that "the home has been overcome." The widow's bed is now let down to the floor. On the sixth day all the mourners bathe. A white cock is killed on the threshold of the house, and the fresh blood is sprinkled inside. The feathers are taken to the crossroads of two paths and left there. In the morning the widow emerges with head up and grief is over. The *Mwesha* returns again, that night he takes the widow out in the bush and sleeps with her for the third and final time. In this third and final sexual contact the widow as the symbolic representative of the village takes the pollution away from the village by sleeping in the bush with *Mwesha*, conclusively transferring the defilement to him. He once again carries the pollution to the remote, undefined outside world (Ibid., 1980).

Thereafter, after a short ceremony in which the widow is inherited by her husband's brother or by one of her children all are free to go home and the funeral is over.

Brown (1980) raises a very important point and question, which theologians and other men of God should ponder when condemning the African Christian Church which at times succumbs to African rituals of death. Brown (1980) asks what a widow is supposed to do when she alone is the only believer (Christian) in her family. How is she going to prevent her brother-in-law from insisting that she fulfills the ritual acts so as to take away the pollution of death? If she refuses to comply, how will she respond to the family's accusation that her failure was the cause of subsequent deaths? Since the widow's children now belong to the brother-in-law, will she ever see them again if she refuses?

Brown (1980) feels that missionaries and pastors might object to the widow succumbing to "tradition". Brown (1980) states, and I agree with him, that it is all very well for the armchair missionaries and pastors to suggest from a distance that the acts and other cultural expressions can and should be used to communicate the gospel. Brown (1980) feels that we have to live with the complexities and the consequences. All the facts must be considered. New options for dealing with such complex religious, cultural and social situations must be courageously addressed by listening carefully to each other in the evaluation and solutions being sought. I fully concur with Brown.

Ghana—The Ga-Adangbe People

The Ga or Ga-Adangbe people live in Ghana. History has it that they founded Accra, the capital of Ghana around AD 1500 as a trading post. Of particular interest and note are the world-famous coffins that their carpenters make. Some even call them "fantasy coffins". The coffins that they make have shapes which symbolically represent interests and activities of the deceased when he/she was alive. Coffins of different shapes are made, for example, coffins in the shape of a plane, shoe, bees, beer, bottle, car, animal, fish, and house, among others. Such coffins are very expensive and their price can be equal to what an average family in Ghana earns in a year (Popovic 2011). As will be shown later in this book the cost of burying Agikuyu today, when one considers the accompanying funeral rituals, amounts to more than an average Kikuyu family earns in a year.

Nigeria—The Urhobo People

The Urhobo of Nigeria believe that death is not the end of the person nor his relationship with the family. The funeral ceremonies performed are to show the everlasting relationship between the living and the dead. These beliefs and characteristics are similar to those of the Agikuyu. The Urhobo communicate with the spirit of the dead and the gods before the burial. The Urhobo want to know the cause of the death. The findings will dictate how the appropriate burial will be organized. It is to be noted that this tradition still exists despite the fact that most Urhobo people are Christians.

Urhobo people believe that death can happen because of old age, witchcraft, accident, illness or abomination. They think that there are two kinds of deaths, good death and bad death. To them good death is associated with people who are 70 or more years old, had a normal life and are not members of some secret cult (Popovic 2011).

Bad deaths are those who died prematurely, also deaths of members due to witchcraft, evil people and those who died a repugnant death. Such people are not given what the Urhobo people call good burial. They are thrown into the forest to be eaten by wild animals. This is done to prevent the reincarnation of their spirit. However, note should be taken that some of the criteria that differentiate good and bad death can be changed. For example, among other factors, having children means a good death. Agikuyu, as mentioned earlier, also used to leave most bodies of the dead to be devoured by wild animals. However, the Agikuyu reason for the bodies being left for the wild beasts was different from that of the Urhobo, as noted earlier.

The Urhobo people believe that funeral rites and ceremonies are needed, because without them the spirit of the deceased will not be able to join the ancestral spirits. Good people are buried in traditional ritual. Urhobo hold prayers for the dead to protect and bless the living.

A young Urhobo person who died prematurely, but had lived a morally upright life would be buried, but without death festivities and rituals. The Urhobo people ensure that in the coffin of the deceased they put some weapons such as cutlass, knife, broken bottle among other weapons to enable the deceased to fight and avenge his death (Ibid., 2011).

English Funeral Rites

Britain colonized Kenya from 1890 to 1963. During that time the English introduced to the Kenya Africans and in this case to the Agikuyu tribe English customs and ways of life. The colonizers affected the culture of the Agikuyu so much that by the time of Kenya independence in 1963 almost all the Kikuyu culture, religion and worldview had been completely changed or modified by Christianity and the colonizers. Today, virtually no Agikuyu practice Agikuyu traditional religion, neither do they believe in the ancestral spirits. Their traditional mode of burial and funeral rites, as will be described in the next chapter, has disappeared and has been replaced by methods and practices from other cultures, some from a few African cultures, but most of them from European cultures; English culture being the largest contributor. It is proper then for this book to analyze modern English funeral rites.

Habenstein and Lamers (1963:561-62) advise that as soon as an English person dies the first question is whether the person's body will be buried or cremated. Two sets of factors, one economic and the other social operate to influence the making of arrangements for the funeral. In England, a considerable number of funerals are undertaken by funeral homes. They obtain an appropriate coffin, and are directed by the family how to keep the body of the deceased, either at the home of the deceased or in the funeral home/chapel. The English are not likely to economize on funeral expense. This contention is supported by an article in the British journal *The Economist* which reported that, "'A death, like a birth or marriage, is one of the most important events in British life, especially for the working classes." The article further advises that "A death provides an occasion for a family to meet and show its solidarity and, as such, is a time when it is felt that no expense should reasonably be spared" (Ibid., 561-2).

This is exactly the view taken by the Agikuyu of today. However, the majority of the Agikuyu are not as financially endowed as the British. Most of the Agikuyu are finding modern funeral expenses too heavy to bear.

Habenstein and Lamers (1963:561-2) note that obituaries are brief and to the point, and appear in the columns of local newspapers to announce the death and funeral. After the funeral, there may be another brief announcement acknowledging flowers and other gifts. This is unlike the obituaries of the Agikuyu which are extremely long and carry too many details of the deceased.

The English obituary notice appearing in the English newspaper is to the point and gives the time, the position or title of the person, residence, the list of relatives, the age, the time and place of the funeral service, the burial arrangements, whether letters of mourning and flowers are desired, and whether there will be a memorial service. It is worthy of note, however, that in the majority of cases paid death notices do not appear in the English newspapers.

A death certificate is issued by the attending physician. Normally the death certificate is issued soon after death. The death certificate is then taken to the local registry of births, marriages and deaths. The officers there issue the disposal certificate. The body is normally viewed at the deceased's home as it is customary for the coffin to be in the family home. On the same day of death, funeral arrangements are made. While fixing the date of the funeral, the bereaved family gives thought to proper clothing. Among the not so well-to-do class, the custom of wearing black during the funeral is disappearing, and nowadays subdued colours are approved. Among the well-to-do, black is still universally used.

Closing the curtains is a custom in England that is observed by all. The curtains are closed on the day a person dies and are kept so until the family returns home from the funeral service. On the day of the funeral the pallbearers close the coffin, and place the wreath of the nearest relative on the lid. They then carry it on their shoulders to the hearse. The family occupies the cars following the hearse without much regard for precedence (Ibid., 561-2).

Except for public persons, owners of large estates and other distinguished persons attendance at funeral services in England is limited to members of the immediate family, and seldom are there more than twenty people present. Habenstein and Lamers (1963:561-2) further observe that most families would take offence at someone not of the immediate family attending the funeral. The number of mourners rarely exceeds eighteen and the minimum is twelve. The sympathy of friends and neighbors is expressed through the media or floral offerings. I understand, however, from a leading theologian of British ancestry that the practice described here was prevalent around the period that Habenstein and Lamers wrote their book in 1963. Gradually the practice has, however, drastically changed. These days I am told that any person who is inclined to attend the funeral may do so and the family would not be offended. Today there is no limited or restricted number of those who may attend. However for a private funeral only relatives and very close friends may attend. The practice of the British of yesteryears is in contrast to the present-day Agikuyu where every funeral be it of an ordinary person, young or old, poor or rich, famous and not famous is attended by hundreds and at times thousands of people. Most of those attending hardly know the deceased or were related to them.

At the Anglican Church, which is the main leading mainstream church in England, the minister leads the procession into the church. The funeral director or the family supplies paper-bound booklets containing the order of service, which show on the front cover the name of the deceased and the place and date of burial. Note should be taken that the booklets are used in the church and the cemetery. When no music is available, the clergy usually extract selected music from the booklets and announce them as he reads them. When hymns are to be sung in the chapel or church a white broadsheet is passed out instead of the grey booklets. They note that the cover of this broadsheet also indicates the name of the deceased and the place and date of burial. After the ceremony the minister takes leave of the family, except in Yorkshire where the minister joins the family and friends at a funeral tea at a public restaurant, where ham is normally served. Hence the English phrase "being buried with ham" (Ibid., 569). Elsewhere in England, it is customary for relatives returning from the funeral to gather at the home of one of them and there partake of light refreshments (Ibid., 569). This is unlike the practice of the modern Agikuyu, where after a funeral lavish meals are provided to all those attending the funeral.

Regarding cremation in England, it is the regulation that bodies which are to be cremated must be held for longer than a week. This makes it possible for any investigation into the cause of death to be carried out, as otherwise, when the body is cremated a day or two after death, there is the possibility of concealment of the cause of death.

Cremation, as will be elaborated in chapter 8 of this study, is an option that increasing numbers of families in the UK are preferring for the disposal of the dead. The reasons for people opting to cremate as opposed to burying the dead are mainly the scarcity of land in England, and the cost of burial which is beyond the means of many people. Additionally, cremation is supported by the medical profession, and has been adopted by the majority of the wealthiest Britons. Cremated remains are usually scattered on a lawn, or buried in a church compound, or in a niche in the family grave.

British royalty is buried with pomp and colour. There is no other time that the English pour forth their affection and respect for an English monarch more than at the time of his death. The ceremonies and procession involved in burying the monarch start from where the body had been lying in state which is in the medieval Westminster Abbey. On the day of the burial it passes through the streets of London, which are lined by hundreds of thousands of people.

Eventually the procession reaches the Windsor Castle's chapel of St George for the last rites conducted by the Archbishop of Canterbury. The Archbishop of Canterbury reads the words of Common Prayer: "For as . . .

Commit the body to the ground, earth to earth, ashes to ashes, and dust to dust." A vault is then opened to receive the body, and as it is slowly lowered, the dowager Queen takes a handful of earth from a silver bowl and drops it onto the casket. Throughout the breadth of England and the British Commonwealth in honour of the dead King, men and women pause in silence for two minutes (Ibid., 571-4).

Some Examples of Bizarre Funeral Rites and Practices

Zoroastrians of Persia and India Funeral Practices

Zoroastrianism was the common religion of the Persians prior to their conversion to Mohammedanism. It takes its name from its great prophet, Zoroaster, or Zarathustra. Zoroastrianism flourished in the first millennium B.C.E. Its sacred books, the *Zend-Avesta*, teach that Ormazd, or Ahura Mazda, lord of light and goodness, wages a ceaseless war, in which he will have final victory, against Ahriman and the hosts of darkness and evil. To aid him in the struggle, Ormazd created man. Today, a remnant of only about 5,000 Zoroastrians survive in former Persia, although over 100,000 of them can be found in India, mostly in Bombay, with isolated pockets in Aden, Lebanon, and Iraq. The Indian Zoroastrians are called Parsis or Parsees, from "Persian", and are descended from Persian refugees (Davies 1999:40-46; Habenstein and Lamers 1963:178).

Preparation of the Dead

When death occurs among the Zoroastrians, the body is borne into the mortuary room in the home for the simple preparation. In ancient times each community set aside a special building for funeral purposes, with separate sections for men, women, and children. Although the custom of the common mortuary still survives in India, it has been lost in Iran, where one room in the house is generally used for funeral purposes (Habenstein and Lamers 1963: 178-9).

There the body is washed, and dressed in a clean, white suit. A well-worn suit is preferred to a new one, as a suit used for a shroud is never worn again. After a member of the family girds the body with a sacred cord, it is laid on the ground or floor with a white sheet beneath it.To provide a bridge across which the departing soul may enter the new life, two relatives, seated at either side, for several hours read sacred writings into the ears of the deceased.

Zoroastrian religious traditions and taboos designate the person who may touch the body and the rules governing such contact. Any violations render the violator unclean, and compel him to undergo a nine day purification ritual, involving, among other matters, a washing of his person with cow urine. As earlier indicated any Agikuyu who touched a corpse had also to be purified by a medicine man, but not with cow's urine.

Contamination is in part avoided by the Zoroastrians delegating many funeral tasks to special funeral servants. Thus, when the two relatives finish their readings to the body, two such servants take over. These unfortunates are much despised, and generally considered unclean.

Habenstein and Lamers (1963:178-80) observe that today all Zoroastrian funerals take place within 24 hours after death, and always in the daylight, so that the body may be exposed to the sun. When death occurs in the evening, the funeral takes place the next morning; when in the morning, the funeral follows late the same afternoon. Agikuyu also used to bury their dead same day of death and at the latest the following day.

When the time for the funeral arrives, the funeral-servants place the body on an iron bier. Wood is never used because the Zoroastrians believe that it can be contaminated by the remains. After relatives have entered the mortuary room for a final viewing, the bier is borne ceremoniously through a special door to begin the procession to the place of final exposure (Habenstein and Lamers 1963:180-84).

The Towers of Silence

The Zoroastrians believe that the earth, fire, and water have a basic purity, which burial, cremation, or putrefaction of a body would contaminate. To avoid this, they expose the dead to scavengers. In communities large enough to maintain them, exposure is made in huge, round "Towers of Silence." In the vicinity of Bombay the Parsis maintain seven of these towers. In smaller communities, bodies are left on a remote mountain or hill.

The procession halts at the entrance of the Tower for a brief ceremony, following which the funeral-servants alone carry the body into the great, round structure. The Tower is generally built of stone, with concentric beds or levels rising from the central pit or well. The unroofed interior is opened to the sky. The Zoroastrians consider this place the most impure on earth, so that only the unclean funeral-servants will enter it, and even they must wear special garments for the purpose.

Vultures look hungrily on while the funeral-servants remove the body from the bier, lay it on the stone bed, and strip it of the white garments.

After these are thrown into the well, the bier is borne from the Tower, and the vultures begin their meal. In the course of a few hours the bones are usually stripped bare. Formerly certain of the Zoroastrians gathered and preserved the bones, but the custom no longer is followed. Now, at intervals, the funeral-servants enter the Tower, gather the bones, and drop them in the central pit. As indicated earlier the Agikuyu used to leave the dead in the bush to be devoured by wild beasts, an equally disgusting practice.

While the bearers are disposing of the body, the other members of the procession retire to a nearby chapel-like room for the reading of prayers.

Habenstein and Lamers (1963:179-184) further advise that funeral process ends with purification ceremonies. The body-bearers enter a prolonged period of ritualistic cleansing. All who participated in the funeral procession wash their hands in cow urine, and on reaching home take a complete bath. Cow urine is used in the home to cleanse all places where the body was laid (cf. Davies 1999:40-6).

Festivals of the Parsis commemorate the phases of creation, Zoroaster's birth and death, the emigration of their ancestors to India and the guardian spirits of the dead. During this last festival, called *Farvardin* or *Muktad* ancestral spirits are thought to return to visit their descendants, and special welcoming ceremonies are held in front of the Towers of Silence. Although bodies are considered the ultimate example of defilement, the spirits of the ancestors do not share this odium, and rites to honor them are highly regarded. This is very similar to the Agikuyu tradition and most other African practices and beliefs regarding the spirits of the ancestors (Habenstein and Lamers 1963: 180-4).

Davies (1999:101-2) narrates almost similar manners of disposing the body of the Jews in the Old Testament, where in Jeremiah 16 God denounces His unfaithful people, and we find therein (In the negation) an account of the nature of subsequent Israelite burial:

> "Thus saith the Lord concerning the sons and concerning the daughters that are born in this place, and concerning their mothers that bare them, and concerning their fathers that begat them in this land: They shall die of grievous deaths; they shall not be lamented; neither shall they be buried; but they shall be as dung upon the face of the earth; and they shall be consumed by the sword, and by famine; and their carcases shall be meat for the fowls of heaven, and for the beasts of the earth" (Jer 16: 3-7,13) (KJV) (cf. 1 Kgs 14:11; 1 Kgs16:4; 1 Kgs 21:24).

One is therefore led to wonder whether leaving corpses to be devoured by birds (fowls of heaven) and the beasts of the earth was not a common practice of disposing the dead in the Middle East and surrounding regions. This is borne out by the fact that Zoroastrian was a Middle East religion which started long before Christianity, and also considering that Persia and the territory of the Jews were in the same geographical area. Additionally Zoroastrian and Judaism started almost at the same period. One further wonders which religion influenced which—Zoroastrian/Judaism or vice-versa.

Funeral Rites—The Poor of the Philippines

An article which appeared in the Kenya *Daily Nation* on Monday 11th October 2010 stated that the residents of the Navotas slum of Manila, Philippines, sleep, cook, eat, bathe, and wash clothes on top of stacked tombs. The article by Cecil Morella-Agence France-Presse, said that Emmalyn Ramos's home has spectacular views of the Philippine capital's skyline, if you don't mind the human bones scattered outside her door. The poor and the dead have little choice but to mingle in a graveyard in the northern Manila port district of Navotas, one of the world's most densely populated areas surpassed only by a few Indian cities. The article indicates that Ramos, a twenty-year-old pregnant woman lives in a tent that is one of several tents pitched precariously on top of a row of concrete tombs, themselves piled five-high, like shipping containers, at the crowded Navotas municipal cemetery. Ramos and her extended family of twelve, plus her jobless boyfriend, are one of about 600 families in the cemetery compound, a community ironically called Bagong Silang (newborn).

The residents of the cemetery sleep, cook, eat, bathe, and wash clothes on top of the tombs, and life can look grisly for an outsider. There are no toilets or running water, garbage piles up among the tombs, and the area is infested with cockroaches that particularly like to parade across the tombs at night. Due to lack of space in the cemetery, old bodies have to be eventually removed from the tombs, and smelly, damp bones are scattered throughout the cemetery or in sacks that have been dumped on tombstones. A spokesman for the Navotas city government explains that local residents get free burial when they die, but the corpses can only stay inside the tombs for five years.

"After that they have to make way for new arrivals", he says. However, life for the cemetery's residents is not completely grim. At sundown, bare-chested men play basketball, karaoke echoes past the tombstones, and children amuse themselves by climbing up the tomb decks or flying kites. 'Sometimes they play with the skulls', Ramos says of her children. And while she says there are no ghosts in the graveyard, her younger brother, sixteen-year-old high school student Marcelo, insists with a smile that there are. In a nation where a third of the population lives on a dollar a day or less, millions of Manila's poor live in sprawling shanty towns, their flimsy houses sitting on swamps, under bridges, and on top of open sewers.

The city official pointed out that Navotas was not the only city with a cemetery full of squatters. He said the city government has bought land south of Manila that would relieve Navotas of some of its squatter problems, but he conceded that its facilities were not enough for all of Bagong Silang's current residents.

The level of poverty reflected above contrasts sharply with the lavish lifestyles and immense wealth of some Filipinos, for example that of the late President Ferdinand Marcos, whose wife owned three thousand pairs of shoes and who was reported to have spent US$ 5.5 million in one shopping tour covering New York, Rome and Copenhagen in 1983 before her husband was deposed (*Daily Nation* Monday 11 October 2010 pages 2-3 (DN2)). Before the Agikuyu of Kikuyu District and other communities across Africa reach such a situation of living among the dead, a solution must be sought urgently. This study is geared to proposing a way out of such a situation.

Funeral Rites of Other Religions

Judaism Funeral Rites

The basic rites followed by Jews are substantially those followed by Judaism with slight modification by force of local or communal traditions. Certain features mark these rites. Among them are reverence for the dead, simplicity, equality between the rich and the poor and rapid burial. The avoidance of cremation, keeping the body inviolate from embalmment, incisions, blood letting, and the existence of burial societies (Habenstein and Lamers 1963:191; Polson 1953:119-82; Jewish Funerals, 2014; Davies 1999:95-109).

As death approaches, confession is heard and the dying person declares, "Hear, O Israel, the Lord our God, the Lord is one". The dead person is placed on the ground and psalms are recited especially Ps 91: "He that dwells in secret place of the most high shall abide under the shadow of the Almighty . . . ." Subsequently the body is washed and wrapped in a white linen shroud. The body of a man is wrapped in his fringed Talith (prayer shawl). In place of the Talith an additional overgarment is placed on a woman's body.

While the law (Deut 21: 23) provides that a body shall not remain unburied overnight; when it is absolutely necessary, for example, to await for the arrival of relatives to the funeral, the burial may be delayed. However, Jews do their utmost to comply with the Orthodox Jewish traditions which prescribe that funerals should take place within twenty-four hours after death (Jewish Funerals, 2014). It is further worthy of note that it is meritorious to accompany the dead to the grave. Relatives should bear the coffin; this is also a task for friends. It is also worth noting that over the last two millennia Jewish tradition requires utmost simplicity and democratic equality at burials. Before placing the body in its final resting place friends ask the departed soul to forgive any slight or wrong and to depart in peace with the world. This is strange, as this seems to be communicating with the departed spirit. The Agikuyu, as stated earlier in this study, used to communicate with the spirit of their departed friends and relatives. This shows that the belief in communication with the ancestral spirits is common to various populations and religions, not just to Africans. After filling the grave with earth, and as people leave the cemetery, Jews pluck some grass to cast over their shoulders saying "He remembereth that we are dust" (Davies 1999:95-109).

Habenstein and Lamers (1963:196-200) further advise that the mourner's first meal on the first day of mourning is called the "meal of condolence". Neighbors supply the food. Mourning rites begin when the grave has been filled. Mourning rites last for seven days. During the first three days of this no labor is permitted even to the poor. On the fourth day, if necessary to secure food, a poor man may work privately in his home. These prohibitions, however, do not apply to a housewife. She may bake and cook.

Cohabitation is forbidden during the seven days. It is of interest that abstinence from sexual union is to be observed by Jews, as it is in most African traditional burial rites as analyzed earlier, including the Agikuyu burial rites.

Tombstones are generally ordered from a stonecutter. The poor use simple markers on the graves of their dead. The rich use more elaborate stones. Sculptured memorials are traditionally not used by Jews: markers however are inscribed. The setting up of a gravestone inscribed with the name of the deceased is encouraged, because it keeps the dead in mind and encourages the living to pray for him. When this is done the relatives, friends and Rabbi gather at the cemetery and "unveil" the gravestone (Habenstein and Lamers, 1963:196-200; Jewish Funerals, 2014).

This is of note in this book, as the Agikuyu Christians of today, one year or so after death gather around the grave to "unveil" or "bless" the cross. The Agikuyu Christians most likely borrowed (without realising it) this custom from the Jewish practice mentioned above. When a new cemetery is being consecrated, those present at the consecration march seven times around the cemetery followed by a sermon and the reciting of Psalms (Habenstein and Lamers, 1963:200; Polson et al 1953:19-182; Davies 1999:95-109). Note should be taken that this is another occasion in Judaism of marching around the perimeter of a given place seven times. The most notable occasion is when they marched seven times round the wall of Jericho (Joshua 6:4). In addition, Judaism regards seven as a lucky number. Cruden (1949:587) observes that seven is a sacred number among the Jews, also indicating perfection or completion. It was used very often in a symbolic manner for the whole of a thing. The number seven entered very largely into the religious life and observance of the Jews (Ibid., 587).

Islamic (Muslim) Funeral Rites

Muslims are only buried not cremated. Most of the customs followed have been laid down in the Shariah (Muslim Laws) which are derived from the Hadith (practices and sayings of Prophet Mohammed) rather than from the Qur'an.

Muslims prefer to die in their homes. They believe in the Day of Judgment and the life hereafter. On approaching one's death it is important to ask for forgiveness of any violation against human beings before asking for forgiveness from God for sins committed. It is a religious recommendation that all ill persons whether an acquaintance or stranger be visited. This is considered a form of worship and "mercy" is showered on such a visitor. When a Muslim dies, the deceased is placed with his or her head facing the Muslim holy city of Mecca. The body is then ritually washed. Male relatives where possible will wash male bodies, and female relatives will wash female bodies. After the ritual washing the body is wrapped in a shroud. This shroud is usually white. The *salat* (prayer) for the dead "*salat ul janaza*" is then performed. This takes the form of the usual Muslim daily salat prayer with some special additions which specifically relate to death.

Muslims prefer to bury the body of the deceased within 24 hours. This is done due to the fact that it is a religious requirement that the body should be buried as quickly as possible, also to avoid decay of the body before burial rendering it revolting. Also as a mark of respect, immediate relatives may not eat until after the funeral. In order to comply with religious requirements and to alleviate the family burden, suffering and distress, burial should take place as soon as possible, preferably within 24 hours after death. Post-mortems are not allowed in Muslim religious customs. Muslims believe that the body is sacred and belongs to God. Agikuyu also traditionally used to bury or dispose of the body immediately death occured, often on the same day of death or at the latest the day following death.

It is generally accepted that Muslim funerals should be as respectful as possible without being extravagant. Coffins, if used at all, are simple wooden boxes with no decorations. According to religious usage, however, Muslims prefer to bury the dead without this. Should the body be brought to the cemetery in a coffin, sometimes to comply with the laws of the land, the funeral committees on arriving at the cemetery may decide to remove the body and bury the deceased without the coffin. The coffin is then donated to the community for use in future funerals.

Muslims are buried facing Mecca. Members of the funeral party, throw a little soil to the grave while reciting 'We created you from it, and from it we will raise you a second time' (Surah 20:25 from the Qur'an). During Muslim burials, public rites are for men only. This is similar to the Agikuyu traditional funeral practices, whereby only males participated in the actual burial. As Islam recognizes no intermediary between humans and God, such as clergy, the ceremony is led either by someone the deceased chose before death, or a close relative, or the family Imam. According to religious laws a Muslim wife is expected to stay in her home for up to four and half months after the death of her husband or, if she is pregnant, until the pregnancy ends. This is important in establishing that the pregnancy was progressing before the death of her husband.

Gravestones are kept simple, marked only by the deceased's name and date of death. Many Muslims will spend money on the poor rather than on an elaborate memorial stone. It is not customary to send wreaths of flowers. No collection is made or donations given. In Turkey, when the burial of a Muslim is over the mourners retreat seven paces from the grave and then return, thus signifying that the dead person sees and recognizes them (Habenstein and Lamers 1963: 129-77; Islamic (Muslim) Funerals 2014).

Hindu Funeral Rites

Hindus believe in reincarnation, and view death as the soul moving from one body to the next on its path to reach Nirvana, "Heaven". Following death, the body is placed on the floor with the head pointing north, (considered the direction of the dead). An oil lamp is lit and placed near the body. People will try to avoid touching the corpse, as it is considered polluting. This is the same attitude that was adopted by the Agikuyu.

A passage by Habenstein and Lamers (1963:118) and Hindu Funerals (2014) is of interest. They indicate that in Hinduism, before a man dies he should attempt as much as possible to be freed from his sins. In India, to accomplish this end, when people grow very old or when it is obvious that death is near, such people are taken to one of the holy cities along the Ganges. There they may either wash away their sins on the banks, or dive in the sacred waters. Relatives sometimes carry the dying into the stream and hold them erect there so that they may breathe their last breath standing knee deep in the cleansing waters. At one of the cities along the Ganges, namely Benares, the river banks in that city are regarded as having a sacred character equal to the river itself. People who are judged mortally ill are sheltered in huts at the river's edge, there to dwell until they die (Hindu Funerals, 2014).

It is interesting to note that this is very similar to the Agikuyu custom, where a mortally sick person was left in a temporary shelter near the homestead to await his death. The Kikuyu custom, however, was done to avoid the impurity that would result when a person died inside his/her hut.

Habenstein and Lamers (1963:118) further assert that immediately death occurs, relatives must be informed, and arrangements must be made for the burial or cremation. The next step is to prepare the body for the funeral. The ritual consists of anointing the head of the body, first with oil and then with soap, nut powder and other preparations. Every participant in the preparation, beginning with the chief heirs, performs this rite. It is noted that both tradition and custom decree that whoever presides at this ceremony is the dead person's successor and inherits his property.

The corpse is usually bathed and dressed in white traditional Indian clothes. If a wife dies before her husband, she is dressed in red bridal clothes. If a woman is a widow she will be dressed in white or pale clothes. The procession to the crematorium is formed at the homes of the dead. In India, this custom is in keeping with the Indian tradition that all important rituals, especially marriages and funerals, take place within the home.

The funeral procession may pass places of significance to the deceased, such as a building, street, and place of work or business among other places of interest. Prayers are said here and at the entrance to the crematorium.

The body is then decorated with sandalwood, flowers and garlands. Scriptures are read from the Vedas or Bhagavad Gita. After the body has been placed on the funeral pyre, the chief mourner, usually the eldest son, circles the body saying the appropriate prayer. He then lights the fire; incense and ghee (cooked and clarified butter) are poured into the flames. Afterwards, the ashes of the deceased are sprinkled on water, and many people take them to the sea near where they live. "*Shraddha*" is practised one year after the death of the person. This is the Hindu practice of giving food to the poor in memory of the deceased. A priest will say prayers for the deceased, and during this time, usually lasting for a month, the family will not buy any new clothes or attend any parties. Sons are responsible for carrying out *shraddha* (Hindu Funerals, 2014).

Funeral matters play a major role in the lives of the people of India (Habenstein and Lamers (1963: 118); Hindu Funerals, 2014). It is observed from the funeral rites website.doc that next to marriage, funerals constitute the most important of Hindu ceremonies, and by the same token exact a heavy financial toll. They observe that although the burden of performing *shraddha* has impoverished many families, yet as one Hindu author points out, the loss of status and position is more feared in these matters than impoverishment. This matter became so serious that in 1958 the government at Delhi issued a "guest control" order stipulating that not more than 50 guests can be given food at wedding parties or funerals. This decree has however not been effective (Hindu Funerals, 2014). Strange things have happened during Hindu funerals. Habenstein and Lamers observe that although legislation outlawed in 1829 the custom of suttee (the self-immolation of the widow on her husband's funeral pyre) yet in 1954 in Jodhpur, Sugan Kunwar, widow of Brigadier Jabar Singh, by her own act perished in the flames of her husband's pyre (according to Habenstein and Lamers this was reported by *Time*, volume 64, November 1, 1954 page 36). The article went on to indicate that by the end of the week 100,000 people had visited the tramped-out fire to scoop into their mouths the dust, now sacred. Emotional wives could be seen worshipping the photographs depicting Sugan Kunwar cradling the head of her husband in her lap as the flames consumed both of them. This episode shows how difficult it is to stop some basic patterns of funeral and worship of the departed spirits of the dead (Hindu Funerals, 2014). Giving further insight into the custom of *suttee*, Irion (1968:14) advises that until its prohibition in 1829 the custom of *suttee,* Hindu wife-immolation, was practiced. The widow was required to jump into her husband's pyre. Irion asserts that it was not simply an act of loyalty or devotion, but had an economic base. It was a custom designed to preserve the widow's dowry and her husband's property for his family by removing her as the heiress.

Buddhist Funerals

Modern trend of Buddhist funeral rites indicates that the country with the overwhelming followers of Buddhist is Japan. Also worthy of note is that modern Buddhists do not rank funerals as high as they used to do in the past centuries. Today funerals are relatively unimportant in Buddhism.

Adherents to Buddhism are noted for concentrating their efforts on the deceased's frame of mind up to and at the moment of death (Buddhist Funerals, 2014).

Simplification of Buddhist funeral rites are noticeable in Japan, where according to Habenstein and Lamers, Japanese funerals have changed worldwide especially over the past several decades. They give examples such as use of cremation, which is now virtually universal in Japan, despite the preference of the Shinto religion for earth burial. Expensive funeral feasts, once the norm, have been simplified. Elaborate gift-giving also has been reduced, since each gift must be returned ceremoniously with another, approximately half the cost. They assert that even with the evident simplification, yet the basic core of sentiment, belief and worship remains virtually intact and of continued significance to urban Japanese as well as to their rural brethren (Habenstein and Lamers 1963:61-2; Buddhist Funerals, 2014).

Humanist Funeral Ceremonies

These can be summarized as follows:

- Humanists believe that there is one life, and that we should make the best of it by living happy and fulfilled lives and helping others to do so.
- They look for evidence or draw on their own experiences—rather than believe what someone else says—in order to form their beliefs and answer questions.
- They accept death as the natural and inevitable end to life. They do not believe in life after death, but rather that people 'live on' in other people's memories of them.
- There are no specific or obligatory rituals to follow at deaths or funerals; however, expressions of sympathy and acknowledgement of the bereaved person's feelings of grief are appreciated.
- Humanists may choose to be cremated or buried, and the ceremony can take place anywhere. If possible, all religious symbols (e.g. at a crematorium) are removed or covered.
- The funeral ceremony is intended to celebrate the life that was lived and properly honor that person's life. Through readings, poetry, music and personal tributes from family and friends, people attending are reminded of how their lives have been enriched through knowing the deceased (Humanist Funerals, 2014).

It is worthy of note that recently the Agikuyu Christians have been announcing in the newspaper, when a person dies, that the funeral is to celebrate the life of the deceased. They might unknowingly be adopting the beliefs and practices of the Humanists. In Chapter 8 of this study, a recommendation will be made that the Agikuyu Christians should stop placing such advertisements in the newspapers. It is pointed out that such advertisements, to an observer, appear from all angles to be in support of funeral practices of the Humanists.

Economy of Burial Grounds

As indicated earlier in this book burial space is today very costly in most parts of the world, especially in or near urban centres. Additionally burial space is becoming extremely difficult to obtain in urban centres, even if one could afford it. To create abundant cemetery space, so that burial spaces are not exhausted and/or to enable close relatives to be buried with their ancestors, as aptly stated in the Bible—to be buried with their fathers, (1 Kgs 14:31, 15:24, 22:50, 2 Kgs 8:24, 12:21, and 20, 15:7), a considerable number of municipalities and communities and religious organizations have come up with an ingenious manner of dealing with this problem. A few examples are given below, but the list is not exhaustive.

The City of Paris

Habenstein and Lamers (1963:513) report that the city of Paris has a monopoly on the operation of cemeteries. Family vaults in Paris cemeteries are usually constructed with a capacity for twenty caskets. When the vault has been filled, and after a lapse of ten years, it is permissible to exhume the remains and place them in a single casket, thus nineteen additional places are provided. Graves may be rented in a Paris cemetery for a minimal rental period of five years. The next longer period is thirty years. The cost difference between the five and thirty years period is not great. Moreover, at the expiration of the contractual period the family has the option of renewing the lease.

It is noted that graves can be rented for a period of one hundred years. If the rental period expires and is not renewed, the city of Paris exhumes the remains and reburies them in a common grave. Sixty five percent of all the five years rentals are not renewed, and non-renewal of thirty years rentals is frequent. This releases additional grave space annually, and makes it unlikely that the cemetery space will be exhausted (Habenstein and Lamers 1963: 513).

Italy

In Italy cemetery space may be purchased for a limited period of ownership or in perpetuity. If a body is given "common ground" burial, it remains buried for a period varying from eighteen months to ten years. After this time the grave is opened, the remains exhumed and the bones are either burned or placed in a small wall niche as the family desires (Habenstein and Lamers 1963: 513).

West Germany

In some localities, because of the acute shortage of land, burial ground is available only in the case of actual death, and is usually leased, with allotment being made by the city registrar for community cemeteries, and by the religious authorities concerned (Catholic, Protestant, or Jewish) for cemeteries under religious jurisdiction. They further note that graves space is leased, never sold.

There are three leases that are available. For social burying grounds (25 years), for family graves (30-60 years), for solidly constructed tombs (60 years). If the contract is not renewed at the expiration date the grave is flattened and the bones are reburied in the same cemetery, but below the normal grave level. At the expiration of the contracted period, if survivors wish, the grave contract can be renewed at half the original fee for another similar period (Habenstein and Lamers 1963: 423-4).

Mexico

In urban areas of Mexico, the poor are buried in the earth; the middle class in walled masonry crypts; and the wealthy in expensive musolea (Habenstein and Lamers 1963:584). Burial in churches has been prohibited since around 1920 (Thompson 1921:311). Also worthy of note is that ordinary grave sites may be purchased or leased. As indicated by Habenstein and Lamers (1963:584) when the rental time has expired, if the remains have not already been taken up by the family, the funeral authorities remove and burn them. However when the family itself has them exhumed, they are placed in a metal container and kept in a small plot purchased by the family and located in another part of the cemetery. In rural areas on the other hand, graves are usually leased for a term of one to seven years. If at the expiration the lease is not renewed, the grave is emptied and the bones cast into a charnal house. It is worthy of note that the comparatively limited area assigned for cemetery uses is one factor leading to the leasing of graves for a limited period of time. Giving an example of how cemeteries in Mexico are sited and used, Habenstein and Lamers (1963:584) indicates that the cemetery of Guanajuato, covers an area of about three acres and is surrounded by eight-foot thick walls, honeycombed with thousands of burial recesses. Many of these spaces are rented for a five year period and each may be occupied by a single body or several bodies of one family. Most of the poor who cannot even afford the low rates charged by the authorities are given earth burial in graves two feet wide, seven feet long and eight feet deep. Such a grave is used for multiple simultaneous burials. As each body arrives, Habenstein and Lamers (1963:584) advises that it is taken from the rental casket (coffin), laid in the grave with its head on a cusion of leaves, and covered with six inches of soil. The grave is then ready to receive another body. For the Agikuyu as well as for other Africans who do not have adequate land to bury their dead, I will in Chapter 8 recommend for adoption by the Agikuyu and other Africans a modified form of this practice of burying subsequent bodies of one family in one grave.

When the rent for each specific grave has expired the bodies are dug up or taken from the wall recesses and placed in a stone tunnel twelve feet high, six feet wide and over a thousand feet long. This tunnel runs benearth the entire periphery of the cemetery. The tunnel also contains many other bodies which had been mummified in the dry air (Ibid., 584-5).

Final Observation about Future Cemetery Space

Reimers (2011) feels that a clear trend in the Western world is an increase in cremation at the expense of inhumation. The article indicates that because urns and ashes require less space than coffins, and there is a growing preference for depersonalized gardens of remembrance instead of personalized graves, it is likely that existing cemeteries will in the future be converted into public parks or gardens. There is also a trend away from ethnic cemeteries, to more heterogeneous graveyards, reflecting the present multicultural society.

The same article further notes that places where practices such as the re-use of graves, and where cremation is common, have no shortage of burial space. It observes that countries that combine low rates of cremation with burial for perpetuity need to continually seek solutions regarding how to manage old neglected cemeteries and how to find new burial space. The author feels that it is likely that most of these countries will in future become more and more reluctant to allow burial in perpetuity, but instead advocate the re-use of graves and cremation (Ibid., 2011). This trend is the one that will be proposed in chapter 8 to be adopted by the Agikuyu and other African Christians.

CHAPTER 3

PRESENT-DAY BURIAL RITES OF THE AGIKUYU CHRISTIANS

Introduction

THE TRADITIONAL AGIKUYU METHODS of disposing of the dead were covered at considerable length in the previous chapter. As a continuation of what was discussed in that chapter, it is reasonable for purposes of comparison, to reflect on the current Agikuyu funeral rites. This is in accordance with the LIM model, the second step of which is to interpret the world as it is, which in this study is to survey and analyze the current Agikuyu funeral rites. This will reveal whether their current funeral practices differ from the traditional funeral rites. Data on the current Agikuyu funeral rites will be obtained by reviewing relevant literature, and from personal experience and observation. Additional data will be obtained from a critical analyzes of radio, television and newspaper announcements. This chapter will also consider recent developments, such as the choice by the Agikuyu to be cremated, having private funerals, not being buried in the dwindling ancestral land, but instead in public cemeteries, and to also note that a number of Agikuyu who die far from home are being buried where they die, and not brought back home for burial.

Information obtained from the above will assist in showing that the present-day Kikuyu funeral rites might not be traditional. What will be presented in this chapter will be the key that will establish whether the current Agikuyu funeral rites embrace scriptural and cultural norms. It will also be of significance when considering those funeral rites that are not practical, and which should therefore be dropped or modified.

Changes that have Taken Place over the Last 120 Years to the Agikuyu Methods of Disposing of the Dead

Agikuyu traditional methods of coping with death have over the last 120 years, that is from the time Agikuyu made contact with Europeans and missionaries in 1889, been progressively reformed. It is worth noting that what is known today as Kenya was formally colonized by Great Britain on first of July, 1895 when Britain declared its take-over of the East Africa Protectorate, which in 1925 came to be called Kenya, including the area between the Coast and the Rift Valley (Were and Wilson 1968:163; Shillington 1995:316). Karanja (1999:10-1) asserts that by 1945 most of the Agikuyu had made contact with Christianity introduced and brought to them by European Christian missionaries, who arrived in Kikuyuland together with the British colonialist. This contact led in time to a lot of Agikuyu tribal customs and values being affected by the teachings of Christianity, and by the influence of the colonizers. Karanja further advises that by that time tribal customs and norms had, in extreme cases, been done away with altogether (Kenyatta 1938: 271; ACK 2001:10-1; Mbugua 2011:48). Among the tribal customs that had been affected were traditional funeral rites.

As indicated above and also in Chapter 2, Christianity, together with Europeans (mainly British), arrived in Kikuyuland in 1889. Anderson (1977:184-5); Langley and Kiggins (1974:276-85); Kariuki (1985:1-8) give a chronological guide to the arrival of various Christian denominations in central Kenya and Nairobi areas as follows:

1887—   Influx of Christian missions to Nairobi area: GMS (1897), CSM (1898), CMS (1901), AIM (1901)

1900—   CMS at Kikuyu

1901—   AIM at Kiijabe

1901 and years following,
    others including numerous Roman Catholic Orders.
    also UMM, LMS, FAM, SDA and others.

These Christian churches introduced to the Agikuyu new and strange ideas. They also made numerous and far-reaching demands of the Agikuyu. Among those demands were that the Agikuyu change and drop their traditional worldview, way of life and religion. Instead the Agikuyu were required to adopt a new worldview which inter alia would embrace to a large measure Christian values. These would undoubtedly be mixed with European culture and worldview.

The first group of the Agikuyu to be strongly affected by these demands was those in close contact with the missionaries and the Europeans. That group included the domestic workers of the missionaries as well as the church workers. Also affected were those Africans employed by Europeans in their houses, farms and business organizations, along with those Africans working in the civil service, parastatals and other government institutions. The Africans had no choice but to comply. That cadre of Africans progressively changed and dropped their cultural norms, adopting instead European mannerisms, mode of dress and worldview.

As can be expected, those demands were not taken lightly by the Agikuyu. Neither were such demands adopted immediately. Noticeable changes took a long time before being effectively felt. Two demands in particular that irritated the Agikuyu were that they stop practicing polygamy, and that they should do away with female circumcision. Both demands brought a lot of resistance and controversy. They were resisted vehemently. Kenyatta (1938:273) indicates that in 1929, a controversy started between the Agikuyu and the Church of Scotland Mission, which among other things started attacking the customs of clitoridectomy (female circumcision by removing the female clitoris). Kenyatta asserts that during the resultant upheaval a large section of the Agikuyu Christians broke away from the main Christian churches. They began to seek other means to satisfy their spiritual hunger without renouncing their social customs. It is to be noted, especially by scholars of African Instituted Churches (AIC), that the Agikuyu who broke away at that time from missionary influence, together with the indigenous population began to form their own churches and educational institutions. Kenyatta (1938:273) asserts that the most popular of these are the independent Kikuyu schools and Karenga schools, which combine religious and educational activities.

From the above it is clear that Christianity was taken with a pinch of salt by the Agikuyu. As indicated by Karanja (1999:73-4) and ACK (2001:42), by 1937 the religious belief of the Agikuyu Christians before Revival (Revival arrived in Kikuyuland in 1937) was not very consistent—it was partly traditional religion and partly Christian. Mbugua (2011:104); Karanja (1999:73-4) and ACK (2001:43) assert that many Africans had become Christians not out of genuine Christian conviction, but through the desire for education. The result was a religiosity that denied the power of the gospel way of life. The same authors observe further that before the onset of Revival among the Agikuyu, the African Church suffered from a flood of practices that were unchristian in nature. They note that drinking excessive alcohol and sexual immorality prevailed so widely that the missionaries lamented the state of the church, and longed for a spiritual revival (Wiseman 1958:7-8; Mbugua 2011:100).

Karanja (1999:73-4) asserts that revivalists stressed the importance of prayer, relevant Bible study and practical holiness. Mbugua (2011:104) observes that most Agikuyu before the Revival would show one face to the missionaries, but at the same time when it suited them, they would end up practicing and observing the Agikuyu way of doing things—both cultural and religious. They would continue practicing the Agikuyu way of life including such practices as female circumcision, polygamy, taking of the Agikuyu traditional alcoholic brew (*njohi*) and observing the Agikuyu funeral rituals including '*kuhukura*', also leaving the bodies of some of the dead in the bush to be devoured by wild beasts. As observed by Mbugua (2011:100), to the Agikuyu Christians, especially after the 1937 revival convention, conversion (being saved or being born again) meant turning from their wicked ways (to the missionaries this meant abandoning all tribal customs and traditional religious beliefs) and accepting Jesus as LORD and Saviour in their lives. The Revival had a tremendous effect on the Christians of Kabete, where, as noted earlier, Revival made its first contact with the Agikuyu at Kabete in 1937. Kabete it should be noted is the scope of this study. Later on, the Revival spread to other parts of Kikuyuland with similar effect.

As one respondent said in Mbugua (2011:81) 'the Revival (Rwanda) taught Christians in Kikuyuland to have and be filled with faith. The revival (Rwanda) taught us what salvation which is true and strong (Unshakeable) was like. Before the Revival the salvation as we know it today was not known.'

Another respondent (Ibid., 82) stated;

> "The strength to refuse anything that might have comprised my faith came from the Bible and much more from the teachings and evangelism of the Revival."

Consequently the converted Agikuyu Christians rejected almost all the cultural practices, including traditional religion, traditional funeral rites and ceremonies and, of course, such practices as polygamy and female genital mutilation (female circumcision).

The dust had not settled from the impact of the Revival on the Agikuyu when the Second World War (1939-1945) drew a lot of European Christian missionaries from their Kikuyuland mission stations to go and serve in the war. The effect of most of the European missionaries going to the First World War (1914-1918) and the Second World War (1939-1945) meant that most of their duties were taken over by poorly educated and trained African clergy, who surprisingly were more zealous than their white bosses in ensuring that their African followers adhered to the "missionaries'" beliefs and way of doing things. This meant, of course, that the Agikuyu were forced to do away with most of their tribal customs, including the way they traditionally coped with death.

As observed by Karanja (1999: 88-9), the First and Second World Wars had a tremendous effect on the socio-religious and political outlook of the Africans and in this case on the Agikuyu. He goes on to assert, for example, that the boundaries that formerly insulated the Agikuyu from the wider world were weakened through increased interaction with other communities. He notes that the First World War took thousands of Agikuyu men (and the same can be said of the Second World War) beyond their boundaries. Karanja observes that out of the 150,000 Africans recruited in Kenya to fight in the First World War, nearly 24,000 lost their lives (cf Mbugua 2011:50). During their tour of duty in those two World Wars, the African servicemen observed the whites at close range. The Africans observed and took to heart a lot of habits from the white soldiers and also from soldiers from other races and cultures. Some of the observations they made and brought home were the seeming lack of fear of dead bodies. Other observations included the way they buried their dead, especially in coffins. They also observed that all the dead had, if possible, to be buried, and none were left to be devoured by wild animals. This of course was unless the war situation was such that the dead could not be buried, but had to be abandoned where they died (Mbugua 2011:50). Cagnolo (2006:278) advises that another observation made by the African servicemen was:

> " . . . the Gikuyu men who were made to take part in the war, were the same people who discovered the great secret that the white man was as vulnerable as anybody else . . . "

When the Agikuyu soldiers came back home from the two World Wars, they introduced to their people foreign practices and characteristics. Within a very short period after the Second World War, the state of emergency in Kikuyuland (1952-1960) was declared by the Governor of the British Kenya Colony and Protectorate on Twentieth October 1952. Mbugua (2011:51) asserts that the state of emergency lasted longer than expected, as it was not lifted until Tenth January 1960. As noted further by Mbugua (2011:50), according to Kenyatta (1968) in his book *Suffering Without Bitterness*, the fundamental origins of Mau Mau were reflectively summarized by Tom Mboya in his book *Freedom And After*. Kenyatta notes that Tom Mboya in his book asserted that Mau Mau was a result of the Africans' economic disempowerment by the colonial powers, exacerbated by their lack of representation in government. Kenyatta further emphasizes in particular the sensitive issue of land. The Europeans, he notes, formed a very small minority of Kenya's population, and yet had acquired huge tracts of the productive land through ignorance, deliberate or otherwise of the land ownership system of Africans, which usually did not involve fencing or even occupation, let alone formal documentation. As a result, he notes that the Africans had been squeezed out of their ancestral land. Kenyatta goes on to note Mboya's observation that social inequalities as a result of racial discrimination were also another reason for the rise of the Mau Mau (Kenyatta 1938:102-4; Mbugua 2011:50).

As noted by Oliver and Atmore (1967:247), during the State of Emergency, the Kikuyu peasantry were rounded up from their scattered traditional homesteads and made to live in villages which could be defended and policed (see also Mbugua 2011:5). During that period, all the Agikuyu from both sides of the divide, that is, the Agikuyu Christians who were seen as being opposed to the Mau Mau and those Agikuyu in the Mau Mau, were severely affected. As stated by one respondent in Mbugua (2011:83-7):

> "The Agikuyu were terribly harassed and persecuted. All the Agikuyu lived in fear. A state of hopelessness prevailed to all the Agikuyu."

All the respondents interviewed in Mbugua (2011) indicated that the state of emergency affected all the Agikuyu, Christians and Mau Mau adherents alike, far worse than anything else had ever affected them in their long history. During the state of emergency, many people were killed, both by the colonizers and by the Mau Mau. Were and Wilson (1968:274-5) indicate that in terms of human life, ten thousand Mau Mau, two thousand innocent Kikuyu, one thousand government troops and fifty-eight European and Asian civilians perished. Isichei gives the official figures of those killed during the war as 12,590 Mau Mau and 58 Europeans (Isichei 1995:259; Mbugua 2011:52).

Those Kikuyu who were killed during those dark days of the emergency were normally buried in mass graves or in simple graves, often without a coffin or ceremony. Their graves were often not marked. Others were killed or died in prison, detention camps or Home Guard posts. A good example of such death and subsequent burial was that of the most famous Kikuyu Mau Mau forest fighter—the late Mau Mau Field Marshal Dedan Kimathi who was hanged on Eighteenth February, 1957 by the British at Kamiti Maximum prison. He was buried without any ceremony within the Kamiti prison compound in an unmarked grave. Up to the present no one has been able to locate the exact spot where he was buried (Cagnolo 2006:281). There was so much death during the state of emergency that the Agikuyu became used to death and subsequently lost their cultural inhibition of dead bodies. (For more information on Mau Mau and state of emergency in Kenya (1952-1960) see also Blundell 1994; Collins 1970; Davidson 1964; Frost 1978; Furedi 1990; Gatu 2006; Granville 1954; Hallet 1974; Isichei 1995; Itote Waruhiu 1967; Kanogo 1987; Karanja 1999; Kariuki 1985; Kenyatta 1968; Kershaw 1997; Langley and Kiggins 1974; Maloba 1994; Muchiri 2009; Muchiri 2004; Mugo 1975; Ngugi wa Thiongo 1976, 1966; Odhiambo and Lonsdale 2003; Ogot and Ochieng 1995; Rosberg & Nottingham 1966; Shenk 1980; Shillington 1995; Upshall 1990; Wanjau 1988; Were and Wilson 1969; Wiseman 1958; Mazrui 1984,1999).

Kenya attained independence in 1963. A few years earlier and up to the present day, Kenyans, and for the purpose of this study the Agikuyu, have migrated in large numbers to the far reaches of the world. Some of the places they have migrated to include Europe, the Americas, Canada, Russia, Australia, China, Japan, India, South Africa, and other neighboring countries. The Agikuyu have one unique albeit strange characteristic, they love their homeland of central Kenya. Wherever a Mugikuyu is in the world, he is always communicating with folks back in Kikuyuland. Consequently when a relative here in Kenya dies, the Agikuyu in the diaspora most of the time send material assistance to the bereaved. On a similar note, most of the relatives in Kenya, when they become seriously sick, often travel overseas for specialized medical treatment. Similarly, when a Kikuyu in the diaspora dies, or when one of the relatives who had gone to visit them or to seek medical treatment dies outside Kenya, the body is often brought back home to Kenya for burial. In most cases, it is not easy, financially, for the concerned family to meet the full cost of bringing the body back to Kenya. The affected family, therefore, is forced to organize a *harambee* (fund raising) for all and sundry to chip in and raise sufficient funds to bring back the body home to Kenya. Ironically the bereaved family might not have sufficient land to bury the deceased. Often the body is buried in a tiny family plot of land, say in a quarter of an acre where the family has its matrimonial home, and so on. In most cases, however, the body is buried in a public cemetery especially the Langata Nairobi County Cemetery.

A good example, out of thousands of cases that have involved the Agikuyu diaspora bringing back to Kenya bodies for burial, is the family members who died on Christmas day 2010. Reporting that incident, the Kenya *Daily Nation* of 30th December 2010 reported:

> "A family is in mourning after losing five members in a road accident in South Africa on Christmas day."

The article went on to indicate that:

> "All the five died on the Oliver Tambo-Johannesburg Road, in a grisly road accident."

One of the relatives of the deceased was reported to have said:

> "Bringing the bodies home will cost about Kshs. 1.3 million. We do not have the money and we cannot even set the burial date."

It was a most tragic accident, and shook all the Kenyans and South Africans who read or heard the story. I was extremely saddened by that accident and I sent my most sincere condolences to the bereaved family. The family was, however, fortunate in obtaining assistance from well-wishers especially from the Government of Kenya, the Kenya High Commission in South Africa, the Kenya diaspora in South Africa, Kenya Airways, Royal Media Services (Citizen T.V.) and other corporations and individuals. As a result it was possible to bring back to Kenya all the five bodies for burial. Very decent and noble for all concerned, but the cost was enormous. Not many Kenya families would obtain such sympathy or financial assistance.

On the issue of bringing bodies back home for burial, one is bound to ask numerous questions such as why do the Agikuyu feel bound to do this, bearing in mind that it is not cultural for them to do so? As was revealed in Chapter 2 any death away from home was traditionally classified by the Agikuyu as a violent death. Additionally, it was revealed that, in case of a violent death the body would be left where it lay, and no one would touch it. Neither would any ornaments on the body be removed. Such a body was not buried, but left to be eaten by wild animals. It is not clear, therefore, what prompted the present Agikuyu to become all of a sudden interested in the dead bodies of their relatives and loved ones to the extent that they would go to any length and spend a fortune to bring the body back home for burial.

As indicated earlier, the influence of Christianity and other cultures started to have a noticeable effect on Agikuyu beliefs and ways of life from as early as 1920 or thereabouts. By that time, Christianity had spread to almost all parts of the Agikuyu homeland. Those Agikuyu who had embraced Christianity started burying their dead in homemade coffins made of rough timber planks. There were insufficient mortuaries, and neither were Africans able to access the few that were available. By the time of Kenya's independence (1963) the only mortuary near Kikuyu District (scope of this study) was the Nairobi City Council Mortuary. Mainly because of lack of mortuaries and lack of adequate transport, when a Mugikuyu died he had to be buried the same day. If on the following day for various reasons he had not been buried, his body would be preserved by being placed in a water basin filled with salt and water or the body would be laid and covered by banana tree trunks (*Miramba*).

In those days and up to the time of the emergency, most Africans had no access to radios. There were a few, but extremely few indeed. Only chiefs or similar "well-to-do" Agikuyu had access to a radio. As such there were no radio announcements made when someone died. Neither were there any newspaper announcements reporting the death of a Kikuyu. The reason for this was that extremely few Africans had access to newspapers, let alone being able to read and write. Death was therefore announced by word of mouth, initially by women screaming (*kuuga mbu*). Luckily, all who knew the deceased were from the neighborhood. Additionally, very few Africans had access to telephones. Note should also be taken that Africans had no TVs, and neither had cell phones been invented.

In those early years (1900-1930), most of the Agikuyu still feared dead bodies, and the majority adhered strictly to the Agikuyu tradition of coping with death. As was revealed in Chapter 2, traditional burial was carried out only by the sons of a deceased elder. As further reflected in Chapter 2, women and other relatives shunned burial, and indeed were barred from participating in the actual burial. Likewise, neighbors were not expected to attend the funeral, nor required to participate in the burial. In other words, burial was, in a sense, a private affair and restricted to the sons and agemates of the deceased, a few elders and a medicine man.

The early Agikuyu Christians *athomi* did not practise traditional funeral rites such as the *kuhukura* (see Chapter 2) or moving the homestead to a new location, nor did they demolish the hut of the widow should she die. In those early days, when the *athomi* started burying their dead the missionary way—in coffins and following the church liturgy, a large number of the Agikuyu stuck to their traditional religion, culture and in this case to the traditional funeral rites. This dual practices portrayed by both sides of the Kikuyu divide, existed side by side until around 1952 when the State of Emergency was declared. Note should be taken that although the two systems were practiced side by side, it was not a harmonious existence. The traditionalists could not tolerate the Christians (*athomi*) and vice versa. For example, the sons of the traditionalists could not marry the Christians' uncircumcised daughters. The Christians on the other hand looked down upon the traditionalists and their sons could not marry their circumcised daughters. The circumcised daughters of the traditionalists could not be admitted in missionary schools. Tension and animosity existed between the two groups, that is, between the Christians (*athomi*) and the traditionalists.

The State of Emergency, as stated earlier, affected the Agikuyu adversely. For instance, in addition to being detained or imprisoned without trial the Kikuyu were moved from their traditional homesteads to villages. These villages were mainly made up of huts built in rows. The Mau Mau suspects had their huts built in one sector of the village. Their huts resembled the circlic traditional huts. The "Royal", that is, those who were Christians and known by the colonialists to be anti-Mau Mau had square houses in another sector of the village. Every activity of the Agikuyu was monitored by the colonialists. The Agikuyu could not practise almost all their traditional way of life including sacrificing to God (*Mwene-Nyaga*). To do so would have required the slaughtering of the sacrificial lamb. These lambs as indicated earlier had to be unblemished and be of one color. Slaughtering of such a lamb during the emergency would have made the colonialist suspect that the blood of the lamb would be used by the Agikuyu for administering Mau Mau oaths (Shillington 1997:387-9; Were and Wilson 1969:274). The Agikuyu could also not dispose of the bodies of their dead in the manner described in Chapter 2, mainly for two reasons. In the first instance, as again indicated in Chapter 2, the colonial government as early as the nineteen thirties had outlawed leaving human dead bodies in the bush to be eaten by wild animals. Secondly, to bury their dead observing traditional burial rites would have necessitated killing a goat or ox to obtain fresh skin (*muguguta*) for burying an elder. Performing such an act would have made the colonialists suspect that the blood of that animal would be used for administering the Mau Mau oaths.

Another reason was that there was no longer a *kiaraini* (rubbish midden) where an elder could be buried. Neither was there a *kibirira* for leaving dead bodies to be eaten by hyenas. The reason for this was that there were no longer any traditional homesteads with a *kiaraini* or with a *kibirira* nearby. These restrictions during the State of Emergency, coupled with the influence of those Agikuyu who had ventured outside the traditional home districts including those who had served in the First and Second World Wars, and also the Agikuyu working in towns, European homes, farms and businesses, as well as those working for churches, missionaries or any government or missionary institution, slowly brought to bear on the rest of the Agikuyu. Such influence led to Agikuyu progressively adopting fresh ways of disposing of their dead.

As indicated in Chapter 2, traditionally Agikuyu did not have kings or chiefs. The Europeans are the ones who introduced chiefs to the Agikuyu society and way of governance. Those chiefs in time became very powerful, but at the same time they became very unpopular (Kenyatta 1938:186-230; Davidson 1964:81; Cagnolo 2006:130-4; Muriuki 1974:174-7). Chiefs have never been fully accepted by the Agikuyu even to this day. By the time of the emergency (1952-1960), the chiefs and their deputies (the headmen) were at the bottom of the ladder of the colonial administration. All deaths during the period of emergency had to be reported to the chiefs, who would give consent for burial. By the time Kenya became independent (1963) an official death permit had to be obtained from the chiefs before burial could take place. A few years after independence and for many years following, up to 2002, any gathering of more than three persons had to obtain a government permit. This restriction of assembly was meant to reduce the number of persons who could attend any social gathering. Restriction of attendance at funerals was, however, not very strictly enforced, as was also the case of the number of persons who could grace a wedding ceremony and reception. Any number could assemble in any functions solemnized by the church. Since funerals and weddings were an extension of services rendered by the church, the government did not therefore intervene as long as there was law and order.

Commencing in 1958 and the following years, the colonizers consolidated the Agikuyu native lands. Each family (*mbari*) after the necessary consultation and survey of their ancestral land was advised of the total acreage belonging to a particular *mbari*. The members of each *mbari* (sub-clan) would then divide their sub-clan acreage in line with traditional Kikuyu land heritage pattern. The manner in which such clan land was divided among the family members was, for example, should the founder of the *mbari* have been a polygamist with, for instance, five wives, the hut of each wife was called *githaku* (veranda) and in such a case, the land given would be divided in such a way that each *githaku* (i.e. sons of each wife) would be allotted an equal share of the ancestral land. So if one wife had only one son then that son would get one-fifth of the family land, while the wife with three sons would be alloted one-fifth of her husband's land, in which case each son of the wife with three sons would get one-third of the one-fifth land allotted to their mother. Rather complex and complicated. As is obvious, this was extremely unfair to the sons of the wife who had many sons. However, frequently most of the elders refused to go by this pattern, instead they allotted land equally to each son regardless of how many sons a particular wife had had. Note should be taken that only male children were allotted land. Females could not own land according to Kikuyu tradition.

The consolidation of Kikuyu land had a profound effect on the traditional way of life of the Agikuyu. Hitherto, the Agikuyu, as was shown, in Chapter 2 were constantly on the move. They would migrate to new lands or locations as soon as the land they had occupied for generations became overcrowded or was no longer fertile and hence not suitable for cultivation. When the number of members of a particular *mbari* became too large, most of them had to migrate in search of greener pastures. Another reason, mentioned earlier, was that when an elder died, his homestead had to be moved to a new location. With consolidation, the Agikuyu became stuck to one spot. They could not move to anywhere else. Their traditional migration had permanently and irreversibly been altered. Or so the colonizers thought. As shown subsequently, the Kikuyu are some of the most dynamic and enterprising people in Africa, if not in the whole world. Soon after independence (1963) the Agikuyu migrated outside their homeland by purchasing (often in cash) large and small tracts of land in places like the Rift Valley, Coast Provinces of Kenya, and even as far afield as Zimbabwe, Zambia, Namibia, South Africa, Tanzania and currently in South Sudan. Of relevance to this study, soon after the said land consolidation, the allottee of a particular parcel of land had to vacate the emergency village and settle on his piece of land. The colonizers insisted that all houses built on the newly demarcated land had to be some metres from the road. The reason for that order was to allow the British administration to inspect any home without any warning or notice. This was to enable them monitor any illegal activity by the Agikuyu, especially the harboring of Mau Mau terrorists. This act by the colonizers did away with the Agikuyu traditional *thome* (entrance to or exit from the homestead). One may ask, "why is this?" As indicated in chapter 2, the Kikuyu traditional homeland is made up of ridges divided by valleys, ravines and rivers. The Agikuyu used to locate their homesteads on the slopes of a ridge; a few metres from the water source which was either a river or a natural spring. The entrance (*thome*) to the homestead would face the water source for ease and convenience of livestock running to the source of water to drink, also, for the convenience of the womenfolk in drawing water for domestic use. Another point to be observed was that when an elder's sons married, the sons would cultivate and build their homestead on fields further up the ridge behind their father's homestead. No son would be permitted, or dare to build their homestead in front of their father's homestead. In other words, no son would build his house(s) in front of his father's *thome*. The significance of this is that with demarcation there was no *thome* in the traditional sense and hence no *kiaraini* where it should have been. The *kiaraini* as noted earlier was normally where an elder was buried.

With demarcation, the elder's home had to be near the road to comply with the government directive. Such roads were on the top of the ridge, and so was the homestead. Therefore, the sons had to cultivate and build their houses towards the river down the slope, which traditionally was the prerogative of the father. So, modern Agikuyu should note that when they state that in accordance with the Agikuyu tradition they wish to bury their parents at the *thome* (entrance) of the family land, they are mistaken, as they are ignorant of the above. To follow the Kikuyu culture and tradition, the parents should be buried down the slope, where, if demarcation had not taken place and no modern road was in place, or if there were no piped water, the traditional homestead of their parents would have been. Of great significance to the burial practice of the Agikuyu is that elders (the few who were buried per se) were not buried at the *thome* (home entrance) but rather at the *kiaraini* (rubbish midden) which it should be noted was outside the perimeter fence of the homestead and to one side of the *thome*. Opposite to the *kiaraini* and still outside the homestead's perimeter fence was the *kibirira* where bodies of almost all the other members of the family were left unburied to be devoured by wild beasts. It should be noted, as indicated elsewhere in this study, an exception was some matriarchs from a polygamous marriage, who were buried behind their huts.

This issue will be of significance in this study when considering why the Agikuyu should stop the trend where most parents are being buried at the entrance of the demarcated land. This issue is thorny one, and one that is causing much animosity among those who inherit the land. After some time, such graves become a hindrance to the economical utilization and development of the ancestral land. For sketch drawings of traditional Kikuyu homesteads see figure 1 and figure 2 below showing the layout of Agikuyu traditional homesteads. Figure 1 is a sketch map of a traditional Agikuyu homestead of a man with four wives. Figure 2 on the other hand is a sketch map of another man having, this time along with four wives, a widowed mother and three married sons. From these sketches, the location of the various facilities in the homestead can be seen, including the *thome* (home entrance), *kiaraini* (rubbish midden) and the *kibirira* (graveyard or cemetery). Similar sketches can be seen in Leakey (1977:132-7) and Cagnolo (2006:53-6).

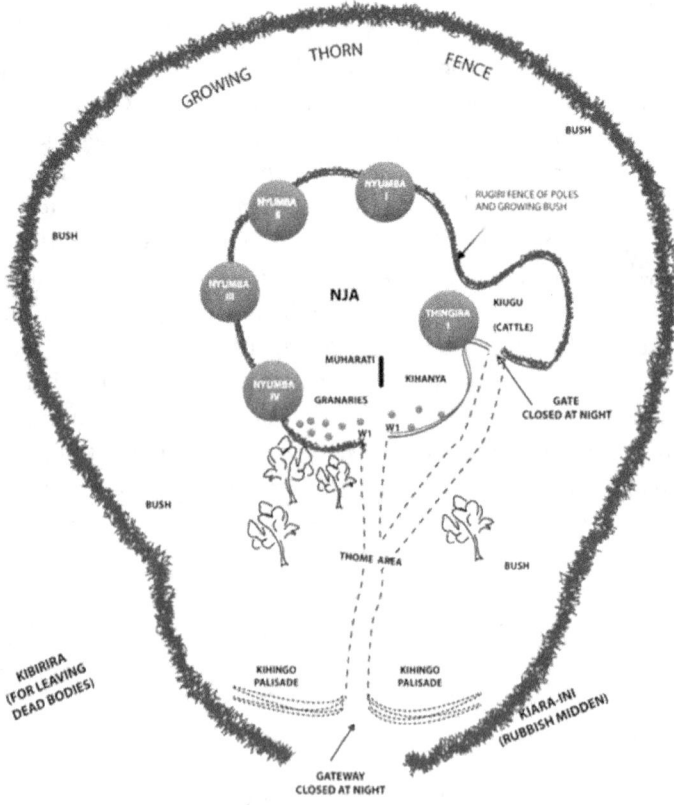

Figure 1: The layout of a traditional Agikuyu homestead of a man with four wives

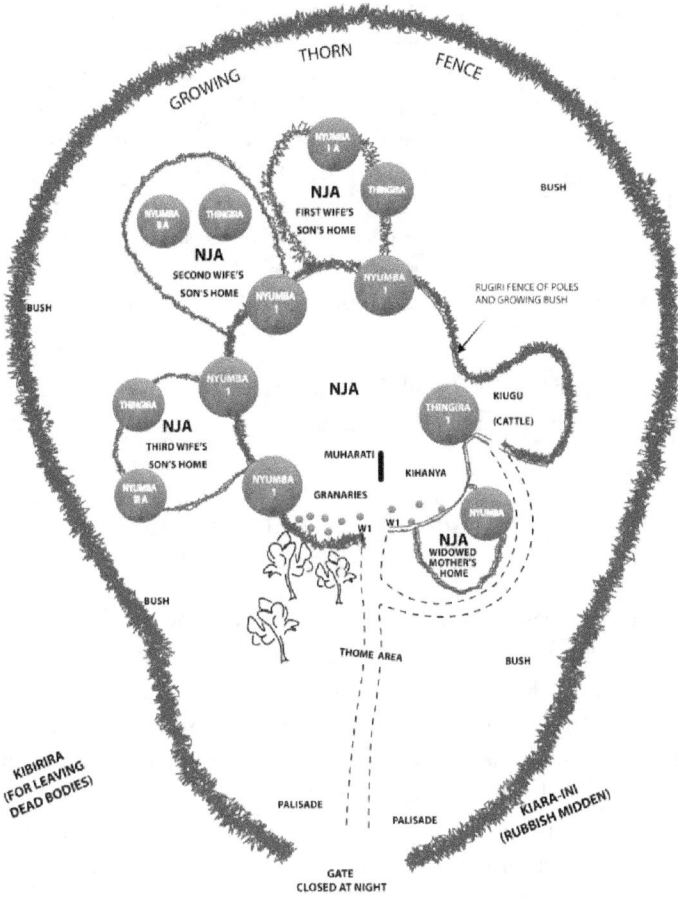

Figure 2: The layout of a traditional Agikuyu homestead of a man with four wives, a widowed mother and three married sons

Commenting on the consolidation of land in Kikuyu land, the movement to villages and the effect this had on the Agikuyu, Macpherson (1970:138) comments:

> "The Emergency made far-reaching changes in the pattern of community life. Hitherto, the Gikuyu people had lived in "dispersed homesteads." Village communities were unknown except in the sense of small family settlements of a temporary nature on a *"mbari"* (extended family) estate. The Emergency ended this traditional pattern. For security reasons, the entire population was resettled in villages and a vast programme of consolidation

of landholdings was planned and gradually carried out over the whole tribal area. The traditional custom whereby each family retained cultivation rights in small parcels of land in various parts of the country was abandoned and by a process of mutual accommodation under the guidance of land consolidation teams, plots were exchanged to provide a single holding of each landowner in one place. When the Emergency ended, landowners were allowed to settle permanently in those consolidated farms, to which they were given a legal title. Landless people remained in the villages and these became a permanent feature of community life."

The so-called landless people have nowhere up to this day to bury their dead. They bury them in public cemeteries.

Noticeable Development of Agikuyu Funeral Rites since Independence (1963)

The Agikuyu have, since Kenya attained its independence in 1963, reformed their funeral rites to some extent. These changes have not been in written form but have developed gradually with time. Some of the new practices which have emerged have been welcomed. However, some, after being used for a brief period have had to be abandoned. For example, in the late nineteen sixties and early nineteen seventies, especially with the expansion and modernization of the Nairobi City Council Mortuary, as well as the construction of the ultra-modern Kenyatta National Hospital mortuary, bodies from Kikuyu constituency would usually be taken to those mortuaries for storage while burial arrangements were being made back home. Kikuyu District (the scope of this study), borders Nairobi City to the West and is a few minutes drive from these two mortuaries. One of the reasons for the body being stored for a few days was that back home the grave had to be prepared. During that period (nineteen sixties and seventies), there was a practice that the inside of the grave and floor had to be built of dressed stones. When the grave was ready, the body would be transported from the mortuary on the day of burial, in a hearse for the well-to-do. Others who could not afford the cost of a hearse used less expensive means of transport, for example, the coffins would be placed on top of a pickup truck or on top of a bus. At the same time, while the grave was being built, other activities would be taking place, such as placing paid announcements on the radio and in the national newspapers. If the deceased was an active church member, on the day of burial the body would be taken from the mortuary direct to the local church. An elaborate funeral service would be conducted with the officiating clergy in their official robes. Choirs, a sermon, and prayers for the family of the deceased, would then be part of the liturgy. Immediately after the church service the body would be taken to the grave. There it would be lowered into the grave with the officiating clergy and a few family members throwing a handful of dust onto the coffin with the words "dust to dust" "ashes to ashes", and so on. Only those handfuls of dust went into the grave. The grave would then be sealed with a concrete slab. This was hardly in accord with the biblical concept of earth to earth and ashes to ashes. The body would remain entombed there, hardly touched by the soil, forever and ever. The body, in my opinion, was therefore not buried in the real sense. After the funeral there was normally feasting for all those attending the funeral. This trend did not last long before the church became uneasy, especially on the issue of feasting and the use of dressed stones and concrete in constructing the grave. The church advised their members to desist from feeding those attending the funeral, as well as to desist from constructing the grave with dressed stones. The church advised the use of simple graves. The only mourners to be fed were those who had travelled from far. Neighbours were not to be fed.

Present-day Agikuyu Funeral Rites

When analyzing the present-day Agikuyu funeral rites, I wish to state that the liturgy of various Christian denominations and the church's role or the duties of their clergy on burial of their members is not part of this study. The study's main concern is the funeral rites of the Agikuyu Christians other than religious roles rendered by the church or their clergy when conducting funerals. Suffice to say that almost all Christian denominations use varying manners and liturgy when burying their members. It is, however, worth noting that in almost all Christian churches in Kikuyuland, funeral services and procedure are to a large measure dependent upon the deceased's standing in the church.

Culturally though, in these days there is hardly any noticeable difference in the burying of an elder, a woman, youth or child (cf. Droz 2011:69). I was astonished a few months ago when a middle-aged man from my area hanged himself, yet he was awarded a Christian burial. By a Christian burial is meant that the church officiated at the funeral ceremony. The main reason I was astonished at the manner of burial of a person who had committed suicide was that both traditionally and from the scriptural perspective, he should not have been buried that way. Culturally, as indicated in chapter

2, suicide was condemned, and when a person committed suicide (usually by hanging), the body when discovered would be lowered to the ground and left at the site of suicide. If suicide took place in the open it would be left there for wild beasts to come and devour. If inside the hut, the body would be lowered, the entrance closed and a few planks at the rear of the hut removed to enable wild animals to enter at night and take the body to devour. Whoever lowered the body would have to be cleansed. From a biblical perspective, Young (1984:518) advises that suicide is the deliberate act of taking one's own life and that the Bible does not call this unpardonable sin. Yet those who practiced it were considered to be utterly filled with remorse or despondency by not seeking God's perfect will (Isa 31:1-13; Matt 27:1-9). Suicide rejects the biblical view that God is the giver and taker of life. Pretzel, (1990:1234), advises that the Old Testament records six suicides (Judg 9:54; 16:28-31; 1 Sam 31:1-6; 2 Sam 17:23; 1 Kgs16:18, 19) and the New Testament one (Matt 27:3-5), none making any value judgement. Pretzel further notes that suicide was a fairly common occurrence in the early church, which tended to approve of self-sacrifice and martyrdom. It was not until St Augustine (AD 354-430) wrote strongly against it that the church began to condemn suicide, and St Thomas Aquinas (AD 1225-74) reaffirmed the Augustine view that suicide is a sin. A very interesting comment is one by Droge (1992:227), who indicates that one of the difficulties Augustine and other theologians had in defending their condemnation of suicide is that neither the Hebrew Bible nor the New Testament explicitly prohibits the act. Boadt (1996:968), summarising his views on suicide, sets out what seems to be the view of the modern Christian church on suicide by indicating that pastorally we should learn the lesson from scripture that suicide is not offered as an option for times of trouble. Suffering can be an important part of God's will for individuals, and we need to turn to God's love and care in dire troubles, when death might seem preferable (Job 3:10-15). Boadt further asserts however, that we also should learn that no suicide should be condemned or dishonoured; it is in God's hands to judge, and in ours to proclaim divine compassion and divine life-giving love (cf. Harran 1989:21-30). In view of the above, and the fact that the liturgies of the Roman Catholic Church, the Anglican Church, PCEA (Presbyterian Church of East Africa) among others, give their clergy guidelines on burying suicide victims, I am therefore, persuaded that the church was justified in burying that middle-aged man. This move, however, reflects how removed the Agikuyu are from their traditional system of handling their dead. In the case of the above suicide, the presiding clergy did not wear the official priestly robes, nor was the body taken to church.

Currently in Kikuyuland when death occurs at home, those who discover the dead body or are the first to witness the death alert the family and neighbours—normally by women screaming (*kuga mbu*). Those who arrive at the scene of death then arrange for the body to be taken to the most convenient mortuary. Should foul play be suspected, for example, murder, drowning, suicide, and so on, the local administration and the police are notified before the body is touched by anyone. If no foul play is suspected, the body is taken to a mortuary such as the Lee Funeral home in Nairobi. This, of course, applies only to those who can afford it. For others the body would be taken to such mortuaries as the University of Nairobi Chiromo Campus Mortuary or to other mortuaries such as the Nairobi County Council mortuary, Kenyatta National Hospital mortuary, PCEA Kikuyu Hospital Mortuary and many others in and around Nairobi. Should death have occurred within twenty-four hours after hospitalization or at home then it becomes a police case. In that case, the body will have to be taken to the Nairobi County Council Mortuary for a post-mortem examination. Such a post-mortem must be undertaken by a police pathologist, who will determine the cause of death. This will establish whether death was due to foul play. The family has the right, however, to be represented by their own pathologist when the autopsy is being carried out. All deaths are reported to the area government administration, where the chief will be asked to issue the burial permit. If a police case is involved, the police will be the ones to give permission for the chief to issue burial permit. The same death permit after burial will be the one to be submitted to the Registrar of Births and Deaths in order for a Death Certificate of the deceased to be obtained. For other than a police case, a post-mortem before the body leaves the mortuary is desirable although not obligatory.

At home, on the first day when death occurs, relatives, neighbors and friends who are near gather at the home of the deceased to comfort the bereaved family. A funeral committee is formed, whose main responsibility is to organise the funeral arrangements. The funeral committee is comprised of all able-bodied adult males of good standing in the community. Nowadays women of good standing are also included. It is important to note that members of such committees must be known to and respected by the family of the deceased. Additionally, they must be conversant with funeral arrangements and procedure. Those selected then choose one of them as their chairperson. The family spokesperson may have indicated that the family would prefer a certain individual to chair the committee. The family choice is often accepted. The committee's initial task is to establish whether the deceased made any request regarding his burial. Secondly, to establish the family's wishes about the burial. Those wishes would be considered by the committee and often respected, provided they do not contravene any government regulation, religious or clan preferences and practices.

On the first day after death, the committee arranges for as many persons to be informed about the death as is possible, through word of mouth, telephone, SMS, by e-mails, radio, newspapers announcements, announcements in local churches and so on. For the rich and famous, in addition to the above, arrangements are made for TV announcements. Such announcements will depend to a large measure on the budget of the committee to meet the costs. A decision is made by the funeral committee as to whether burial should be delayed to await the arrival of those coming from far away. Seating arrangements for the committee and the times of meetings are agreed upon, as well the seating and catering arrangements for those who will be coming to the home to console the family, and additionally for those who will come for prayers and for those who will be bringing material assistance. The committee will also decide who will be singing every evening. There is a trend these days whereby, at the home of the deceased from the date of death to the day before burial, Christian volunteers come to the home to sing every evening from about 9:00 pm to midnight. No one has been able to establish the purpose of such singing, which at times is incoherent. Some families do not allow such singing, as it sounds strange. If the deceased was affiliated to a particular church, that church is notified immediately death occurs. The minister of that church is requested to indicate the day that would be most convenient for him to officiate at the funeral. Additionally, he has to indicate what sort of services the deceased will be accorded—for example, whether the body will be taken to church, the hymns to be included in the funeral programme and other details. The date and time the minister gives are often the time and date that are set by the funeral committee and the family for burial. The funeral committee meets often, almost every evening to finalise funeral and burial arrangements. Some of the issues addressed by the committee include setting the date of burial, place of burial, identifying the exact spot where the grave will be dug; deliberating on issues such as whether a post-mortem will be done, and if so when and by whom; deciding the clothes the deceased will be dressed in, and the coffin (casket) to be selected, paid for and delivered to the mortuary. Arrangements for the transport of the body (hearse) are discussed and decided upon as well as transport arrangements for close family members and other well-wishers. A decision is also made on the clothes to be worn on the burial day, especially by the female family members of the deceased. The issue of catering for the funeral committee, the family, visitors and other well-wishers is also considered; placement of radio and newspaper announcements and the wordings of such announcements, as well as the photogragh of the deceased that will appear in the advertisement. Payment of any outstanding hospital and mortuary bills. These have to be settled, often before the body can be released by such institutions. In consultation with the church, the hymns to be sung on that day are agreed on and the choirs that will participate. Arranging for daily prayers at the home of the deceased is organized by the church. As indicated above, the wording of the advertisements on the radio and in the newspapers is decided by the funeral committee. The radio and newspaper announcements give names of the deceased, name of the spouse, names of children, parents and names of the in-laws, the number of the grandchildren, and great-grandchildren. Additionally, they also indicate where the deceased was working, his position in the community or church and where his ancestral home is. The date and time and place of burial appear. Also the time when the body will be collected from the mortuary and the time and place where burial will take place. Should the body be taken to church before burial, the name of the church is given. The advertisement in the newspaper carries a colored or a black and white passport-size recent photograph of the deceased. A shorter version of the announcement is read on the radio. If there is a fundraising requirement, to offset medical bills, to assist in bringing the body home from afar or for meeting outstanding medical and funeral expenses, the place, date and time of such fundraising is shown. Recently, a mobile phone number via which contributions can be sent via electronic media (here in Kenya referred to as *m-pesa*) is given. My opinion regarding this is that too many names and details are given, to such an extent that one does not bother to read even a fraction of those names. For further comments on this issue, see Chapters 7 and 8 of this book. Should the body be out of the country, the funeral committee organizes how the body will be brought back home; this is done only if it is the family's wish. Often fundraising is organized to assist the family meet the cost. The funeral committee also makes contact with the Kenya Embassy and the Kenya diaspora for them to assist in bringing the body back home. The funeral committee also produces a funeral programme that is made up of a number of pages, the simplest one being four pages of A5 size paper. The front page carries a photograph of the deceased. Full names are given and his standing in the Christian faith (born again, elder, deacon, and so on.) The page also indicates that it is the funeral programme of that named individual. The second page will show who will be the master of ceremonies, transport manager, the speakers during the ceremony, name of the church minister officiating, names of the ones to give votes of thanks, and the Bible passages to be read; in other words the second page contains the events of the burial day. The third page contains the eulogy, which is a compressed life history of the deceased. The eulogy is often written in two languages—the third page carrying the version in Kikuyu language, while on the next page is the English version. For the four-paged programme, however, only one version is given. The fourth page contains selected hymns agreed upon by the church minister. The funeral committee ensures that enough copies of the programme are produced and distributed to each person attending the funeral. If, for example, there are one thousand people expected to attend the funeral, one thousand programmes are produced. The cost of producing those programmes is met by the funeral committee from funds raised from the family as well as from well-wishers. The cost of producing such programmes can be enormous. For the well-to-do, the funeral programme resembles a booklet. At times, it might be up to 20 pages of A4 size paper. The front page contains the deceased's colour photograph, his full names and date of burial. Other details are as given for the simple ones other than the eulogy, which covers numerous pages covering the deceased's journey through his earthly life. It bears colour photographs of his childhood, youth, school days, college days, graduations, marriage, children, place of work, honors bestowed, workmates and so on. Some of those programmes, in my view, are too elaborate and contain unnecessary details. They also cost a lot of money. Such a display of wealth is not necessary, and one is bound to wonder wether it is done just to show off. The day before burial, young men from the neighborhood are shown by elders where to dig the grave. The young men volunteer to dig the grave free of charge. They do not demand, nor are they given, any payment. The bereaved family only provides them with lunch, which is prepared by the ladies from the neighborhood. During the day of the funeral, those going to the mortuary to collect the body gather at the home of the deceased or at a convenient meeting place usually before 8 a.m. After brief prayers, the vehicle proceeds to the mortuary. At the mortuary, the family or representative of the funeral committee finalizes all formalities required, such as payment of all the mortuary outstanding bills, completion of all forms required and anything else. The body is then released to the family. Prior to this, the body would have been bathed (washed) by the mortuary attendants and clothed with appropriate attire. The clothes would have been delivered to the mortuary beforehand by the family. Ladies are normally dressed by other ladies (relatives or very close friends). Men are usually dressed by the mortuary attendants. Note should be taken that bodies of those who are members of a particular fraternity in the church, such as the Woman's Guild (PCEA), Mothers Union (ACK) are clothed in their official church uniforms. After the body has been released, it is then placed in the coffin that, as described earlier, should have been delivered to the mortuary beforehand. Brief prayers are said, and then those who wish to view the body are given a chance. It is not advisable for the body to be viewed by everyone—only those who are courageous enough should do so. The lid of the coffin is then closed, and the coffin borne to the waiting hearse or other means of transport. The mode of transport varies according to the economic ability of the family. It might be a hearse, a pickup, or the coffin might be loaded on top of a public transport bus. Very close family members (usually male) normally sit in the hearse or in the vehicle carrying the body. Other vehicles carrying close family members—usually the ones carrying the widow/widower, children of the deceased or parents follow the hearse; these are followed by other vehicles. At times, the motorcade can be as many as 100 vehicles. The convoy then travels to the church or burial site. Family photographs are taken there before the funeral service commences. The clergy then call the congregation to order. The coffin, if the funeral service is to be held inside the church, is carried inside the church by members of the fraternity of which the deceased was a member. For example, the coffin of a church elder is carried by other church elders, the coffin of a lady who was a member of say, ACK Mothers Union or of PCEA Woman Guild is borne by members of that religious order. The service then follows the order laid down in the funeral programme, namely hymns, prayers, eulogy, speeches, choirs, reading of the scriptures, sermons, and prayers for the family of the deceased while standing around the casket (coffin). Depending on the officiating clergy, there might be a number of alterations to the funeral programme as the funeral service progresses.

At the conclusion of the church funeral service, which takes from two to three hours, the master of ceremonies usually thanks all those who have attended the service as well as those who have assisted in any way. He then gives directions as to how to proceed to the location of the burial. The minister's car leads the motorcade to the gravesite followed by the vehicle carrying the coffin. This is followed by the vehicle carrying very close relatives namely the widow (widower) and children.

At the graveside, the coffin is borne by those designated to do so. For those holding a church position the coffin is borne by members of the fraternity of which he was a member. For the uniformed individuals (police, military and so on) the body is borne by officers of the same rank as the deceased. Some nephews and friends bear the coffin of relatives who are not designated to be borne as otherwise indicated above. Interment follows in accordance with the order stipulated by that particular denomination. The grave is then filled with earth. Flowers are normally placed on the grave. The first one, made in the shape of a cross, is placed at the head of the grave by the minister of the church. The second one, designed as a heart, is placed next by the widow (widower) and children of the deceased. A third one, preferably also in shape of a heart, is placed by the parents of the deceased.

Other flowers are placed by brothers, sisters, other close relatives, friends, workmates and others. The officiating clergyman finally inserts a cross at the head of the grave "in the name of the Father, the Son and the Holy Spirit". The graveside ceremony is over after that. At the home of the deceased, the clergyman and his entourage are given a room to change their official gowns. They are also provided with a meal. Those visitors from afar are also given a meal. All leave after that, other than close friends, members of the family and members of the funeral committee. Immediately after the funeral, the funeral committee meets to make arrangements for ensuring that all matters relating to the funeral are concluded satisfactorily and promptly. Issues to be attended to include the payment of outstanding bills relating to the burial, also to making sure that all items hired or borrowed are returned. This may include tents, chairs, tables and public address system. After a day, or at most a fortnight, the committee meets to "wind up" its affairs. At that final meeting, they analyze all that has taken place. They go through the finances and ensure that the balance after settling all bills and expenses is handed over to the most deserving person(s). For children who have lost both parents a trustee is normally identified to take care of the welfare of such children. For a woman who has lost her husband, she is given the money, provided she is responsible and of good character. For a husband who has lost his wife, he is given the money, provided he is not an alcoholic` or of questionable character. Usually the funeral committee ensures that the Government Death Certificate is obtained. This is necessary, as it will be a key document in winding up the estate of the deceased. If desirable and affordable, the family or the funeral committee places an advertisement in one local newspaper thanking all those who attended the funeral or assisted in any way. A year after the funeral, or within a reasonable time thereafter, the family after erecting a gravestone, preferably with a marble cross and an appropriate engraving, places an advertisement in the newspaper(s) inviting all who can attend to assemble at certain date, to "unveil" the cross. Additionally, and as an alternative, a similar notice is circulated to the surrounding churches as well as to the church where the deceased was a member. The function is officiated by a clergyman. Speeches are offered by close friends of the deceased. The family spokesperson then thanks all attending as well as all those who from the date of the funeral have kept the family in their thoughts and prayers.

It is most strange that currently, when a man dies there are no arrangements made by the family or clan about who will be looking after the widow and the children. In other words no one is appointed by the clan to take over the role of the dead husband and father to his children. It should be noted that in no way am I advocating "wife inheritance". Additionally, it is worthy of note that traditionally the Agikuyu did not, as was revealed in Chapter 2, force the widow to be inherited. Rather a brother or nephew was appointed by the elders to take over the responsibility of looking after the widow. This did not give him any conjugal rights over her. He would be responsible for her children. The widow could, however, take a lover if she so decided. No one would mind if she was inclined to do so. Should she have children with that lover or lovers, any children born of that union would be regarded as belonging to the dead husband.

The one who "inherited" her would be responsible for the welfare of the children she got with her lover(s). Such children would be named in line with the deceased's family tree. When mature, such children would inherit the assets of their deceased father's estate (not the estate of the lover). Very interesting indeed (see also Chapter 2 of this book).

As will be argued in Chapter 7 of this book, the current mode of burial of the Agikuyu Christians and the accompanying funeral rites, differ substantially from the Agikuyu traditional funeral practices, as well as from those of early Christians. Additionaly, they are not in line with those observed and practiced during biblical times as revealed in Scripture. Present-day Kikuyu burials are very expensive and a considerable number of the Agikuyu are unable to meet such costs. Often they are forced to organize fundraising to collect funds from well-wishers. An indication of today's cost of burying the dead, especially the ones who die far from home, was given earlier in which five members of one family died in South Africa in December 2010. The gross cost of burial and freight of those five family members was estimated at Kshs. 1.3 million.

According to the official charges of a leading National newspaper in Kenya, the cost of funeral advertisements and related matters is as follows:

INSERTION RATES PER DAY-DEATH ANNOUNCEMENT

Size (cm x column)	BLACK & WHITE (Kenya Shillings)	COLOR (Kenya Shillings)
6.5 cm x 2col	11,250	19,500
8cm x 2 col	14,500	23,000
10cm x2col	18,250	27,500
13cm 2col (one-eighth page)	27,000	41,500
15cm x 2col	30,000	43,500
17cm x 2col	33,250	46,500
18cm x 2col	38,500	52,500
Quarter page	80,000	107,000
Half page	121,000	189,000
Full page	290,500	526,500

Table 1: Death Announcement charges by a leading newspaper in Kenya

APPRECIATION/MEMORIAL (VAT INCLUSIVE)

Size (cm x column)	BLACK & WHITE (Kenya Shillings)	COLOR (Kenya Shillings)
6.5 cm x 2col	13,050	22,620
8cm x 2col	16,820	26,680
10cm x 2col	21,170	31,900
13cm x 2col (one-eighth page)	31,320	48,140
15cm x 2col	34,800	50,460
17cm x 2col	38,570	53,940
18cm x 2col	44,660	60,900
Quarter page	92,800	124,120
Half page	140,360	219,240
Full page	336,980	610,740

Table 2: Charges of Announcement of appreciation and memorials on death by the same leading Kenya newspaper.

Similar to the newspaper announcements, the costs of radio announcements are also high. One radio station in Kenya currently charges Kenya shillings 1,800 for each funeral announcement. The costs of coffins are also extremely high. In January 2012, one Kenya leading newspaper reported that the cost of a coffin to bury a Kenya dignitary was Kenya shillings Forty Thousand while the suit to dress the body of the same dignitary was to be purchased for Kenya Shillings Twenty Thousand. In my view this extravagance is ridiculous, especially when one bears in mind that the per capita income of the majority of Kenyans is less than USA $2 per day. Simple and speedy burial with few rites and requirements is therefore called for, and should be adopted as soon possible. Most of the current funeral rites should be altered and some done away with as will be shown and recommended in Chapters 7 and 8.

Recent Development Touching on Modern Agikuyu Christian Funeral Rites

Over recent years, there has been considerable number of Agikuyu who have opted to be cremated. Among the most notable Kikuyus who chose to be cremated were the late Archbishop of the Anglican Church of Kenya Manasses Kuria and his wife. Mrs Kuria died and was cremated in 2002 AD in a simple ceremony at the Langata Nairobi City Council Crematorium, attended by only a few very close friends and a few relatives. Her husband Archbishop Kuria, the second Archbishop of the Anglican Church of Kenya, died in 2005 AD. At the end of his life, he chose to break with Agikuyu tradition and convention of his time by arranging that after his death, his body should be cremated in a simple ceremony attended only by relatives and close friends. His wish was fulfilled when his body was cremated in the manner he wished in 2005 at the Nairobi City Council Crematorium. More recently on Saturday Eighth October, 2012, another Kikuyu, the Nobel Peace Laureate Professor Wangari Maathai, although she was awarded a state funeral by the Kenya Government, nevertheless was cremated in accordance with her wish. Her simple cremation ceremony was attended only by relatives and close friends at the Hindu Crematorium, Kariokor in Nairobi.

In one of the Kenya Newspapers in January 2012 there was an advertisement that in part read:

> "The family of . . . In accordance with his wishes the body has been cremated. . . . there will be a memorial service at (church named)."

This is an indication that there is a trend developing whereby immediately after death the body is cremated and a memorial service held at a later date.

In recent years there have appeared numerous newspaper advertisements where it is indicated;

> "Memorial services will be held at (a given church) followed by private burial thereafter"

This shows that private burials, as opposed to funerals attended by all and sundry, are slowly being opted for by the Agikuyu. Their wishes are being honored and respected. In recent years also, numerous funeral announcements have appeared in local newspapers giving notification of death of named individual *mugikuyu* and advising that burial has already taken place or will take place in such and such a cemetery in a given city in an overseas country. This shows that a number of the Agikuyu, are being buried far away in overseas cities. Thus, their bodies are not being brought back to Kenya for burial.

As was indicated in Chapter 2 of this study very many Agikuyu, most probably out of ignorance and without realizing the magnitude of those words, are indicating in their funeral advertisement;

> "Celebration of a life well lived"

When one analyzes the description of the deceased appearing in his death announcement, one clearly sees that the deceased was a practising Christian and not a Humanist. Humanists, as stated in chapter 2, do not believe in life after death and neither do they believe in any religion. When a humanist is being buried, all religious symbols must be removed or covered. They believe among other things that the funeral ceremony is intended to "celebrate" the life that has been lived, and properly honour that person's life. It is obvious that humanists are unchristian, and Christians should therefore refrain from having or practicing anything humanist. By placing advertisements of that nature, we are promoting humanist ideologies without realising it.

The chapter that follows (Chapter 4) will be an attempt to show what the scriptures, in this case the Old and New Testaments of the Holy Bible say about funeral rites and burial practice. There is an attempt to establish whether there are funeral and burial practices that are explicitly mandated in scripture, and possibly shown as normative, which ought to be adopted and incorporated in Agikuyu practices of coping with death.

CHAPTER 4

BURIAL IN THE BIBLICAL PERIOD

Introduction and Methodology

BURIAL RITES OF EVERY race and tribe are influenced by many factors including culture, religion, environment and other external factors. In chapter 2 of this book the Agikuyu traditional burial and funeral rites were explored. Also considered and explored were the traditional funeral rites of some other African tribes, the funeral rites of the English, as well as funeral rites of selected world religions. Additionally explored was how a few countries are coping with limited burial space as well as burial excesses. Chapter 3 dwelt on the present-day burial rites of the contemporary Agikuyu Christians.

In this chapter, an attempt will be made to explore and analyze burial and funeral rites in both the Old and the New Testaments. This is according to the third step of the LIM model, whose requirement is to interpret the world as it should be, which in this case is based on a selection of scriptural texts on burial, and looking at classic theological and church teachings on burial rites. The latter is covered in Chapters 5 and 6. This analysis will aim to reveal whether there are biblical burial practices that are mandated or are normative, and therefore ought to be incorporated in Christian funeral practices, including those of the Agikuyu and other African Christians. This chapter will also reveal whether the biblical funeral practices resemble or have in anyway influenced the current Agikuyu burial and funeral rites.

I believe that the best way of conducting the Biblical survey and analyzes is to work through the Bible materials from start to finish. To accomplish this, the theological discipline utilized will be that of Biblical Theology. As indicated by Yarbrough (2000:61-2), Biblical Theology is the study of the Bible that seeks to discover what the biblical writers, under divine guidance, believed, described, and taught in the context of their own time. We learn further from him (2000:61-2), that Biblical Theology is related to but different from three other major branches of theological inquiry. Practical Theology he asserts focuses on the pastoral application of biblical truths in modern life. Systematic Theology articulates the biblical outlook in a current doctrinal or philosophical system. Historical Theology investigates the development of Christian thought in its growth through the centuries since biblical times (Ibid., 61-2).

He (2000:61-2), further asserts that Biblical Theology is an attempt to articulate the theology that the Bible contains as its writers addressed their particular settings. The scriptures, it should be noted, came into being over the course of many centuries, from different authors, social settings and geographical locations. The whole Bible is given by God. While what it unabashedly affirms and reflects is human authorship, it is no less insistent on its divine origin and message. Since God is the ultimate author of the Bible, and since truthfulness characterizes His communication to mankind, Biblical Theology is justified in upholding the full reliability of the Bible rightly interpreted. The theology of the Bible unfolds in the course of the events it describes and sometimes precipitates (Ibid., 61-2).

Erickson's (1989:21) views are similar when he indicates that to him Biblical Theology is the organization of theological teachings in terms of the portions of the Bible where they occur rather than by topic. Biblical Theology Erickson further asserts makes no attempt to restate the biblical expressions in a contemporary form.

Barr (2004:452) is of the view that Biblical Theology has the Bible as its horizon; its source material is the biblical text; its subject is the theology which lies behind or is implied by the Bible, and its scope is determined by the meanings as known and implied within the time and culture of the Bible. In answering the question often asked as to the relevance of biblical theology for the present day, or actualization (as one might call it) he queries whether biblical theology only tells us what the theology of biblical times was and explains to us its inner relations and connections as the people of the Bible understood them, but also explains how that theology is to be interpreted and realized in the actual life and thought of the religious community today? He observes that within modern Biblical Theology, different currents have answered this question in very different ways, and some he feels have evaded the question and tried to sit on the fence. He (1999:17) asserts that various strands of Biblical Theology in modern times have been affected by complexity of motives, issues and contracts. He feels that there is at present no simple definition that can be given to the many-sided character that attaches to the idea of Biblical Theology as Old or New Testament theology. When concluding his book he (1999:607) indicates that to him Biblical Theology has proved itself as something that will be a part of the scene, as a fully academic level within biblical studies, and as a participant in the consideration of doctrinal theology.

He (1999:4) is further of the opinion that "biblical theology" has clarity only when it is understood to mean theology as it existed or was thought or believed within the time, languages and cultures of the Bible itself. Only then, he asserts, can its difference from doctrinal theology, from later interpretation, and from later views about the Bible be established. What we are looking for, he contends, is a theology that existed back there and then, and hence descriptive rather than prescriptive. He indicates that however closely we define "then", for example, whether we refer to the time of events referred to or to the time of original writing of the texts or to the time of their finalization, the answer is that any or all of these are included or may be so.

For this study the most appropriate methodological option of conducting the appropriate survey of burial rites during biblical times is the canonical treatment of the relevant biblical materials. This will also incorporate discussions of elements of dating as it relates to the treatment of specific texts. Giving his reasons for advocating a canonical approach to the study of Old Testament theology, Childs (1986:6) indicates that a canonical approach to the Old Testament is unequivocal in asserting that the object of theological reflection is the canonical writing of the Old Testament that is the Hebrew Scriptures which are the received traditions of Israel. He (1986:6) asserts that the canonical approach he advocates is explicit in developing an approach which is consistent in working within canonical categories. He further indicates that the discipline of Old Testament theology derives from theological reflection on a received body of scripture whose formation was the result of a lengthy history development. The process, he asserts, began in the early pre-exilic period of Israel's history and extended through the final structuring by the Jewish synagogue during the Hellenistic era. Central to its history, it should be noted, was a hermeneutical activity which continued to shape the material theologically in order to render it accessible to future generations of believers. According to him canonization proper, which was the final stage in the process, established the scope of authoritative literature. The Christian church, he observes, recognized the integrity of the Old Testament for its own faith within its canon of authoritative scriptures. He (2004:250) is of the view that it is a basic tenet of the canonical approach that one reflects theologically on the text as it has been received and shaped. Yet he feels the emphasis on the normative status of the canonical text is not a denial of the significance of the canonical process which formed the text.

Childs' works and views have faced frequent criticisms. These include among others those of Vanhoozer (2005:217-9) who indicates that Childs fails to develop a sufficient argument for taking the final form as theologically authoritative. To address this shortcoming Childs needs to locate the canon in the theo-dramatic context, that is, in the context of God's own speech and action. This criticism has arisen from the observation made by Vanhoozer that Childs stipulates that "canon" refers not simply to the final form of scripture, but to the historical process in which Israel and the church shaped their respective scriptures so that they might have a continuing authoritative function in the believing community. Vanhoozer further observes that Childs employs the term "canon" to describe the practices of communities of Jews and Christians who have recognized and read the books of the Bible as normative. He additionally indicates that Childs' "canonical" practices are those not of the original authors but of the interpretative community. To me these are most interesting observations. The strongest critic of Childs' works and views on Biblical theology and canon is the late scholar Barr (1924-2006), who when critiquing Childs' works used rather strong language, for example where he (1999:438) indicates, 'Professor Childs wrote as if he is the only theologian in the world or at least the only one among living Biblical scholars'. However, he (1999:438) indicates that Childs touched on aspects which for many are religiously very important, and these are likely to produce further expression in the future.

Giving support to some of the above contentions, Sailhamer (1995:16) asserts that for one to study Old Testament theology, one needs to ask oneself whether such a theology is to be understood as normative for the Christian today. He wonders whether one's theology should be taken as binding, because it is a restatement of what God himself has revealed. Additionally he asks whether theology is merely the description of human beliefs about God. In short has God spoken? Is the Bible a record of what God has said? Can we claim or dare to speak God's word as it has come to us in the Old Testament? He is of the view that the Bible is the word of God, and that in the Bible God has spoken. This should be the attitude of those calling themselves Christians, and in this case the Agikuyu Christians. He further asserts that the Bible is not merely a record of what God said in the past; it is in fact, a record of what God is saying today. By means of the words of scriptures, God has spoken and speaks to us today. He asserts that if God has spoken in the Bible, then the task of theology is made considerably clearer. He feels that this is so as the task of theology is to state God's word to the church in a clear and precise manner. He indicates that to him what is expected of theology is an understandable restatement of the word of God. He asserts that theology is the restatement and explication of God's revelation, which to him is the Bible. The Bible, Sailhamer asserts, intends to state what should be heard as normative for the truth and practice of the Christian believer. However, he is of the view that theology, like all other fields of study, is a human endeavour. As such, it is subject to all the limitations of human fallibility. It should be noted, however, that no statement of the Bible's theological message can claim to speak with the same authority as the Bible itself. Only the Bible is infallible, not our theological systems.

He (1995:237) indicates that a canonical theology of Old Testament arranges what is revealed in the Old Testament diachronically. The historical dynamics of the formation of the Hebrew Bible, are such that a diachronic survey of its theology is the most appropriate method. He (1995:16) argues that given a specific purpose to the study of the Old Testament, a synchronic survey may be preferred. However, should the general purpose be to understand the theology in its own terms, then a diachronic survey is preferred.

Erickson (1989:43) indicates that diachronic survey is the study of the development of a concept through successive periods of time. This approach, Erickson asserts, contrasts with the synchronic survey which is the study and comparison of several simultaneous concepts. Since the purpose of this study is specifically to survey and analyse burial and funeral rites in both the Old and New Testaments then a diachronic survey is preferred.

In chapter 4 a canonical approach will be applied. As indicated by Sailhamer (1995:222), when applying a canonical approach it should be borne in mind that a canonical theology of the Old Testament is based on the canonical text of the Old Testament rather than a critically reconstructed one. He indicates that because the approach begins with a theological premise, that is the verbal inspiration of the scripture, he believes that the biblical text must be taken as authoritative, that is, as canonical. The canonical approach will proceed to treat the writings of both the Old and the New Testament in canonical order.

The word canon was applied in the early church to religious laws and doctrine and to a list of writings understood to provide an authoritative standard of faith. The various books of the Bible thus constitute a canon, and those included are termed "canonical". The process of settling the canon of scripture is the one referred to as canonization. Erickson (1989:26) advises that the term canon refers to the collection of books deemed authoritative by the church. As indicated by Beckwith (2000:27-35), every book has a text, but not every book has a canon. Only a book like the Bible, which is also a collection of books, has a canon. The biblical canon is a collection of authoritative sacred texts. Their authority derived not from their early date, not from their role as records of revelation (important though these characteristics were), but from the fact that they were believed to be inspired by God and thus to share the nature of revelation themselves. He (2000:28), goes on to indicate that this belief, expressed at various points in the Old Testament, had become a settled conviction among Jews of the intertestamental period, and is everywhere taken for granted in the New Testament treatment of the Old Testament. It is indicated further by Beckwith, that the New Testament writings share this scriptural and inspired character is first stated in 1 Timothy 5:18 and 2 Peter 3:16. Pagan religion it should be noted also could speak of "holy scripture" and attribute them on occasion to a deity, but the Jewish and Christian claims were made credible by the different quality of biblical religion and biblical literature.

He (2000:34-6), asserts that when Christians refer to the Bible as "scripture", they express their conviction that the Bible is the written word of God. The term "holy scripture(s)" was used by the Jews to denote an established body of writings of divine origin, possessing authority for the people of God as well as for the individual. The early Christians shared this view; the (Old Testament) scripture is "utterances of God" (Rom:3:2; cf 1:2) even when the speaker is not God himself (cf.the quotation of Isa 28:11-2 in 1 Cor 14-21). We learn further that Jewish and the early Christian tradition agree that "what scripture says, God says". Jewish and Christian interpretations of various statements in the Hebrew Scriptures differed, but the divine origin and the normative nature of scripture were acknowledged by both groups. The first Christians, it should be noted, extended the notion of the "Word of God" to the apostolic account and explanation of the person and ministry of Jesus Christ (cf. Thess 2:13), just as specific words of Jesus were regarded as authoritative (cf. 1 Cor 7:10), and soon the term "scripture" was used for the letters of the apostles (cf. 2 Pet 3-16).The conviction that scripture is the word of God was the undisputed tradition of the church until the seventeenth century. He (2000:34), observes that in the seventeenth century, philosophers and theologians began to challenge the truthfulness and authority of scripture with reference to human reason. However, today it is generally felt that as human reason is affected by the fall, and thus by the malaise of sin, it cannot be the source of truth. If truth about God is not revealed to us, we have to remain agnostic. Without revelation we cannot know God. This is the reason why our understanding of scripture as the word of God has to be derived from the scripture itself.

Biblical theology, which is the one applied in this study, seeks to present a synthesis of the message of scripture. It presupposes, therefore, a coherent and established canon of biblical books. It is precisely for this reason that the nature of the Bible as scripture is of central importance (Rosner 2000:3-11).We learn further that in order to understand what is entailed by the conviction that the Bible is scripture, we need to understand that the Bible is a collection of historical texts written over a long period of time, utilizing different literary forums and manifesting diverse perspectives, and as the word of God who spoke and continues to speak through its books. Biblical theology acknowledges the multidimensional nature of scripture (Schnabel 2000:36).

Numerous theological works have commendable observations of the sequence of biblical events. The works that have been of extreme assistance and which have enabled me to follow the sequence of biblical events, and hence helped me carry out the required survey of the Bible in regard to the theme of this study namely burial rites and mourning as they appear in the Bible, include numerous works on concordance, including but not limited to: Concordances edited by Whitaker 1988; Strong 2007; Young 1982; Cruden 1949; Ellison 1972; Hartdegen 1977; Kohlenberger III 1991; Kohlenberger III 2000. Following the order of the biblical burial events as they appear in the above works, I was able to carry out a diachronic survey based on a canonical approach. The survey and subsequent analysis comprise two major aspects, namely burial rites and the accompanying mourning at times termed in the Bible as lamenting.

As advised by House (1998:53) several methodologies for composing Old Testament theology exist. House asserts that Old Testament theology itself can be defined as "the task of presenting what the Old Testament says about God as a coherent whole". "Only by keeping God at the forefront of research", House feels, "can one compose a viable and balanced theological work". He goes on to indicate that there is a growing conviction that theology must address the world in some normative fashion. Totally descriptive theology is waning at the moment. He feels, and I concur with him, that truly Old Testament and Biblical theology can be obtained when one explains in a way that highlights God's nature, person and actions. By stating what the Old Testament says about God's nature and will, Old Testament theology moves from beyond description of truth into prescription of action. House argues, if interpreters agree that the Old Testament teaches that God commands certain behaviour, it seems evident that a description has discovered a norm. One may obey the normative command or not, but the fact that a norm has been uncovered remains unchanged.

Based on what is said above, it is now possible to summarise the methodology that will be applied in this chapter. The methodology applied is the new biblical theology method, which attempts to relate the Old and New Testaments to one another. The chief proponent of this method is Childs, who utilizes and recommends a canonical approach to biblical theology. The canon as indicated earlier will be treated as scripture, which will be construed to mean divinely inspired texts that claim to have, and are accepted as having authoritative status. Those texts that comprise and are recognised by the church as providing authoritative standards of faith are termed "canonical".

In this chapter a canonical approach will be applied, which as indicated earlier will be basically an analysis of biblical burial and funeral rites. The canonical approach applied, and the subsequent analysis, will be God centred, intertextually oriented, authority-conscious, historically sensitive and devoted to the pursuit of the wholeness of the Old and New Testaments. Additionally, it will mean theological reflection that intends to deal carefully with the uniqueness of theological reflection of the Old Testament, so that its influence on the New Testament can be better understood. It will enable one to read the events in the Old Testament and New Testament as authoritative scripture born in history, intended for the ages; it will be an approach that bridges gaps between the Old Testament and New Testament, and thereby will contribute to an informed and valid biblical theology (House 1998:52-7). Adopting the canonical approach to biblical theology will enable the achievement of one of the objectives of this study, which is to analyze what the scripture has to say about funeral rites including mourning (cf. Bromiley 1960:95-7), also to establish and show whether the scripture gives an explicit, that is, normative manner of coping with death.

Burial in the Biblical Period

Burial is the disposition of a human corpse to prevent its desecration. Davies (1985:141), indicates that the Jews uniformly disposed of the corpse by entombment where possible, and failing that, by interment; extending this respect to the remains even of the slain enemy and malefactor (1 Kgs 11 15; Deut 21:23), in the latter case by express provision of law (Payne 1979:556-60).

Tenney (1973:77) asserts that burial is the interment of a corpse including the accompanying ceremonies. Cole (2000: 203-5), indicates that terms for burial in the Bible may refer to the burial preparation process, the interment of the body or the place of burial (Eccl 6:3, Isa 14:20; Jer 22:19; Matt 26:12) or the burial place (Gen 47:30; Deut 34:6; 2 Kgs 9:28; 21:26; 23:30). Cole further observes that biblical texts tend to be brief descriptions of burial practices rather than lengthy prescriptions of burial rites. Cole also notes that among most people of the ancient near East, burial was an especially sacred act. A disturbance or desecration of the burial place was considered a heinous act. Even in times of war, conquering armies allowed for the proper disposition of the dead (Payne 1979:556-60; Burdick & Rea 1975: 279-80).

Burial of Patriarchs and Matriarchs—Old Testament

The first mention of burying anyone and the necessity of use of a grave in scripture (Holy Bible) is by Abraham in Genesis 23:4, where is recorded his concern and care for the burying of Sarah (Wheaton 1975:107). Genesis 23:1

indicates that Sarah died at the age of 127 years. Spence (1950 vol 1:290-1) observes that Sarah as the wife of Abraham and the mother of believers (Isa 51:2; 1 Pet 3:6) is the only woman whose age is mentioned in scripture. Of great interest is an observation by Willmington (1987:46) in which he indicates "There are those today who would advocate the adoration of Mary (Mother of Jesus), but in the New Testament it is the life of Sarah that is called to our attention" (see 1 Pet 3:1-6). Pfeiffer (1978:28-9), advises that Sarah died at Kiriath Arba (that is Hebron) in the Land of Canaan (Gen 23:2). When Abraham learned of her death he went to mourn for Sarah and to weep over her. This is the first occasion in scripture which mentions mourning and weeping for a dead person. Beside wailing and otherwise loudly manifesting his grief he broke forth into weeping. The Hebrew words for mourn and weep carry both ideas (Pfeiffer 1978:28-9). In due course, after his sadness had abated somewhat, he expressed his anxiety to obtain a secure place in which "to bury his dead out of sight". This as observed by M'Clinlock & Strong (1894:921) is the attitude almost all people have naturally regarded as the proper mode of disposing of the dead.

Abraham instead of taking Sarah's body back to his ancestral homeland of Ur of the Chaldeans (Gen 11:28), chose to find a sepulchre in the land God had given him (Gen 15:18-21). He bought a cave for her tomb; namely the cave of Machpelah. This purchase was his first land acquisition in the land of Canaan. It is reported that the Hittites offered one of their sepulchres, but Abraham preferred to buy and utilize his own cave. The cave in question belonged to one Ephron (v.8), but the decision to convey it to Abraham's use evidently rests with the people of Hebron as a whole—the people of the land (vv.10-13). Abraham, who is regarded by the Hebronites as a "mighty prince" (v.6) is first offered a choice of burial places but not legal ownership. He insists that the latter is what he seeks; and finally succeeds in buying the entire field, taking it (vv.12-3) at a high price (400 shekels of silver). The transaction was then finalized in the presence of all the Hittites at the city gate, the place of legal and business dealings (cf.19:1). In this cave were buried not only Sarah but also Abraham (25:9), Isaac and his wife Rebecca, and Jacob and Leah (49:29-31, 50:13). The point of this event was to ensure that the cave and field would be Abraham's possession. He was not presumptuous. In faith he bought the land, taking nothing from these people (cf.14:21-4). It is important, then, where people buried their dead; burial was to be done in their native land. Thus, to Abraham there was no going back. Though Abraham was an alien and a stranger among the people (23:4) his hope was in the land (Pfeiffer 1978:28).

According to Smick (1975:10-11), the exact date for the birth of Abraham cannot be pinpointed by means of archaeology, though most authorities place it on the early second Millennium. By using Biblical figures and assuming no gaps, a date of c.2000 BC for the birth of Abraham may be obtained. This, Smick notes, fits well with the archaeological date. Unger (1998:233) gives a slightly different date for the birth of Abraham, when he indicates that Abraham was born in the town of Ur in 2160 BC. Pfeiffer (1978:30) observes Abraham came to the end of his earthly sojourn and expired at the age of 175,. The expression is derived from the Hebrew *gå̄wą̄*, "to breathe out his breath", "to fail", "to sink". Immediately, it is further observed, Abraham was gathered to his father's kin (literally) and took up his residence in Sheol, the place of departed spirits. Abraham died at a full and good old age. Of great interest is the fact that he was buried in the sepulchre at the cave of Machpelah by his two sons (v.9), whom he had loved with unsurpassed attention. Isaac and Ishmael were united in common grief at the loss of their beloved father.

As observed by various authors including Smick(1975:10-1), and Pfeiffer (1978:28), today, on what is thought to be the burial site of Abraham and other members of the patriarchal family, stands the Moslem Mosque of Hebron, which covers a cave thought to be the cave of Machpelah. As indicated in 2 Chronicles 20:7 and James 2:23 Abraham is called the friend of God. The universality of this title for the father of the Hebrew nation is reflected in the name of the Mosque in honour of Abraham at Hebron, AL-KHALIL ("The Friend"). No one can be sure that this mosque stands over Abraham's burial cave in the field of Machpelah, but Genesis 23:19 states that it was indeed in the area of Hebron (Coogan, 1993:277) (cf. Barabas 1982:5-6).

The majority of residents of Kikuyu District, the scope of this study, are Christians. However, there are other residents who profess other faiths including Muslims, Hindus, Kikuyu traditional religions, atheists and others. For those who profess Christian, Muslim and Judaic faiths, and who might not be aware of the close relationship and common ancestry of their faiths, it is worthwhile for them to learn that as pointed out above, as well as by Boyd (1939:20-2), on Abraham's grave is a Moslem mosque. The fact of the matter is that Abraham is held in extremely high regard by the world's three major monotheistic religions namely Judaism, Christianity and Islam. Numerous scholars have expounded on this matter, among them Boyd (1939:21), who indicates that to the Muslim, Abraham is of importance in several ways. He is mentioned in no less than 188 verses of the Qur'an, more than any other character except Moses. He is reputed to be one of the series of prophets sent by God. He is the common ancestor of the Arab and the Jew. Boyd goes on to advise that Abraham played the same role of religious reformer to his idolatrous kinsmen as Mohammed himself played. Abraham is credited by the Muslims with having built the first pure temple for God's worship (at Mecca!). As in the Bible so in the Qur'an, Abraham is the recipient of divine covenant for himself and for his descendants, and exhibits in his character the appropriate virtues of one so highly favoured; faith, righteousness, purity of heart, gratitude, fidelity, compassion. Boyd (1939:21-2), observes that he received marked tokens of divine favor in the shape of deliverance, guidance, visions, angelic messages (no theophanies for Mohammed), miracles, assurance of resurrection and entrance into paradise. Abraham is called "Imam of the people" (Qur'an, 2.118; Boyd 1939:18-22).

The early patriarchs and matriarchs were reported after death that, "he/she slept and was gathered to the ancestors". Giving meaning to this idiom, Byron (2006:509-10), indicates that when referring to death and burial, the Bible often indicates that a person "slept and was gathered to their ancestors" (e.g Gen 25:8; 35:29; Judg 2:10; 2 Kgs 22:20) in a then-traditional bench tomb (Iron Age bench tomb); the bones of the dead would eventually all end up beneath one of the benches in a bone repository. Over long periods of time, the repository would have to hold the bones of all the deceased members of the family or extended kin group who used the tomb. It meant then that when an individual's bones were placed into the repository at the time of secondary burial, that individual's identity would disappear into the collective ancestral heap (Metzger 1993:277-9; Byron 2006:509-10; Burdick & Rea 1975: 279-80).

Traditionally the Agikuyu did not know nor adapt such practices. Neither do their present-day descendants, most of whom are Christians, practice such methods. My view and suggestion, as will be elaborated in chapters 7 and 8 of this book, is that it is a high time that the Agikuyu Christians and other Africans commenced using a bone repository; that is, that after a suitable period after burial, the remains (bones) would be exhumed and placed in a common family repository. That way, fresh graves would be made available to the family all the time. Additionally, all the members of the family would eventually all end up in the ancestral heap. This, as was the case with the Jews, would satisfy the urge to be buried with "our" forefathers or with our ancestors.

Burial of other Biblical Patriarchs and Matriarchs

Bloch-Smith (1992:1-785), reports that in the patriarchal period it is impossible to distinguish Israelite from Canaanite burial. Unger (1988-232) gives patriarchal to the Davidic Era as c.2000—1000 BC. Unger additionally gives, as indicated earlier, Abraham's birth at Ur as c.2160 BC. During the patriarchal period, with the exception of Rachel, the patriarchs and matriarchs were, interred in the cave of Machpelah purchased as shown earlier by Abraham (Gen 49:29-31). Bloch-Smith further states that in accordance with their wishes to be buried with family, the embalmed remains of Jacob and Joseph were transported from Egypt to Canaan (Gen 47:29-30; 50:15; Exod 13:19; cf Gen 50:5). Interment at the location of death and in proximity to a tree was also attested in this period and later. Rebecca's nurse, Deborah, was interred where she died near Bethel under an oak tree (Gen 35:8), and the people of Jabeshgilead cremated the bodies of Saul and his sons and then buried their bones under a tamarisk tree(1 Sam 31:12-3). The tree signified divine presence, as demonstrated by Abraham planting a tamarisk tree and calling on the name of God at a treaty site (Gen 21:32-3). Burial under a tree also expressed the desire to propagate and to perpetuate the memory of the individual. The tree was long associated with immortality, as illustrated by the "tree of life" in the Garden of Eden (Gen 2:9; cf. Isa 56:3, the eunuch as a "withered tree"). Rachel was also buried where she died. Various traditions locate her burial on the way to Ephrath where a *masseba* was erected (Gen 35:19-20) and in Zelzah in Benjaminite territory near the Ephraim border (1 Sam 10:2) (cf. Hachlili 1992:789-94; Payne 1979:556-61; Kitchen 1962:170-2; Cole 2000:203-5; Nicol 1898: 331-3; Payne 1979:556-60).

It was customary during the times of the patriarchs for successive generations to be buried in the family tomb (cave or rock-cut); thus, as indicated earlier, Sarah (Gen 23.19), Abraham (Gen 25.9), Isaac and Rebekah, Leah (Gen 49.31), and Jacob (Gen 1.13) were all buried in the cave of Machpelah, east of Hebron. Individual burial was sometimes necessitated by death at a distance from the family tomb; so Deborah near Bethel (Gen 35.8) and Rachel on the road to Ephrath (Gen 35.19, 20) their tombs being marked by an oak and a pillar respectively. During that period, besides weeping, mourning included rending one's garments and donning sackcloth (Gen 37:34, 35), and lasted for as long as seven days (Gen 1.10). The embalming of Jacob and Joseph and the use of a coffin for Joseph in Egyptian fashion was exceptional (Gen 1.2, 3, 26). Mummification required removal of the viscera for separate preservation, and desiccation of the body by packing with salt (not brine); thereafter the body was packed with impregnated linen and entirely wrapped in linen. Embalming and mourning usually took seventy days, but the period for embalming could be shorter, as for Jacob (Kitchen 1962:170; Cole 2000: 203-5; Nicol 1898: 331-3; Payne 1979:556-60).

As is evident from the above description of early biblical burials, the burial places of patriarchs and matriarchs were not consistent, nor governed by any law or custom. Some were buried in family tombs; others had to be transported from distant lands so as to be buried with their ancestors.

Others were buried where they died. We can therefore deduce from the incidences reflected in the Bible, that one can be buried anywhere, especially where one died, and depending on the circumstances revolving around a particular death. Of course, there were preferences, for instance, Judanine kings were buried in Jerusalem while Abraham's family was initially buried in the cave at Machpelah. However, there is nothing normative that dictates the place of burial, manner of burial or rites performed after burial. This issue will be considered when making recommendations in chapter 8 with reference to the Agikuyu and other African funeral practices.

Burial During the Period of the Exodus and Conquest Generations

Due to the diverse opinions regarding the dating of the Exodus, the period is generally dated from the fifteenth through the early thirteenth century BCE. Unger (1988:234; 384-8) gives the date of Israel quitting Egypt at 1450-1425 BCE. Bloch-Smith (1992:785-6) on the other hand claims that this period is generally dated from the sixteenth through early eleventh century BCE. These dates have, however, been questioned by numerous scholars. No one is as yet certain about the exact dates that these events took place. Like Rachel and Deborah, members of the Exodus generation were interred at the location of their death: Miriam in Kadesh (Num 20:1), Aaron on Mount Hor (Num 33:39, but see Deut 10:6), and Moses in Moab (Deut 34:6; Ibid., 785). Burial at the death locale deviates from the patriarchal practice, for just as the bones of Jacob and Joseph were carried from Egypt for burial on family land (Josh 24:32), so could the remains of Miriam, Aaron and Moses have been transported (Ibid., 785). Based on this we can conveniently conclude that as indicated above, burial places were neither normative nor cultural (cf. Nicol 1898: 331-3). Most were buried where they died or where it was most convenient.

Beginning with the conquest generations, family burials established a visible, perpetual claim to the patrimony (*nahala*), which sometimes functioned as a territorial boundary marker, as in the cases of Rachel (1 Sam 10:2) and Joshua (Josh 24:30). Joshua was buried on the border of his inheritance in the hill country of Ephraim (Josh 24:30), Joseph on family land in Shechem (Josh 24:32), and Eleazar the son of Aaron at Gibeah in the hill country of Ephraim (Josh 24:33). The only other burial from this period was that of the five Amorite kings killed by Joshua. After being hanged from trees, their bodies were thrown into a cave, the mouth of which was sealed with stones (Josh 10:26; Ibid., 785-6). It is worthy of note that all these were earth burials. This point will be reflected in chapter 8 while making my recommendations (cf. Nicol 1898: 331-3).

Burial During the Period of the Judges

Bloch-Smith (1992:786) writes that by the period of the judges, family tombs of inherited lands were well established, and so individuals were interred "in their father's tomb" or "in their hometown." For Gideon, Samson, and Asahel, the record specifies that they were buried in their father's tomb on family land (Judg 8:32; 16:31; 2 Sam 2:32). She further indicates that only the fact of burial locale is given for the remaining judges: Tola in the Shamir hill country of Ephraim (Judg 10:2), Jair in Kmon, Gilead (Judg 10:5), Jephthah in the cities of Gileod (Judg 2:7), Ibzah in Bethlehem, Zebulum (Judg 12:10), Elon in Aijalon, Zebulun (Judg 12:12), Abdon in Pirathon, Ephraim (Judg 12:15), and Samuel in Ramah (1 Sam 25:1; 28:3). Ramah may refer to the city Ramathaim-Zophim as well as to an elevated place. Important individuals were buried in prominent places where their tombs would be visible and accessible. For some of those individuals, little is known except for their burial location. Men who enjoyed a special relationship with Yahweh during their lifetimes were thought to continue that relationship after death, and so it was important to know where they were buried (Bloch-Smith 1992:786; Kitchen 1962:170-2; Cole 2000:203-5; Nicol 1898: 331-3; Miller & Miller 1961: 83-4; Payne 1979:556-60). The burial practice applied to such persons was not normative, and was not mandated to be applicable to future Christians.

Burial During the Monarchic Period

Beginning with David's reign, kings and religious and administrative high functionaries (2 Chr 24:15-8; Isa 22:15-6) were buried in their capital cities. David who reigned between 1004—965 BC (Unger 1988:234) initiated burial in the City of David (1Kgs 2:10) and was joined by his son Solomon (1Kgs 11:43; 2 Chr 9:31). Other recorded family burials from the period of the united monarchy include Abner and the head of Ishbaal (Ishboshet) in Hebron (2 Sam 3:32; 4:12), Ahitophel (2 Sam 17:23), Barzillai in Gilead (2 Sam 19:38), and Joab in the wilderness (1 Kgs 2:34; Bloch-Smith 1992:786; Cole 2000:203-5).

Following the death of Solomon and the division of the country into Israel in the North and Judah in the South, monarchs were buried in their capital cities of Tirzah or Samaria and Jerusalem respectively (Bloch-Smith

1992:786). Of kings and prophets, it is recorded that they were sometimes interred in proximity to holy sites: prophets of Judah and Bethel near the Bethel altar (2 Kgs 23:17-8) and later Judahite kings adjacent to the Jerusalem temple (Ezek 43:7-8). The deaths and burials of the kings of Israel were recounted solely in Kings. The books of Kings present royal interment in a formulaic, consistent manner, perhaps in an attempt to fabricate a positive record for the Judahite kings in homage to the house of David. Varying accounts of the burials of Judahite kings are preserved in Kings and Chronicles. The Chronicler's supplemental information has been discounted as glorifying favoured kings and discrediting others. The Chronicler may have expressed judgment, not through manufacturing new material but in choosing which references to include and which to delete (Cole 2000:203-5; Bloch-Smith 1992:786).

Bloch-Smith (1992:786) asserts that relatively little was written about the burial of the kings of Israel. Of several kings, including Nadab, Elah, Zimri, Ahaziah, Zechariah, and all subsequent kings, no details of burial are given (1 Kgs 15:28; 16:10; 18; 2 Kgs 1:17; 15:10). For most of the remaining kings only the fact of burial in the royal city was mentioned: Baasha in Tirzah (1 Kgs 16:6), and Omri, Ahab, Jehu, Jehoahaz, Joash, and probably Jeroboam in Samaria (1 Kgs 16:28; 22:37; 2 Kgs 10:35; 13:9, 13; 14:16, 29). In Judah, as indicated earlier, David and his descendants were buried in the Jerusalem City of David, a small ridge bounded by the Kidron, Hinnom, and Tyropoeon valleys. according to the account in Kings, all kings from Rehoboam through Ahaz were buried "with their fathers in the City of David" (1Kgs 14:31; 15:8, 24; 22:51; 2 Kgs 8:24; 9:28; 12:22; 14:20, 22; 15:7, 38; 16:20; Neh 3:16). Subsequent kings were buried elsewhere, Manasseh and Amon in the household garden of Uzzah (2 Kgs 21:18, 26) and Josiah in his own tomb (2 Kgs 23:30). There is no reference to the burial of Hezekiah or of Josiah's successors (cf. Burdick & Rea 1975: 279:80).

The Chronicler noted no such harmony in burial arrangements observes Bloch-Smith (1992:786); while commendable kings were buried with their predecessors in the City of David, sinful and ailing kings were denied interment with their fathers. A *kabod* (honor) was prepared for the righteous king Hezekiah. The honor certainly entailed lamenting (1 Kgs 13:30; Jer 22:18) and offering sacrifices (Isa 57:7; 2 Chr 16:14). Jehoiadah the priest was also accorded burial with the kings in the City of David (2 Chr 24:16). Among the discredited kings, Asa was buried in his own tomb. Mortuary practices included laying the body " ... in the resting place (*miskab*)" which was filled with spices of all kinds; expertly blended; a very great fire was made in his honour (2 Chr 16:14; Ibid., 786). The "very great fire" probably resembled in appearance and intent the burnt-offering sacrifices of sweet savour presented to Yahweh (Gen 8:20-21; Lev 1:9, 28). Others denied burial in the royal tombs included Jehoram, Ahaziah, Jehoash, Amaziah, Uzziah, Ahaz and Amon (2 Chr 21:19-20; 22:9; 24:25; 25:28; 26:23; 28:27) (Bloch-Smith 1992:786). Burials of monarchs in different manners and different locations show that burial of monarchs such as in the royal tombs or with pomp and great honor was neither consistent nor normative.

Isaiah described rock-cut tombs and mortuary practices in a condemnation of the cult of a dead. Isaiah 57, the so-called "Third" Isaiah, is usually dated to the last quarter of the sixth century BCE, but the text describes Jerusalem bench tombs, which had attained their post-exilic form by the seventh century BCE. It should be noted that the so-called "Third" Isaiah is an historical perspective that is rejected by evangelical scholars. Accordingly, since the scholarly community is divided about the date and authorship (Isaiah as a unified work dating from the eighth century BCE is the evangelical view, whereas liberal scholars tend to support two or three "Isaiahs" and date the last 27 chapters to much later than the eighth century BCE). For further scholarly comments on "Third" Isaiah see Unger (1988:628-31). According to Isaiah 57:7-9, tombs were hewn high in the mountainsides. A door and door-post opened into the chamber with a resting-place (*miskab*) for the deceased and a mortuary stele perhaps in the shape of a phallus (*zikron yad*) near the door. At the tomb sacrifices were offered (cf. also Deut 26:14 and Ps 16:3-4) and the dead consulted (cf. also 1 Sam 28 and Isa 8:19-20). To conclude the diatribe, Isaiah refuted the role of the ancestors in ensuring control of the patrimony—true inheritance passes not through the ancestral dead (and the family tomb) but through Yahweh (Isa 57:13; Cole 2000:203-5; Bloch-Smith 1992:786).

Bloch-Smith (1992:786-7), goes on to indicate that a variety of mortuary practices existed within Israelite society to eighth Century BCE, not all of which were widely practiced or acceptable by later prophets and the Deuteronomistic editor(s). According to Browning (2009:85) the deuteronomistic editor(s) were unknown editor(s) in Judea, who imposed a theological view with a distinctive oratical style on the books of the Old Testament, especially from Deuteronomy to 2 Kings which are often called "the Deuteronomistic History". They cover the period from the death of Moses in Deuteronomy 34 to King Jehoiachin's release from prison in 561 BCE and the reversal of fortune in Babylon (2 Kgs 25).

Browning further advises that the intention was to explain the nation's fate as due to its apostasy from the true worship of God. This was because there was a covenant (Deut 7:12) which God for His part would keep, but peace and prosperity for the peoples depended on their faithfulness. The prophecies of Jeremiah (and some would add many other prophetic collections) seem to have been edited to express the Deuteronomist point of view. Browning asserts that the collapse of Judah in 586 BCE and the exile are interpreted as vindicating Deuteronomy's prophesy of punishment if they were faithless (Jer 36.29). Freedman (1982:226-8) is of the view that in the last analyzes, it must be admitted that Deuteronomic history is not a given part of the Hebrew Bible as we have it. However, Freedman notes it is closely related to the original form of Deuteronomy and the editors of both (i.e. Moses and Deuteronomist) had similar concerns.

During the Monarchic period, according to Bloch-Smith (1992:786), the majority buried their dead in the family caves and bench tombs located in proximity to the patrimony. Biblical references and inscriptions on a tomb at Khirbet Beit Lei testify to family burial, but there is currently no osteological evidence. It is noted that Isaiah rebuked Shebna, an official of King Hezekiah, for having hewn an ostentatious individual tomb in Jerusalem, rather than being buried with his family (Isa 22:15-6). The common burial ground in Jerusalem's Kidron valley was considered by some, an illegitimate form and place of burial as suggested by Josiah's scattering Asherah ashes over the ground and Jehoiakim's casting in the body of the assassinated prophet Uriah (Jer 26:23; 2 Kgs 23:6). Both royalty and commoners sacrificed children in the *tophet* in Jerusalem's Hinnon Valley, and as further indicated by Bloch-Smith (1992:787) presumably buried them as at Carthage (see Stager and Wolf 1984:30-51), demonstrating official sanction during certain reigns of a practice considered abhorrent and unacceptable at other times (2 Kgs 16:3; 2 Chr 28:3; Jer 7:31).

Burial markers preserved the memory of the righteous, the sinner, and men without offspring. A *masseba* and *siyun* ("pillar" and "monument") marked the graves of the righteous Rachel (Gen 35:20) and the unnamed prophet (2 Kgs 23:17) respectively. A circle of stones served to show contempt for Israel's enemies and those who challenged Yahweh's anointed: Achan, the King of Ai, the five kings of the Southern coalition, and Absalom (Josh 7:26; 8:29; 10:26; 2 Sam 18:17-18). Monuments serving to perpetuate the memory of men without descendants, literally to "memorialize the name," have been associated with death cult activities (Pitard 1979). During his lifetime Absalom erected a pillar, literally, "hand/phallus (Heb. *yad*) of Absalom" (2 Sam 18:18; cf. also Isa 57:8) and Yahweh promised the faithful eunuch through His temple and holy city "a monument and memorial (*yad wasem*) better than sons and daughters", a perceptual testimonial which cannot be destroyed (Isa 56:5; cf. 2 Sam 14:7) (Bloch-Smith 1992:787)

The Pentateuchal Legislation on Burial and Mourning

As indicated by Kitchen (1962:170), prompt burial, including that of the bodies of hanged criminals was the norm (Deut 21:22, 23). It is observed that contact with the dead and formal mourning brought ceremonial defilement. Mourning by weeping, rending the garments, and unbinding the hair was permitted to the Aaronic priests (Lev 21:1-4), but not to the High priest (Lev 21:10-11) or the Nazirite under vow (Num 6:7). Expressly forbidden to priests (Lev 21:5) and people (Lev 21:27-28; Deut 14.1) were laceration ("cuttings in the flesh"), cutting the corners of the beard, baldness between the eyes, and "rounding" (mutilation?) of the corner(s) of the head. Additionally eating of tithes in mourning or offering them to the dead (Deut 26:14) was also forbidden. These were heathen Canaanite practices. Women captured in war might mourn their parents for one month before marrying their captors (Deut 21:11-3). The national leaders Aaron (Num 20:28, 29; Deut 10:6), and Moses (Deut 34:5-8), were each accorded thirty days' national mourning after burial (Kitchen 1962:170; Cole 2000:203-5). There is no evidence or statement given in scripture indicating that any of these burial practices were normative.

Burial Practices—Israel in Palestine

When possible, people were buried in the ancestral inheritance in a family tomb: so Gideon and Samson (Judg 8:32; 16:31), Asahel and Ahithophel (2 Sam 2: 32; 17:23), and eventually Saul (2 Sam 21:12-4). Burial in one's "house", as of Samuel (1 Sam 25:1, cf. 28:3) and Joab (1 Kgs 2:34) may merely mean the same, unless it was literally under the house or yard floor. The body was borne to rest on a bier (2 Sam 3:31). Lack of proper burial was a great misfortune (1 Kgs 3:22; Jer 16:6). Tombs were usually outside the town. There is limited archaeological evidence for the family tombs having an irregular rock-cut chamber (or chambers) with benches, reached by a short, sloping shaft blocked by a stone cut to fit over the entrance. As indicated earlier the upstart treasurer Shebna drew Isaiah's condemnation in hewing himself an ambitious rock-tomb (Isa 22:15, 16). Pottery and other objects left with the dead became a pure formality during the Israelite period, by contrast with elaborate Canaanite funerary provision. Memorial pillars were sometimes erected in Israel as elsewhere in antiquity; 2 Samuel 18:18 is an anticipatory example. Outside Jerusalem was a tract of land set aside for 'the graves of the common people' (2 Kgs 23:6; Jer 26:23). This doubtless, was for simple interments, and was paralleled by similar cemeteries at other towns (Kitchen 1962:170-1).

The grave of an executed criminal or foe was sometimes marked by a heap of stones. Examples are the sinner Achan (Josh 7:26), rebellious Absalom (2 Sam 18:17), the King of Ai, and the five Canaanite kings (Josh 8, 29:10. 27). Cremation was not a Hebrew practice, but in difficult circumstances a corpse might be burnt and the remains buried pending proper burial in the ancestral tomb, as with Saul (1 Sam 31:12, 13) and probably envisaged in Amos 6:10 (Cole 2000:203-5).

It is worthy of note that In Palestine in the second and first millennia this mourning included: (1) baldness of head and cutting the beard; (2) lacerating the body; (3) rending garments and sackcloth; (4) scattering dust on the head and wallowing in ashes; and (5) weeping and lamentation. Not all of these were favoured by the law. Good examples of Hebrew mourning were those displayed by David (2 Sam 1:11, 12, 13:31), the woman of Tekoah (2 Sam 14:2), and the allusions in the prophets (Isa 3:24; 22:12; Jer 7:29; Ezek 7:18; Joel 1:8; Amos 8:10; Mic 1:16). For Tyrian seafarers, Philistia and Moab see Ezekiel 27:30, 32, Jeremiah 47:5; Isaiah 15:2, 3 and Jeremiah 48:37 (Kitchen 1962: 170-1).

Notable deaths sometimes occasioned poetic laments. So David lamented over Saul and Jonathan (2 Sam 1:17-27) and Jeremiah and others over Josiah (2 Chr 25:25). For professional mourners see Jeremiah 9:17, 18; Amos 5:16. After a funeral a breaking-fast meal was possibly given to mourners (Jer 16:7; cf. Hos 9:4). A "great burning" sometimes marked the funeral of Judaean kings (2 Chr16:14, 21:19, 20; Jer 34:5) (Kitchen 1962:171; Payne 1979: 556-60; Burdick & Rea 1975:279-80). None of these Jewish burial practices as far as can be judged were normative.

Burial Practices in the New Testament

Jewish practices in New Testament times differed little from those described in the Old Testament, though there are certain extra details given. The corpse was first washed (Acts 9:37); it was then anointed (Mark 16:1), wrapped in linen garments with spices enclosed (John 19:40), and finally the limbs were bound and the face covered with a napkin (John 11:44). The scene in Acts 5:6 may perhaps suggest that some young men's fraternity had the duty of seeing to such matters (Payne 1962:172; Cole 2000:203-5; Peterson 2001:195-6).

Weeping and wailing and beating the breast are, of course, typically oriental, and are evidenced in the New Testament too. As in the Old

Testament, professional mourners might be employed. Matthew 9:23 refer specifically to flute players. It may be that Jesus did not much care for this noisy and professional mourning. He Himself, we read, wept quietly at the tomb of Lazarus (John 11:35). Commenting on Jesus weeping quietly unlike the Jews custom of wailing loudly, Blum (1983:314), observes that Jesus weeping did indeed differ from that of the other people who were wailing loudly, (v.33). Blum is of the view that His weeping was over the tragic consequences of sin. Blum feels that the crowd, however, interpreted His tears as an expression of love or frustration of not being there to heal Lazarus. However, when he finally raised Lazarus from the dead the crowd was amazed.

This incident in my view clearly indicates that wailing for the dead was a custom to the Jews. It was not normative. Therefore, following the example of Jesus, we believers should control our emotions and if one has to weep then to weep quietly.

As was the normal practice during the Old Testament; so it was in the New Testament, when the actual interment took place as soon as possible after death, normally on the same day (Payne 1962:172). Burial places and grounds were usually outside the city or town. Common burial grounds did exist (cf. Matt 27:7), but individuals and family tombs were widely used. Some men, such as Joseph of Arimathea, liked to prepare their burial place beforehand (cf.Matt 27:60). Coffins were not used to transport the dead to the place of burial; instead the dead were carried on simple biers (see Luke 7:12, 14) (Ibid., 172). Cremation was never a Jewish practice. Eager (1939:530), advises that cremation found no place in Jewish law and custom. He (1939:530) indicates that Tacitus (Hist V.5) expressly says, in noting the contrast with Roman and Greek customs, that it was a matter of piety with the Jews "to bury rather than burn the bodies". It is worthy of note that cremation was not common in primitive times, but in the ancient civilized world it was the normal custom except in Egypt, Judea and China. Cross (1988:430) advises that belief in the resurrection of the body made cremation repugnant to the early Christians, whose use of burial as indicated in chapter 5 of this study is confirmed by the evidence of the catacombs in Rome. However he (1988:430) asserts that by the fifth century Christian influence had caused cremation to be abandoned throughout the Roman Empire. It was, however, revived in the nineteenth century largely in free-thinking circles. Today he (1988:430) notes other than the Orthodox Church that forbids cremation, other Christian denominations including all the protestant churches allow it. Even the Roman Catholic Church recognizes the legitimacy of cremation by the 1969 Canons (B 38) which add that,

"Save for good and sufficient reasons the ashes of a cremated person should be interred or deposited . . . In consecrated ground."

There were several types of burial place. There were ordinary graves in the earth, some unmarked (cf. Luke 11:44). Then there were rock-hewn tombs or caves, which might well have monuments or pillars erected over them. Family tombs often had a number of separate chambers. In these were fashioned ledges (*arcosolia*) or niches *(kokim)* to accommodate the bodies. Here the bodies might be placed within receptacles, such as stone coffins or sarcophagi. Another practice of the New Testament period was to place bones in small stone coffers known as ossuaries—a custom perhaps borrowed and adapted from the Roman boxes to hold ashes after cremation (Payne 1962: 172; Payne 1979: 556-60).

Thus, if a family tomb became over-filled, dry bones could be taken from the ledges and niches and placed in ossuaries. Ossuaries might house the bones of more than one person. These various receptacles usually bore designs and motifs of various types; although among the very orthodox Jews very little in the way of embellishment was permitted. Names were also frequently inscribed on ossuaries. The practice of adornment and embellishment of tombs appears to have been common in the time of Jesus, judging by His denunciation of the Pharisees in Matthew 23:29. He made scathing reference also to the practice of whitewashing tombs (Matt 23:27). The purpose of this was doubtless to render them conspicuous (especially at night), thereby preventing passers-by from touching them accidentally and so incurring ritual defilement (Payne 1962: 172; Payne 1979: 556-60).

To prevent too easy access into the tomb, in view of jackals and thieves, the doorways were firmly closed by hinged doors, or less commonly by large flat stones like millstones, which could, with difficulty, be rolled sideways from the tomb entrance. There are a number of tombs in and around Jerusalem which date from within a century or two of the time of Christ, notably those of Absalom, Jehoshaphat, St James, Zechariah, the Herod family, and "the Kings" (most of these names are fictional, it should be added) (Payne 1962:172).

It is worthy of note that in the New Testament we are told In Matthew 14:12 that after he had been beheaded, the disciples of John the Baptist took his body and buried it. No details are given as to how he was buried. In Luke 16:22 the beggar died and the angels carried him to Abraham's side. No indication is given as to what happened to his body. The rich man also died and was buried. No details are given as to how he was buried. The next reported burial in the New Testament was that of Jesus. We have sufficient information regarding His burial, which in actual fact followed to the letter the Jewish burial custom. The main reason for this was that by then Christianity had neither been established nor taken hold. In fact by the time of Jesus death (AD 33), Jesus and His disciples were observing Judaism and obeying Hebrew laws, tradition and culture. The death of Jesus, His resurrection and His teachings are the ones on which later Christians obtained their ideas of Christian behavior, and in this case their mode of burial. We learn from numerous authors, among them Milligan (1926:241-2) that immediately it was established without any doubt that Jesus was really dead, Joseph of Arimathea obtained permission to take possession of His body (Matt 27:57; cf. the merciful provision of the Jewish law (Deut 21:23). Haste was required, as the Jewish Sabbath was close at hand, and the body, after being, perhaps, bathed, was at once wrapped "in a clean linen cloth" (Matt 27:59), the "roll of myrrh and aloes", of which Nicodemus had bought about a hundred pounds weight (John 19:39), being apparently crumbled between the folds of the linen. It was then borne to the "new tomb wherein was never man yet laid," and reverently laid on the rocky ledge prepared for the purpose, while the whole was secured by a "great stone" placed across the entrance, which was afterwards at the wish of the Jews sealed and guarded (Matt 27:62; cf. Gospel of Peter, 8). There the body remained undisturbed over the Jewish Sabbath. It is worthy of note that the tomb where Jesus was buried was not the normal place of burial of the majority of the inhabitants of Palestine. Rather it was similar to the burying of a noble or rich man. In this instance the tomb had been prepared by a rich man known as Joseph of Arimathea for his own burial. It was common for some persons to prepare their burial places beforehand (cf. Matt. 27:7). When on the morning of the first day of the week the women visited the tomb, bringing with them an additional supply of "spices and ointments" to complete the anointing, which the lack of time had previously prevented, it was only to find the tomb empty, and to receive the first assurance of their Lord's resurrection (Luke 24:1) (Ibid., 241). In connection with this visit, he (1926:241) has drawn attention to the fact that the law expressly allowed the opening of the grave on the third day to look after the dead (Bible Educator, iv. p. 332). In entire harmony with this incident is the account which St John has preserved for us of his own and St Peter's visit to the tomb of Jesus (John 20:1). He himself, when he reached the doorway, was at first content with stooping down and looking in, and thus got only a general view of the linen cloths lying in their place. But St Peter on his arrival entered into the tomb, and "beheld"—the word used points to a careful searching gaze, the eyes passing from point to point—not only the linen cloths , but the napkin that was about Christ's head "rolled up in a place by itself" (Ibid., 241; Peterson 2001:195-6).

These particulars have sometimes been used as evidence of the care and order with which the Risen Lord folded up and deposited in two separate places His grave clothes before He left the tomb. But it has recently been shown with great logic that what is probably meant is that the grave-clothes were found undisturbed on the very spot where Jesus had lain, the linen clothes on the lower ledge which had held the body, the napkin 'by itself' on the slightly raised part of the ledge which formed a kind of pillow for the head. The empty grave-clothes, out of which the Risen Lord had passed, became thus a sign not only that no violence had been offered to His body by human hands, but also a parable of the true meaning of His resurrection: "all that was of Jesus of Nazareth has suffered its change and is gone. We—grave-clothes, and spices, and napkin—belong to the earth and remain" (Milligan 1926:242).

Milligan (1926:242), asserts that, apart from these more special considerations, it is sufficient to note that the very particularity of the description of the burial of Jesus is in itself of importance, as emphasizing his true humanity and the reality of His death. From nothing in our fate did He shrink, even the sad accompaniments of the grave. On the other hand, the empty grave on the morning of the third day has always been regarded as one of the most convincing proofs that "the Lord is risen indeed". Had it not been so, then His body must have been stolen either by friends or by foes. But if by the latter, why in the days that followed did they not produce it, and so silence the disciples' claims? If by the former, then we have no escape from the conclusion that the church of Christ was founded "not so much upon delusion as upon fraud upon fraud springing from motives perfectly inexplicable, and leading to results totally different from any that could have been either intended or looked for" (cf. Dayton 1983:153).

Regarding the burial of Jesus, Wheaton (1975:107), is of the opinion that Paul mentions the burial of Christ as part of the gospel (1 Cor 15:4) since it attested to the reality both of the death which preceded it and of the resurrection which followed. Wheaton goes on to indicate that it has its place in the Apostles' Creed from earliest times. It should be of interest to all believers to note how Jesus was buried as well as the significance of his burial for us. The Agikuyu Christian and other Africans should, where possible and practicable, emulate what took place during Jesus' burial.

The next burial in the New Testament after the burial of Jesus which is narrated with reasonable detail is that of Ananias (Acts 5:6). It is reported that the young men wrapped him around and carried him out and buried him. No further details are given regarding the mode of burial. In Acts 5:7-10 we learn that Ananias' wife Sapphira fell at Peter's feet and died. It is reported that the young men came in and finding her dead, carried her out and buried her beside her husband. No details as to how she was buried are given either (Milligan 1926: 241-2).

Summary of the Biblical Rites of Burial and Burial Customs

This summary is heavily dependent on the works of numerous authors shown subsequently but more so on the works of Nowack and Paton 1936 (cf. Bloch-Smith 1992: 151; Bender 1894:317-47).

Preparatory to Burials:—Preparation of the body. Customs and usages connected with death reach back into remote antiquity, and show the family to have been even then a social-religious unity. When death occurred, it was a duty to close the eyes (Gen 46:4), probably also the mouth of the person. It is true this is distinctly mentioned only in the Mishna (cf. Tract. Shabbath 23:5—codified about C.E. 200), but the custom certainly antedates this tractate. Kissing the dead (Gen 50:1) was probably exceptional. The body was washed (Acts 9:37) and anointed (Mark 16:1; Luke 24:1; John 12:7, 19:40). It was wrapped in a white linen sheet (Mark 15:46), the hands and feet being bound (John 19:40) with grave-bands and the face with a napkin (kerchief) (John 11:44). How ancient these customs were it is not possible to determine (Nowack & Paton 1936:117-18; Payne 1962:172). These burial customs, it should be noted, were practices of the Jews in those Biblical days and were not normative.

Burial—Interment Ceremonies:—The Israelites did not embalm their dead (cf. Gen 50:2, 26). From Isa 28:14; Isa 14:9; Ezek 32:27, we must conclude that in the ancient period the dead were buried with the garments they had worn while living. According to Jeremiah 34:5; 2 Chronicles 16:14, 21:19, spices were burned beside the bodies of prominent men. Later it was the custom to bury together with the dead objects which had been used by them during life, for example, inkhorns, pens, writing-tablets, keys, and similar items. Herod furnished Aristobulus his funeral spices and other articles (Josh. Ant. 15, 3:4). Probably this custom goes back to older times (cf. Josh. Ant. 15, 8:4; 16, 7:1) (Nowack & Paton 1936: 117-8; Payne 1962: 172).

Conventionally the Agikuyu had a similar custom. As revealed in chapter 2 of this study traditionally the Agikuyu who were buried, mainly elders and elderly women, (but not all of them only selected ones who deserved that respect) would be buried together with objects they had used during their lifetime. For the elders this would include his ornaments, snuff pouch and his beer drinking horn.

Cremation, as indicated previously, was not practiced in Israel (cf. Comm. On I Sam 31:12; Amos 6:10); the usage was rather to bury the dead, while cremation, for example, of criminals (Lev 20:14, 21:9; Josh 7:25; cf.Deut 21:23), as indicated earlier appears to have been a disgrace added to the penalty of death (Mishna, Tract. Aboda Zara 1, 3 rejects cremation as a heathen practice. cf. Tac.Hist; 5, 5:4) (Nowack and Paton 1936:117-9; Mare 1982:672; Payne 1962:172).

Importance of Burial:—Not to be buried was considered by the Israelites, as by other peoples of antiquity, a frightful fate which one wished visited only on one's worst enemies (Amos 2:1; cf. Jer 16:4; Ezek 29:5; 2 Kgs 9:10). (Nowack and Paton 1936:117-9; Mare 1982:672-74).

Mode of Burial:—In all probability burying came usually on the very day of death. The body was carried to the place of burial on a litter or bier (2 Mittah 5:3-31; cf Luke 7:14) and was followed by mourners who chanted lamentations (Nowack and Paton 1936:117-9).

Place of Burial:—The grave. In view of the belief that family unity survived death, we can understand the importance attached to the custom of placing bodies in a household grave; it was thus that connection with the family was preserved after death (cf. Gen 15:15, 25:8, 17, 35:29,). In ancient times these household graves were located on land belonging to the family and in proximity to the house (cf. Gen 23:19; Isa 25:1; accordingly the tombs of the kings down to Ahaz are found in the citadel, later in the "garden of Uzza", which in any case is to be sought for in the vicinity (cf. Ezek 43:7). Preferably such caves were located under shade-tree (sacred trees, Gen 35:8; Isa 31:13), or in gardens (2 Kgs 21:18, 26). Gradually the habit prevailed of placing them outside of inhabited districts and of making use of clefts and of caves, which abounded in the country. For the most part, however, the graves were excavated, and an effort was made to place them on the rocky hillside and often on heights difficult of access (Isa 22:16; 2 Kgs 23:16); but in view of the dangers from beasts of prey, their openings were closed with heavy stones. The sepulchre was always strictly regarded as family property, in which no stranger should be laid. Only in later times, as older views were relaxed, did strangers, in exceptional, circumstances, find burial in them (2 Chr 24:16; Matt 27:20). For the destitute (2 Kgs 23:6; Jer 26:23) and for pilgrims (Matt 27:7) there were common, that is, public cemeteries, where criminals also were interred (Jer 26:23; Isa 53:9; 1 Kgs 13:22) (Nowack and

Paton 1936:117-8). These customs, it is worthy of note, were observed by the Jews during those biblical times, and there is no indication in Scripture that they were normative.

Sanctity of the Grave:—In view of the fact that the graves of ancestors were in earlier times places of worship (shrines), and as such, holy ground, it is easy to understand that over the tomb of Rachel a *maststsebhah* (pillar) was raised (Gen 35:20). It appears probable that the sacredness of some shrines rests upon the fact that they were burial-places of heroes (cf. Hebron, Gen 23:20, 25:9, 49:31; Shechem, Josh 24:32; Kadesh-Barnea, Num 20:1). The tomb of Deborah was under a sacred tree near Bethel (Gen 35:8). In later times sepulchres as a whole were regarded as unclean, because of being associated with another worship, that is, the worship of the spirits of the departed as contrary to the worship of Yahweh, and the custom arose of whitewashing the stones which covered them in order to render them distinguishable from afar and keep passers-by from ceremonial pollution (Matt 23:27) (Bailey 1993:95-6; Nowack and Paton 1936:117-8). These customs, it is again worth noting, were not normative. They were Jewish customs intended for the Jews.

Mourning—Customs of mourning:—Upon the news of the death of a relative it was customary to rend the clothes (2 Sam 1:11) and cover oneself with the mourning garment (cf. 2 Sam 3:31), which originally was probably nothing but a loincloth. Among the Arabians the custom prevailed of going about naked as a sign of mourning. Whether this was practiced in Israel is doubtful (Mic 18; Isa 20:2 are not clear evidences of such a usage). But it was customary to go bareheaded and barefoot (Ezek 24:17; 2 Sam 15:30), to sprinkle dust and ashes on the head (Josh 7:6; 2 Sam 1:2), to cover the head, or at least the beard (Ezek 24:17; Jer 14:3; 2 Sam 15:30), or to place the hand on the head (2 Sam 13:18), and to sit in dust and ashes (Jer 6:26, Job 2:8). In addition, various disfigurements and mutilations were self-inflicted. The head was shaved (Jer 16:6, 47:5); the beard was cut off, or at least clipped (Jer 41:5, 48:37; Isa 15:2; Lev 19:27); gashes were made on the whole body, or at least on the hand (Jer 16:6, 41:5,). It was quite usual upon the occurrence of a death to follow the widespread custom of holding a funeral repast (Hos 9:4; 2 Sam 3:35; Jer 16:7; Ezek 24:17, 22). In addition there were separate offerings of food and drink which were placed upon the grave (Deut 26:14). This custom continued until quite late. Also widespread was the custom, while the women of the house were sitting upon the earth weeping, for professional female mourners to come and chant particular rhythmic lamentations beginning with "ekh" or "ekhah". Evidently, this custom of funeral lamentation was a religious usage regulated by closeness of relationship (cf. Zech 12:10) (Kitchen 1962:170-2; Reed 1962:474-6; Bailey 1993:96; Mare 1982: 672-3; Nowack and Paton 1936:117-8; Bloch-Smith 1992:151; Bender 1894:317-47). These customs as far as can be ascertained were not normative.

Conclusion

As revealed earlier in this chapter when analyzing the pentateuchal legislation on burial practices and mourning, prompt burial (preferably same day of death) was the norm. This was similar to the Agikuyu tradition and practice. Contact with the dead brought ceremonial defilement. This was similar to Agikuyu belief and observance, which stipulated that should anyone touch a dead body he/she had to be cleansed. Expressly forbidden to the Jews was the eating of tithes in mourning or offering them to the dead. These practices, as mentioned earlier in this chapter, were Canaanite heathen practices. National heroes, for example Aaron and Moses, were accorded thirty days national mourning. A requirement that was emphasized was that all the dead should be buried or in exceptional circumstances their bodies disposed of in some other manner, such as the burning of bodies of persons under a serious curse (e.g. the bodies of Achan and his family referred to earlier) (Josh 7:25). Others could in extremely serious circumstances have 'their carcasses . . . be meat for the fowls of heaven and for the beasts of the earth' (Jer 16:3-7, 13) (cf. 1 Kgs 14:11; 1 Kgs 16:4; 1 Kgs 21:24). As was shown earlier, reformation of the Jewish mode of coping with death took place, but very gradually. It was rare that such reformation occurred suddenly. It occurred to suit prevailing circumstances. The Jewish mode of coping with death was not normative, but meant to be observed by the Jews at that time.

In the New Testament, burial practices initially followed the Jewish religious and cultural practices (e.g. burial of Jesus). However, in the first three centuries AD burial practices evolved which were a modification of Jewish procedure, and were practices which would suit Christian teachings and principles. Such methods in particular were introduced to facilitate Christians moving away from pagan burial practices. Cremation, as observed, was not a Jewish practice. Christians also refused cremation, not because of the Jewish beliefs, but because Christians felt that their bodies should not be destroyed as they believed that their same bodies would be the ones to be resurrected. The practices and attitude of the early Christians will be researched in depth in the next chapter (chapter 5). Suffice to say that judging from what has been revealed in chapters 3 and 4, there does not seem to be any similarity between the biblical mode of coping with death and the one currently practised by present-day Agikuyu Christians. As shown and discussed so far in this study, neither the Agikuyu traditional burial practices were explicitly mandated to be observed or obeyed by the contemporary Agikuyu, nor were scriptural burial practices normative. It will therefore be necessary in chapters 7 and 8 of this study to critically look at those biblical teachings and methods on burial and mourning that could (if at all) be adopted by the present-day Agikuyu and other African Christians.

Chapter 5 which follows will explore, analyze and reflect on how the early Christians coped with death. Also explored in Chapter 5 is whether the early Christian fathers indicated how Christians should conduct their funerals. If at all they did, an analyzes will be done to show whether the advice they gave in this regard is binding on present-day Christians to follow and implement in their funeral practices. The findings will also reveal whether the early Christians adopted Jewish customs, pagan customs or whether they practiced other methods when coping with death. Whichever method(s) they adopted, an attempt will be made to establish whether their methods have in any way influenced the present-day Agikuyu Christian practices, and if not, then to find out why not. A further analyzes of those burial practices of the early Christians will determine whether they could be adopted by the present-day Agikuyu and other African Christians.

CHAPTER 5

BURIAL RITES FOR THE EARLY CHRISTIANS FROM 33 AD TO 600 AD, AND ALSO DURING THE MIDDLE AGES

Introduction

SO FAR IN THIS book I have explored and analyzed numerous issues touching on burial. It was explored and analyzed in chapter 2 how the Agikuyu coped with death before embracing Christianity and before interacting with other cultures. Also analyzed was how a few other tribes, races and religions coped with death. Additionally, how a few countries are coping with limited burial space. Chapter 3 analyzed and revealed how the contemporary day Agikuyu Christians cope with death. It was shown that the contemporary Agikuyu hardly know or incorporate in their burial practice any traditional custom of coping with death. Chapter 4 dealt with what scripture, namely the Old Testament and the New Testament of the Holy Bible say about burial, also, how burials were handled during biblical periods. At the end of that chapter it was shown that burial customs in scripture were Jewish funeral practices and were not normative. This chapter aims at exploring how the early Christians from 33 AD to 600 AD, and also during the Middle Ages, coped with death. Also to be explored is whether the early Christian fathers indicated how Christians ought to cope with death, and additionally to reflect whether whatever they said is binding on us to implement in our funeral practices. A further aim is to bring to light the funeral practices of the early Christians, as well as to analyze those teachings and arguments that were advocated by the apostles of Jesus and the early Christian fathers relating to how the followers of Jesus should conduct themselves when coping with death, among other issues.

Similar to what was indicated at the beginning of Chapter 4, the analyzes of the teachings of the early church fathers follows the LIM model, which requires looking at theologicalclassic and church teachings on burial rites.

The methodology applied will include a thorough discussion of what the term "early Christianity" represents as applied and referred to in

Christian history and theology. It will then be necessary to obtain and critique relevant data from the writings of some of the early church fathers. This will involve listing the church fathers to be consulted, as well as showing the periods that they represent. The primary and secondary sources consulted will be reflected. It will then be necessary to engage as appropriate with scholarly interpretation of the relevant writings of those church fathers. This will be in line with the methodology underlined in chapter 4 of this book regarding doing biblical theology. This is because the approach of the two are similar. It is worth noting that the methodology of studying the history of the early church, just like biblical theology, is descriptive and historical and seeks to state the theology implied by the biblical books themselves, as well as the writings of the early church fathers (Barr 1999:247). Additionally he contends that the Bible is studied not merely historically or phenomenologically but with a truly theological interpretative purpose. It is the same with the study of early Christian funeral rites examined in this chapter. Principally, and in essence, the engagement with the writings of the early church fathers is meant to present and interpret their writings, and seek to understand the theological themes they contain with regard to the topic under discussion

Towards the end of the presentation, it will be necessary to move towards the synthesis of the data. This will then enable relevant recommendations and conclusions to be made.

Synopsis of Early Christianity

The period chosen for the coverage of early Christianity in this book extends from the death of Jesus (AD 33) to approximately AD 600. The latter date (as indicated in the preface to the second edition of Ferguson 1997: Vii) is arbitrary, but conventional and is not observed rigidly. Boer (1976: 134) terms the history of that period (AD 33 to AD 600) as ancient church history. He calls period AD 33 to AD 312 the first period of ancient church history, and the history from AD 313 to AD 600 as the second period. Rutherford (1990:6-12) breaks the same period into two. He terms the first three centuries (AD 30 to AD 313) "the church of the martyrs", while the four centuries following (AD 313 to AD 600) he terms "the church of the empire".

Concurring with the above authors, and the division they give to that period Needham (1997:17) advises that historians usually divide the history of the church into different stages. The first stage, which he labels "Early church period", began with the birth of the church on the day of Pentecost and lasted for some 600 years. Austin (1983:11-84), in giving the history of early Christianity labels the period AD 33 to AD 312 as, "Period of fullness of time and of the martyrs" while the next period (AD 313 to AD 590) he refers to as, " Period of the Over-comers".

The earliest Christians did not consider themselves followers of a new religion (González 1984:20). All their lives, he observes, they had been Jews and they still were. This it should be noted was true of Peter and the twelve, also of the seven (these are the seven including Stephen who had been appointed by the apostles to "serve" tables) (Acts 6:5-6) and of Paul (Ibid., 19). Their faith was not a denial of Judaism, but rather the conviction that the Messianic age had finally arrived. Paul would say that he was persecuted "because of the hope of Israel" (Acts 28:20). He claims that the earliest Christians did not reject Judaism, but were convinced that their faith was the fulfilment of the age-long expectation of a Messiah (Ibid., 20).

The above contention is supported by Needham (1998:44), who asserts that Early Christianity and the early church were what we could call a Jesus Movement. In the first years, he observes this was a religious movement, which blossomed exclusively within the confines of Judaism, and revolved around Jerusalem as its spiritual home. The original followers of Jesus, he indicates, were all Jews, and they had no intention of being anything other than faithful and pious Jews. They continued to worship in the Jerusalem temple, to obey the Law of Moses, and to have a negative attitude towards Gentiles. He (1998: 45) further asserts that the early church started as a purely Jewish movement, a sect within Judaism. Yet, by the end of the first century, he observes, events had transplanted the church from its original Jewish soil into the Gentile world, where it became an almost exclusively Gentile movement.

Boer (1976:3) sheds further light on the matter by advising that the roots of the Christian church reach back deeply into the history of religion of Israel, ""Salvation said Jesus is from the Jews"(John 4:22),"Jesus came not to destroy but to fulfil the Law and the prophets" (Matt 5:17), "Those who belong to Christ are Abraham's offspring, heirs according to the promise" (Gal 3:29). He observes that as Palestine was part of the Roman Empire, so the church is related, and very deeply so, to Israel, the people of Palestine. He asserts that the earliest church was wholly Jewish, its savior was a Jew, and the entire New Testament was probably written by Jews. MacCulloch (2009:115) sheds further light on this issue by indicating ". . .a significant pattern for the future: Christianity was not usually going to make a radical challenge to existing social distinctions". The reason for this he feels was that Paul and his followers assumed that the world was coming to the end soon, and so there was not much point in trying to improve it by radical action.

The relevance of the above, and of the following section, to the theme of this chapter, which among other subjects deals with the funeral and burial rites of Early Christianity is the fact that it is necessary to understand what is meant by early Christianity, and also because the ante-Nicene and post-Nicene literature originated from the early church fathers who lived and wrote within the period of early Christianity, which as expressed above was within the first six centuries of Christianity.

Baillie (1970:15-30) asserts that the most striking facts about early Christian literature are its variety and its exclusively Gentile authorship. He observes that outside the New Testament writings, little belongs to the first century. However, the second century saw an increasing literary activity among Christians, which swelled to a flood toward its end. The earliest Christian writings after the New Testament are customarily known under the title "Apostolic Fathers" (Ibid., 15). Expounding further on the issue of Apostolic Fathers, O'Collins & Farrugia (2000:17) advise that this was the name for the oldest non-biblical and Orthodox Christian writers.

Austin (1983:68), however, indicates that the erroneous idea that the Apostolic Fathers were taught by the Apostles has long died, but the title remained. According to current thought, those listed as Apostolic Fathers should include only those authors who were directly connected with the apostles and whose mentality was close to the New Testament. Accordingly, O'Collins & Farrugia (2000:17) indicate that this suggests listing as Apostolic Fathers only St Clement, St Ignatius of Antioch, St Polycarp, and Papias, as well as St Quadratus (second century) who around AD 124 addressed to Emperor Hadrian the oldest apology for Christian faith. The contention that some Apostolic Fathers were taught by the Apostles is supported by the writings of some church fathers namely Ignatius and Iraneus respectively, who wrote, "Polycarp was a personal disciple of the Apostle John, and served as the bishop of Smyrna for many years . . . " (Ignatius (c.AD 105); Bercot 1998:526). Also "Polycarp also was instructed by apostles, and he spoke with many who had seen Christ. Not only that, but by Apostles, in Asia he was appointed bishop of the church in Smyrna and also by Iraneus" (c.AD 180) "And these things are borne witness to in writing by Papias, the hearer of John, and a companion of Polycarp". Iraneus wrote, " . . . Polycarp to forego the observance (of his Easter customs) in as much as these things had been always observed by John the disciple of our Lord, and by other apostles with whom he had been conversant" (Bercot 1998: 526—27).

Expounding further on the issue of "Apostolic Fathers", Browning (2009:19) and Austin (1983:70) advise that the Apostolic Fathers, whom they list as Clement of Rome (c.AD 96), Ignatius (c.AD 35–107), Hermas (c.AD 100-40), Polycarp (c.AD 69-155), Papius (c.AD 60-130) as well as the authors of the Epistle of Barnabas, the Epistle to Diognetus, 2 Clement and the Didache (Teaching of the Twelve Apostles) form the literary link between the New Testament period and later Christian generations. The writings of the "Apostolic Fathers", asserts Baillie (1970:15), do not form a unity either in date or in type. The earliest is Clement's letter about AD 96. This was a letter to the church of Corinth. What marks those writings, taken as a whole, he feels, is their literal simplicity, their earnest religious conviction and their independence of Hellenistic philosophy and rhetoric. He observes that they are closer to the New Testament in their artlessness, and while they may lack something of its spiritual depth, they reveal an intense concern for its basic message. He (1970:17) points out further that they come from a time when the church was warring on two fronts—against pagan attack and internal schism. Their particular concern is for order, their dominant themes being the unity of the church around its leaders and the preservation of the faith from perversion. In consequence, the religious spontaneity of the New Testament writings gives place to a more moral and ecclesiastical note. Concurring with most of the views expressed above, Austin (1983:70) comments that the writings of the Apostolic Fathers were intended to furnish the churches with instruction and inspirations, which in this case were intended to advise the followers of Jesus how to cope with death. Such instructions were advisory in nature. They were just guidance. and should therefore not be construed as binding on future Christians. In other words, they were neither mandatory nor normative. As indicated earlier, even the burial of Jesus was not normative. The writings of the Apostolic fathers tended to be moralistic and considerably below the spiritual level of the New Testament. Austin goes on to advise that the vast world of non-Christians did not understand these writings, nor the message of the church. To address the question and opposition of unbelievers, another important group of Christian thinkers developed (Ibid., 70).

Those Christian writers who first addressed themselves (c.AD 120-220) to the task of making a reasoned defence and recommendation of their faith to outsiders are known as Apologists (Austin 1983:70). The Apologists were Christian writers primarily in the second century, who attempted to provide a defence of Christianity and criticisms of Greco-Roman culture (The New Encyclopaedia Britannica Vol 1. 1986:486). Austin asserts that the Apologists met head-on pagan philosophy and Jewish objections. They applied Old Testament prophecy to Christianity and defended the divinity of Christ in relation to monotheism. Austin (1983:70) advises that the Apologists were not primarily theologians. Rather they were devoted thinkers who desired to present Christianity to emperors and to the public as politically harmless. Their intent was also to defend Christian morality, which was under attack. He (1983:70-1) gives the names of those referred to as Apologists who include Aristides (second century), Justin Martyr (c.AD 100-65), Tatian (c.AD 160), Athenagoras, Theophilus and Minucius Felix, (Ibid., 70-1). Gamble (1997:81), states that apologetics is a reasoned defence of belief or behaviour. Apologetics was a persistent task of the ancient church owing to the suspicion, criticism, and hostility encountered by Christianity. According to him (1997:81), Christian apologists all defended Christianity against criticism. Many and varied examples appear during the first five centuries, but second century Christianity is sometimes called "The age of the Apologists". Yet those apologists, he asserts, only strengthened a concern that had appeared here and there in the New Testament, and their work was continued by Christians of the third through fifth centuries, who, it should be noted, composed some of the most important apologies. He further advises that the apologists of the early church faced two distinct fronts, the Jewish and the Greco-Roman and thus created two discrete bodies of apologetic literature namely Apologetics towards Judaism and Apologetics toward the Greco-Roman world.

Christian writers who followed the early Apologists were the early Catholic theologians. As observed by Austin (1983:77), the word "Catholic" is derived from a Greek word meaning general or universal. One of the earliest appearances and use of this word is in the writings of Ignatius of Antioch (c.AD 115). According to O'Collins & Farrugia (2000:36) Catholicity (Gr. "Universality") is the all embracing character of the true and undivided church that gathers into the one people of God those of different races, languages, and cultures. To combat the growing heresies of the second and third centuries, the term (Catholic) became widely used in making the distinction between orthodoxy and heterodoxy. Doctrine which agreed with the Holy Scriptures and the faith of the church was received as catholic or universal, and every departure from the general sentiment of the church was considered as heresy. The concern of the church to preserve apostolic tradition and teaching resulted in the emergence of some great scholars and theologians. According to Austin (1983:78-82), these included Irenaeus (c.AD 130-200); Tertullian (c.AD 160-220), and Origen (c.AD184-254).

The period from Apostolic Fathers to the time of the early Catholic theologians was one of doctrinal development and systematic defence of the Christian faith (Austin 1983:78-80). Intellectual activity however, was not the only pursuit of the church during this period. Political machination was at work and the structure of the church government was taking shape. He (1983:80-1) advises that the notion of one bishop at the head of the church has a hazy and uncertain beginning, but accelerates into a well-documented movement relatively early in church history. The main church leaders whose thoughts and writings brought about the Monarchical Episcopate and laid the foundation for the development of the church into the Roman hierarchy, which led to its ultimate authority in the Roman See, included Ignatius of Antioch (c.AD 115), Callistus (Bishop of Rome AD 217-22) and Cyprian (Bishop of Carthage AD 200-58).

The final group of early Christian writers whose writings have relevance to chapter 5 of this book are the "Church Fathers". We are accustomed to call the authors of early Christian writings "Fathers of the Church". In ancient times the word "Father" was applied to a teacher; for in biblical and early Christian usage, teachers are the fathers of their students. In Christian antiquity, the teaching office was the bishop's. Thus the title Father was first applied to him. In the third century it was given especially to those bishops of the past who were cited as witnesses to the doctrine of the Church (Quasten 1950:9). As witnesses to the tradition of the Church the bishops of bygone ages became a definite body, "the Fathers". Doctrinal controversies of the fourth century brought about further development. The use of the term Father became more comprehensive; it was now extended to ecclesiastical writers insofar as they were accepted as representatives of the tradition of the Church. Thus St Augustine numbers St Jerome among the witnesses to the traditional doctrine of original sin, although he was not a bishop (Ibid., 9).

In summary, it is worthy of note that the history of the church fathers can be divided in the following periods:

The origins of the Church Fathers' Literature (AD 70-313):—This is the beginning and emergence of Christian literature from the apostolic age to the emancipation of the Church in AD 313 by Constantine. In this era we can make the following divisions: (1) The earliest writers put Christian truths in concrete formulas for simple instruction. Such were the Apostolic Fathers. (2) As the Church grew and spread Christian writers came to grips with the religious, political, and philosophical ideas of the Roman Empire. This period produced the great Apologists, who include Aristides, Athenagoras, Tertullian and Justin Martyr. (3) The beginning of the third century saw the start of scientific presentation of the truths of Christianity such as the *Adversus haereses (Against Heresies)* of Irenaeus and *The Fundamental Doctrines* of Origen (Dirksen 1959:2).

The Golden Age of Church Fathers' Literature (AD 313-430):—In this period appeared the most powerful minds in the history of the Church such as Athanasius, the Cappadocians Basil, Gregory of Nyssa and Gregory of Nazianzus, Ambrose, Jerome, John Chrysostom and Augustine. Moreover, the great doctrinal controversies on the Trinity and grace were fought out. The Trinitarian problems were solved by the Fathers of this period in such a fashion that later centuries have but to record and uphold their teaching (Ibid., 2).

The Last Centuries of Church Fathers (AD 431-800):—This period is sometimes unfairly called the decadent centuries. (1) In the first part of this period, from the council of Ephesus (AD 431) to the second council of Constantinople (AD 553) there occur the great Christological controversies. The councils reach a definitive solution to these problems. It is also in this time that the Western part of the Roman Empire was destroyed. The Church is confronted with the Barbarians. (2) In the second part of this period, from AD 554-800, the Fathers of the Church such as St Gregory the Great (AD 540-604) in Italy, St Gregory of Tours in Gaul (AD 540-94), St Isidore in Spain (AD 560-636) and the Venerable Bede in England (c.AD 673-735) try to enlighten the Barbarians and to win them over to the Church. Of course, there were also numerous Eastern writers (Ibid., 2).

As indicated above, the writings of the early church fathers addressed numerous critical issues of continuing importance, which were initially addressed in the debate between Christianity and the classical tradition (Gamble 1997:86). He (Ibid., 86) goes on to state that these included the relation of God and the world, the status of Jesus and His relation to God, the problem of faith and reason, the role of Christianity in society, the status of Christianity among other religions, including Judaism, the historical reliability of scripture, and the proper means of scripture interpretation. He feels further that the intellectual challenge laid down by pagan critics compelled Christian thinkers to give more careful consideration to the elements of Christian belief, to specify their connections and implications, and to set them forth in clear and systematic fashion. Thus, he concludes, early Christian apologetics provided the context in which Christian thought moved beyond its early Biblicism and took up the systematic and philosophical tasks of theology proper.

As indicated by Rush (1941:1) the Christian concept of death, and in this case the concept of how Christians should cope with death, arose from scripture as well as from the manner in which Jesus himself was buried. Subsequently, the way in which Christians should cope with death was developed by the writers and fathers of the church, and manifested practically in the lives as well as in the funeral practices of the first Christians. As indicated earlier, instructions of the early Christian church fathers were advisory in nature, intended to give guidance on how the Christians should conduct themselves when coping with death and other issues touching on their lives. The fathers did not issue explicit mandate as to how Christians should conduct their funerals.

Some of the views of the early church fathers on how Christians should cope with death will be considered, and those deemed relevant to this book will be incorporated where appropriate in the following section(s).

Early Christian Burial Rites

Introduction

Meyers and Strange (1981:170) write that the first Christian century is diverse in cultural matters and is pluralistic in social and religious elements. They assert further that the Judaism of the first century AD is more than a grouping of religious sects. They further observe that the earliest Christianity cannot be monolithic either. They note that they (archaeologists) have only scarce materials from early Christianity until the establishment of Christianity by Constantine the Great (AD 285-337). They are of the view that Jewish Christianity remains one of the most tantalizing of all questions in the study of origins of Christianity, and that much of the data purported to be Jewish Christian is artifactual in nature. They (1981:108) further advise that the question of early Christian evidence is intimately tied to the study of Jewish tombs. They note that the church and synagogue were interdependent in the formative period of Christianity. They express their amazement that such a situation might obtain in a period of supposed animosity between Jews and Christians. This, they feel, is evidence that the two communities remained in close contact (Ibid., 109). They note that archaeological findings reveal that early burial rites and customs in Palestine were based on Judaism and there was apparently no difference between the burial of Christians and those of Judaic Jews.

Furnishing almost similar views, Rowell (1977:1) is of the view that the cultural practices and norms of the early Jewish Christians were no different from Judaism. He further observes that evidence of burial rites and customs of the Christian church for the early centuries is scanty.

The contention that in the first two centuries no distinctively Christian burial forums are known is also borne by White (1997:197), when he additionally advises that initially the early Christians observed ancestral or local customs and conditions in burial. Expressing similar views, Peterson (2001:195), indicates that there is lack of early Christians' burial customs. White (1997:197), asserts that the first evidence of uniquely Christian concerns in burial arises in the late second century. Rowell (1997:19) is of the view that although the care of the Christians for the burial of the dead was noted, information about the details of the Christian practice is not easy to obtain. This is so as the rites of burial during the period of early Christianity were not controversial matters, and according to him did not feature in apologetic or polemical works. References to them are only incidental. Rutherford (1990:6) advises that during the first three centuries of the life of the church aptly called, as indicated earlier, "the church of the martyrs", the earliest witnesses to Christian care of the dead are the cemeteries themselves. These were public cemeteries and not, as popular piety once believed, secret burial places of the persecuted Christians. Very few date from before the fourth century. He indicates that they reveal that Christians and pagans were buried in a similar manner, sometimes even side by side in the same cemetery. Only the decorative representation and inscriptions indicate any distinction between these early graves. Certain apparently neutral pagan motifs continued to appear with Jewish and Christian ones on the same grave (Ibid., 6). Even these early decorations proclaimed in their pristine manner that for the Christians their dead were no mere shades whom they remembered with sadness and resignation. These were the ones who had gone before to the paradise of the shepherd, 'to the place of refreshment, light and peace' (Ibid., 6).

Childers (1997:443), observes that in the early church, Christians tended to accommodate contemporary non-Christian funeral practices in ways that emphasized Christian monotheism and the well-defined Christian belief in the resurrection of the dead. He goes on to indicate that no early sources set out to present a complete account of Christian funeral practice. Practices varied from place to place and evolved through time. Numerous early texts and archaeological data, however, provide incidental details that allow the construction of a typical picture of the matter.

Brigham (1979:558) asserts that contrary to the pagan conviction that proper burial was essential for an individual's happiness in the afterlife, the Early Christians insisted that this was not so. St Augustine writes, "And so there are indeed many bodies of Christians lying unburied; but no one has separated them from heaven, nor from that earth which is all filled with the presence of Him who knows whence He will raise again what He created...Wherefore all these last offices and ceremonies that concern the dead, the careful funeral arrangements, and the equipment of the tomb, and the pomp of obsequies, are rather the solace of the living than the comfort of the dead" (St Augustine, *The City of God* 1.12). Nevertheless, out of reverence for the body as the temple of the Holy Spirit and in view of the future resurrection, they were zealous in their care for the dead. The first Christians, as detailed earlier, naturally followed Jewish burial customs, but these were modified under the influence of local practices and Christian hope (Ibid., 558).

Among the many points of contrast between the Christian church and the systems which it supplanted, the treatment of the departed furnished one of the most conspicuous. Side by side with their unprecedented hospitality and their austere purity of life, Julian enumerates their care for the burial of the dead as one of the means by which the Christians against whom he strove, had succeeded in converting the empire (Julian, *The Letter to Arsaces*, XLIX). What was characteristic of the new faith was not only its belief in the resurrection of the body, but its reverence for that body as sharing in the redemption, and this showed itself in almost every incident connected with the funeral rites (Smith & Cheetham 1875:251).

Acts Performed Before Death—Early Christianity

Certain rites were performed before death, which were intimately linked with each other, namely, the stretching out of the feet of the dying, the administration of the *Viaticum*, the catching of the last breath and the imparting of the final kiss (Rush 1941:91). On the approach of death, the relatives and friends of the dying person gathered around his bed, and as he drew his last breath, his nearest relative gave the last kiss so as to catch the soul which was breathed out (Rowell 1977:9; Toynbee 1971: 43-64). The stretching out of the hands and feet, which was one of the first acts performed in the laying out of the body after death, really began while the person was in his death agony (Rush 1941:1). The stretching out of the feet was intended as a means of laying out the body when the soul takes its departure. *Viaticum* (Eucharist) in Christianity was the reception of the body and blood of Christ at the time of death, which was supplied to the dying person and was meant to be of great supernatural and spiritual help.

Furnishing more information on the issue of *Viaticum*, Donohue, (2001:366), indicates that the reception of the Eucharist for the dying person (food for the journey, or *Viaticum*) was regarded as so crucial for the journey to the next life—Ignatius of Antioch (ca. AD 35-ca. AD 107) referred to the Eucharist as "the medicine of immortality and the antidote preventing death . . . leading to life in Jesus Christ forever" (Eph, 20:3). According to the council of Nicaea Canon 13, it states that "Concerning the departing, the ancient canonical law is still to be maintained, to wit, that, if any man be at the point of death, he must not be deprived of the last and most indispensable *Viaticum*. But, if any one should be restored to health again who has received the communion when his life was despaired of, let him remain among those who communicate in prayers only. But in general, and in the case of any dying person whatsoever asking to receive the Eucharist, let the Bishop, after examination made, give it him".

As a result of the great importance attached to the reception of *Viaticum*, however, a widespread abuse grew up in the early funeral rites. This was the custom of giving the Eucharist to the dead (Rush 1941:99). The abuse was not localized but was widespread. It became so serious that it was even discussed and prohibited by certain councils. This shows all the more how serious and widespread it was, for the bishops gathered in councils would only enact a public prohibition for a public use (Ibid., 99). The prohibition is met with as early as the Council of Hippo of AD 393. This was an important council because bishops from all over Africa attended it; it is on this account that St Augustine refers to it as a "Plenary Council of all Africa" (Augustine, *Retractationes* 1:16). The Council of Hippo made a public prohibition against the giving of Eucharist to corpses. Over the following centuries various councils including the Council of Carthage (AD 397), Council of Carthage (AD 525), Council of Auxerre (AD 578), Council of Trullo (AD 692) all issued prohibitions against giving the Eucharist to the corpses, noting that the dead could neither take nor eat the Eucharist (Donohue 2001:366). In addition to the councils, numerous church leaders denounced the practice. St John Chrysostom inveighs against the practice of the dead being baptized, and of giving the Eucharist to corpses. He shows that when Christ said, "Unless you eat my flesh and drink my blood. . ." He was speaking to the living and not to the dead (Chrysostom, *Homilia* 40 in 1 Corinthians 1). On this account, Chrysostom denounced this practice. Giving the theological reason for the prohibition of giving Eucharist to the corpses, the Third Council of Carthage held in AD 397 refers to the words of Christ, "Take and eat" and then points out that corpses cannot fulfil the condition of eating the Body of Christ (Rush 1941:100).

The catching of the dying breath was associated with the final kiss. In the rites of Christian burial, there was a ceremony of imparting the kiss of peace, but this was not given in conjunction with the catching of the dying breath. Rather, it formed an integral part of the burial service. This was the Christian kiss of peace bestowed upon the dead (Ibid., 103). The liturgical kiss is a sign of reverence, signifying the supernatural charity existing among Christians. The kiss of peace, therefore, in the burial service shows the intimate bond of union and charity existing between the living and the dead and this forms one aspect of the doctrine known as the Communion of Saints. Treating the dead in this manner, Christianity introduced a custom which was at variance with the Jewish and pagan tradition. Contact with a corpse entailed a legal defilement in Judaism (Num 19:11-14). In Roman burials also, the purpose of placing branches before the door of the house in which the wake for the deceased was being held was to warn the passers-by and especially the priest not to enter, because the priests were defiled by the sight of a corpse (Pliny, *Natural History*, 16, 10, 49). To the Christians, however, the body, even of the dead, was something sacred and holy. Therefore, does the *Didascalia* urge Christians to flee from the observations of Judaism with all its ritual purifications (*Didascalia* VI, 22, 1- 4). The body of the dead person, it says, is something sacred and holy (*Didascalia* VI, 22, 4). Hence, Christians should touch and handle the bodies of the dead without incurring any legal defilement or without having any recourse to ritual purifications (*Didascalia* VI, 22, 5). Not only did the Christians touch their dead, but they developed a formal liturgical rite in their burial services which involved contact with the dead, namely, the imparting of the kiss of peace (Childers 1997:443).

Acts Performed Soon After Death

When a Christian died, the body was prepared at home for burial. Relatives closed the eyes of the corpse calling out their loved one's name to verify the death (Childers 1997:443). Concurring with this, Rush (1941:105) indicates that the first act performed after death was the closing of the eyes and mouth of the deceased. St Augustine, who closed the eyes of his mother St Monica, said that he closed her eyes and his heart was overwhelmed with sorrow "I closed her eyes; and there flowed a great sadness into my heart, and it was passing into tears, when my eyes at the same time, by the violent control of my mind, sucked back the fountain dry, and woe was me in such a struggle!" (Augustine *Confessions* IX, 12, 29). What followed next was, as indicated above, calling the loved one's name (Ibid., 443). He (1941:108) calls this act "*conclamatio*". He indicates that the intention was that the loud shouts of calling the deceased's name would awaken the person if he was not really dead. As far as can be ascertained, the *conclamatio* did not continue with Christianity as a formal rite.

The next act was the setting of the various members of the body. The process was to ensure that the feet were drawn out, the arms stretched out along the side of the body. At times, however, the arms were reposed on the chest in form of a cross (Ibid., 110). This process is commonly known as the laying out of the body. The body was then washed with warm water. This duty of washing the body was frequently performed by women chosen from the nearest kin. In later times, it was performed by one of the domestics or by the undertakers (Ibid., 114). The washing of the corpse, he (1941:113) observes, is frequently mentioned by Latin writers. For instance, as Virgil describes the funeral pyre, "First they raised a huge pyre, heavy with cut oak and pine, weaving the sides with dark foliage, set funereal cypress in front, and decorated it above with shining weapons. Some heated water, making the cauldrons boil on the flames, and washed and anointed the chill corpse. They made lament" (Virgil, *Aeneid* VI, 218-19).

The washing with warm water had the same purpose as the *conclamatio* namely to make sure that death had ensued, for the hot water would revive a person if he were only apparently dead. The first mention of washing the corpse in Christian burials came from the first Christian community of Jerusalem. Hence, it is seen that these Jews carried over into Christianity the Jewish custom of washing the corpse. Speaking of the death of Dorcas, a woman of that community who was noted for her charity, the Acts of the Apostles (9:37) mention that her body was washed and laid in an upper chamber. Another occasion was when Joseph of Arimathea is reported to have washed the body of Christ when he was taken down from the cross (Gospel of Peter 6, 24). Though the gospel of Peter is not part of the canonical books of the Bible this shows that the practice was there in the early Christian times.

After washing the body it was then anointed, John 12:7; Acts 9:37 (White 1997:196; Brigham 1979:558). Rush (1941:121) notes that the more usual practice was anointing the body to preserve it for a while, and especially for the lying in state of the body.

It should be noted that writers both from the East and the West speak of the Christian practice of anointing the dead. St John Chrysostom, speaking of the burial of Christ takes it for granted that the anointing of the body was a funeral rite well known to his hearers. He mentions the care that Joseph of Arimathea and Nicodemus bestowed upon Christ, and he speaks of the sweet spices whose special nature is to preserve the body (Chrysostom, *Homilia* 85 in Joannem, 3; Rush 1941:124).

During early Christianity, formal embalmment was not frequent, and was confined mainly to Egypt (Rush 1941:124). Expounding on this Rush states that this practice in Egypt led to abuse which St Antony, the hermit, tried to eradicate. According to Rush, the Egyptians were accustomed not to bury the dead underground, but to place them on couches and keep them in their homes. St Antony fought against this and wanted all Christians to be buried in the earth after the manner of the patriarchs and the LORD, "And thus saying, he showed that he who did not bury the bodies of the dead after death transgressed the law, even though they were sacred. For what is greater or more sacred than the body of the Lord? Many therefore having heard, henceforth buried the dead underground, and gave thanks to the Lord that they had been taught rightly" (Athanasius *The Life of St. Antony*, 90). St

Augustine's views expressed in his *Sermon* 361,12 has relevance for this when he condemns the practice of preserving the body because of the resurrection, pointing out that if the preservation of the body were a prerequisite for the resurrection, then only the Egyptians would believe in it, because they diligently cared for the dead. This care, according to Augustine consisted of the Egyptian custom of drying the corpse and of making it as hard as metal. White (1997:197), is of the view that embalming techniques, as in Egyptian mummifications, were not widely used in Jewish custom although they are known (Gen 50:2-3, 26) and seem to have continued into the Roman period especially among wealthy pagans and later among Coptic Christians.

Clothing of the Dead

When a person died and after the body had been washed and anointed, it would next be wrapped in linen as a sign of immortality. It would then be dressed in the clothes worn during life (Brigham 1979:558). White (1997:198), observes that in addition to washing and anointing the body (John 12:7; Acts 9:37) wrapping or binding was done to prevent undue distortion or swelling (John 11:44; 19:40). Childers (1997:443) asserts that the body was dressed according to the social status of the deceased. The manner in which the Christians clothed their dead can be traced back to similar practices in Jewish and other ancient burial rites. At times, linen garments were employed; at other times, the corpse was clothed with the best kind of garments worn during life. Among the Christians, there was a tendency to go to excess in this matter; and this called forth denunciation from certain of the fathers as shown below. Ecclesiastical writers mention linen clothing, which was used at burial. St Gregory of Nyssa, speaks of clothing of pure linen, which was used in preparing the body of bishop Meletius for burial. Prudentius speaks of it as a custom to spread the clothing of pure whiteness over the corpse. St Jerome, in his account of a woman who was beheaded, says that the clergy, whose duty it was, wrapped the bloodstained corpse in a linen winding-sheet. Besides clothing the dead in linen, the Christians at times buried their dead in the ordinary clothing worn during life or more usually in special clothing. When possible, however, special burial garments were procured (Rush 1941:129-130).

Narrating the baptism of Constantine, Eusebius says that Constantine, at the conclusion of the ceremony of his baptism, arrayed himself in shining imperial garments brilliant as the light. Then he reclined on a couch and refused to clothe himself with the purple any longer after being received in the church. It was in this baptismal robe that he died, and thus clad he was buried (Ibid., 131). This is an indication that in all probability, the mentality of early Christians demanded that outstanding persons should be clad in special garments. The tendency to adorn the dead in special garments led to excess. Certain fathers denounced this, and it is from these denunciations that the Christian practice of attempting to procure special and costly burial garments can be seen to greater advantage. St Basil, attacking this abuse among the wealthy, asks them in a very pointed manner if it is not better to adorn one's heirs with splendid and sumptuous attire than to have these precious vestments decay together with the corpse. He says, "What? Should we not in fact accessorize present company with expensive, swanky apparel, rather than bury a dead person's most valuable garments along with him? What good is a monument over the grave, and a pompous burial, and useless expenditure? It is right that things needful for life be made use of by the living" (Basil, *Homily for the Rich*, 9). St John Chrysostom bitterly inveighed against the extravagance of Christians who clothed their dead in precious apparel and often in silks and gold. After showing that Christ rose naked from the tomb, he refers to the extravagance of Christians as madness and urges them to cease from such excess (Chrysostom, *Homily* 85). To him it was a superfluous and unprofitable expense, because it brought no gain to the departed and much loss to the mourners. He did not forbid accepted funeral observances, but he bade them to clothe their dead with moderation, so as not to consign their bodies to the earth naked. In opposition to the gold and silken clothing with which the Christians were adorning their dead, Chrysostom sets before their minds the garment of immortality which the body is to put on, and which is more glorious than garments of gold and silk (Chrysostom, *Homily* 85).

The practice of clothing the dead in better and more precious garments resulted in a peculiar abuse which became prevalent in Gaul. The council held at Clermont in Auvergne in AD 535 decreed that the bodies were not to be wrapped in palls which were used for the divine services (Canon 3 (Mansi VIII, 860). It likewise legislated that not even the bodies of priests were to be so attired when carried to burial (Canon 7 (Mansi VIII, 860). Later on in the same century, the Council of Auxerre (AD 578) repeated the same prohibition and said that it was not permitted to wrap the bodies of the dead in veils or palls (Canon 12 (Mansi IX, 913).

Crowning the Dead and Significance of Crowns in Early Christianity

According to Rush (1941:137) Christianity was one culture in which funeral crowns played no part. Funeral crowns were likewise foreign to the Jewish culture, and it is partly in the light of this antecedent that Christianity looked on the custom of crowning the dead as specifically pagan. Note should be taken that crowning the dead was common in many cultures of the pagan antiquity. The Christian teaching on God, death, and the afterlife necessitated the rejection of crowning the dead. The struggle against the use of funeral crowns can be seen in the *Octavious* 12, 6 of Minucius Felix. Here, *Octavious* goes on to defend the Christian rejection of crowns with a positive reason taken from the teachings of Christianity and says, "we arrange our funerals as simply as our lives; we twine no fading crown but await from God a crown blossoming with eternal flowers" (Minucius Felix, *Octavious* 38, 4). The struggle against the use of crowns among the Christians in Alexandria can be seen from the writings of Clement of Alexandria; he prohibits the use of crowns because of their association with idolatry and he says, "We must in no way have communion with demons. Nor must we crown the living image of God after the manner of dead idols" (Clement of Alexandria, *Pedagogy* 11, 8, 73, 1). Besides linking the rejection of crowns with their connotation in pagan culture, Clement brings forth a reason of fitness drawn from the teachings of Christianity. He mentions that Christians delight in the holy Passion of Christ who was crowned with thorns. Therefore it is an insult to the Passion of Christ for a Christian to be crowned (Clement of Alexandria, *Pedagogy* II 8, 73, 3). These are some of the early Christianity sources indicating the Christian struggle against the pagan practice of crowning the dead.

The practice of crowning the dead was thus rejected by the Christians. However, Christianity made no violent breaks with the culture of the past. Rush (1941:141) asserts that when a particular practice was rejected, the church set about the task of drawing its adherents away from it only gradually. This it did by bringing forth new concepts drawn from the teachings of Christianity, and these were to be Christian substitutions for the cultural custom, which was rejected. In opposition to the funeral crown of the pagans, the belief was stressed that God Himself was the crown of the Christians. He who was converted to Christianity and found there such soul-satisfying doctrines, and especially he who thereby came to the knowledge of the one true God and found salvation, began to glory in the fact that he had God Himself as the crown. Tertullian told the Christians that their crown was Christ, the flower of Jesse (Tertullian, *On the Military Garland* 15).

Another crown spoken of in Christian antiquity was the crown of life. St Paul, who could well adapt himself to the cultural background of his hearers, drew on the analogy of athletic games to show that a crown of victory was awaiting the Christian when the struggle of life was over. Writing to the Corinthians, he says: "Know you not that they that run in the race, all run indeed, but one receiveth the prize? So run that you may obtain. And everyone that striveth for the mastery refraineth himself from all things; and they indeed that they may receive a corruptible crown; but we an incorruptible crown" (I Cor 9:24-25). Regarding his own death, St Paul wrote to Timothy: "I have fought a good fight, I have finished my course, I have kept the faith. As to the rest, there is laid up for me a crown of justice which the LORD, the just judge, will render to me in that day; and not only to me but to them also that love His coming" (2 Tim 4: 6-8). He (1941:143) advises that throughout the New Testament, the crown of victory is held out to those who are loyal in following Christ. Addressing the Elders, St Peter urges them to be true shepherds of souls and tells them that when the Prince of pastors shall appear they shall receive a never-fading crown of glory (I Pet 5:4). St James expressly refers to this crown as the crown of life when he says; "Blessed is the man who endureth temptation; for when he hath been proved, he shall receive the crown of life, which God hath promised to them that love Him" (Jas 1:12). Similarly, St John, at the express command of Christ, wrote to the bishop of Smyrna: "Be thou faithful until death and I will give thee the crown of life" (*Apocalypse* 2:10). In like manner he was bidden to write to the bishop of Philadelphia: "Behold I come quickly; Hold fast that which though hast, that no man may take thy crown" (*Apocalypse* 3:11).

The early Christians awaited a crown in death. However, instead of having it put on their head by men, they preferred to forego the funeral crown in order that they might have the happiness of receiving the crown of life from the hands of God. That is the reason why Clement of Alexandria says that a beautiful crown of amaranth is laid up for those who have lived well. This flower, he says, the earth is not able to bear; heaven alone can produce it (Clement of Alexandria, *Pedagogy* 11, 8, 73, 2). Tertullian, too, arguing against the use of crowns, reminds Christians that they should keep for God His own property untainted. After citing texts from the New Testament referring to the crown of life awaiting the Christian, he says, "Why do you condemn the brow which is destined for a diadem to a little chaplet or twisted headband? For Christ Jesus has made us kings to God and His Father. What have you in common with the flower which is to die?" (Tertullian, *On the Military Garland* 15).

From what is discussed above regarding the funeral crown it can be seen that the church made no violent break with the culture of antiquity.

It drew its adherents away from the pagan practice of crowning the dead, which it looked upon as idolatry, by setting a Christian substitute before them. This Christian substitute for the pagan funerary crown was fourfold. In the first place, God was regarded as the Crown of the Christians. Secondly, the Christians could reject funerary crowns, because they looked forward to receiving from the hands of God the crown of life. Thirdly, the martyrs needed no fading crown, because their martyrdom was their crown. Finally, a Christian life dedicated to the service of God began to be looked upon as a second martyrdom, and this too received its crown, the crown of lilies (Ibid., 149).

The relevance of Crowns in this book is deemed important especially to the Agikuyu and other African Christians, who frequently in the funeral eulogies of their loved ones and especially in the newspapers' funeral advertisements (obituaries) when announcing deaths of their loved ones often quote 2 Timothy 4:6-8 and reflect their deep conviction that their beloved will receive a Crown of Justice from the LORD. It is therefore necessary when analyzing death rites of early Christians to show what led St Paul to making those statements. Additionally, for them to understand the background to the concept of the heavenly crown to be bestowed by God to those who love and obey Him.

The Wake Held Over the Dead

After being washed, anointed and dressed, the body lay in state at home on a specially fashioned bier (Childers 1997:443). Wake in the modern sense is a night or nights spent keeping watch by a dead person's body before it is buried (Hornby 1992:1431). Another definition is a gathering to watch and grieve over a dead person on the night before the burial, sometimes with drink and food (Hornby 1992:1431; Quirk 1989:1182). Merriam-Webster Dictionary indicates that "Wake is a watch held over the body of a dead person prior to burial and sometimes accompanied by festivity."

The first account of a wake is that which was held in connection with the burial of Dorcas, a woman of the first community of Jerusalem, who was noted for her charity. The Acts of the Apostles state that Dorcas was laid in an upper chamber (Acts 9:37). The great mourning, which the devout men observed over Stephen, indicates some period of mourning, which ensued after death and before burial (Acts 8:2). Hence it is that the converts from Judaism took over with them into Christianity the Jewish practice of having the body exposed for some time after death before being brought out to be buried. Converts from paganism, who before entering Christianity were so well acquainted with the practice of holding wakes for the dead, must have in the same way continued the practice when they became Christians (Rush 1941:154). The account of the death of Constantine shows the splendor of the wake in the case of an Emperor. Eusebius mentions that Constantine was laid out in one of the principal rooms of the palace, where he was attended by a group of soldiers for several days and nights. So much splendor surrounded this wake that Eusebius says it was a sight such as was never seen before (Eusebius, *Life of Constantine* IV, 66). Although the wake for the ordinary faithful was not as magnificent as that for an Emperor, still there are references both in the East and the West which testify to the practice of "waking" the person for a while in his home before burial. St John Chrysostom, attacking excessive mourning practices, shows that it was the custom for the people of his time to hold wakes over the dead in their homes. Speaking of the wake which was held over the daughter of Jairus, St John Chrysostom shows that Christ cast out those who were making a row. Then he sharply reproached those Christians who, when waking their dead, bring in pagan *praeficae* only to increase their grief (Chrysostom, *Homily* 31). Again, he shows that, in accordance with the new concept of death, psalms were to take place of wailings during the laying out of the body (Chrysostom, *Homily* 31). Flowing from this concept, he says that wailings are an insult to the dead and only defeat the purpose of bringing in singers and priests (Chrysostom, *Homily* 4). From these abuses, therefore, which St Chrysostom set out to correct, it can be seen how general a practice it was for Christians of this time to have the body laid out in their homes for some time after death.

Among the *Canons of Athanasius*, there is one, which has reference to the conduct of the Christians during the wake. It is worded; 'And if the dead be a beloved or an only son, his people shall not despair by reason of grief of heart, but the priests shall chant and read to them until the hour when the dead is borne forth, while they pray each hour that comfort may be given to the sorrow of their hearts lest sorrow increase upon them and they die' (*Canons of Athanasius* 100).

Writers in the West mention at times the wake, which was held in the home of the deceased. Speaking of the death of his mother, St Monica, St Augustine refers to the many brethren and religious women who came to pay their last respects to her (Augustine, *Confessions* IX, 12, 31). From the *Gelasian Sacramentary* Rush (1941:157) indicates that it was the accepted practice to hold a wake in the home of the deceased. This *Sacramentary* contains two sets of prayers to be used on such occasions. The first set comprises those prayers to be recited immediately after death; the second set contains a list of orations to be recited before the deceased was carried out to be buried.

When burial took place very soon after death, a vigil was often held at the grave. As indicated previously, among the Jews it was the practice to bury on the day of death. St Augustine's account of the death and burial of his mother, St Monica, seems to imply that she was buried on the day of her death (Augustine, *Confessions* IX, 12, 31-32). Under these circumstances, the wake or vigil would be kept at the grave. In Jewish thought, this vigil at the grave, as Rush referring to the works of E. Freistedt observes, was linked with the eschatological belief that the soul hovered near the body for three days after death. This belief it should be noted did not carry over into Christianity.

A development peculiar to Christianity was to hold the wake in a church. It was only in the fourth century with the peace granted to Christianity that the Church could openly establish festivals to commemorate publicly the death and anniversaries of the martyrs (Rush 1941:160). At this time, Christian life tended to centre more and more around the Church. Not only were the deaths and anniversaries of the martyrs celebrated in the church, but the death of the faithful was linked with church services. Thus originated the practice of bringing the deceased to the church, and there holding a wake over him. This became the usual practice throughout Christendom.

From all the above discussion, it can be seen that the Christians took over the practice of holding wakes over the dead. The wake was held at times in the house. At other times the vigil took place at the grave, especially in cases where it was the practice to bury as soon after death as possible. Finally, Christianity introduced a new manner of solemnizing the wake over the dead, namely, by holding it in a church. This later practice was a development, as indicated earlier, after peace came about for the church.

Early in Christianity one of the problems St Paul had to deal with was excessive mourning. Writing to the Thessalonians, who were giving way to excessive grief for their dead, St Paul consoles them with the thought of the future resurrection, and brings forth what was to be the position of the new religion in this regard, when he writes: 'We will not have you ignorant, brethren, concerning them that are asleep, that you be not sorrowful even as others who have no hope' (1 Thess 4: 13).

When St John Chrysostom took up the attack against pagan mourning survivals, he referred to the whole affair as nothing else but disgracing the dead (Chrysostom, *Homily* 31). To his mind, all excessive mourning was forbidden to Christians who lived under the certain hope of the resurrection. Therefore, he asks by what right do the Christians mourn over the dead after the manner of the pagans, as though they were Bacchanalians (Chrysostom, *The Consolation of Death* 2, 6). He says: "But at this point my mind is aroused to bitter grief, realizing to what heights Christ has raised us and how far we have lowered ourselves. For seeing the mourning indulged in public, the wailing over those departing life, the lamentations and other unbecoming practices, believe me, I feel ashamed before the heathens, Jews and heretics who see it and who deride us on this account" (Chrysostom, *Homily* 4, 5). In their attempt to eradicate the surviving pagan mourning practices, the leaders of Christianity had to direct special attention to the women, for they were especially attached to such display. In Christian times it was the women especially who continued pagan practices, and it was against them that denunciations were often directed (Rush 1941:182). St Gregory of Nyssa speaks of the sad wailings of the virgins that sounded in his ears, and he speaks of it as a bitter and irrepressible cry (Gregory of Nyssa, *The Life of St. Macrinus*). It was then that he directed them to turn their lamentations into psalmody (Gregory of Nyssa, *The Life of St. Macrinus*).

In Christianity, the denunciation of such conduct had its effect and the singing of psalms gradually replaced the pagan dirges. To assure the triumph of Christianity in this regard, it was the desire of the church that the teachings of Christianity should permeate the lives of the faithful, so that everything out of harmony with this might disappear. St Cyprian said that the fear of death would depart when the thought of immortality took root, and he recommended to his flock that they should show that this was what they believed so that they should not mourn (Gregory of Nyssa, *The Life of St. Macrinus*). St Ambrose said that tears and mourning will cease when the soul heeds salutary remedies (Ambrose, *The Death of Satyri* 1, 70). St John Chrysostom admonished his flock to devise what consolation they could for the departed, but instead of seeking it in tears and lamentations they should rather seek it in the Christian substitutions of alms, prayers and oblations of the dead (Chrysostom, *Homily* 21). Finally, St Augustine observed that, according to St Paul, Christians are not enjoined to refrain from weeping, but not to weep as those who have no hope. It is necessary that sadness results from the death of friends, but he pointed out that Christian hope should be a source of consolation for one in sorrow (St Augustine, *Sermon* 173, 3). Then after setting before his people the hope of the resurrection, he said; "Let sadness perish where there is so great a consolation; let sorrow be plucked from the heart and let faith drive away sadness" (Augustine, *Sermon* 173, 3).

The Funeral Procession

The Christian church gave to the funeral procession somewhat of the character of a triumph (Smith & Cheetham 1875:253). Childers (1997:443) writes that after lying in state, the body was covered and carried to a cemetery outside the city in a procession of friends and relatives who sang psalms along the way. While partaking of the nature of a religious triumph, the Christian procession was much simpler than those in vogue among the pagans. The music and the mourning associated with the pagan concept of death were supplanted by the singing of psalms. Tertullian recommends the exclusion of instrumental music whereby he says that it was not fitting for a Christian to become a soldier because in death he would be disturbed by the trumpet blast of the musician, while he was awaiting to be awakened by the trumpet of the angel (Tertullian, *On the Military Garland* II). Hence, the Christian procession should be limited to the corpse and its bearers and to the participants who joined in the procession. It was the general rule for the participants to follow the corpse, with the relatives of the deceased taking the lead. St Jerome, in a letter of condolence to Julian who had lost his wife and two daughters within a short time, speaks of him as leading the funeral procession in which his comforting friends took part (Jerome, *Letter* 118, 2).

The deceased was placed on a funeral litter (*lectica*) and was carried by up to eight pallbearers. As a rule, only four pallbearers were employed. Among the Christians, this was the customary manner of transporting the corpse to the grave. It is in the history of the highly organized first Christian community at Jerusalem that mention of pallbearers is first encountered. The Acts of the Apostles states that when Ananias expired, 'the young men rising up, removed him and carrying him out buried him' (Acts 5:6). The same young men also carried his wife, Sapphira, to burial (Acts 5:10). The details of the burial of St Stephen, the first martyr, were arranged by "devout men" (Acts 8:2). Not only the first Christian community, but others likewise, provided for the burial of their members, especially the poor. This is indicated very early in Christianity when Aristides says that when one of the poorer members of Christianity passes out of this world each one of the Christians, according to his ability, gives heed to him and carefully sees to his burial (Aristides, *Apology* 15, 8). Moreover, he says that at such a time the Christians rejoice and accompany his corpse as if he were merely going from one place to another (Aristides, *Apology* 15, 11). Tertullian refers to the special trust fund of piety that was set aside for the burial of the poor (Tertullian, *Apologetics* 39, 6). The *Canons of Athanasius* prescribed that if the deceased were poor, the church would provide for his burial (Canon of Athanasius 100). In these cases, it is probable that the church in providing for the burial would likewise provide pallbearers for the carrying of the corpse to the grave. It is known that Constantine at Constantinople set aside a group of *lectiarii* whose office it was to take over the entire charge of the burial and of carrying the dead to the grave (Justinian, *Novellae* 43). They were likewise to provide for the burial of the poor, without cost, and to carry them to the grave, at least where there were endowments for this purpose (p. 59). St Jerome speaks of clerics whose official duty it was to provide for burial (p.59). St Augustine states that all the details of the funeral of his mother Monica were arranged by those whose duty it was. No special mention is made of the ones who carried her body to the grave, and it is probable that it was these officials who acted as pallbearers.

The Christians, like the Greeks and Romans, often employed persons of note to act as pallbearers and thus honor the deceased. This happened in cases of prominent ecclesiastics. At the funeral of St Basil, holy men acted as pallbearers (Gregory of Naziunzus, *Prayer* 43, 80). St Fulgentius, the Bishop of Ruspe, was borne by priests to the church of the city where he was buried, the first one to receive the honor of being buried in that basilica (*The Life St Fulgentius* 65). The clergy at times acted as pallbearers in the case of outstanding Christians. At the funeral of St Macrina, Araxius the bishop of the place ordered all who shared the priesthood with him to bear the body (Gregory of Nyssa, *The Life of St Macrinus*). As her body was being borne in the procession, St Gregory of Nyssa and Araxius were the pallbearers at the feet of the bier, while two other distinguished clerics were at the head of the bier (Gregory of Nyssa, *The Life of St Macrinus*). St Ambrose acted as pallbearer for his own brother Satyrus (Ambrose, *The Death of Satyri* 1, 36). St Jerome mentions it as a special mark of honor that St Paula was borne by bishops who even put their shoulders to the bier (Jerome, *Letter,* 108, 29). Sidonius Apollinaris relates that priests acted as pallbearers for a woman of outstanding holiness (Sidonius Apollinaris, *Letters* 11, 82).

Black and red were the colours especially associated with the cult of the dead. In pagan antiquity black, especially, was the colour of the mourning garments worn by people on the occasion of a death. In the light of their cultural antecedents, it was only to be expected that Christians should carry over the practices of wearing mourning garments. However, since the use of such garments was associated with pagan beliefs, the leaders of the Christianity inveighed against the practice among the Christians. This struggle against the use of mourning garments manifests itself in the writings of St Cyprian. To such an extent did the Christians take over the practice of wearing mourning garments that even during the calamitous times of the plague then raging they still had the resources to wear mourning. Denouncing this practice, St Cyprian says; "How often has it been revealed to us also, the last and the least, how frequently and manifestly I have been commanded through God's vouchsafing that I should bear witness constantly . . . that dark garments should not be worn here, in as much as they have already assumed white garments there?" (Cyprian, *Mortality* 20). This language of Cyprian is clear and strong. A public abuse called for a public correction, and it is evident from this that the early Christians took over the practice of wearing mourning garments. It is likewise evident that the leaders of Christianity did their utmost to eradicate this custom which they regarded as a remnant of paganism and something out of harmony with the Christian outlook on death. White, therefore, was the color which Christian leaders thought should be associated with the dead. White was regarded as the color of life and immortality, and that was the only color which should be associated with those who had gone forth to eternal life (Rush 1941: 216-217).

Regardless of when the procession took place, the torchbearers were an integral part of the funeral pomp. At the beginning of Christianity, there was opposition to the use of lights and candles by the Christians. By reason of their association with the pagan cult of the dead, the church forbade the use of candles. It was only when the practice lost its pagan connotation that it was adopted by the Christians. St John Chrysostom, speaking of the candles used in the funeral procession says; "Tell me, what is the meaning of the bright torches? Is it not that we send the dead before us like athletes?" (Chrysostom, *Homily 4* in Hebrews, 5). And strangely enough, when the body of St John Chrysostom was brought back to Constantinople, the crowds flocked to the bay of the Bosphorus with torches (Theodoret, *Church History IV*, 36, 1). Among writers in the West, St Jerome mentions the use of candles at funerals. Describing the funeral procession of St Paula, he states that some of the priests carried lights and candles (Jerome, *Letter 108*, 20). St Jerome in his time had to defend the Christian practice of using lights and candles, for example, when he makes a vehement retort, saying that the Christians did not burn candles during the day, but only at night to temper the darkness while they watched until the morning (Jerome, *Against Vigilantius* 7). Even if some did burn the candles during the day through misguided piety, Jerome says it was done as a means of honouring the martyrs. Then he says that in the churches of the East candles are lighted when the Gospel is being read, even when the sun is shining. This is done, he says, not to dispel the darkness, but to manifest joy. Thus, it is seen that the candles were given a spiritual symbolism by the Christians. The candle became a symbol of Christ who was the light of the world. It symbolized the Christians who were the "children of light." The torch too, was a symbol of life. This symbol is still retained in birthday celebrations. On the birthday cake are placed candles corresponding to the number of years already lived by the one celebrating the birthday. In the centre of the cake a larger candle is placed, "the light of life", as a symbol of a wish for many more years of life. Death to the Christians was a *dies natalias*. The light of the candles was a symbol of life. It represented the eternal light or the eternal life to which the soul had gone. It is this for which the church prays when it says: *Lux perpetua luceat eis* (Rush 1941:228).

The Singing of Psalms during the Christian Procession

Christianity introduced the singing of psalms during the procession to supplant the pagan *planctus* and *nenia*, and likewise the pagan music. Christianity, in keeping with their joyful concept of death, introduced the singing of psalms and hymns, which was regarded as a true spiritual help to the dead.

The spirit of the Christians procession is confirmed by Aristides when he says that at the departure of one of the faithful from this world, the Christians rejoice and give thanks to God, accompanying the corpse as if it were merely going from one place to another (Aristides, *Apology 15* II). This spirit of rejoicing and thanksgiving is seen in the account of the procession of St Cyprian, where it is stated that his body was conducted with prayers in great triumph to the burial ground of *Macrobius Candidianus* (Rush 1941:232). As well as demonstrating how accepted a practice it was to have psalms sung during funeral procession of the Christians, St John Chrysostom brings out the spiritual significance attached to this Christian substitution for pagan dirges. Stressing the Christian concept of death as an antidote to mourning, he asks; "What is the reason for the hymns? Is it not that we praise God and thank Him that He has crowned the departed and freed him from suffering, and that God has the deceased, now freed from fear, with Himself? Is this not the reason for the singing of hymns and psalms? All this is a sign of joy, for it is said; "Is anyone cheerful, let him sing" (Chrysostom, *Homily* 4). The joyful character of the procession is seen when Augustine states that they went and returned without tears when Monica was carried to burial (Augustine *Confession IX*, 12, 31).

The *Apostolic Constitutions* prescribe that psalms should be sung in the procession of the Christians because, "precious in the sight of the Lord is the death of His saints" (*Apostolic Constitution Vi*, 30). From this, it can be seen that the people chanted Psalm 115, which is a song of thanksgiving to God. When St John Chrysostom upbraided his people for their excessive mourning practices, he recalled to their minds the sentiments of the psalms, which they sang when they carried their dead to burial. Here he tells them to recall that when they sing; "Turn, Oh my soul into thy rest because the Lord has been bountiful to thee," and, " will fear no evil, for thou art with me", and "Thou art my refuge from the trouble which hath encompassed me" (Chrysostom *Homily 4*). From this, it is evident that they sang psalms 114-115 just as had been noted in the *Apostolic Constitutions*. The second verse indicated by Chrysostom shows that they sang Psalm 22, which is a song in praise of the Lord as shepherd and host. The last verse quoted by Chrysostom shows that they sang Psalm 31, in which the psalmist sings of the joy of a pardoned sinner. All these psalms are songs of praise and thanksgiving and they indicate what a contrast all this was to the funeral dirges of the pagans. This contrast is manifested all the more when it is realized, as St Jerome relates, that the strains of *Alleluia* were heard at the funeral of Fabiola. The *Alleluia* is an expression of great joy, and its use at this funeral gives an indication of the joyful outlook of these Christians on death.

Interment and Why the Early Christians Were Against Various Pagan Practices

In some respects there was the great similarity between Christian and pagan funeral rites. In others, there were great differences. It is especially in the manner in which the Christians buried their dead that the main difference is most apparent. From the beginning, the Christians rejected the practice of cremating the body. In reply to the criticisms of the Christians' refusal to cremate the bodies of their dead, Octavius the defender of Christianity on cremation states; 'We do not as you (pagans) believe, fear any loss from cremation. Rather, we adapt the ancient and better custom of burying in the earth' (*Minucius Felix*, Octavius 38, 10). Burying the dead in the earth has been so associated with Christianity that the fact might be lost sight of that Christians, in the words of their own exponents, were simply following the old and better custom of earth burial (Rush 1941:237). Christ, was buried after the manner of the Jews, and among them cremation was not the manner of disposing of the dead. Regarding the burial practices of the Jews, Tacitus says; "They choose to bury the bodies of their dead rather than burn them, following in this the Egyptian custom" (Tacitus, *History V*, 5). Not only the Jews in Palestine buried their dead in this manner, but the Jews of the Diaspora did likewise. The existence of Jewish catacombs in Rome prior to the advent of Christianity shows that the Jews preserved the custom of burying their dead in the earth. The manner in which the Christians buried their dead is to be found in the practice of the land that was the cradle of the new religion and from which many of the first converts came (Rush

1941:242-3). This is borne out in the account of the first deaths in the Christian community in Jerusalem. Ananias (Acts 5:6), Sapphira (Acts 5:10) and St Stephen (Acts 8:2) were not cremated but buried. From this, it is seen that the church in Jerusalem continued the practice of earth burial. Not only the community in Jerusalem, but the other Christian communities adhered to the old and better practices of earth burial. It is noteworthy though, that as shown in Chapter 4 of this book, earth burial was not normative per se. Rather it was the burial practice that was preferred by the Jews.

The insistence on burying the body in the earth can best be seen from an account in the *Life of Antony*. St Athanasius, the biographer of this saint, says that the Egyptians followed the practice of not burying holy persons, and especially the martyrs, underground, but that they placed them on couches and kept them in their houses. St Anthony fought against this practice, urging the bishops to command that this be abolished. He himself taught the people that the practice was neither lawful nor pious. He said that those who did not bury their dead underground were transgressing the law and Christian practice. The bodies of the patriarchs and the body of Christ were laid in tombs, and it was for that reason that the bodies of the Christians should be interred under the ground (Athanasius, *The Life of Antony*, 90). Knowing this abuse of the Christians in Egypt, his dying words were; "Do not allow my body to be brought back to Egypt, lest they place it in the houses, for it was for this reason that I betook myself to the mountains and came here. You know how I always upbraided those who did this and commanded them to put a stop to this practice. But bury my body and hide it in the earth" (Athanasius, *The Life of Antony*, 90). St Athanasius says that as a result of St Anthony's exhortations many began to bury the dead in the earth. Tertullian, too, ridiculed the pagan practice of cremation when he pointed out the inconsistency of using fire to dispose of the corpse and then using fire to offer sacrifices to the dead. In this connection he says; "But I will deride the ordinary lot of mankind, especially when it cremates the dead most cruelly and afterwards feeds them most gluttonously, thereby propitiating them and offending them by one and the same fire. O piety that amuses itself with cruelty! Is it sacrifice or insult which it offers when it burns its offerings to those it has already burnt?" (Tertullian, *The Resurrection Of the Body* I). These retorts do not, however, give a positive justification for the Christian practice of earth burial. They simply ridicule the pagan practices such as embalmment and cremation. There was no legalized prohibition against cremation and embalmment in Christian antiquity. None was needed, for the Christians by reason of their belief abhorred them. A very powerful motive for earth burial, as indicated above, was the burial of Christ Himself. Those who imitated Christ during their lives also wished to imitate Him in death and be buried after the manner of His burial. The desire to give the body back to earth, whence it had its origin, was another reason for preferring earth burial. In this connection, Lactantius says; "We will not allow the image and workmanship of God to lie as a prey for animals and birds, but we will return it to the earth whence it came" (Lantantius, *Divine Institution VI*, 12, 30). Still a third reason for the Christian practice of earth burial was respect for the body as the workmanship of God. Tertullian attests that there were some who abstained from undergoing cremation out of deference to the soul; and then he shows that respect for the body should prohibit such a procedure. In this connection, he says: "And yet certain men still hold to this opinion (belief in the partial survival of the soul). Hence they say that the body should not be cremated, intending thereby to spare what remains of the soul. There is another reason for this pious practice, not as if meant favoring the relics of the soul, but as if averting cruelty even in regard to the body; since being human, it certainly does not deserve to have such a punishment inflicted upon it" (Tertullian, *On the Soul* 51, 4). Moreover, in Christian thought the body was looked upon as something sacred. The soul, supernaturalized by sanctifying grace, had dwelt in it and the body was considered as a temple of the Holy Ghost (I Cor. 3:16; 6:19). It had cooperated as the instrument of the soul in the work of the sanctification and redemption of the deceased. Therefore, reverence for the body as the instrument of the soul was another motive for not subjecting the body to the funeral pyre. Origen brings this out when he says; "It is the reasonable soul which we honor, and we commit its bodily organs with due honours to the grave. For it is not right that the dwelling place of the rational soul should be cast aside anywhere without honor, like the carcasses of beasts; and so much the more when we believe that the respect paid to the body redounds to the honor of the person who has received from God a soul which has nobly employed the organs of the body in which it resided" (Origen, *Against Celsus VIII*, 30). St Augustine brings this out when he says; "The bodies of the dead are not on this account to be despised and cast aside; least of all the bodies of the just and faithful, which the spirit has holily employed as organs and instruments for all good works" (Augustine, *The City of God* I,13). The main reason for burying the dead in the earth was respect for the body that was one day to rise in glory from the tomb. Rush (1941:250) is of the view that although respect for the body which was to rise formed the basis for the practice of burying the dead in the earth, the Christians were convinced that it made no difference how they met death or in what way their bodily remains were disposed of. They knew that nothing which might befall them would prevent their resurrection. So unconcerned was St Ignatius the Martyr about the manner in which his body was disposed of that he wrote to the Romans: "Suffer me to be eaten by the beasts, through whom I may attain to God. I am God's wheat, so let me be ground by the teeth of wild beasts that I may be found to be the pure bread of Christ. Rather entice the wild beasts that they may become my tomb and leave no trace of my body that when I fall asleep I be not burdensome to any. Then shall I truly be a disciple of Jesus Christ when the world shall not even see my body" (Ignatius, *The Letter to Romans* 4, 1-2). Rush (1941:253) indicates that St Augustine is at pains to bring out that nothing the enemy might do to the body could prevent its future resurrection. Therefore, he wrote: "The earth has not covered the body of many a Christian, but nothing has separated a one of them from heaven and earth which is filled with the presence of Him who knows whence He will raise up what He has created" (Augustine, *The City of God*, I, 12). The pagans however were convinced that the Christian practice of burying their dead in the earth was prompted by their fear of not rising from the dead. Therefore, out of the hatred for this Christian belief, they did all in their power to prevent the bodies of the martyrs from being buried. Various tortures were devised by which their bodies would be completely destroyed (Mbugua 2011:28-40; Bercot 1998:427-32 and 509-14; Austin 1983:59-66). It was in this way that the pagans hoped to thwart their future resurrection. Condemning the cruelty of Romans persecuting Christians and even denying them a place to bury their dead, Lactanius (c.AD 304-313) wrote with bitterness: "No one can fittingly describe the cruelty of this beast (i.e. Rome) that . . . not only tears in pieces the limbs of men, but also breaks their very bones and rages over them with ashes—so that there will be no place for their burial. As though those who confess God aimed at this: that their tombs would be visited rather than that they themselves may reach the presence of God. What brutality it is! What fury, what madness! To deny light to the living and earth to the dead" (Bercot 1998:81).

The Christian Vale

As the Christian outlook on death was different from that of the pagans, so too was the departing ceremony at the grave especially touching on the words of farewell spoken at the funeral. The farewell greetings of the Christians to their dead are preserved in the funeral inscriptions, and these form a decided antithesis to the farewell wishes of the pagans. The farewell prayers of the Christians manifest a vivid belief in the fact that death, instead of being the end of life, is in reality the beginning of true life. The Christians adopted the practice of pronouncing a funeral oration before the assembly of the faithful over those who had been honored by the church. It was natural for the Christian bishops to clothe their funeral orations in the form and style of the orators and writers of the day. If the Christian bishops were to sow the seed of Christianity and to make their influence felt on the learned who were coming under the influence of Christianity, they saw that it was necessary to clothe their instructions, sermons and funeral orations in the form of pagan oratory, for the people of that time looked upon everything as inferior which was not preached in the popular style of the times. Norden (1898: Vol II, 516), says that for Christianity to expand and make its influence felt on the learned, it was necessary for the leaders of the new religion to adapt themselves to the style of the times which was dominated by the sophists; and it was in this way that the teachings of Christianity were to be proposed to the pagan world. Thus Norden says that the good news of Christianity was received in the language of fishermen, but was proposed in that of the Sophists (Norden 1898: Vol II, 516).

Place and Mode of Burial

As indicated earlier, the body was carried to the grave on a bier borne by pallbearers. At the grave, hymns and prayers were renewed, and followed by an address from the bishop or clergy (Smith & Cheetham 1875:253). Either in the church or at the grave it was customary, as early as the fourth century to have a celebration of the Eucharist in token of the communion that still existed between the living and the dead. With these were united special prayers for the soul of the departed. The priest first, and afterwards other friends, gave the corpse the last kiss of peace (Dionys. *Arcop. Hierarch, Eccles*, C.7). They (1875:253) further advise that as observed earlier, for some centuries in spite of repeated prohibitions by councils of the church, the practice prevailed in Northern Africa, in Gaul (France) and in the East, of placing the consecrated bread itself, steeped in the wine, within the lips of the dead. When the body was lowered into the grave it was with the face turned upwards and with the feet towards the east in token of the sure and certain hope of the coming of the Sun of Righteousness and the resurrection of the dead (Chrysostom *St. Hon*. CXVi. t. Vi). They (1875:253) further indicate that the insignia of office, if the deceased had held any such position—gold and silver ornaments, in the case of private persons—were often flung into the open grave, and the waste and ostentation to which this led had to be checked by an imperial edict (*Cod. Theodos*. XI. tit.7,1.14), which does not, however, seem to have been very rigidly enforced. The ancient practice of a solemn prayer while the first handfuls of earth were thrown on the coffin, is not, according to them (1875:253), traceable to any early period. When the grave was closed, the service ended with the LORD'S prayer and benediction.

While expressing views that are similar to the above, but more elaborate, Childers (1997:443), observes that once the bearers had laid down the bier at the burial site, family members bestowed a final kiss upon the brow or lips of the deceased making an acclamation of farewell. Prayers were said for the deceased, perhaps a eulogy, and in some cases the Eucharist was cerebrated on their behalf. The survivors sometimes adorned the grave with flowers. The wealthier a person was, the more elaborate the tomb or monument was likely to be. In Christian thought, the burial was a *deposition,* a temporary placement of the person until the day of resurrection—the term appears in many Christian funerary inscriptions. Christians nearly always practised inhumation, not cremation. As with non-Christians' burials personal items were often buried with the body. Children's burials sometimes included toys. From the fifth century, martyrs' relics became popular burial accoutrements. During the fourth to the seventh centuries, the body was sometimes buried with the elements of the Eucharist on its chest or in its mouth. He (1997:443) indicates further that the burial was followed by a funerary meal, the *refrigerium*. Family or friends tended the grave of the deceased. On special days, such as the anniversary of the death, they might adorn the grave with flowers or lanterns, or even anoint it with oil. By the fourth century, it was common to pronounce regular prayers for the dead. Especially in the case of martyrs, lists of the dead were maintained in churches for the purpose of prayer. Celebrations commemorating the deceased took place periodically at the site of the burial, perhaps in a chapel below ground or in gardens above ground. The latter were landscaped occasionally around a grave or *martyrium*. Such gardens were associated with the concept of *paradeisos,* the blissful Eden of eternity. In most of these practices, the influence of contemporary non-Christian practice is evident. Yet Christian optimism about the state of the righteous soul after death transformed the context of typical funerary practices, so that they took on distinctive meaning. He (1997:443) advises that this is nowhere more obvious than in the hopeful funerary inscriptions and artwork adorning Christian places of burial, which stand in contrast to the cynical—even bitter—funerary inscriptions left by non-Christians. Moreover, Christian faith and charity provided help for the living; the assurance of an honorable funeral and a dignified burial regardless of one's social standing and provision for the welfare of survivors. Habenstein and Lamers (1963:61) indicate that no regulation required that the dead must be buried in a coffin. They further advise that the early canon law laid down simple requirements for the burial of the dead, asking only that the body should be buried in consecrated ground. A decree of the council of Auxerre held in AD 578 forbade the priest to bestow the ceremonial kiss upon the dead and prohibited the practice of clothing the corpse in rich raiment (Ibid., 61). As indicated earlier, early Christianity preferred very simple burials. Sumptuousness in funeral arrangement was frequently condemned. Giving an example of such condemnations Rowell (1977:24) observes that Augustine, for instance warns against imitating lavish funeral rites for the rich, who expire on ivory beds and are borne to the graves amidst the mourning of their entire household establishment (Enarrati in Ps 33 (2), 14). Regarding exorbitant funeral charges by lay priests or churches, the church fathers condemned such practices.

Burial options of Christians did not come into use overnight. The chosen burial option of the early Christian and Jewish communities in Rome itself was the catacomb, located, as were all Greco-Roman burial sites, outside the city walls. Davies (1999:191-2) states that the Roman catacombs varied in origin, being sometimes the "linking-up" of smaller hypogea or smaller, older, underground burial sites, sometimes the adaptation of old watercourses, cisterns and quarries. We learn from him further that there is evidence, for both Jews and Christians, that the larger catacombs were designed and purpose-built. Eventually, over a thousand kilometres of galleries extended under the outskirts of Rome, providing burial space for something in the order of six million people (Shaw 1996:101). Davies (1999:192) is of the view that construction, even underground, on this scale could not have been "invisible" to either the authorities or the populace of Rome, so there cannot be much sense in the idea that the catacombs were dug to hide funerals and bodies.

Jews and Christians, in their respective catacombs, over the late second to early fifth century CE, buried their dead in either *loculi* of about six feet by two feet by two feet cut into the walls of the galleries, giving a "beehive" effect, or in *cubicula*, (chambers with benches covering the actual graves) for two or more burials. Decorative effect might be enhanced by an arch over the benches, producing an *arcosolium*, a mini-temple effect (Shaw 1996:101; Ferrua 1991:19-21). It is indicated further that the *loculi* were, for both the religious groups; the most used form of interment, followed by the *arcosolia*, and then *forma* (straight into the ground), *sarcophagi* and *amphora* (Davies 1999:193).

Some of the Christian catacombs were highly decorated, using biblical motifs. In contrast, the main Jewish catacombs were, until late on, relatively undecorated (no "graven images") (Rutgers 1995:56). Inscriptions, for both sects, were in Greek. Burials were of full-body cadavers: neither Jews nor Christians allowed cremation. Davies (1999:193) observes that while the catacombs of Jews and Christians looked very similar, they were exclusive: Jews in their tombs, Christians in theirs, more apart, perhaps, in death than they were in life. Indeed, in death contradicting, to some extent, the inevitable interaction between the diverse faiths and ethnic groups of cosmopolitan Rome.

He (1999:193) writes that at the end of the fourth century CE, especially after the peace of the church brought by the conversion of Constantine, Christians began to abandon the Roman catacombs, and above-ground Christian burial sites associated with churches began to appear within city walls, proclaiming the new and dominant status of Christianity. This move, architecturally very visible—whereas the catacombs were both hidden and extramural—is associated with two other aspects of Christian life in the late Roman Empire. These were the development of the cult of the martyred saints of the periods of persecution and the exigencies of church government and administration in the periods of tolerance and eventual supremacy.

It is worth noting that the original name for the Christian churches was "martyries", and these buildings became the shrines of civic, localized cultic worship and pilgrimage. Also worthy of note is that in this sense, and in this sense only, the cult provided some continuity with the civic and localized cults of paganism (Ibid., 193).

As Fontaine (1989:213) said, the nature of the Christian beliefs about death produces in late antiquity the image of Christian witness, of the dead colonizing the cities of the living. The dead of all other religious cultures had been kept outside the city walls. Progressively there developed the familiar image of a Christian church located at the centre of the city, town, or village, with attendant graveyard and, for important or martyred saintly Christians, burial within the church itself in a shrine, the whole being frequently placed on top of older, defeated pagan religious and burial sites (Deroche 1989:2713-26). Painter (1989:2049) feels that by the end of Ancient Christianity, the Christian dead had indeed colonized the central places of the living. Even where extramural cemeteries were maintained, Christians proclaimed their separate and theologically different status. An example of this is at Poundbury near Dorchester (United Kingdom), a huge fourth century CE Christian cemetery with about 4,500 interments, which is clearly separated from the adjacent pagan burial area. It is further noted that the Christians were buried naked other than for their burial shrouds. The pagans on the other hand were fully clothed and equipped with grave-goods. Thus, in death, in dress separation was absolute (Davies (1999:193).

As emphasized by Brown (1981:7) there was a rather different but parallel process to the "urbanizing of the dead" going on in the eastern parts of the Empire. Here, the shrines of the martyrs were either located in extramural cemeteries, which became in effect "cities of the dead", or in remote desert places, where they became places of pilgrimage, associated with monastic and ascetic styles of Christianity, somewhat at odds with the this-worldly concerns of the growing number of bishops and other functionaries of the nascent church. There are, therefore, surely twin developments, together saying to the pagan world that it was through its dead that the new religion lived—and it was the colonization of the cities by the dead, which was the most startling reversal of ancient practice. This is how as indicated by Brown (1981:7) Julian the Apostate saw it, when with increasing fury he sought to rid the Roman Empire of the new religion in whose practices he saw the ruin of Rome:

> "You keep adding many corpses newly dead to the corpses of long ago. You have filled the whole world with tombs of sepulchres . . . The carrying of the corpses of the dead through a great assembly of people, in the midst of dense crowds, staining the eyes of all with ill—omened sights of the dead. What day so touched with death could be lucky? How, after being present at such ceremonies, could anyone approach the gods and their temples? (Julian, in Brown 1981:7)."

Davies (1999:195) indicates that the corpses of the newly dead referred to above were those of the martyrs and saints, often the same people.

Early Christians did not insist on being buried in the ancestral land or place of birth, nor burial with their close relatives. This contention is supported by Miles (1990:620), where she indicates that Augustine's mother, St Monica, at the end of her life, shared with Augustine the mystical experience recorded in *Confessions* 9.10. Important and of great relevance to this book is that St Monica died at Ostia, Italy and that she no longer insisted on burial with her husband, as she was confident of resurrection. This contention is further supported by Rowell (1977:24) who indicates that St Augustine (*Confessions* IX) records Monica's own wishes for the manner of her burial. For she, when the day of her death drew near, did not want her body to be sumptuously adorned, or embalmed with spices, nor desired any special monument, or to be buried in her own land. She did not recommend these things to us, but desired only to be remembered at the altar where she used to assist continuously without even a break of a single day.

It is my wish and prayer that all committed Christians should adopt such conviction and attitude that their mode of burial or where they are buried should not matter, but rather that they might be certain of resurrection when they will rise from their rest and be given a new spiritual body.

Christian Burial From the Middle Ages

Although this chapter as will be observed in chapter 1 of this book was intended to be a survey and analysis of burial rites for the early Christians from AD 33 to AD 600, I felt as my research for this book progressed that it would be prudent and appropriate to comment briefly on the Christian mode of coping with death in later centuries of Christianity. This, I further feel, has some bearing on this book especially in relation to what the European Christian missionaries introduced to their Agikuyu and other African Christian converts when they made contact with them.

According to Caspari (1911:309), the western church of the Middle Ages also knew only earth burial as a means of disposal of the dead. Charlemagne (AD 768-814) forbade the conquered Saxons to cremate corpses, on pain of death. The place in which a Christian was buried was considered holy ground. Patrons or spiritual dignitaries were entombed in churches as a token of distinction. Every Christian was to be buried in consecrated ground, but if special emergencies, like war or shipwreck, necessitated a burial in unconsecrated ground, the grave had to be provided with a cross. The dead were washed, dressed in linen or penitential robes, or, in case of one in holy orders, in official dress. On the day of the funeral he was carried by his peers, the layman by laymen, and the clergy by clergy; first to the church, where mass was celebrated, and afterwards to the grave, in which he was laid, with his face turned towards the east. Various ceremonies had their specific meaning; the holy water sprinkled on the body protected it from demons; charcoal indicated the presence of a grave at that spot, and thus kept it from profanation; incense kept away the odour of decay, and was a symbol of prayer for the dead, also implying that he was a sacrifice well pleasing to God; ivy and laurel symbolized the imperishable life of those who die in Christ (Ibid., 309).

The custom of throwing three shovelfuls of earth upon the body was known in the Middle Ages, although it appears that the present Roman ritual does not mention it. The modern Roman Catholic Church has retained the old Christian view that the death of children who have been baptized is a joyful event, and that their burial should have the character of joy. As far as protestant churches are concerned, the Reformation totally removed the existing burial rites, insofar as they presupposed the doctrines of purgatory, mass and the meditation of the church, but it adhered to the view that the dead body is not a worthless thing, but is to rise again, no matter how it had decayed. For this reason it should have a Christian burial and the burial-places must have a fitting appearance. The burial was a matter for the church, and the congregation should take part in it, if possible, and should also attend the funerals of the poor. Accordingly, bells called the congregation together (Ibid., 309).

The church was represented by the minister, also present were schoolchildren, the sexton and the grave-digger. As the procession was moving to the cemetery, the children or the mourners sang Christian funeral hymns, and at the grave such biblical passages as 1 Thessalonians 4:13-18 or John 11 were read and prayer was offered, while basins were also placed to receive alms for the poor. In some countries, the congregation recited the creed after the closing prayer. The desire to instruct the congregation on every occasion was expressed in the burial service by the reading of scriptures and the singing of hymns. A short discourse on death and the resurrection was read in the home, in the church, or at the grave, although a special sermon might be requested from the minister if he was specially paid for it, and in such cases, he referred particularly to the life and death of the subject of his address. Thus arose the funeral sermon, which was originally designed to instruct the congregation in eschatology, and to honor the memory of the departed (Ibid., 309).

Conclusion

As shown in various sections of this chapter, and as so well indicated by Brigham (1979:558), contrary to the pagan convictions that proper burial was essential for an individual's happiness in the afterlife, the early Christians insisted that this was not so (St Augustine, *The City of God* 1, 12). Nevertheless, out of reverence for the body as the temple of the Holy Spirit and in view of the future resurrection, they were zealous in their care for the dead. The first Christians naturally followed Jewish burial customs, although as shown in Chapter 4 of this book, the Jewish funeral practices were not normative. The said Jewish funeral customs were later modified under the influence of local practices and Christian hope. Also shown in this chapter and worthy of note, is that the early Christian fathers did not issue explicit mandate as to how the Christians ought to cope with death. Rather they went to greath lengths to give advice on how they felt Christians should conduct themselves when coping with various issues touching on their lives, and in this case how they ought to deal with issues surrounding death.

Numerous differences have emerged in this book on how the early Christians coped with death and how the current Agikuyu Christians are buried. What has been discussed in this chapter are the numerous ways of coping with death practiced by the early Christians, most of which are not practiced or known by the present-day Africans including the Agikuyu

Christians. These issues will be analyzed and some recommendations made in chapters 7 and 8 for adoption by the Agikuyu and other African Christians.

Chapter 6, which follows, will analyze the issue of the resurrected body; it will dwell mainly on scriptural analyzes and a literature review of resurrection and resurrected body. The aim of chapter 6 will be to establish whether it will be our earthly bodies that will be resurrected or whether we will be given new spiritual bodies which will have nothing to do with the material substance of our earthly bodies. Also to be discussed will be the effect cremation has on the resurrected body, and whether the view held by a considerable number of Agikuyu Christians as well as by other Africans and members of the Christian community worldwide, that their body, if cremated, will result in the inability of it to be resurrected is justified. An attempt will be made to come up with an acceptable explanation and persuasion to remove such antipathy.

CHAPTER 6

THE ISSUES OF THE RESURRECTION AND OF THE RESURRECTED BODY

Introduction

THIS CHAPTER AIMS AT exploring what the scripture, early Christian fathers, theologians and scholars have said about the resurrection and also about the resurrected body. Additionally to analyze the findings obtained and subsequently to attempt to establish whether what will have been presented has in any way influenced or shaped the present-day Agikuyu Christian and other Africans funeral rites. Additionally this chapter will address how to overcome the aversion to cremation which is apparently felt by a good number of Africans, other Christians on the globe and in this case by the Agikuyu Christians.

The methodology applied in this chapter as far as scriptural matters are concerned will be that of a more selective treatment of Biblical theology i.e. it will be of lesser scope than the one applied when doing Biblical theology in the previous chapter (4) which dwelt on biblical study of burial practices. This is so as this chapter will aim, as indicated above, at exploring what scripture has to say about the resurrection and more specifically about the resurrected body. A canonical approach will be utilized as far as scriptural matters are concerned. This approach is as was indicated and expounded at considerable length in chapter (4). The analysis of what scholars and theologians have said about the resurrection and the resurrected body will involve an in-depth literature review and analysis of their works. It is worthy of note that a more selective treatment of LIM model is applicable for this chapter. It is part of the third step of the LIM model which among others requires looking at theological classic and church teachings on burial rites. Resurrection of the body, as explained elsewhere in this book, is deemed necessary to be explained to the Agikuyu Christians and to most other Africans because of the aversion some have to cremation.

The Concept of Resurrection and its Development among the Jews and Christians

Johnston (2000:446) asserts that in the past scholars often suggested that post-exilic Israel absorbed Persian notions of resurrection and post mortem judgment. More recently, he asserts, some scholars have proposed an earlier influence from Canaanite notions of Ba'al as a dying and rising god, as shown in the Ugaritic texts. For example, J. Day according to Johnston traces this influence progressively, with the concept "demythologized" to refer to the nation in Hosea and Isaiah and "remythologized" to refer to individuals in Daniel. In contrast, Johnston further indicates that others argue for an inner-biblical development: reflection on God's creative power prompted belief in His recreative, resurrecting power. For instance, he (2000:446) observes that BC Ollenburger notes this strong motif in the second century martyr account of 2 Maccabees 7, and traces it back to the Old Testament. Johnston states that these approaches are not mutually exclusive and that it was the threat and then the reality of exile which led to the prophetic development of the motif, perhaps one already known from Canaanite religion(s). He, however, asserts that the development was a distinctly Israelite one—not of a dying and rising deity, but initially of a moribund and revived nation, and then of dead and resurrected individuals. Confirming this contention, Segal (2009:1979), indicates that "resurrection was an innovation in Hebrew thought".

Muller (1988:145), is of the view that Israel probably encountered the Persian belief in resurrection during the exile, when national hopes were lowest and the eschatological dimension of prophesy was strong. Yet even then, he contends, there was no wholesale appropriation of foreign belief, only a reinforcement of elements already in Israelite religion that pointed toward an eschatological culmination of the divine plan in a renewed Israel.

Expounding as to why and how the idea of the afterlife and resurrection originated and developed among the Jews, Schmid (1975:1445) observes, that the question has much been discussed, and has often been answered affirmatively, whether the influence of Zoroastrianism was operative in the origin and particularly in the further formation of the Jewish belief in the resurrection. Belief in the resurrection of the dead in Zoroastrianism is attested in Greek sources from the fourth century BC (Theopompos in Diogenes Laertius, Proem 9). The principal argument for assuming Zoroastrian influence is the connection between resurrection and judgment found in both cases. The possibility of such influence is of course admitted in principle. It must, however, be remembered that the fully developed concept of retribution and the problems to which it gives rise in the actual experience of life, provided the conditions for the rise of belief in the resurrection, yet this belief only appeared in Judaism at a time when the Palestinian Jews no longer lived under Persian but Greek rule (Ibid., 1445).

Davies (1999:110) asserts that in the 800 years or so bisected by the birth of Christ, "Jewish political and military structures were firstly extended and consolidated, then fractured in a civil war, then later on annihilated by Roman armies and subsumed into the Roman Empire as just another conquered territory". He writes that "as part of the process, whatever there might have been of Jewish political and religious unity was pulled apart. Consequently, the cultural and religious life of these centuries was characterized by a most exotic flourishing of rival sects and religious movements". He further asserts that "the world for the Jews turned upside down".

Davies (1999:111) further states that "in revolutionary times, people often die and have to be buried or otherwise disposed of. In such occurrences, epitaphs are produced during those occasions". He (1999:111) asserts that "epitaphs then as now, vary considerably". Some of them evidenced a blessing and the hope of life after death. Van der Horst (1991:37) and Davies (1999:111) indicate that during the period which they wrote about, 300 BCE to 700 CE, there was (and is) considerable controversy about both the nature and the development of Jewish beliefs in the afterlife or resurrection. There is no reason to believe either that there was uniformity on such matters or that any "official" policy was generally adhered to.

John Sawyer, according to Davies (1999:111), produces a very interesting observation when he indicates that with some methods of interpretation almost any verse in the Old Testament can provide support for the concept of the resurrection of the dead (Sawyer 1973:228). He (1999:111)asserts that the subject was a "'live issue" at the time of writing of the Targum, the Mishnah and the New Testament (231), and that it had assumed a "central position" from the second century BCE although there was powerful resistance to such an idea in both Jerusalem and Samaria (227). He (1999:111) observes that "the general expectation of an afterlife is most clearly stated in Sanhedrin in both the Mishnah and in the Babylonian Talmud, though again the general assurance is qualified by both the need for righteousness ("All Israel have a portion in the world to come, for it is written, 'thy people are all righteous'") and by an admonitory and minatory list of those who are to be excluded from the general resurrection" (*The Babylonian Talmud: Seder Nezekin*, 111, *Sanhedrin*, 601).

He (1999:111) writes that in "ordinary times" the comforting idea of an afterlife must have persisted as part of the funerary ethos of most Jews as they contemplated life and death. The Beth Shearim epitaph indicates, though, that there was perhaps a degree of uncertainty, as well as mordant wit, about the subject of an afterlife; Van der Horst's study of ancient Jewish epitaphs supports such a view.

Segal (2009:769), observes that "the First Temple period survived quite nicely without the idea of *anastasis*, (rise up), (resurrection)". He further advises that what was believed in this long period of time is a puzzle, because the early texts in the Bible have so little to say about afterlife in general. He goes on to say that 'Archaeological remains, which include grave-goods, suggest that there were popular notions of afterlife among the Israelites that differed very little from Canaanite customs". He (2009:769), further asserts that "where the text gives us details, it appears as though the dominant understanding of the afterlife in First Temple times was that the dead went to *SHEOL*". This according to Segal "was a dark place where all the dead went regardless of their moral or immoral life on earth" (compare Deut 32:22; Amos 9:2). He indicates that it "was not a reward or a punishment for anything". Segal notes "in the famous recall of Samuel from the dead (Sheol), Samuel said to Saul "Why have you disturbed me by bringing me up?"" (1 Sam 28:15).

Additionally, Segal asserts:

> "We find no extended discussion of the notion of life after death or the realm of the dead in biblical thought, not because it did not exist in popular Israelites thought probably, but because the Bible is reticent about opening the door to what it calls idolatry or the Canaanite veneration of spirit or ghosts (Segal 1997:92)."

Davies (1999:112) writes that political and military events were, though, tending towards a strengthening of a belief in an afterlife, and a differentiated afterlife at that. In the two centuries each side of the birth of Christ, he (1999:112) observes "war and death in war impinged more and more on "ordinary" life". As observed by Klassen (1992:869)Aelius Aristides, writing early in the second century of the Common Era, felt that war was a thing of the past and advises that for the 150 years or so which Aristides had in mind there had been about 200 wars in Palestine.

Millar (1993:348), referring to Cassius Dio's *Roman History*, describes the wars leading to the destruction of the temple and the transformation of the Jewish city of Jerusalem into the Roman city of Aelia Capitolina, and the Jewish land of Judea into the Roman province of Syria Palaestina. These wars, Davies claims resulted in the destruction of 50 Jewish fortresses, 985 villages and the deaths in battle alone of 580,000 Jewish men. Jewish prisoners of war were fed into the Roman arenas, either as play for the beasts or as gladiators forced to fight and to kill one another. The Romans systematically built or rebuilt "Greek" cities, fully equipped with public cultic and imperial sacred spaces and places. The territorial and missionary expansion of the Maccabeans was reversed. The Jews became a predominantly rural population. Davies (1999:112) observes that the culture and space of the one-time Jewish settlement area was subsumed into the general pagan world and practices of the Roman Empire. It was into this world, with that history, that Christianity emerged.

He (1999:114) observes that authors such as John Sawyer, Gila Rowland and Alan Segal see a radical change in the tenor of life in the 800 years or so bisected by the birth of Christ. "These years see a series of Jewish revolts, short-lived victories and long-term defeats. What to Aristides was the Pax Romana, was to the Jews in their several Judaisms the tyranny of an alien empire which oppressed and eventually destroyed the Jewish way of life—or perhaps the Jewish ways of life. Jewish history becomes a tragedy of such enormity that the rationality and sedateness of the biblical barriers to an extended discussion of death, of its place in creation and the role and the very point or purpose ('"the face") of God, are shattered' (Ibid., 115). "Jewish society is fragmented by war, destroyed by defeat in war, and when some kind of peace descends it is of a type that creates yet further problems of identity and orthodoxy, problems of fission as much as of fusion" (Ibid.,115).

Segal (1997:97) finds the first explicit reference to resurrection in the Hebrew Bible in Daniel 12:1-3. Daniel, writes Segal, can be dated quite accurately to 168 BCE, that is, to the period of the massacres and persecutions surrounding the Maccabean War. However, it is felt that this is the date held by liberal theologians which is not accepted by numerous other theologians such as the Evangelicals. This date has been criticised, as it is felt that it is built on a number of highly plausible fallacies (Unger 1988:276).

Young (1984:160) is of the view that traditionally, the Book of Daniel is considered a sixth century BCE document written by Daniel the Prophet. Young observes that "many evangelicals support this, but other scholars assign to it the date of 165 BCE and say the author is unknown". In this study, I accept and agree with the date of sixth century BCE. This date and view is supported by Pentecost (1985:1323).

Daniel 12:1-3 reads:

> "At that time Michael, the great prince, the protector of your people, shall arise. There shall be a time of anguish, such as has never occurred since nations first came into existence. But at that time your people shall be delivered, everyone who is found written in the book. Many of those who sleep in the dust of the earth [or 'the land of dust'] shall awake, some to everlasting life,

and some to shame and everlasting contempt. Those who are wise shall shine like the brightness of the sky, and those who lead many to righteousness, like the stars forever and ever" (Daniel 12: 1-3; Segal 1997: 97).

Resurrection—the Biblical Teaching

The Bible clearly promises the resurrection of the believers (Erickson 2005:1200). Byrum (1982:546-7) is of the view that the doctrine of resurrection of the dead is commonly believed by Christians, though there are differences of understanding concerning what is signified by the expression. Seely (2000:1120), indicates that "resurrection is the concept of a person being brought back from a mortal death to a state of immortality usually involving the reunification of the spirit or the soul with an immortal body". Seely further writes that "in the Old Testament, there is no single word for resurrection; in the New Testament the most common Greek term is *anastasis*, "rise up"". The Old Testament according to Erickson (2005:1200) gives several direct statements on resurrection, the first being Isaiah 26:19

> "But your dead will live;
> their bodies will rise.
> You who dwell in the dust,
> wake up and shout for joy.
> Your dew is like the dew of
> the morning,
> the earth will give
> birth to her dead" (cf. Ezek 37:1-14; Dan 12:2).

Likewise, Schmid (1975:1444), is of the view that the oldest testimony which is still primarily a profession of joyful belief in God's just rule is found in the "Apocalypse" of Isaiah (Isa 24-27). The restoration of the dead to life, Schmid asserts, is linked here with expectation of the time of salvation for the whole nation (i.e. the nation of Israel). To complete the redeemed community, the just dead must also be added.

However, Segal (2009:770), asserts that the imagery of resurrection (Isa 26:19; Ezek 37:1-14) appears in the Bible before the actuality of the promise. According to Segal, the first sure reference to resurrection occurs in Daniel 12:2, which is a prophecy of the end of time, and which is basic to all other Jewish, Christian and Muslim views of resurrection of both the believer and the wicked: "Multitudes who sleep in the dust of the earth will awake; some to everlasting life, others to shame and everlasting contempt".

The doctrine of resurrection, he (2009:772), feels, "is first securely manifested in Biblical writing in Daniel 12". He indicates further that "the resurrection may be generally defined as the doctrine that after death the body will be reconstituted and revivified by God as a reward for the righteous and/or faithful".

Segal asserts further that "it is one thing to know that God has promised resurrection to the righteous faithful in Daniel, presumably in his own way and at the appropriate time, and another to express what exactly happened to Jesus on the first Easter and how those who heard his message might gain the same reward".

He further indicates that "the most famous of preparatory prophecy of resurrection is Ezekiel 37:1-14". These passages, he states, are "where the prophet envisions corpses being reassembled from their bones to become fully realised human beings on earth".

This vivid description of the dead being reassembled in their flesh he asserts "seems like it is the parade example of resurrection but careful reading reveals that it is merely a metaphor for the prophecy, a vision that does not prophesy the future, but signifies that the prophet's own preaching of the Spirit will soon reanimate the people who are depressed and demoralised by exile". He is further of the view that "rather than personal immortality it is the more relevant consolation that, although punished, God has not left them (i.e. the Israelites) and continues to guide Israelites' existence".

The above view is also held by, among others, Schmid (1975:1444), who asserts that "in Ezekiel 37:1-14, the resurrection of the dead bones does not, it is true, signify the resurrection of the dead abiding in Sheol, but the restoration of the nation". He goes on to indicate that "the revivification described by Ezekiel actually takes place in the living, not in the dead; for the dead bones signify the nation in the "dead condition" of exile, to which a return home is promised".

Regarding the issue of dry bones Browning 2009:197; Young 1984:112; Ungers 1988:178; Willmington 1987:220; 1981:112; Dyer 1985:1298, give similar interpretations regarding Ezekiel 37 as the one given by Schmid above. They advise that the dry bones of Ezekiel's vision represent the scattered Israelites in exile, and their coming together represents the regathering and coming to life again of Israel as a nation. Likewise, according to Seely (2000:1121), two passages directly allude to resurrection in the context of national resurrection (Ezek 37:13-14; and Hos 6:1-2).

The views and comments expressed above touching on the dry bones should be of paramount interest and significance to most Christians who hitherto thought and believed that since the dry bones mentioned in Ezekiel 37 rose to life and were filled with flesh, so likewise when people die, at the resurrection the bones of the dead will rise up, be filled with flesh, and those bodies will come back to life although spiritually. From my discussions with numerous African Christians and others, this notion of dry bones of the dead being filled with flesh and coming to life has contributed in no small measure to a substantial number of Christians, and in this case the Agikuyu Christians, insisting on earth burial as opposed to being cremated. They are convinced that it is their earthly bodies that at the resurrection will rise from the grave. They are therefore reluctant to have their bodies cremated.

On this issue, Mitchiner (2011:11) observes that 'there are Christians who object to the practice of cremation. Their arguments are based on the Biblical concept that one day the bodies of those who have died in Christ will be resurrected and reunited with their souls and spirits'. This teaching according to Mitchiner "assumes that if a body has been destroyed by fire (or by any other means, I may add), it is impossible for it to be resurrected later and reunited to the soul and spirit". This contention is however contrary to the following two verses from scripture:

> "(1 Cor 15:35-55)
> It is the same way for the resurrection of the dead. Our earthly bodies are planted in the ground when we die, but they will be raised to live forever. Our bodies are buried in brokenness, but they will be raised in glory. They are buried in weakness, but they will be raised in strength. They are buried as natural human bodies, but they will be raised as spiritual bodies. For just as there are natural bodies, there are also spiritual bodies ... then, when our dying bodies have been transformed into bodies that will never die, this Scripture will be fulfilled: 'Death is swallowed up in victory. O death, where is your victory? O death, where is your sting?"
> (Excerpt Verses 42-44; 54-55 NLT)

> (1 Thes 4:16)
> "For the Lord himself will come down from heaven, with a loud command, with the voice and with the trumpet call of God, and the dead in Christ will rise first" (NIV).

Schmid asserts, as explained earlier, that a considerable further step is taken in the Maccabean period, in Daniel 12:2: "Many of those who sleep in the dust shall awake, some to everlasting life, the others to shame and everlasting abhorrence. The teachers of the law shall shine like the brightness of the firmament and those who have instructed many in righteousness, like the stars for ever and ever". This passage is not merely much more definite than the previous one. It is also distinguished from the former by the fact that not only the just but also the impious will rise again. The reference is to the martyrs of the time of persecution under Antiochus IV Epiphanes, when many Jews suffered death for their faith, and to their persecutors. He observes that there is no thought of a general resurrection, nor of the great figures of the ancient history of Israel. It is also clear that it is not God's power alone which is to be manifested thereby, but also his retributive justice.

As pointed out by Seely (2000:1120-1), evidence for belief in resurrection in the Old Testament is scarce and often ambiguous. He indicates that as God formed man's body from the dust of the earth and gave him life by breathing the breath of life into him (Gen 2:7), so upon death the breath leaves the body and the body returns to the dust (Ps 104:29).

He advises further that the realm of the dead in the Old Testament is Sheol which is described as a dark and gloomy place, a place where the dead are separated from the living and God (Ps 6:5; 30:9; 88:1-12; 115:17), where they are forgotten (Ps 88:14; Eccl 3:19-21; 9:5-10) and as a final destination and a place "of no return" (Job 7:9-10; 16:22; Isa 38:10). On the other hand, he points out "several texts describe the power of God over Sheol (Job 12:22; 26:6; Ps 139:8; Prov 15:11; Amos 9:2) and that the LORD will deliver from Sheol (Ps 49:15)". Additionally, Seely notes "several passages specifically allude to YHWH's power over death (Deut 32:29; Sam 2:6; Isa 25:4)".

In addition to direct statements on resurrection, Erickson (2005:1201) indicates that the Old Testament intimates that "we can expect deliverance from death or Sheol". Erickson is of the view that this verse is supported by Psalm 49:15 which says "But God will redeem my life from the grave; he will surely take me to Himself". Erickson goes on to advice that "while there is no statement about the body in this passage, there is an expectation that the incomplete existence in Sheol will not be our final condition".

Smith (1975:449), is of the view that "whatever be the exact translation of the difficult passage in Job 19:26-27, here is deep conviction of the truth of resurrection from the dead" (cf Job 14:13-15).

It is worthy of note that Psalm 17:15 speaks of awaking in the presence of God: "And I—in righteousness I will see your face; when I awake, I will be satisfied with seeing your likeness". Some expositors according to Erickson (2005:1201) see similar intimations in Psalm 73:24-25 and Proverbs 23:14, although the latter is questionable (Berkhof 1981:721).

Job 14:12 asks "if a man die, shall he live again?" Job answers: "All the days of my appointed time will I wait till my change come. Thou shalt call and I will answer thee ... " Killen (1975:1460), observes that in Chapter 19, Job takes up the subject again. Job knows his redeemer lives and will stand upon the earth in the latter days and he is sure that even though worms destroy his body in the grave yet "from" his flesh and with his own eyes he will see God at that time (Job 19:25-27). He further asserts that both LXX and Jerome support the view that Job is referring to his future resurrection. However, numerous scholars have given differing views on the interpretation and meaning of Job 19:25-7. For example, Schilling (1970:758), indicates "the text of Job 19:25 is unfortunately corrupt, with the result that although the Vulgate takes it as referring to the resurrection, this interpretation has not been so far confirmed".

Segal (2009:780-1), states that "there are a few ambiguous places where Sheol is depicted as being under the power of God (Job 8:3-7; 26:6; Ps 139:8; Amos 9:2). These passages underline the constant biblical refrain that God is the only God. They contradict the notion that Sheol contains no presence of God. It is hard to know whether this represents an evolutionary step in the development of monotheism or merely an alternative poetic trope that the psalmists and prophets could use. In these passages YHWH is God of the living and the dead, of this world and the next". He feels that "the statements are probably part of the biblical polemic against other gods, in this case, against the notion that there is another god who is "lord of the underworld". Psalms 49:15 and 73:26 seem to suggest that the good will remain with God forever, and this may imply the beginning of a new notion of life after death, even as early as the First Temple period, but it is only a hint, and Psalms and Job are particularly difficult to date. It would be incautious to conclude that this demonstrates resurrection or any specific notion of afterlife". Note should be taken that Segal's view on the evolution of monotheism discussed above is a distinctly liberal idea. As for an Evangelical reading of scripture, there was no "evolutionary development of monotheism". God revealed Himself as the one and only God from the beginning.

"While we must exercise care not to read too much of the New Testament revelation of resurrection into the Old Testament", Erickson (2005:1201) warns, "it is significant to observe that Jesus and the New Testament writers maintained that the Old Testament teaches resurrection". He observes further that "when questioned by the Sadducees, who denied the resurrection, Jesus accused them of error due to lack of knowledge and scriptures and of the power of God (Mark 12:24), and then went on to argue for the resurrection on the basis of the Old Testament: "How about the dead rising—have you not read in the book of Moses, in the account of the bush, how God said to him, "I am the God of Abraham, and God of Isaac, and the God of Jacob"? He is not the God of the dead, but of the living. You are badly mistaken" (vv 26-27).He further asserts that "Peter (Acts 2:24-32) and Paul (Acts 13:32-27) saw Psalms 16:10 as a prediction of the resurrection of Jesus. Hebrews 11:19 commends Abraham's belief in God's ability to raise persons from the dead". Additionally, he is of the view that "Abraham reasoned that God could raise the dead, and figuratively speaking, he did receive Isaac back from death".

Resurrection, asserts Segal (2009:772), is central to Christianity in a way that it is not to any other of the first century sects of Judaism. Regarding this contention, he is further of the opinion that "because the resurrection of Christ was experienced as an event for the early Jesus movement, Christianity needed to define what resurrection was in a way that was not necessary to other Jews in the first century CE".

Centrality of Resurrection in the New Testament

Belief in the bodily resurrection of Jesus Christ is central to the Christian faith (Perkins 1997:979). It is so foundational to the faith that the apostle Paul viewed both faith and preaching as futile if Christ were not raised (1 Cor 15:14). From the Christian viewpoint, "the resurrection of Jesus Christ was the most significant event in history" (Root 2001:596). Why is the resurrection so crucial? First, the resurrection validates Jesus Christ's claims about being God and Savior. Second the resurrection establishes the truth of the gospel. Jesus's death secured our forgiveness and his resurrection our justification (Rom 4:25). It is the resurrection of Christ that assures us that our salvation was really accomplished at Calvary (Morris, 1962:1086-9). If Christ did not rise, our sins are not forgiven (1 Cor 15:14, 17). Third, the resurrection of Christ serves as both the pledge and the paradigm for the bodily resurrection of believers (Harris 1988:581; cf. 1 Cor 6:14; 15:20, 23, 48-9; Col 1:18). If Jesus did not rise, neither shall we, but if Jesus rose, we shall rise as he did (Morris 1962:1088). Thus the resurrection of Christ establishes both the fact that we shall rise from the dead, and the form in which we shall rise.

As expressed by Harris (1988:581-2), five types of resurrection may be distinguished in New Testament usage: "(1) the past physical resurrection of certain individuals to renewed mortal life (e.g. Luke 7:14-15; John 11:43-44; Heb 11:35); (2) the past bodily resurrection of Christ to immortality (Rom 6:9); (3) the past spiritual resurrection of believers to new life in Christ (Col 2:12); (4) the future bodily resurrection of believers to immortality (1 Cor 15:42, 52); (5) the future personal resurrection of unbelievers to judgement (John 5:29; Acts 24:15)". However, Harris (1988:581-2), asserts that occasionally resurrection refers to mere reanimation, but it generally also implies transformation (1 Cor 15:52, "raised immortal") and exaltation (Acts 2:32-33; 5:30-31). In its fullest sense, resurrection is God's raising of persons from the realm of the dead to new and unending life in His presence. It is an event leading to a state (Harris 1988:581). The resurrection of Christ is a central item in the New Testament Kerygma, the proclamation of Good News (Purkiser 1983:452). The apostle Paul declares it to be a crucial truth without which faith is worthless and sin is without remedy (1 Cor 15:12-19). He is further of the view that "against all efforts to "spiritualize" or "demythologize" the resurrection, the New Testament clearly indicates that the body of the crucified LORD was raised from the dead and ascended into heaven, leaving behind an empty tomb and a believing Church".

The New Testament indicates that Christ's resurrection is the prototype and guarantee of ours (John 14:19; 1 Cor 15:21-26) and His resurrected and glorified body is our best clue to the nature of the eternal state of the redeemed (1 Cor 15:49-15; Phil 3:20-21; 1 John 3:1-3). The resurrection of Christ is for the above reasons evident in scripture as few other facts are (Purkiser 1983:453).

Theologically, he (1983:453), advises that "the Resurrection is central to Christology as well as soteriology or doctrine of salvation. Without the Resurrection, Jesus was a martyr; with it, He is "declared with power to be the Son of God'" (Rom 1:4, NIV). "The Resurrection was the Father's seal on both Christ's life and teachings, and His atoning death" (Acts 17:31) (cf Killen 1975:1459; Smith 1975:451-2; Morris 1962:1086-9).

As observed by Killen (1975:1459), the resurrection of Christ is historically attested by: (1) the fact of the sudden changes in the lives of the apostles. It is worthy of note that the eleven were "cowards" at the crucifixion, but men ready to give their very lives 50 days later at Pentecost; (2) the descent of the Holy Spirit on the day of Pentecost, in fulfilment of Jesus' promise (John 14:16; 15:26; 16:7; cf. 7:37-39; Acts 2:32-3); (3) the changing of the day of worship from the Jewish Sabbath to the first day of the week as a testimony to the day upon which Christ arose; (4) the sudden and amazing growth of the Christian Church; (5) the existence of the New Testament whose very message hinges upon the authenticity of resurrection.

The bodily resurrection of Jesus is the best attested event in ancient history (Ibid., 1459). As pointed out by Killen, Tenney sums up that "the resurrection is relevant to the human need for purpose of assurance ... The event is fixed in history; the dynamic is potent for eternity".

Denials of Resurrection

Irrespective of the concrete proof of resurrection analyzed in the above section, several theories have been suggested which deny the bodily resurrection of Christ (Killen 1975:1458). It is worthy of note that "critics of Christianity have often concentrated their criticism on the resurrection" (Root 2001:596). He asserts that "Christian faith does not centre on a set of mere moral principles nor does it give checklists or formulas for successful living". The Christian faith, he feels, centres on the fact that man is fallen and in desperate need of repair. The death and resurrection of Jesus Christ as an historical event provides the means for forgiveness of sins, reconciliation with God, and beginning of the believers' pilgrimage toward the complete restoration of the image of Christ (Rom 8:28-29). Detractors attack the historic event of the resurrection in order to minimize the doctrines which are substantiated by it.

Giving illustrations of the various attempts to explain away the resurrection, he, (2001:597), observes that they began soon after the event took place. "The Gospels record that the religious leaders paid the soldiers who had guarded the tomb of Jesus to say that while they were sleeping the disciples came and stole the body (Matt 28:11-15)". Of course, sleeping soldiers could hardly be convincing, testifying to what occurred while they were fast asleep. Throughout the ages other suggestions have been attempted to explain away the empty tomb. G.D. Yarnold suggested that the body simply decayed over time through natural processes (*Risen Indeed*, 1959, 59). Three days after Christ's crucifixion, when the tomb was declared empty, hardly enough time had elapsed for natural processes to have eliminated the body. Kirsopp Lake explained that the women most likely went to the wrong burial place on that Sunday morning. They simply made a mistake and went to another tomb which happened to be empty (*The Historical Evidence for the Resurrection of Jesus Christ*, 1907, 250-53). It remains difficult to believe that the women who cared for Jesus would have mistaken something so important to them. It is equally difficult to believe that the disciples and others would make the same mistake. This view is even more incredible since the Scriptures indicate that Jesus' body was not placed in a tomb in a cemetery but in the garden tomb of Joseph of Arimathea (Matt 27:59-61; John 19:38-42). David Strauss suggested that Jesus never actually died on the cross; that he somehow survived crucifixion, revived in the coolness of the tomb, and on the third day he was mistakenly believed to be resurrected (*The Life of Jesus for the People*, 1879, vol. 1, 412). It is difficult to believe a man crucified and confirmed dead by a Roman soldier's spear thrust into his side could revive after three days without medical attention. It is even more difficult to believe that such a person, beaten, bruised, bloody, could convince anyone of his triumphant resurrection from the dead. Joseph Klausner suggested that Joseph of Arimathea stole the body (*Jesus of Nazareth, His Life, Times and Teaching*, 1925, 357). It is hard to believe that Joseph had either the motive to steal the body or the strength to pull off the theft before the soldiers guarding the tomb. Many other views have been suggested. Each has various weaknesses. On the other hand, the New Testament narratives recount that over five hundred people were eyewitnesses to the resurrection of Jesus Christ (1 Cor 15:3-8) (cf Lewis & Demarest 1996:464-71; Morris 1962:1086-8; Purkiser 1983:453).

The Resurrection of Believers and the Resurrected Body

Jesus rose and assuredly one day all men too will rise (Morris 1982:1088). The general New Testament position is that resurrection of Christ carries with it the resurrection of believers. Paul tells us that "since death came through a man, the resurrection of the dead comes also through a man. For as in Adam all die, so in Christ all will be made alive" (1 Cor 15:21, 22; cf. 1 Thess 4:14). The resurrection of believers follows immediately from that of their savior. So characteristic of believers is resurrection that Jesus could speak of believers as 'the children of God, being the children of the resurrection" (Luke 20:36).

Resurrection in the Old Testament connotes God's returning the righteous to life at the end-time. In Christian writings it is the resurrection of Jesus after his crucifixion. Less frequently, the wicked are also spoken of as resurrected to suffer punishment (e.g. the "second death" in Rev 20:11-15). Unlike immortality, an inherent property of the soul in contrast to the perishable body, resurrection is an act of divine power in calling persons to a new form of life eternally in God's presence (Perkins 1997: 979).

I concur with the observation by Young (1984:454), that biblical resurrection is rising from the dead. Young asserts further that in the biblical concept, man in a disembodied state is incomplete. The departed soul is waiting for the redemption of the body. At the resurrection of the body, the two are joined again for eternity (Rom 8:23; 2 Cor 5:37) (see also Unger 1988:1075). Resurrection of the body (Gr. *anastasis*, "to make to stand" or "rise up") according to Unger (1988:1075) is the union of the bodies and souls of men that have been separated by death. Unger advises that "this is rightly held to be an important article of Christian belief though it is left by the revelation of scripture obscure in many details".

As indicated earlier, numerous places in the New Testament contain references to the resurrection mainly of believers as well as of Jesus (Erickson 2005:1202-3). We note that John, for example, reports several occasions when Jesus spoke of the resurrection. One of the clearest declarations is in John 5: "I tell you the truth, a time is coming and has now come when the dead will hear the voice of the Son of God and those who hear will live . . . Do not be amazed at this, for a time is coming when all who are in their graves will hear his voice and come out—those who have done good will rise to live, and those who have done evil will rise to be condemned" (vv. 25, 28-9). Other affirmations of the resurrection are found in John 6:39-40, 44, 54, and the narrative of the raising of Lazarus (John 11, especially vv. 24-5). Although the raising of Lazarus is regarded by a number of theologians as a temporary revivification, as Lazarus even after coming back to life did at the end of his earthly life eventually die.

At the resurrection, believers will all be transformed and into the image of His son (Segal 2009:781). They will have bodies constituted like that received by Christ (Phil 3:21) and suitable for the soul's eternal state (Killen 1975:1460).

Perhaps as indicated by Morris (1962:1088), we can gain some help by thinking of the resurrection body of Christ, for John tells us that "we shall be like him" (1 John 3:2), and Paul that "our vile body" is to be fashioned 'like unto his glorious body' (Phil 3:21). Thus on some occasions He was recognised immediately (Matt 28:9; John 20:19) but on others He was not (notably the walk to Emmaus, Luke 24:16; cf. 21). He appeared suddenly in the midst of the disciples, who were gathered with doors shut (John 20:19), while in contrary fashion He disappeared from sight of the two at Emmaus (Luke 24:13). He spoke of having "flesh and bones" (Luke 24:39). On occasion, he ate food (Luke 24:41-3), though we cannot hold that physical food is a necessity for life beyond death (cf. 1 Cor 6:13). It would seem that the risen Lord could conform to the limitations of this physical life or not as He chose, and this may indicate that when we rise we shall have a similar power (Ibid., 1088).

The Apostles' Creed declares "I believe . . . in the resurrection of the body" (Wilson 1983:453). Other Early Church creeds echo and amplify the teaching of scripture that the bodies of the dead shall be raised. Jesus declared "I am the resurrection and the life" (John 11:25). Because of the empty tomb, believers have been assured of final victory over death (1 Cor 15:57). The apostle gave words of reassurance to believers that loved ones who had died in the faith would not be left out in the coming of Christ: "The dead in Christ shall rise first" (1 Thess 4:16) promptly to be followed by believers living and remaining. Before Felix the governor, Paul testified that "there shall be a resurrection of the dead, both of the just and unjust" (Acts 24:15; Ibid., 453).

Wilson (1983:454), asserts that the scriptures go beyond the Greek concept of "the immortality of the soul" to declare a reunion of soul and body. Instead of non-material, ghostlike phantoms, recognisable bodies of loved ones who have died would come forth from the graves. The resurrected body will assure a preservation of personal identity, without being identical atomically and biologically. Rather the resurrected body will be changed, and made "like unto his glorious body" (Phil 3:21).

It is revealed that the believer shall be like his Lord (Phil 3:21; 1 John 3:2), having a tangible body "like his glorious body" (Killen 1975:1460-1). The identity will be retained between the mortal body and the new resurrection body, even though this does not necessitate a reconstitution from the same atoms. Even in this life the materials of the body change constantly. They are entirely replaced in a progressive manner within the span of a few years. He (1975:1460), further indicates that resurrection "does not have to be a particle-by-particle re-gathering and reconstitution of the old body of flesh, since the resurrection body is one with entirely different qualities from the old body; but it does mean the constitution of a body like that received by Christ (Phil. 3:21) and suitable to the soul's eternal state".

Furnishing further enlightenment on the resurrected body, Erickson (2005:1204) advises that a contrast must be drawn between the "natural (soulish) body" that is sown and the "spiritual body" that is raised (1 Cor 15:44). It should be noted that there is a significant difference between the two, but we do not know the precise nature of that difference. There are explicit statements that exclude the possibility that the resurrection body will be purely physical. Paul says near the end of his discussion of the resurrected body "flesh and blood cannot inherit the kingdom of God, nor does the perishable inherit the imperishable" (1 Cor 15:50).

Additionally, Erickson observes there is the problem of how one's body can be reconstituted from molecules that may have become part of another person's body. On this Erickson (2005:1204) indicates: "see Augustus H. Strong's question" "Who ate Roger Williams?" in *Systematic Theology* (Revell, 1907:1019). Erickson asserts that cannibalism presents the most extreme example of this problem. Human bodies serving to fertilize fields where crops are grown and the scattering of human ashes over a river from which drinking water is drawn are other cases in point. A ludicrous parody of the Sadducees' question: "At the resurrection whose wife will she be?" (Mark 12:23), arises, namely 'At the resurrection whose molecules will they be?".

We know the resurrected bodies will be immortal: "Neither can they die anymore" (Luke 20:36) (Byrum 1982:549). Matter as we know it is constituted internally and so conditioned externally that it is subject to dissolution. God will so change the resurrection body, as to internal constitution and so condition it that it will be incorruptible. In view of the power of God to do this, the immortality of matter is not impossible. The resurrected body is raised in "glory", whatever that may mean. It may reasonably be assumed from the words "it is raised" that the resurrected body will be free from all defects and mutilations. Byrum indicates that Christ's body bearing the scars was probably an exception for a special purpose (Ibid., 549).

Supporting this contention, Erickson (2005:1205) is of the view that our resurrection body will be like Jesus' present body, not like that body he had between his resurrection and ascension. We will not have those characteristics of Jesus' post-resurrection earthly body that are inconsistent with the descriptions of our resurrection bodies (e.g. physical tangibility and the need to eat).

In conclusion of the issue of the resurrection body, he (2005:1206) is of the view that 'there will be a bodily reality of some type in the resurrection. It will have some connection with and derive from our original body, and yet it will not be merely a resuscitation of our original body. Rather, there will be a transformation or metamorphosis'. An analogy here, Erickson indicates, is the petrification of a log or a stump. While the contour of the original object is retained, the composition is entirely different (cf. Badham 1976:65-94). We have difficulty in understanding because we do not know the exact nature of the resurrection body. It does appear however, that it will retain, at the same time glorify, the human form. Additionally it is worthy of note that we will be free of the imperfections and needs we had on earth (Erickson 2005:1206).

As to how the resurrected believers will identify each other, Byrum (1982:547) is of the view that in some sense the resurrection body will be identical with the body which is placed in the grave. Byrum then argues if the body in which we die is not the subject of the resurrection, then that future body will not be a resurrected body, but a new creation. But the Scriptures teach a resurrection of dead bodies, not a transmigration of spirits to newly created bodies. That this is true was exemplified in Christ, who was the first fruits of them that slept. His dead body which was laid out in the tomb was raised to live again. Jesus said to those who required a sign, "Destroy *this* body, and in three days I will raise *it* up again". He did not say he would find or create another body if the first were destroyed (Ibid., 547).

But there may be distinguished an absolute identity and also a proper identity (Byrum 1982:549-50). An absolute identity requires every particle of which the body is composed at a particular time. A proper identity requires only such a degree of sameness as is true of the body at widely separated periods of the present time. We are told that each seven years throughout life every atom of the body is exchanged for another. If we meet a friend after a lapse of ten or twenty years we recognise him, though he has an entirely new body as to the matter of which it is composed. Yet in a proper sense he possesses the same body as formerly. It is practically identical as to shape, size, and appearance. It is identical in a real sense. This at least illustrates the possibility of the practical identity of the resurrection body with that which dies without its being absolutely identical (Ibid., 546-50).

Conclusion

The majority of Christians do frequently state when reciting The Apostles' Creed: "I believe . . . the resurrection of the body and the life everlasting". This is the belief and attitude of almost all the Christians of Kikuyu District, the scope of this study.

In the New Testament, Young (1984:454) judges to be one of the simplest statements, "there will be a resurrection of both the righteous and the wicked" (Acts 24:15). The certainty of resurrection and the nature of it are described by St Paul at great length in 1 Corinthians 15:12-54. Our resurrected bodies will be like our Lord's after his resurrection (Phil 3.20, 21; 1 John 3:2).

On the issue of the natural body and the spiritual body, Eiselen (1929:1192) observes that St Paul in 1 Corinthians 15:35-49 turns to the doctrine of bodily resurrection to remove difficulties by explaining its true meaning. The main obstacle to this issue is a materialistic view of resurrection. Eiselen indicates that by the parable of the grain of wheat, we are reminded of the difference in outward form of the present and the future body. The present body must perish (v. 36); God gives a new body according to his own creative decree (v. 38). Commenting on the parable of the grain of wheat, he (1929:1192) is of the view that our present life is the seed-time, marked by perishableness, dishonor, weakness (cf. Rom 8:10, 21; 2 Cor 13:4). Through death we pass to the state of incorruption, glory, power (cf. Rom 8:18-23). He (1929:1193) further asserts that corresponding to these two conditions are two different kinds of body, one natural, the other spiritual. The first corresponds to the needs of the soul in this order of physical existence, fulfilling the requirements of thought, feeling, will, and is thus in the process of adaptation for the higher service of the life above the realm of the senses (cf. Gal 6:8). In speaking of bodily resurrection St Paul has no material body in mind. At the advent of Christ we shall be changed whether dead or alive. Our mortality then will be replaced with immortality. Eiselen indicates that the notable feature of Paul's teaching is his insistence on the spiritual nature of the future life, and the spiritual character of the resurrection body. The body that decays in the tomb Eiselen advises does not rise again. "Flesh and blood cannot inherit the Kingdom of God, nor does the perishable inherit the imperishable" (1 Cor 15:50) (cf. Erickson 2005:1204).

Furnishing additional enlightenment on this issue of the resurrected body, Erickson (2005:1195) observes that St Paul clearly believed and taught that there is to be a future bodily resurrection. The teaching on the resurrection by St Paul is especially pointed in 1 Corinthians 15:51-2 where it is stated "Lo! I tell you a mystery. We shall not all sleep, but we shall be changed, in a moment, in the twinkling of an eye, at the last trumpet. For the trumpet will sound, and the dead will be raised imperishable, and we shall be changed". He (2005:1195-6) further asserts that there are several passages in the New Testament which affirm that the body will be restored to life. One of them is Romans 8:11 "if the spirit of him who raised Jesus from the dead dwells in you, he who raised Christ Jesus from the dead will give life to your mortal bodies also through his spirit which dwells in you". Erickson observes that in Philippians 3:20-21 Paul writes, "But our commonwealth is in heaven, and from it we await a Savior, the LORD Jesus Christ, who will change our lowly body to be like his glorious body, by the power which enables him even to subject all things to himself". In 1 Corinthians 15, St Paul says "It is sown a physical body, it is raised a spiritual body. If there is a physical body, there is also a spiritual body" (v. 44). It is to be noted that there is a significant difference between the two. We do not, however, know the precise nature of that difference. He (2005:1199) asserts further that there are explicit statements which exclude the possibility that the resurrection body will be purely physical. One of the key statements to this effect, as indicated earlier, is what St Paul said in 1 Corinthians 15:50 that "Flesh and blood cannot inherit the kingdom of God, nor does the perishable inherit the perishable". He is of the view that resurrection is more than a post death survival by the spirit or souls; this something more is not simply a physical resuscitation. In the New Testament we observe that there is a utilization of the old body, but a transformation of it in the process. Some sort of metamorphosis occurs so that a new body arises. This new body has some connection or point of identity with the old body, but is differently constituted. St Paul speaks of it as a "spiritual body" (1 Cor 15:44) but does not elaborate. He uses an analogy of a seed and the plant that springs from it (v. 37). What sprouts from the ground Erickson asserts is not merely that which is planted; however, it issues from that original seed.

Giving further insight on what God can do or not regarding the reconstructing of our bodies, especially on the misconception that God cannot handle the ashes at the second coming of those whose bodies have been cremated, Hammons (2011:1) is of the view that "God can do anything as far as His character will allow Him. The resurrection of our bodies is nothing for Him whether our bodies become dust through natural decomposition or they are ashes through incineration (cremation). If God can take dust and turn it into a man as He did with Adam, He can take the dust or ashes of our bodies and do the same". This should be the attitude of all believers, as God is all powerful and His ability is not limited. It is my prayer and trust that this explanation and others given in this study will remove the aversion to cremation felt by a number of Christians on the globe, Africans and Agikuyu Christians included. Should our bodies be cremated, God in His might and power will give the cremated individuals fresh spiritual bodies just as He will give those whose bodies that had been accorded an earth burial.

From all the above, it can be argued that at the resurrection there will be a bodily reality of some type. It will have some connection with and derive from our original body, and yet it will not be merely a resuscitation of our original body (Erickson 2005:1199). Rather, Erickson feels there will be a transformation or metamorphosis. We do not know the exact nature of the resurrection body and hence our difficulty in understanding. However, he (2005:1199) asserts that it will retain and at the same time glorify the human form. We will be free of the imperfection and needs we had on earth.

As shown in chapter 1 of this study, chapter 7 that follows will mainly be a critical correlation of all the chapters so far undertaken, so as to bring the findings obtained so far into dialogue with one another in an attempt to formulate a model for the Agikuyu Christians and other Africans' funeral rites that integrates relevant cultural, scriptural and practical norms.

CHAPTER 7
CRITICAL CORRELATION OF THE STUDY

A Table Offering a Visual Summary and Correlation of the Funeral Practices of the Various Traditions Discussed in this Study

EVENT	AGIKUYU TRADITIONAL PRACTICES	BIBLICAL	PATRISTIC	CONTEMPORARY AGIKUYU PRACTICES
1. How the idea of burial arose	Not known.	The Jews developed with their own ingenuity their funeral practices. These, however, were not normative.	Early practices based on Judaism. Also from scripture and the manner of burial of Jesus. These funeral practices were not mandatory for future Christians to observe.	From practices of numerous other cultures, religions and their own ingenuity.
2. Actions performed before death	For the elder making an oral (verbal) will; dividing his fields; blessing his people and indicating where to be buried.	For the patriarch blessing his people; making an oral (verbal) will; indicating where to be buried.	Stretching out the feet; administration of the Viaticum; giving the dying the last kiss and catching the last breath (soul).	The Roman Catholics anointing the sick; administering viaticum. Other denominations prayers and solace for the dying.
3. Actions performed soon after death	For the elder, all sons to be notified; urgent meeting of elders to supervise the funeral. Elder's body laid in correct position for burial; ornaments to be removed.	Corpse washed; anointed; wrapped in linen garments and spices; face covered with napkin.	Closed eyes of the corpse; laying out of the body; body washed with warm water; anointing the body including perfuming the body.	Alerting the immediate family and neighbors; body wrapped in sheets or bedcovers; taking the body to mortuary; advising the relevant government officials.

EVENT	AGIKUYU TRADI-TIONAL PRACTICES	BIBLICAL	PATRISTIC	CONTEMPO-RARY AGIKUYU PRACTICES
4. Clothing of the dead	For the elders, body wrapped in skin garments; whole bundle tied with bark and roots of a plant called "*muoha akuu*" (one that ties the dead); face of dead person not to be covered to allow him to see what was happening.	Old Testament, no information given; New Testament—the bodies were washed and wrapped in clean linen cloth.	Body washed, anointed and wrapped in linen as sign of immortality. Then it would normally be dressed in the clothes worn during life.	On the day of burial, body dressed either in their church uniforms (e.g. Woman's Guild) or in the clothes they wore during life. Occasionally some dressed in new clothes and shoes.
5. Crowning the dead	The dead were not crowned.	The dead were not crowned.	The dead were not crowned.	The dead are not crowned.
6. The wake held over the dead	The Agikuyu did not hold a wake over the dead.	Wake was a Jewish custom. A good example is the wake over the body of Dorcas (Acts 9:36-41). Holding a wake is not normative.	Early Christians took over from Judaism holding of wake. Later, introduced solemnizing wakes in the churches.	No wake per se is held. Largely because the body is at the mortuary from death to burial.

EVENT	AGIKUYU TRADITIONAL PRACTICES	BIBLICAL	PATRISTIC	CONTEMPORARY AGIKUYU PRACTICES
7. Mourning	Did not "mourn" unduly.	Mourned excessively; body mutilations and disfigurements, sprinkling ashes and dust on the head; engaging professional female mourners.	Not mourned "unduly".	Not mourning "unduly".
8. Funeral procession	For the elder, led by a medicine man carrying a burning torch. Body carried by sons. All the carriers on the same side of the bundle by the man's back. Then followed the officiating elders and the age mates of the deceased. However, burial not attended by other close family members not even by wives, neighbors or friends.	Almost no information on this is recorded. Of note, however, is that the corpse was lifted on a bier or litter which was carried on shoulders to the tomb. Chief mourners followed the bier accompanied by the specially robed professional lamenters (cf. Gen 50: 7-11).	Funeral procession had the character of a triumph: singing of hymns; deceased carried on a bier; wearing white encouraged. The procession attended by many Christians.	Very complex; body accompanied by a convoy of many vehicles, even at times headed by motorcycle outriders.

EVENT	AGIKUYU TRADITIONAL PRACTICES	BIBLICAL	PATRISTIC	CONTEMPORARY AGIKUYU PRACTICES
9. Time of burial	Same day as death or the following day—"*mundu athikwo riua riianathua*" meaning to be buried before the sun sets.	Same day as death.	Same day as death.	On the average, one week after death, but often many weeks or months after death.
10. Interment	For the elder, body laid inside the grave; ornaments laid near the stomach; body covered with a fresh wet skin of an ox or goat (*muguguta*). Branches of acacia tree placed by sons on the grave. Bodies of the greater proportion of the Agikuyu were, however, not buried per se but left at the "*kibirira*" (cemetery) or in the open to be devoured by wild beasts.	Body carried to the grave on a bier; accorded earth burial; buried in clothes worn during life.	Earth burial was the norm.	Follows the Liturgy of the Church; body borne in a coffin; flowers placed on the grave after burial and a cross inserted on the grave. Recently in accordance with their wishes a few cremated.

EVENT	AGIKUYU TRADITIONAL PRACTICES	BIBLICAL	PATRISTIC	CONTEMPORARY AGIKUYU PRACTICES
11. Place of burial	For the elder at the "*kiaraini*"—rubbish midden. For the matriarch behind her hut. The rest left in the bush to be devoured by wild animals.	Graves located on the family land; later outside inhabited districts and making use of clefts or caves. Secondary burial was the norm.	Similar to those of the Jews. Later, the majority in catacombs. Secondary burial was the norm for most families.	Graves dug on family ancestral land; public cemeteries, and so on. Recently a few who die overseas are buried where they die.
12. Rituals performed after burial	"*Kuhukura*" ceremony one month after burial; cleansing by a medicine man of all who made contact with the body; wife inheritance.	A *masseba* and *siyum* (pillar and monument) constructed; circle of stones to show contempt for Israel's enemies; Levirate marriages.	At the anniversary of death, relatives and friends adorned grave with flowers or lanterns and anointed it with oil; pronounce regular prayers for the dead.	One week after burial, an announcement placed in newspapers thanking all who participated in the funeral; one year after a ceremony of "unveiling" the cross and gathering of family and friends for prayers and remembrance of the deceased.

EVENT	AGIKUYU TRADITIONAL PRACTICES	BIBLICAL	PATRISTIC	CONTEMPORARY AGIKUYU PRACTICES
13. Life after death	On death one went to the land of the ancestors.	In Old Testament, all went to Sheol without distinction meaning there was no question of punishment or reward; in New Testament, the righteous went to heaven, the sinful to hades.	Early Christians believed that if righteous on death they would go straight to heaven; the sinful to hades; they also believed in the resurrection of the body and of the life everlasting.	They believe that if you are righteous, on death one will go to heaven, the sinful to hell; believe in the resurrection of the body and of the life everlasting.
14. Economy of burial grounds and spaces	The Agikuyu were, in those days, not bothered about this as they had sufficient land and furthermore the large proportion of the populace were not buried.	Second burial and burying in caves and cliffs.	Second burial, catacombs.	Not yet established. This book might furnish the solution to this issue.

Regarding this Chapter

This chapter will principally be a critical correlation of all aspects so far undertaken in this book. In other words it will basically put all the pieces together, and bring together all that has been undertaken so far. It will also explore how the various pieces of the puzzle relate or fit together. The objective of doing this will be to bring the findings obtained so far into dialogue with one another in an attempt to formulate a model of Agikuyu Christian and by extension other African ethnic communities funeral rites that integrates relevant cultural, scriptural and practical norms.

In essence, it will be necessary to explore areas of similarity and conflict between various trends of traditions pertaining to funeral practices. The resulting evaluations and appraisal will assist in arriving at appropriate proposals for the Agikuyu Christians as well as for other people, showing them how they might have arrived at their present practices. Additionally, it will show them how they may value elements of that practice, and where it is felt necessary, lead to their changing most of their current funeral practices and while doing so still remain faithful to Christ.

The best method of achieving this is to analyze what has been presented principally in chapters 2 to 5 of this book on each aspect of coping with death. This will involve comparing and contrasting what the study has revealed as having been believed and done in various stages and order of funeral practices, in other words, to show a close resemblance or contrast between funeral practices exhibited in the chapters. For example, it will be necessary to compare where the people involved in each chapter obtained their idea(s) of burial. Analyzes undertaken will enable me to correlate, for example, what was traditionally observed by the Agikuyu just before death, what acts are performed just before death by the current Agikuyu, what acts were performed during biblical times by the Jews before death and how early Christians conducted themselves when death was near. This approach will reflect at a glance how each aspect and stage of disposing of the dead was viewed and handled. The analyzes will then enable me to deduce whether the current Agikuyu funeral practices bear any resemblance to the Agikuyu cultural and traditional manner of disposing of the dead, to the biblical practices and also to the burial practices of early Christians. The analyzes will also aim to reveal whether the various peoples and periods involved in this study have borrowed from each other, and whether such practices have close resemblance to each other, and if so, then analyze what led to such characteristics. Additionally, an attempt will be made to explore the relationships and connexions between the parts. I then hope to recommend in chapter 8 the best way forward. This will be based on the consideration of all aspects presented in this book, especially on whether any Agikuyu traditional practices, any scriptural practices and those of early Christianity can be adopted in shaping fresh Agikuyu and other Africans funeral practices that will integrate relevant cultural, scriptural and practical norms. The recommendations in chapter 8 will be based not only on what is discussed in this book, but in addition, any relevant information from scripture, from the writings of the early Christian church fathers, from views obtained from a number of secular leaders, pastors and other Christians, as well as views from other scholars and from works done so far on reformation of funeral rites by a number of other prominent scholars.

How the Idea of Burial Arose

No one is certain of the origin of mankind's practice of coping with death. For the Agikuyu, no information is available as to how the Agikuyu formulated their traditional methods of coping with death; neither how they acquired their traditional religion, worldview, nor how they developed their belief in their ancestral spirits. Suffice to state that the methods and beliefs developed and were acquired over the last four thousand years or thereabouts as the Agikuyu migrated from West Africa to their current ancestral homeland of central Kenya. During that migration the Agikuyu intermarried and adopted cultures, practices and beliefs of numerous other peoples they came across. One such practice they may have acquired was how to cope with death. The said migration, popularly referred to as the Bantu migration, was analyzed at length in chapter 2 of this book.

As presented in chapter 3, over the last one hundred years or so, the Agikuyu, soon after interacting with other races, tribes and peoples, as well as having been colonized by the British, and also having been influenced by other religions and worldviews of other cultures, started to acquire religious beliefs and funeral practices which, as shown in Chapter 3 of this study, are in almost all respects at variance with the traditional Agikuyu religion, worldview and the Agikuyu traditional mode of coping with death. From 1898 when they made contact with Europeans and Christian missionaries, the Agikuyu have progressively reformed their mode of coping with death. Other factors that have influenced those reforms have among others been the enactment of by-laws by the colonizing British requiring that all the dead must be accorded an earth burial.

The Jews, on the other hand, have over the ages developed on their own initiative their practices and observance of coping with death. No information is available as to exactly how and when their burial practices developed.

However, it is certain that the Jewish burial practices did not originate as described in the Mohammedans' (muslims') fable so well narrated by Wakeford (1890:5) which reads that, "Cain, the first murderer in the frenzy of horror and remorse, caught up the corpse of Abel in his arms and fled he knew not whither. For days he wandered about without being able to rid himself of his ghastly burden, till at last, overcome by fatigue, he sank upon the ground. Just then, two crows alighted near him and engaged in mortal combat. When one of the two was stretched lifeless upon the ground, the victorious survivor scratched a hole with his talons and covered the dead bird with earth. Cain profited by the lesson, and digging a grave with his hands, buried his dead out of his sight" (cf. *Qur'an*, cxiv.30). Wakeford (1890:4-5) goes on to indicate that the truth underlying this fable is that very early in the world history the problem, "how to dispose of the dead, had to be faced". The words of scripture (Gen 4:10, 11) might suggest that Cain hid Abel in the ground. "The voice of your brother's blood crieth unto me from the ground. And now cursed art thou from the ground, which hath opened her mouth to receive thy brother's blood from thy hand" (KJV). As discussed in chapter 4 there seems to be the likelihood of the Jews having acquired some of their practices of coping with death from other people in the Middle East and surrounding territories. Likely sources in this regard include, but are not limited to, nations such as the Canaanites, the Egyptians, Persians, Mesopotamia, also from religions of other people in the vicinity such as from the Zoroastrians of Persia, from the Ugaric Ba'al of the Canaanites, and so on. However, the notion that the Jews acquired their idea of coping with death from other people and religions has been questioned by numerous theologians. It is now generally held that the Jews developed their methods of coping with death on their own, and these evolved and were transformed over the ages. The Jews, where possible, followed the manner in which their ancestors and kings were buried. A good example is how the Jewish patriarchs and matriarchs, such as Abraham and Sarah, were buried, also how their kings such as David and their High Priests, such as Aaron, were buried. It was noted in chapter 4, however, that the Jews did not have a normative method of coping with death (Decker 2006:16; Decker 2007:9).

According to Meyers and Strange (1981:109), archaeological findings reveal that early burial sites and customs for early Christianity in Palestine were based on Judaism, and there was apparently no difference between the burials of Christians and those of Judaic Jews. Rush (1941:1) is of the view that the Christian concept of death, and in this case the concept of how Christians should cope with death, arose from scripture as well as from the manner in which Jesus himself was buried. Subsequently, the way in which Christians should cope with death was developed by the writers and early church fathers, and this manifested practically in the lives as well as in the funeral practices of the first Christians. There were, however, numerous areas and aspects of contrast between the Christian church and the systems which it supplanted. One of the most conspicuous is the treatment of the departed. This point stands side by side with the Christian unparalleled hospitality and their austere purity of life. Additionally, the Christian care for the burial of the dead was one of the means by which the Christians had succeeded in converting the Roman Empire (Julian *Epist and Arsac*, XLIX). Smith and Cheetham (1879:251) are of the view that one of the most conspicuous characteristics of the new faith was not only its belief in the resurrection of the body, but also its reverence for the body as sharing in the redemption. This showed itself in almost every facet of the funeral rites.

It is evident from the above that the origin and developments of funeral practice reflected in each chapter differ markedly from each other. The only one that appears to have some resemblance to another, is the way in which the early Christians' funeral practices were to a large extent based on the Jews' practices. As indicated earlier, this was not because the Jews methods were normative, but because their burial rites and customs were based on Judaism. It is worthy of note that Judaism was the religion that Jesus and his disciples as well as the very early Christian Jews were observing and practicing. The origin of the current Agikuyu funeral practices differs substantially from the traditional Agikuyu funeral practices, the scriptural, as well as from the early Christian practices. It will therefore be necessary in chapter 8 for me to recommend to the current Agikuyu faithful, and other Africans, funeral practices that are practical and faithful to God and his requirements, while at the same time being faithful and relevant to their culture (s) and traditions.

Actions Performed Before Death

There is evidence described in this study of correlation between actions performed before death in the Agikuyu, Biblical and early Christian funeral practices. This can be seen in all the three traditions in the way the person about to die, behaved, spoke or acted in each instance. Additionally, the way relatives and those who were close family members, as well as those close to him, became involved at that time with the dying person.

As was shown in chapter 2, both my respondents and Cagnolo (2006:151) indicated that when an Agikuyu man who had a family found himself on the point of death, called his relatives and where possible trustworthy elders around his death bed to express his last will. It was shown that in such circumstances relatives took great care not to offend the dying in any way, a complaint or worse still a curse from his lips would be the beginning of an endless trail of troubles. The dying man would then proceed to divide his field and family property. Cagnolo and my respondents further indicate that the will was made orally, but in the presence of numerous trustees. It is worth noting that no one would ever think of challenging the will, because of the belief that the spirit of the dead maintained his interest in the affairs of the family and would visit with heavy penalties anyone who transgressed his will. As indicated further in chapter 2, a considerable number of Agikuyu even today fear the curse (*kirumi*) of a dying person. In the case of other members of the family, except the family matriarch, who were accorded almost similar respect to that accorded to the family patriarch, when they were taken seriously ill, were carried out alive to the *kibirira* (an area in the bush set aside near the homestead or in that ridge for the disposal of the dead). The relatives and friends made a temporary shelter and lit a fire for him. The relatives took turns watching over their dying relative. They removed all ornaments on him when he was still alive and laid them beside him. When he died, the relatives left the body there in the bush to be eaten by wild beasts. As was observed in chapter 2, often the wild beasts did not come immediately, and the body would rot infecting the surroundings with the stench. Many times, at night, the relatives would hear from their huts, the sound of hyenas, jackals and leopards crunching the bones of the departed. They would huddle silently around the fire with their heads on their knees and sigh "*uhoro ni muthiru*" (meaning "all is over"). If several days elapsed before the corpse was devoured by wild beasts, this was taken as an evil omen. A testimony which is proof of how the Agikuyu left those seriously ill in the bush to die there and when dead for their bodies to be devoured by wild beasts was given very recently on First May, 2013 at the burial of a church elder at the ACK St Joseph Church, Kanyariri. In the eulogy of the deceased, which he had dictated to his son when he was still alive, he narrated an incident in which his uncle (his father's elder brother—"*baba mukuru*") together with one of his baby sisters had accompanied their mother on a journey. The sister became very sick and in accordance with Agikuyu traditional practice the old lady abandoned the sick child still alive in the bush. The uncle of the deceased very early the following morning went to check on his sister. Unfortunately she had been devoured by wild animals and only her head remained.

Events performed before death in the Bible are not easy to equate, because of the scanty details in which they are described (Jones 2010:337). However, there are a few occurrences that are mentioned and which afford reasonable insight to what was said or done. For example, Isaac in Genesis

27:2-4 said to Esau his firstborn son, "I am now an old man and don't know the day of my death . . . prepare me the kind of tasty food I like and bring it to me to eat, so that I may give you my blessing before I die". This shows that in the early days of the Old Testament, fathers used to bless their firstborn sons just before they died. Sometimes, however, as in the case of Jacob, they blessed all their sons, divided their assets among them and indicated where and how they should be buried as shown in Genesis 49:28 which reads ". . .when he blessed them, giving each the blessing appropriate to him" and then in verses 29-33 he charged them with instructions where he would be buried. The text reads: "I am about to be gathered to my people. Bury me with my fathers in the cave in the field of Ephron the Hittite, the cave in the field of Machpelah . . . breathed his last and was gathered to his people".

This act of blessing the sons as well as indicating where they would be buried has some similarity with the way the Agikuyu left their wishes and blessings when they were about to die. In modern Judaism a practice worthy of note is the one where as death approaches, confession is heard and the dying person declares, 'Hear, O Israel, the Lord our God, the Lord is One". The dead person is then placed on the ground and psalms are recited especially Psalms 91, ". . .He who dwells in the shelter of the Most High will rest in the shadow of the Almighty . . . "

In early Christianity, as was noted in chapter 5, certain rites were performed before death, which were intimately linked with each other, namely stretching out of the feet of the dying, the administration of the Viaticum, the catching of the last breath and the imparting of the final kiss. As was further discussed in chapter 5, on the approach of death, the relatives and friends of the dying person gathered around his bed and as he drew his last breath, his nearest relative gave the last kiss, so as to catch the soul which was breathed out. It is worthy of note that this practice was more similar to the then church (Catholic) tradition rather than Biblical Christianity, and hardly seems to have any theological basis in scripture. As observed by Rush (1941:1) the stretching out of the feet was intended as a means of laying out the body when the soul takes its departure. It was further observed that according to the thinking of early Christianity the stretching out of the feet was a help in the natural order, while the admission of the Eucharist (Viaticum) was a help in the supernatural order.

It is evident from the above, and worth noting, that relatives of the dying person gathered around his bed in early Christianity in the same way as done in the Agikuyu tradition. The point of departure from the Agikuyu traditional practices is seen, however, in the events that were performed on and for the dying person in early Christianity. In Chapter 8, it would be prudent to recommend to the contemporary Agikuyu and other African

Christians, to give solace, comfort, prayers where possible and practicable and to assist the dying in confessing and repenting their sins. Additionally, for them to register the last words and wishes of the dying person.

For contemporary Agikuyu Christians, there is hardly any specific act or laid-down rite to be performed or observed for the dying before death. However, there are exceptions depending on the denomination with which one is associated. For example, the Roman Catholic Agikuyu, in addition to the prayers offered for the one at the point of death, whoever is seriously sick can make a request for the sacrament of the anointing of the sick as well as Viaticum to be administered. This practice is still very much alive among the practising Agikuyu Roman Catholics. Numerous other Christian denominations often have their pastors pray and give solace to those seriously sick as well as to those who appear near death.

Currently, among contemporary Agikuyu Christians, when one is taken seriously ill, one is either taken to a hospital, clinic or suitable healthcare centre. Should the person be suffering from an ailment that the medical profession has been unable to treat, or when the family has exhausted all its resources for meeting medical bills, and hence the family cannot afford to continue maintaining the relative in a hospital, then the family takes care of the sick at home in the best way they can until death takes place. Unlike in the past, the dying person may indicate their dying wishes, but such wishes are often not taken as seriously as in the past. The trend now is for the dying person to have divided his assets or written a legally-binding will. Additionally, the dying person might indicate or might have indicated how and where they wished to be buried. Fulfilment of such wishes would depend on what the family and friends can afford. Also, they might decide to honor most of those wishes, ignore most of them, modify some or ignore all of them. It is worth noting that due to the numerous conflicts that arise after the demise of the head of the family, today most of the churches, the NGOs (Non-Governmental Organisations) as well as the Kenya Government are encouraging people to draw up written wills to avoid such occurrences. It is unfortunate, however, that to a large extent such efforts seem to be falling on deaf ears, as contrary to this appeal, the Agikuyu, both educated and not so educated, poor, rich, religious and not so religious, hardly ever make written or verbal wills. Indeed, they are very reluctant to apportion their lands and assets to those entitled to receive them. This is strange, as often most of what they own, they themselves inherited them from their ancestors. Consequently, lengthy, expensive and seemingly unwarranted court cases ensue after death to determine how the assets of the deceased should be apportioned to those entitled to them. Additionally, hardly ever do the dying bless their people.

This section has shown that from the four traditions, namely the Agikuyu, Biblical and early Christianity, as well as those followed by contemporary Agikuyu Christians, there are elements as elaborated above and in the study, that show a correlation of events performed before death, which, where appropriate, will be considered for recommendation in Chapter 8.

Actions Done Soon After Death

As shown in Chapter 2, traditionally for the Agikuyu only the death of selected elders or of selected matriarchs were given prominence. The rest of the populace were not buried per se, but their bodies were taken to the *"kibirira"* to be devoured by beasts of the wild. Should death occur far from home, the body was left where it lay to be devoured by wild animals and birds. For the elder, as soon as death was confirmed and his death pronounced, normally by women screaming (*kuga mbu*) messengers were sent to all his sons asking them to come home at once. It should be noted that an "elder" does not mean any elderly man or married man, but a married man with more than one wife whose standing was that of a respected elder and who had sons of his own old enough, in other words, who were circumcised and hence able to take part in a burial ceremony. The body of an elder could not be disposed of until all his sons were present. In practice, however, it was regarded as sufficient if the eldest sons of each wife were present and as many of the others as possible. Other measures that were done soon after death of an elder were presented in depth in Chapter 2; these commenced with an immediate and very urgent meeting of elders, which gave guidance regarding burial, as very few persons were conversant with burial procedures as *the ceremony of burying anyone was performed very rarely*. Other issues that were attended to were that the elders instructed the senior son of the deceased how to put his father's body in the correct position for burial. This was necessary, as the dead man had to be laid on his right side in the "sleeping position", namely with his legs slightly flexed and his right hand under his cheek and his left hand by his breast. All the ornaments on his body were removed. The ornaments would be buried with him. Other matters attended to, as detailed in chapter 2, are hardly known or effected by the Agikuyu of today.

There seems to be no resemblance at all between the traditional Agikuyu practices described above and those practised in biblical times by the Jews. As presented in Chapter 4, in biblical times the corpse was first washed (Acts 9:37); it was then anointed (Mark 16:1); wrapped in linen garments with spices enclosed (John 19:40) and finally the limbs were bound and the face covered with a napkin (John 11:14). The scene in Acts 5:6 may perhaps suggest that some young men's fraternity had the duty of seeing to such matters. In respect of the treatment of the human remains, Jones (2010:347) is of the view that "the body is theologically significant; thus, both the act of and the imagery conveyed by the treatment of the deceased ought to be weighed carefully". As indicated in Chapter 6, and as will be discussed later on in this section, the remains of the human mortal body are relevant to the resurrected body, and hence the importance of taking care of the deceased. He (2010:343) asserts further that biblical characters showed great care and respect to the bodies of their deceased and loved ones. He (2010:340) additionally advises that the Jewish practice of preparing a body with perfumes and spices, such as was done for King Asa (2 Chr 16:14) and Jesus (Luke 24:1; John 19:39-40) was an expression of care, not an attempt at embalming or mummification. Following the examples given above, the Agikuyu and other African Christians should treat the bodies with respect, but with moderation as will be argued and recommended in chapter 8.

Although there is no resemblance between the Agikuyu traditional practices and those practised in Biblical times, there are, however, numerous resemblances between those practised in the Old Testament and the ones practised by the early Christians. As presented in chapter 5, in early Christianity times, when a Christian died, the body was prepared at home for the burial. Relatives closed the eyes of the corpse calling out their loved one's name to verify the death. The intention of calling out the name was that the loud shout of calling the deceased's name would awaken the person if he was not really dead. This act known as *conclamatio* did not pass into Christianity as a formal rite. The next act was the setting of the members of the body commonly known as the laying out of the body, which principally was to ensure that the feet were drawn out, the arms stretched out along the side of the body, although at times the arms were reposed on the chest in the form of a cross. The body was then washed with warm water. This was to ensure that death had occurred, for the hot water would revive a person if he were only apparently dead. After washing the body, it was then anointed (John 12:7, Acts 9:37). The reason for anointing was so that it would be preserved for a while, and especially for the lying in state of the body. In the Acts of Peter 40, it is related that Marcellus cut seven "minae" of aloes and Indian leaf and perfumed the body of Peter. White (1997:197), is of the view that embalmment was not widely used in Jewish custom although the practice was known in the Roman period and was adopted among Coptic Christians.

As was discussed in chapter 3, customarily in these days for the Agikuyu there is hardly any noticeable difference in the burying of an elder, a woman, youth or child. Likewise actions done soon after death are the same for everyone—elder, child, and so on. On discovering death, just as was done traditionally by their ancestors, the first act is to alert the family and neighbors normally by women screaming (*kuga mbu*). The body is then wrapped usually in a blanket, bed sheet, bed cover, or similar, and then taken to the most convenient mortuary. Should death occur in the hospital, the hospital staff cover the body and wheel the body to the mortuary. Should the hospital not have a mortuary or should the family select another, then an ambulance is called to take the body to the mortuary desired by the family. This is done as soon as the family settles all the outstanding hospital bills.

It is evident from the above that actions done soon after death by the current Agikuyu Christians, other than the women alerting their neighbors by the traditional screaming (*kuga mbu*) have no resemblance to those that were performed by their ancestors, neither those that were observed in scripture and nor those performed by the early Christians. Based on what has been presented in this study on this matter, appropriate recommendations to be adopted on this aspect by the current Agikuyu and other African Christians will be reflected in Chapter 8.

Clothing of the Dead

Chapter 2 outlines how traditionally for the few Agikuyu who were buried, namely selected patriarchs and matriarchs, all the ornaments that the deceased was wearing had to be removed immediately after death. The ornaments would then later be buried with him, but were never to be left on him. The body was then carefully wrapped in the skin garment of the deceased, after this had been knotted at the corners. His skin sleeping mat was also folded around him, and then the whole bundle was tied like a parcel with the bark and roots of a plant called *Muoha Akuu* (one that ties dead bodies). It should be noted that at that time the Agikuyu slept on beds made of animal skins. They also wore skin garments. Blankets, sheets, and so on, were introduced to them by the Europeans, Indians and Arabs. Chapter 2 explained that care was taken not to cover the face of the dead man, which had to be allowed to peep out of the bundle. This was to allow the dead man to see what was going on.

It is not possible to compare the above practices of the Agikuyu with the biblical practices, as in the Old Testament there is almost no mention as to how the dead were clothed. Presumably they were dressed in the clothes they wore during life. However, in the New Testament some information may be gleaned, for example, regarding burial of Jesus. We note in Matthew 27:59 that Jesus' body, perhaps after being bathed as was the Jewish custom, was "wrapped" in a clean linen cloth. There is a correlation between the New Testament practice and that of the Agikuyu regarding the wrapping of the body. However, there is a difference, as the Jews used to wash the body before wrapping it with linen while the Agikuyu did not wash the body. Also, the Agikuyu wrapped the body with animal skin garments, not with linen as done by the Jews.

In the early Christian era, as was presented in chapter 5, when a person died and the body had been washed and anointed, it would then be wrapped in linen as a sign of immortality. This practice was similar to that of the Jews. After wrapping the body, it would then normally be dressed in the clothes worn during life, but at times in special clothing.

In addition to washing and anointing the body (John 12:17, Acts 9:37), wrapping was done to prevent undue distortion or swelling (John 11:44, 19:40). Childers (1997:443), asserts that the body was dressed according to the social status of the deceased. It should also be noted that the manner in which the Christians clothed their dead can be traced back to a similar practice in Jewish and other ancient rites. Often, linen garments were employed, but at other times, the corpse was clothed in the best kind of garments worn during life. However, as indicated previously, when possible special burial garments were procured. Chapter 5 showed that among the Christians, there was a tendency to go to excess in this matter, and this called forth denunciation by certain of the fathers of the church. Numerous early church fathers condemned excess in clothing the dead. Among them was St. John Chrysostom in his *Homilia* 85, where he bitterly inveighed against the extravagance of Christians who clothed their dead in precious apparel and often in silks and gold. After showing that Christ rose naked from the tomb, he refers to the extravagance of Christians as madness and urges them to cease from such excess (Chrysostom, *Homily* 85). To him it was a superfluous and unprofitable expense, because it brought no gain to the departed and much loss to the mourners. As was also revealed in chapter 5, it is worthy of note that Chrysostom did not forbid accepted funeral observances, but he bade them to clothe their dead with moderation, so as not to consign their bodies to the earth naked. As opposed to the gold and silk clothing with which the Christians were adorning their dead, Chrysostom drew their attention to the garments of immortality which the body is to put on, and which are more glorious than garments of gold and silk (Chrysostom, *Homily* 85).

For today's Agikuyu Christians, a large proportion of bodies from date of death to date of burial are at the mortuary. Prior to the date of burial, the family or its representatives would have taken appropriate attire to the mortuary for clothing the dead. Early in the morning of the day of burial, the body of a dead lady is dressed by other ladies (relatives or very close friends), or should the family so desire, by the mortuary attendants. Men are normally dressed by the mortuary attendants. It should be noted that the bodies of those who are of a particular fraternity in the church, such as Mother's Union (Anglican) or similar, are usually dressed in their official church uniforms. The act of dressing such ladies is often done by fellow members.

It is evident from these descriptions of the practices of the contemporary Agikuyu, as well as what was discussed in Chapter 3, that there is no resemblance of the Agikuyu current practices to those of their ancestors, nor to biblical practices, nor to those of early Christianity. The only common factor is that they occasionally dress their dead with expensive attire, often new, including new shoes! In Chapter 8 it will be recommended that Agikuyu and other Africans should heed the advice of the early church fathers, and dress their dead in moderation, and also bear in mind that such garments will decay along with the body. In the case of those being cremated, the clothes will be burned along with the corpse. It should also be borne in mind that the corpse is not aware of how you dress it. Such attires are entirely meant to impress those attending the funeral, and have no benefit whatsoever to the one being buried. Additionally, such behaviour is neither cultural, or scriptural, and was not advocated by the early church fathers.

Crowning the Dead

There is correlation in this aspect, as all the four traditions, namely that of the Agikuyu, biblical, early Christianity, as well as that of the current Agikuyu Christians did not and do not crown the dead.

Traditionally, the Agikuyu did not practise or think of crowning the dead mainly due to the fact that crowning anybody or anything living and dead was foreign to them. As presented in Chapter 2, traditionally the Agikuyu did not have any crowns either secular or religious. The nearest to this was the headgear or hat worn by literally all and sundry who so desired, which in Kikuyu language is often referred to as *"thumbi"*. Additionally, the Agikuyu had no king or chiefs and, as indicated earlier, the idea of crowning anybody was foreign to them. Because of this there was therefore no practice or thought of crowning the dead.

As observed by Rush (1941:137), funeral crowns played no part in Jewish culture. This was unlike the practice of numerous other cultures during the biblical period. As indicated by Browning (2009:73), a crown in the Bible was used as a token of kingship (a different word in Greek) symbolizing power (Rev 9:7) and glory (1 Pet 5:4). Browning further asserts that Paul looked on his servants as his crown (Phil 4:1).

It is generally held that following Jewish culture, Christianity was one religious movement in which funeral crowns played no part. Additionally, it was in the light of Jews not crowning the dead that Christianity looked upon the custom of crowning the dead as specifically pagan. Note should be made, that crowning the dead was common in many cultures of the pagan community. The Christian teaching of God, death and the afterlife necessitated the rejection of crowning the dead.

Currently, the Agikuyu Christians do not understand or practise crowning the dead. The only reference to the word crowning in connection with burial is where in a considerable number of funeral announcements 2 Timothy 4:7-8 is quoted, where St Paul writing to Timothy wrote: "I have fought the good fight, I have finished the race, I have kept the faith. Now there is in store for me the crown of righteousness, which the Lord, the righteous Judge, will award to me on that day—and not only to me, but also to all who have longed for his appearing". The meaning of this, especially its reference to a crown of justice, was expounded in chapter 5 of this study. Likewise, St Peter while addressing God's elect urges them to be true shepherds of souls and tells them that when the Chief Shepherd appears "you will receive the crown of glory that will never fade away" (1 Pet 5:4). This is the expectation the African Christians and others should continue upholding, as the only true and lasting crown will be the crown of justice, which at times is referred to as the crown of glory that they will receive from their Lord and Saviour Jesus Christ in heaven together with all other righteous.

The Wake Held Over the Dead

Traditionally, for the Agikuyu burial took place the same day of death or at the latest, the following day. There was no wake held over the dead. Another reason was that the Agikuyu feared touching or being near a dead body. Should one have touched a dead body, one had to be cleansed by a medicine man.

Unlike the Agikuyu, however, a wake was a Jewish custom as was discussed in chapter 4. This contention is exemplified by a wake that was observed in the city of Joppa over the dead woman named Dorcas (Acts 9:36-41). She had died and her body had been taken to an upstairs room, which when Peter arrived was filled with weeping widows. After Peter had requested all present to leave the room, he prayed and turning to the body he said, "Get up Dorcas". She opened her eyes and when she saw Peter, she got up.

As was presented in Chapter 5 of this study, in early Christianity before the peace of Constantine, Christian converts from Judaism took over with them into Christianity the Jewish practice of having the body exposed for some time after death before being brought out for burial. However, it should be noted that early writings are meagre on the practices of Christians, including how the wake was held. After the peace of Constantine, the church, which in other words means Christians, was at liberty to develop its own practices and celebrate them publicly, and it was then that the custom was introduced of solemnizing the wake by holding it in the church. For the majority of Christians, the wake and funerals as a whole were, according to the words of Minucius Felix, (Octavius 38, 4) "We arrange our funerals as quietly as our lives". This certainly gives some indication of the simplicity of these early funerals. For dignitaries, and in particular the wake held over Emperor Constantine it was full of pomp and splendor. Eusebius mentions that Constantine was laid out in one of the principal rooms of the palace where he was attended by a group of soldiers for several days and nights. So much splendor surrounded this wake that Eusebius says it was a sight such as had never been seen before (Eusebius, *Vita Constantine IV*, 66).

Chrysostom, in his *Homilia 31*, indicates that wakes were held at the homes of Christians before burial. Additionally, Chrysostom shows that with the new concept of death, psalms were to take place of wailings during the laying out of the body.

When burial took place very soon after death, a vigil was often held at the grave. As indicated, among the Jews it was the practice to bury on the day of death. Under these circumstances, the wake or vigil would be kept at the grave. In Jewish thought, this vigil at the grave was linked with the eschatological belief that the soul hovered near the body for three days after death.

Currently, for lack of a better word, the Agikuyu hold a wake of some sort for (not over) the dead. Why do I say this? According to Hornby (1992:1431) a wake in the modern sense is a night, or nights, spent keeping watch over a dead body before it is buried. A wake can additionally be defined as a gathering to watch and grieve over a dead person on the night before the burial, sometimes with drink and food (Quirk 1989:1182). It is worthy of note that a similar definition is given by the website version of the Merriam-Webster Dictionary. These days, the Agikuyu dead are preserved in the mortuary from the date of death to the date of burial. Thus, there is no occasion when the body is available to be kept at home, church or a convenient place to enable family and friends to keep watch over the dead body. However, a form of wake is held, in the sense that while the body is at the mortuary, at home or at the church, a group of family members and friends meet for prayers, making funeral arrangements. In my view, and also that of the Agikuyu of Kikuyu District, this might be construed as a "wake". Such gatherings are held from the date of death to the day before the funeral. As the body is therefore not physically at home during the whole period between death and burial, it would not be correct to term the meeting of persons at the home of the deceased a "wake".

Thus there is no resemblance between what was practiced by the Agikuyu ancestors, and what was practiced in biblical times and by the early Christians. As the Agikuyu dead are at the mortuary from the date of death to date of burial, it is most unlikely that the Agikuyu would contemplate changing their attitude, and keep the body at home or church to facilitate holding a wake over their dead. Another point of consideration is that holding a wake over the dead will be foreign to the Agikuyu, as there is no history of their having ever done so. Accordingly, in Chapter 8 it will be reasonable to recommend that they continue with their present habit of not holding a wake as such, but to gather at the home of the deceased or other suitable places for funeral preparations while the body is still at the mortuary.

Mourning

Whilst traditionally the Agikuyu felt sorrow at the death of a loved one, as such feelings are natural and cannot be wished away, yet as indicated in Chapter 2, my respondents as well as Leakey (1977:937-8) asserted that the Agikuyu did not "mourn" unduly. This was so as they were comforted by two beliefs namely: (1) The dead person's spirit would always be near at hand, and as death was inevitable, there was therefore no need for regrets, such as that perhaps the life could have been saved if more had been done. (2) As also observed by Leakey (1977:1103) and my respondents, the Agikuyu side by side with the worship of *Ngai* (The Supreme Deity or High God) practiced what missionaries called ancestor worship. However, Kenyatta (1938:57, 253-8) and Leakey (1977:1074-1119) assert that this was not ancestor worship, but a belief in a spirit world, and in the ability of the spirits of those who had died to exert their influence over the living. As such, the Agikuyu did not mourn all that much, as they believed that the spirits of their loved ones would continue to be present among the living.

There is a correlation of the above with the practice of the current Agikuyu Christians who have, in more ways than one, adopted a similar attitude of not mourning unduly for the dead. This, however, is for very different reasons. Their ancestors did not mourn for reasons given above, which are scarcely known, practiced or believed in by the current Agikuyu. The modern Agikuyu, although they feel sorrow at the death of their loved ones, yet they are convinced that the dead go to heaven should they have been righteous. Additionally, the living believe that they will join them when they themselves die. They also believe that when the righteous die they join in heaven other righteous loved ones who had gone before. It is worthy of the note, however, that immediately after death, especially when viewing the corpse and also when the body is being lowered into the grave, a number of persons weep. Generally, however, the Agikuyu are able to contain their feelings.

A similar attitude of not mourning unduly is also observed in early Christianity. This is evident from the writings of early church fathers including St Paul himself who discouraged the faithful from excessive mourning. A good example is when St Paul had to address the excessive mourning by the Thessalonians (1 Thess 4:13). The text reads, "brothers we do not want you to be ignorant about those who fall asleep or to grieve like the rest of men, who have no hope" (NIV). Other church leaders who advised the Christians not to indulge in excessive mourning included Origen, Tertullian and others. St Cyprian, for example, in his treaties wrote ". . ..our brethren who have been freed from the world through the summons of the Lord, should not be mourned . . .." (Cyprian, on Mortality 20). Others were Commodian and St Chrysostom. The latter admonishes his flock to devise what consolation they can for the departed, but instead of seeking it in tears and lamentations they should rather seek it in a Christian substitution of alms, prayers and oblations of the dead (Chrysostom, *Homily 21*). St Augustine, for his part, observes that, according to St Paul, Christians are not commanded to refrain from weeping, but should not weep as those who have no hope. It is necessary that sadness results from the death of friends, but he points out that Christian hope should be a source of consolation for one in sorrow (St Augustine, *Sermon 173*.3). As discussed previously, unnecessary mourning was regarded by the early Christians as ungodly and was associated with pagan practices. The righteous were expected not to resort, under any circumstances, to the pagan type of behavior including mourning unduly. Even when an unbelieving loved one died without accepting Christ, they were encouraged not to resort to pagan type of mourning, but rather to seek solace in the Christian substitutions of alms, prayers and oblations of the dead.

In the Middle Ages, the Christians naturally felt sorrow on the death of their loved ones, but mourning as such had been curbed. Instead, as explained in chapter 4, the burial of a Christian was a joyous occasion.

The Old Testament practices of mourning are the only ones that are substantially different from those of all the others.

As presented in chapter 4, the Old Testament gives numerous details of customs of mourning. The Jewish mode of mourning included rending the clothes; going bareheaded and barefoot; sprinkling dust and ashes on the head; covering the head; and sitting in the dust and ashes. Additionally, various disfigurements and mutilations were self inflicted. There was also observance of separate offerings of food and drink, which were placed upon the grave. Additionally, professional female mourners were engaged to come and chant particular rhythmic lamentations.

It is gratifying that the Agikuyu Christians appear to have unknowingly adopted the pattern of their ancestors of not mourning unduly, which was also similar to that adopted by the early Christians. Similarly Christians during the Middle Ages did not mourn unduly, and their funerals were a joyous occasion. This is one custom that I would recommend to the Agikuyu Christians and other Africans to adopt and continue to exercise when death occurs. They should regard death as an inevitable act of God, and treat it and burial as a joyous occasion, since if the deceased was righteous, then on death he would have gone to be with the LORD.

Funeral Procession and Time of Burial

As indicated previously, traditionally among the Agikuyu, it was the custom to bury the body the same day the person died, or at the latest the following day. This was in strict observance of the then deeply-held tradition of "*Athikuo riua ritanathua*" (to be buried before the sun sets). As also indicated previously, a large proportion of those who died were never buried at all. It was extremely few Agikuyu who were buried as such, namely, a selected number of respected elders and matriarchs from a polygamist marriage. For the elder, the body was taken to the grave after being wrapped in the manner described previously. The procession was led by a medicine man carrying a burning torch. The senior unmarried son took his father's head, with the other sons who had helped in digging the grave taking the feet and supporting the back. It is worth noting that a dead body was not to be carried like an ordinary body or load. It was carried in the position in which it had laid immediately after death, with all the carriers on the same side of the bundle, by the man's back. Additionally, it should be noted that the deceased's feet were carried first through the door of the hut in which he died, and similarly through the main entrance of the homestead. The burial was not attended by close family members including wives or even neighbors and friends. Agikuyu as described in chapter 2 feared and avoided funerals. Only the sons participating in the actual burial were present together with the officiating elders, the medicine man and the agemates of the deceased.

As was discussed in the study, relatively little was written about funeral processions in scripture. However, it is evident that prompt burial, including that of the bodies of hanged criminals was the norm. The actual funeral took place as soon as possible after death, normally on the same day as the death. The body was carried to the place of burial on a litter or bier (2 Mittah 5:3-31; cf Luke 7:14) and was followed by mourners who chanted lamentations (Nowack & Paton 1936:117-9).

From the foregoing, it is evident that there are a few similarities between the Agikuyu traditional practices and those of the Jews, especially prompt burial on the same day as death. However, there are differences between the two, especially concerning how the body was carried to the place of burial, as well as by whom, and how the body was followed. As shown below, the practices of early Christianity differ substantially from those of the Agikuyu ancestors, the ones in scripture, as well as those of the contemporary Agikuyu Christians.

As presented in Chapter 5, in early Christianity, the church gave the funeral procession something of the character of a triumph. After lying in state, the body was covered and carried to a cemetery outside the city in a procession of friends and relatives who sang psalms along the way. The music and mourning associated with the pagan concept of death was largely replaced by the singing of psalms. Musical instruments were, however, excluded because as Tertullian indicated "the dead would be disturbed by the trumpet of the musicians while he was waiting to be awakened by the trumpet of the angel". The procession was a religious service, and hence there was no room or allowance for actors and entertainers to participate. Other key activities worth noting were; the deceased was placed on a funeral litter (*lectica*) and was borne by pallbearers. At other times, such as during the period of plague and public calamity, the bearing of the dead to burial was the work of private friends. The wearing of black garments for mourning was condemned by church fathers, especially Cyprian, who, while condemning the use of black garments, recommended the wearing of white garments, since the departed have already assumed white garments there, namely in heaven. Regardless of when the procession took place, the torch-bearers were an integral part of the funeral procession. The Christians introduced the singing of psalms during the procession to supplant the pagan *plantus* and *nenia,* and likewise, the pagan music. The singing of psalms is an expression of great joy, and their use and the singing of them give an indication of the joyful outlook of the early Christians on death. It is also worthy of note that burial normally took place on the same day as death.

Today, for the Agikuyu Christians, this question of funeral processions has become extremely complex and involved, and the processions bear no resemblance to those of their ancestors or those in scripture, nor to those of early Christianity. As indicated earlier, almost all their dead bodies are preserved at the mortuary, on average for a week or so. Sometimes the body can be kept at the mortuary for weeks or months for several reasons. On the day of the burial, at the mortuary after the body has been embalmed, washed, clothed and a little perfume sprinkled on the body, the body is then placed in a coffin. Those brave enough to view the body are then invited to do so. Very rarely is the whole corpse viewed. Only the face is viewed through the aperture provided at the top-side of the coffin for that purpose. The aperture is then closed after viewing. The coffin is next taken to the hearse or mode of transport by the pallbearers who are usually members of the church, family members or very close friends. The convoy, of as many as one hundred vehicles then travels to the church/graveside led by the hearse, followed by the vehicle carrying the clergy, widow/widower, children and others. Recently there has emerged a tendency for the hearse to be headed by motorcycle outriders, resembling the motorcade of a king or president of a nation!! The whole entourage then proceeds to the church/graveside where after the funeral service, the coffin is then borne by the appropriate pallbearers to the grave where interment takes place.

It is evident from the above that current Agikuyu Christians have scarcely borrowed or adopted any aspect of funeral procession or of an immediate burial from their ancestors, from scriptural practices, or from the practices of early Christianity. It will, therefore, be necessary in chapter 8 to recommend those aspects that seem appropriate to be adopted by the modern Agikuyu and other African Christians in line with the theme of this book.

Interment

There are similarities in some aspects and differences in others regarding the interment of the dead, amongst all the traditions discussed in this study. To show any correlation between them, it is necessary to give a summary of the practice of each tradition, and thus facilitate the comparison.

Traditionally, for the Agikuyu when burying an elder, the funeral procession on reaching the burial site laid the body carefully in the grave on its right side facing the homestead. The ornaments that the deceased was wearing when he died, and which had been removed soon after death, were all laid in the grave near his stomach. Then the wet skin (*muguguta*) of the goat or ox that had been slaughtered earlier in the day was laid over the bundle containing the body, care being taken not to cover the face and the eyes.

Other events closely related to the actual interment included; the grave was filled with earth and stones; every son of the deceased had to bring a branch of *Mugaa* (acacia thorn tree) and lay it over the pile of stones; the young men who had dug the grave and carried the body were then cleansed with the stomach contents (*tatha*) of a fleshly slaughtered virgin ewe. The meat and the skin of the slaughtered ewe was thrown away for the hyenas to eat, all except a small portion which the elders had to eat so that, "*mburi ndigateo ta mundu*" (the ewe not to be thrown away like a person). This certainly proves that to the Agikuyu mutton was of greater importance than the body of the dead! The married sons of the deceased went back to their homes but until the concluding "*hukura*" ceremony had been performed they took care not to have sexual intercourse with their wives or with any other woman. They slept in their own hut, but not in the hut of any of their wives.

The Jews also had elaborate practices of burying their dead, but these differed substantially in many respects with the ones of the Agikuyu indicated above.

As presented in chapter 4, the Israelites did not abandon their dead (Gen 50:2, 26). From Isaiah 28:14, Isaiah 14:97; Isaiah 14:19; Ezekiel 32:27 we note that in the biblical period the dead were carried to the grave on a bier and buried in the garment they had worn while living. According to Jeremiah 34:5; 2 Chronicles 16:14; 21:19, spices were burned beside the bodies of prominent men. Later it was the custom to bury together with the dead objects which had been used by them during life, for example inkhorns, pens, writing tablets, keys . These days, as observed by Habenstein and Lamers (1963:191), the basic funeral rites by the Jews are those specified by Judaism. Certain features mark rites observed and practiced within Judaism, which include reverence for the dead, simplicity, equality between rich and poor, rapid burial, the avoidance of cremation, keeping the body inviolate from embalmment, incisions and blood-letting. Some of these practices and observances will be recommended for adoption by Africans including the Agikuyu in their funeral practices. Modern Judaism now encourages the establishment of burial societies wherever Jew communities reside. As indicated further by Habenstein and Lamers (1963:191-192), today practically all the local burials of Jews are carried out by burial societies, which operate mostly according to the tradition of the Hevra Qadisha (Holy Brotherhood). These, according to Habenstein and Lamers, are non-profit organizations of pious people who have assumed the responsibility for conducting funerals of Jews. A typical brotherhood sets up four aims; (i) to acquire land in its town's administrative area and to fence and divide it, construct roadways through it, provide it with service buildings and otherwise improve it so as to be a cemetery suitable for Jews. (ii) to keep this cemetery in good condition, (iii) to organize the members into an effective staff capable of supervising funerals and burials, and to engage in other good works and (iv) to co-operate with the authorities in any public venture initiated and sponsored by them and to accept authoritative rabbinical guidance (Ibid.,191-2). The Agikuyu including other Africans in the diaspora residing far from the their ancestral homeland in Africa will be encouraged in Chapter 8 to adopt such arrangements and form similar organisations for coping with death of their fellow tribesmen instead of bringing them all the way back to their African country of origin.

In early Christianity, earth burial was the norm. As has been presented in this study, the Christians in Jerusalem and other Christian communities adhered to the old and better practices of earth burial. It is worthy of note that the bodies of the early Jews patriarchs and matriarchs, as well as the body of Christ, were laid in tombs. It was probably on that account that early Christians felt that the bodies of Christians should be interred under the ground. Christians did not cremate their dead, although as far as can be ascertained, there was no legal prohibition of cremation and embalmment in Christian antiquity. None was needed, however, for the Christians by reason of their belief detested them. The Christians imitated Christ during their lives, and wished to imitate him in death and be buried after the manner of his burial. The desire also to give the body back to earth, whence it had its origin was another reason for preferring earth burial.

In the Middle Ages, the western church knew only earth burial as the means of disposal of the dead. Charlemagne (AD 768-814) forbade the conquered Saxons to cremate corpses on pain of death. The dead were washed, dressed in linen or penitential robes, or, in case of one in holy orders, in official dress. On the day of the funeral, the dead person was carried by his peers, the layman by laymen and the clergy by clergy, first to the church, where mass was celebrated, and afterwards to the grave in which he was laid with his face turned towards the east. The church adhered to the view that the dead body is not a worthless thing, but is to rise again, no matter how it had decomposed or decayed. For this reason it had to have a Christian burial, and the burial places must have a fitting appearance. The burial was a matter for the church, and the congregation was required to take part in it if possible, and should attend the funerals of the poor. Accordingly, bells called the congregation together. At the graveside, among other activities, basins were placed to receive alms for the poor. In some countries, the congregation recited the creed after the closing prayer. The desire to instruct the congregation on every occasion was expressed in the burial service by reading of scriptures and the singing of hymns. A short discourse on death and the resurrection was read in the home, in the church or at the grave, although a special sermon might be requested of the minister if he was specially paid for it, and in such cases, he referred particularly to the life and death of the subject of his address. Thus arose the funeral sermon, which was originally designed to instruct the congregation in eschatology, and to honor the memory of the departed.

These days, for the Agikuyu Christians, interment follows the liturgy of the Christian denomination which is conducting the burial. As presented in chapter 3, unlike the practice of their ancestors which had distinct methods of disposing of the bodies of the various categories of individuals, there is hardly any recognizable difference between the interment of a child, youth, women or men. In my view, such traditional categorizing was discriminatory, as all should be accorded similar burial as exercised today by the Agikuyu Christians. The coffin is borne to the grave by pallbearers who, when instructed to do so by the officiating clergy/pastor, lower the coffin into the grave. After the grave has been filled with soil and a few stones laid on top, the pastor officiating then plants a cross and blesses it. When doing so he intones the words, 'in the name of the Father, the Son and the Holy Spirit'. Flowers are then placed on the grave by the pastor (church) (a flower in the shape of the cross), next by the widow/widower and children (a flower in the shape of a heart). Others present then place flowers on the grave or plant shrubs or tree seedlings.

It is apparent from the above that currently the Agikuyu Christians do not follow the practices of their ancestors. Neither do they follow most of the practices observed in the Old Testament or the New Testament. However, there seems to be a lot that they have borrowed from practices of the Christians in the Middle Ages, which include care of the body, affording their dead a Christian burial, including taking most of the bodies to the church during the funeral service. It is worthy of note that it is only the bodies of staunch Christian believers and sincere church members that are accorded this privilege. Other aspects similar to those of Christians in the Middle Ages include funerals being attended by as many Christians as possible, reciting psalms or verses of scripture, reading of scripture, reading or giving a eulogy and a sermon being given by the pastor. There seem, however, to be two major habits that the Agikuyu Christians have not adopted, namely all the Christians being obliged to attend funerals of the poor as in the Middle Ages, and secondly, at the graveside to place basins to receive alms for the poor. Contrary to the decree by Charlemagne, the grounds where Christians are buried do not appear to be consecrated. It was during that era, that the church seems to have insisted that all Christians should receive a Christian burial. In chapter 8 that follows a number of recommendations to be adopted by the current Agikuyu as well as by other African

Christians will be made, based on what is shown in this section, especially collecting alms for the poor at the funeral.

Place of Burial

Chapter 2 explained that the Agikuyu only buried respected elders and matriarchs. The rest of the Agikuyu were dumped in the bush mainly in the "*kibirira*" and their bodies left to be devoured by wild beasts and birds. The patriarch was buried in the "*kiaraini*" (rubbish midden). As analysed at length in chapter 2 (regarding the "*kiaraini*") and in chapter 3 (regarding "*thome*") the *kiaraini* (rubbish midden) was sited to one side of the home entrance and outside the perimeter hedge of the traditional Agikuyu homestead. The location of the main entrance or gate (*thome*) to the traditional family homestead is misunderstood by the current Agikuyu, as it is not where they assume it to have been. This issue has been analyzed in considerable depth in chapter 3. I would hope that the arguments presented herein are read and understood as mistakenly elders are being buried where they should not be. Elders as presented in Chapter 2 of this study, and as indicated above, were buried in the *kiaraini* (rubbish midden) located near the home entrance (*thome*) but not at the *thome*. Granted, the *kiaraini* was found at one side of the *thome,* but it was in the *kiaraini* that elders were normally buried. Today, an elder cannot possibly and practically be buried in the *kiaraini* as traditionally after burial of an elder, the homestead had to be moved to a new location to facilitate, among other reasons, the founding of a new *kiaraini* for use by the new homestead. Today, most of the Agikuyu of Kabete have permanent or semi-permanent residences. Additionally, most have no available land or space to move to. There can therefore be no question of relocating the homestead. The elders should be buried in another convenient place but not at the *kiaraini* and definitely not at the *thome*. I would urge the Agikuyu to have a better understanding of the location of *kiaraini* (rubbish midden) of a traditional Agikuyu homestead as it would lead to a better utilization of the family land and be extremely beneficial to those left behind. Even nearer home and easier to help the current Agikuyu generation comprehend the concept of where traditionally an elder ought to be buried is for them to ask themselves where even in the modern Agikuyu homestead the rubbish midden (*kiaraini*) is located. It is definitely not at the main entrance of the homestead, rather at the back of the homestead. If therefore Agikuyu tradition were strictly adhered to, that is where an elder ought to be buried.

The exact position in the *kiaraini* where the elder would be buried was left to be decided by the elders unless the deceased, before he died, had chosen a spot himself and marked it with a peg. When the exact site had been agreed upon, the grave digging was started by the senior and circumcised unmarried son of the deceased, or, if there was no circumcised unmarried son, a circumcised unmarried nephew of the deceased. The married sons had to be present, and the son who started the digging was later assisted by some of the junior brothers and nephews. For an old married woman in a polygamist marriage, in all details as indicated by Leakey (1977:957) and my respondents, the method of digging the grave and of burying the body were the same as for an elder, except in the following four points namely; (i) the woman was buried lying on her left side and not on her right (ii) the grave was not dug near the rubbish midden (*kiaraini*), but in the bush immediately behind the hut of the deceased woman (iii) a dead woman might not be carried out through the main entrance of the homestead, but instead had to be carried out through a gap made in the fence at the side of the hut; additionally her body was not wrapped with *muguguta,* but only in her sleeping mat and animal skins she had worn during life (iv) no elders were called in to give advice, as her husband was an elder (Leakey 1977:955-6; my respondents).

There is hardly any similarity between the Agikuyu and the Jews' belief and practice regarding the place of burial. As was discussed in Chapter 4, in view of the belief that family unity survived death, scripture shows that, the Jews placed great importance on a household grave. Such graves were located on the land belonging to the family and in proximity to the house.

Gradually, however, the habit prevailed of placing them outside inhabited districts and of making use of clefts and of caves. The openings were closed with heavy stones. The sepulchre was always strictly regarded as family property, in which no stranger should be laid. Only in later times in exceptional circumstances were strangers buried in them. For the destitute, pilgrims and the like, there were common, namely public, cemeteries, where criminals also were interred.

Regarding the place of burial, there were areas of resemblance between scriptural practices and those of early Christianity. Burial options of Christians did not happen overnight (Davies 1999:191-2). The chosen burial option of the early Christians and Jewish communities in Rome itself was the catacombs, located as were all Greco-Roman burial sites outside the city walls. Shaw (1996:101) asserts that eventually over a thousand kilometres of galleries extended beyond the outskirts of Rome providing underground (catacombs) burial space for something in the order of six million people. As observed in the study, catacombs are ancient underground burial sites containing niches hewn in the rock (*loculi*) and found not only in Rome but in numerous other places around the Mediterranean Sea. It should be noted as observed in Chapter 5, that Jews and Christians, in their respective catacombs, from the late second to early fifth century CE, buried their dead in either *loculi* of about six feet by two feet by two feet cut into the walls of the galleries, giving a "beehive" effect, or in *cubicula*, chambers (with benches covering the actual graves) for two more burials. Davies (1999:193) advises that the *loculi* were, for both the religious groups; the most used form of interment, followed by the *arcosolia*, and then *forma* (straight into the ground) sarcophagi and amphora.

Among the Jews and also during the period of early Christianity, secondary burial was widespread in Palestine during the first century CE (McCane 1990:34). "While there is evidence for variety in the practice (e.g. Ossuaries, Loculi, shelves and even pits) a consistent pattern is nevertheless easily discernible", indicates McCane. It should be further observed according to McCane that people who used the tombs all buried their dead in two stages; first they placed the body of the deceased in the tomb, and later, after the flesh of the body had decayed, they returned to rebury the bones. McCane observes further that secondary burial was the final ritual of mourning for the dead. Second burial is neither known nor practiced by most African communities including the Agikuyu. In chapter 8 it will be recommended for them to consider practicing it, especially for those families who are facing acute shortage of land for burying their dead, but who at the same time would wish almost all their dead to be buried in the same place, that is, in the ancestral land.

Currently, other than the very few who are cremated, the majority of the Agikuyu are accorded earth burial in the family parcel of land or in a public cemetery. Additionally, in the Kikuyu District for ordained ministers and lay-readers (and their spouses) of ACK St Joseph Kanyariri church, and ordained ministers, elders and their spouses of the PCEA Kimuri (Church of Torch), they are buried at the ACK St Joseph Kanyariri Church cemetery, or in the PCEA Church of Torch (Kimuri) cemetery respectively. Next to the PCEA Kikuyu Hospital there is a Church Cemetery for other members and families of the PCEA Church. As indicated elsewhere, there is an acute shortage of space for earth burial in Kikuyu District. In Chapter 8, alternative means of disposing of the dead other than by earth burial will be proposed to be adopted by those communities with limited land to bury their dead.

Rituals Performed After Burial

From what has been presented in this study, it is apparent that traditional rituals observed by the Agikuyu after burial differ substantially from those in scripture and those of early Christianity. There is seemingly no similarity between the practices of any of them.

This study shows that traditionally for the Agikuyu, every death involved the performance of a ceremony of *kuhukura* (the purification ceremony to free the home from the plight of death) which was considerably more complicated in the case of an elder than it was otherwise. The *kuhukura* ceremony was analyzed at length in Chapter 2. Principally, it involved the widows of the deceased having ceremonial sexual intercourse with a stranger referred to as *mwendia ruhiu* (one who sells his penis). However, the younger brother of the deceased is the one who had to have ceremonial sexual intercourse with the senior widow. The *kuhukura* ceremony took place one month after burial and lasted for eight days. As was revealed in Chapter 2, if during the course of the eight days of the *kuhukura* ceremony, any of the men who had been partners of the widows should have formed a special friendship with his partner, then that man might, from this time on, claim a special right to come and have sexual intercourse with her and even beget children by her. Such children did not rank as children of their physical father but as children of the deceased man. Although the responsibility for looking after, feeding, and clothing the widow was inherited by one of the male relatives of the deceased who had inherited her, the widow could not be prevented from having her partner from the *hukura* ceremonies as her lover if she wished it (Chapter 2 of this book: Leakey 1977:942-52; my respondents).

The occurrence narrated above relates to the *hukura* ceremony where an elder had died. However, where an old married woman died during the life of her husband, one month after burial of the woman, the husband carried out a ceremony of *kuhukura* for the deceased wife. As indicated by Leakey (1977:958) as well as by my respondents, most details of such a *hukura* ceremony for the wife were exactly the same as the ceremony performed for an elder, though there were a few important points of divergence namely: (i) no men were called in as partners for the woman's co-wives, since the husband was alive and would perform the necessary sex acts (ii) these ceremonial sex acts were performed only by the wife next senior to the one who had died; other co-wives of the deceased were not involved (iii) during the eight nights of *hukura* ceremony, all unmarried children of the deceased woman had to sleep in the hut of the next senior wife to their deceased mother where the *hukura* ceremony was being performed by the father, and thus participate by their presence in the ritual acts of "sacrifice" by sexual intercourse (iv) only the husband, the next/senior wife, and the children of the deceased woman and of the co-wife who performed the sex acts wore *ngoka* rings, or took part in the ceremonies in any way.

Regarding the *kuhukura* ritual, as well a number of other archaic traditional Agikuyu customs and sacrifices, Leakey (1977:1103) is of the view that the nature of this observance and sacrifices and the power which they had is quite obscure, and it is probable that the original significance has been completely lost. Leakey further feels that "the whole conception of the meaning of these ceremonial sex acts (*kuhukura* and others) of sacrifice for Agikuyu was that of a purification rite and yet it was called a sacrifice". These rituals Leakey further feels "had in the past had a different meaning and had been in the nature of an act of worship to some deity that had been superceded by the Agikuyu High God (*Ngai*)". The significance of *kuhukura* will be referred to further in chapter 8 regarding its close resemblance to the ritual practiced by the Wa Sukuma of Tanzania, which was analyzed in chapter 2. A recommendation will be made for further research to be undertaken to establish whether the Agikuyu borrowed from the Wa Sukuma or vice versa, especially during the Bantu migration.

Other rituals carried out by the Agikuyu after death include among others; the hut (*thingira*) in which the elder died was not pulled down immediately, however, the male members of the family continued to live in it. After a short interval, according to my respondents and Leakey (1977:981), the whole homestead was moved to a new homestead; As for the hut (*nyumba*) of a woman, according to my respondents and Leakey (1977:966), when she died, one of two things could be done according to the decision of her husband, or if she had been a widow by the son or the brother-in-law who was responsible for her, namely (a) he could gather every member of his household and together they could pull the whole hut down at once. This was done as soon as the body had been disposed of. When the hut had been pulled down, every plank, pole, piece of thatch and all the hearthstones were carried out by way of the main entrance of the homestead and deposited in the bush in a pile to rot and decay, (b) alternatively the man responsible for the widow would leave the hut where it was and then after the *hukura* ceremony had been performed he would move the whole homestead one hundred metres or so, leaving the hut of the deceased standing deserted. Such a deserted hut was called a *kĩgĩgĩ* (a hut deserted because of death).

As revealed in Chapter 2, according to my respodents and Middleton (1953:51) shortly after the elder had been buried and the *kuhukura* ceremony performed and finalized, a few other activities took place thereafter which included among others "wife inheritance" mentioned earlier. The senior member (son) usually the firstborn son (but in exceptional circumstances, another more able son with leadership qualities) of the senior widow could inherit his father's authority. He would have more often than not become the trustee (*muramati*) of the assets belonging to the *mbari*, in other words he would be the head of the *mbari* (family). Additionally, my respondents and Middleton advise that as indicated earlier, the senior wife (*nyakiambi*) may not remarry. She is inherited by the husband's younger brother or by his sons. Note should be taken that a man may not inherit the wife of his deceased son nor the widow of a younger brother, because he stands in the relation of father to her. Middleton indicates that if a widow has no brother-in-law, a stepson could inherit her. If not, she passed to a man of her own clan (Middleton 1953:51; my respondents).

It is worthy of note that all of the aforementioned Agikuyu traditional after-burial rites are barely known by the current Agikuyu generation. Additionally, none of them is practiced today as far as I have been able to ascertain. Due to the fact that they are obviously unchristian, I would not recommend them to be reinstated in part or in whole.

In scripture there is limited information regarding rituals performed after burial. In the Old Testament we note that a *masseba* and *siyum* (pillar and monument) were constructed as markers of the righteous. A circle of stones served to show contempt for Israel's enemies. Worthy also of note is the fact that the law expressly allowed the opening of the grave on the third day to look after the dead.

A practice found in scripture, and which might be classified as a rite, is that of levirate marriages. This according to Hirsch (1939:526), was the marriage of a childless widow to her husband's brother, which was an ancient custom followed at the time of the patriarchs (Gen 38:8), and later incorporated into the Law of Moses (Deut 25:5-10). This issue is discussed at length in Chapter 2, but of note is the purpose of levirate marriage, which was a requirement for a brother or the nearest male kin of the deceased to raise up seed to the name of the deceased. This practice had a remote similarity with the Agikuyu's custom of "wife inheritance", but with a different angle, in the sense that the purpose for the Agikuyu doing so was principally to look after the widows and the children of the deceased. The male relative who "inherited" the widow was not required by custom or by the Agikuyu religion to have sexual relationship with the widow unless she voluntarily consented to such as arrangement. The widow would, however, as indicated earlier seek the affections of other men, who would then give her children. Children from such relationship, however, would belong to the deceased and be looked after by the male relative who inherited the widow. Giving further insight on the issue of Levirate marriage, Bozman (1958:734) indicates that Levirate was an "institution by which a widow is inherited by her deceased husband's successor, but her later children are legally those of her dead husband, not of her new husband". Bozman asserts further that "it is found among anct Hebrews and many African and other peoples today".

For the early Christians, on special occasions such as the anniversary of death, relatives and friends might adorn the grave with flowers or lanterns or even anoint it with oil. By the fourth century, it was common to pronounce regular prayers for the dead.

These days for contemporary Agikuyu Christians, there are hardly any rituals performed after burial other than that within a week or so after burial an advertisement, for those who can afford it, is placed in one local newspaper thanking all who participated in the funeral. One year after, for families who can afford it, a tombstone is placed on the grave, then the family and friends gather at the grave-side to "unveil" the cross. The aspect of "unveiling the cross" in my view is of modern creation, and as far as can be ascertained, has no theological basis. As indicated in Chapter 8, I would strongly recommend to the Agikuyu to do away with this rite.

As indicated earlier, another rite observed by the Jews and some early Christians was the practice of second burial. This is where after some suitable time, namely after the flesh had decayed and only the bones remained, the bones would be exhumed and reburied. Such remains would be reburied in ossuaries. One ossuary might hold the bones of numerous generations of one family. This is what in scripture is termed "being buried with one's fathers". As again elaborated earlier, the way this was done was that initially burial was individual, but as indicated by Decker (2006:14) after a corpse had decomposed so as to leave only bones, the bones were transferred to an ossuary (a stone or pottery bone box or pottery jar) to make room for additional burials of family members. This was done principally to comply with the custom and to create more space for burying the dead. This method of "second burial" as indicated earlier will be recommended for consideration by the Agikuyu, whose land especially of the majority of those living in Kikuyu District (the scope of this study) is extremely limited, and most of whom would not like their remains to be cremated but interred in their ancestral land. As again indicated earlier one problem in this is the fact that to exhume a body in Kenya one must obtain a Court Order. This can be overcome if appropriate legislation is enacted to allow the exhumation of bodies to be done without the need for dealing with much red tape.

Life After Death

Regarding this aspect, there is correlation in the beliefs of the four traditions considered in this study, namely between the traditional Agikuyu, scripture, early Christianity and the contemporary Agikuyu. Some beliefs in the afterlife are similar, while others differ as shown below.

As was presented in chapter 2, the Agikuyu did not fear death. As a matter of fact, they used to long for death, as they were certain that after death they would go to the land of their ancestors, where they would be welcomed warmly by their departed kith and kin. Additionally, they believed that life in the land of the ancestors was literally a duplicate of the life they had lived here on earth with cattle, sheep, goats, plenty of food and all their life's requirements. It is strange, however, for reasons that no one has so far been able to discern they feared dead bodies. The Agikuyu also believed in reincarnation. They believed that when a child is born to their kith and kin and named after them, they were automatically reincarnated in that child. This is strange as such reincarnation or naming of a particular child often takes place when the one being named or "reincarnated" is still alive. Another odd aspect of this practice and belief is that often, one might, while still living, have numerous children bearing his/her name; thus according to this thinking, being reincarnated in many children. Strange, but it is true, and happening even today among staunch Christians. The Agikuyu are even today very insistent on how children born in the family are named, mainly because of this tradition and belief.

Another angle to the practice of incarnation, followed and observed in those pre-colonial days by the Agikuyu, was that of ensuring that some particular category of individuals was reincarnated. For example, in cases where the firstborn child died at infancy, a subsequent child of the same sex born to the same mother later on would "replace" the firstborn child that had died. This child would, however, not be given the same name as that of the dead child, but would be given the name *Muriuki* or *Kariuki* (meaning one who has been "reincarnated") for a boy child or *Njoki* (meaning the one who "replaces"') for a girl child (cf. Leakey 1977:516).

In the Old Testament, Muller (1979:145-50), advises that the souls of those who died were believed to have departed to Sheol. This is at times referred to as the abode of the dead. Additionally, in the Old Testament, Sheol is used in reference to the afterlife. Muller is of the view that Sheol denotes a grey and shadowy existence in which the dead persist without much joy or comfort. Further Muller asserts that in the Old Testament all go to Sheol without distinction, meaning that there is no question of reward or punishment. He (1979:900) is further of the view that although the New

Testament description of the abode of the dead differs little from the Old Testament the destinies of the righteous and the unrighteous are more carefully distinguished.

Early Christians believed in the resurrection and early church fathers taught their followers not to fear death, and instead the root of immortality should be embraced and exercised in their lives.

For today's Agikuyu Christians, they do not welcome death. They, for want of a better word, dread death. Their attitude to death is one of defeat, sorrow, loss and at times bitterness as to why death should take place. This attitude is evident even in staunch Christians when approaching death, or when one of their own dies. This attitude is both strange and surprising, because one is left wondering why they should feel that way, when their ancestors did not fear death, and likewise why fear death if they are certain that when they die they will go to heaven, which is by far a better place than this world. Additionally, if they believe that to die is to be with Christ, as death when one is righteous opens the doors for one to go to heaven. The only gratifying thing about the current Agikuyu attitude is that after death, they believe in the resurrection of the body and of the life everlasting. Currently the large majority of Agikuyu Christians respect the bodies of the dead and take good care of the corpse. This is mainly because they believe that it is the same body that will be resurrected. This notion was analysed in chapter 6, and will be clarified again in a following section.

As discussed in Chapter 6, and as indicated by Young (1984:454), one of the simplest statements is, "there will be a resurrection of both the righteous and the wicked" (Acts 24:15). The certainty of resurrection and the nature of it are described by St Paul at length in 1 Corinthians 15:12-54. Our resurrected bodies will be like our Lord's after his resurrection (Phil 3:20, 21; 1John 3:2). All faithful Christians should therefore be convinced and believe as I do in the resurrection of both the just and the unjust, and in the eternal blessedness of the children of God. So there is no need to fear death, since if one is righteous, one is destined to go to heaven and be with Jesus for evermore.

As presented in chapter 6, at the resurrection there will be a bodily reality of some type. It will have some connection with, and derive from, our original body, and yet it will not be merely a resuscitation of our original body (Erickson 2005:1199). As further shown earlier, there will be a transformation or metamorphosis. No one knows the exact nature of the resurrection body, and hence our difficulty in understanding. However, it will retain and at the same time glorify the human form. We will be free of the imperfection and needs we had on earth. The spiritual body which Paul speaks of in 1 Corinthians 15:44 will have some connection or point of identity with the old body, but will be differently constituted, as the old body of flesh and blood cannot inherit the Kingdom of God, nor does the perishable inherit the imperishable (1 Cor 15:50; Ibid., 1199).

Economy of Burial Grounds and Spaces

As was presented in the study, especially in chapter 2, due to dwindling burial space in some parts of the world, ingenious methods of dealing with the problem have evolved. A few examples were shown in the study, including the Jewish method of "second burial" whereby after the initial burial, which was mainly individual burial, the corpse would be exhumed after all the flesh had decayed and only the bones remained. These bones would be placed in ossuaries, thus creating room for more bodies to be buried. This might, as indicated earlier, be a long-term solution for the Agikuyu of Kikuyu District as well as for numerous other Africans, who are facing an acute shortage of burial space. Other methods instituted for dealing with this problem include, but are not limited to, the City of Paris where cemeteries are usually constructed with a capacity for twenty caskets. When the vault has been filled, after a lapse of ten years, it is permissible to exhume the remains and place them inside a single casket, thus nineteen additional places are provided. In Italy, cemetery space may be purchased for a limited period of ownership or in perpetuity. If a body is given "common ground" burial, it remains buried for a period varying from eighteen months to ten years. After this time the grave is opened, the remains exhumed and the bones are either buried or placed in a small niche as the family desires.

As was discussed in chapter 2, places where practices such as the reuse of graves and where cremation is common have no shortage of burial space. In chapter 8, a recommendation will be made for the Agikuyu and other Africans to consider seriously putting a stop to burial in perpetuity, but instead introduce "second burial", reuse of graves and cremation. Additionally for them to consider, is the donating of bodies for use by medical schools.

The Chapter that Follows

Chapter 8, which follows, will contain my recommendations based on what has been discussed in this study, on my own views, on the views obtained from a number of Agikuyu Christians and pastors, as well as on the views and works of other prominent theologians and scholars towards formulating a model for Agikuyu Christian and other Africans funeral rites that would integrate relevant cultural, scriptural and practical norms. The chapter will also include my recommendations on areas of further research, especially dwelling on issues encountered in this book.

CHAPTER 8

RECOMMENDATIONS, CONCLUSION, AREAS OF FURTHER RESEARCH AND CONTRIBUTION TO THE FIELD OF PRACTICAL THEOLOGY

Introduction

HAVING CONSIDERED AND ANALYZED numerous issues touching on funerals, including the Agikuyu traditional mode of coping with death, how currently they are coping with death, how funerals were handled during biblical times, during early Christianity, as well as having considered the issues of resurrection and the resurrected body, and additionally having analyzed how some countries are coping with limited burial spaces, it is now appropriate for me to express my recommendations, based on what has been discussed in this study, on how the Agikuyu Christians of Kikuyu District (the scope of this study) as well as for other African ethnic communities should cope with death. This is in accordance with the fourth and final step required of the LIM model, which involves interpreting contermporary obligation and considering what should be the ideal method of burial, which in this case is the ideal method of burial for the Agikuyu Christians as well as for most other African communities.

From what has been discussed in this book, the funeral practices of the contemporary Agikuyu bear almost no resemblance to those of their ancestors or those practiced during biblical times and those of early Christianity (cf. Droz 2011:69). The contemporary Agikuyu Christians can therefore adopt and indeed design fresh modes of coping with death, which where possible should resemble the practices of those three above. However, as will be observed subsequently, great care will be taken to ensure that the proposed new model of coping with death by the Agikuyu Christians and by other Africans is based on scriptural and Christian principles; it will respect the dead as well as the families of the deceased; will be dignified and at the same time will respect some of the modern "customary" methods practiced today by the Agikuyu and other African Christians.

Note should be taken that there are biblical absolutes in terms of what we believe about life and death, but according to Decker (2007:9), how we handle the death of a loved one is not specified. It is also worthy of note that Christianity as discussed in this book does not permit that the dead body be cast into a hole without ceremony, and neither is there any example or evidence of encouragement given to justify the lavish expenditure which has become the rage among most of the Agikuyu Christians, and indeed among the majority of peoples worldwide.

As so well expressed by Decker (2007:9), often there are cultural practices, but for a Christian they should be local customs which have been evaluated and modified in light of biblical teaching. In answering the question why mankind has funerals, he (2007:9) is of the view that it is traditional to have funerals. For the Agikuyu, however, traditionally they did not have funerals as such, only for a very few respected elders and matriarchs, whilst the large proportion of the dead were left in the bush to be devoured by wild animals and birds. If being traditional, however, is not a compelling reason, which as indicated above applies to the Agikuyu, then one is left to wonder why do we bother with what is usually an expensive, time-consuming affair (Ibid., 9). Note should be taken that though burial is not a biblically mandated practice, as indicated above, the very fact that it is nearly universal in all cultures (biblical and otherwise) including the contemporary Agikuyu Christians, and other Africans, suggests that there is some wisdom in such a practice (Ibid., 9).

Perhaps the most basic function of a funeral asserts Decker (2007:9) is the time to say goodbye, to accept the fact of death, to deal with the inevitable grief, and prepare to move on without a loved one. Joseph Bayly, in (Decker 2007:9), is of the view that the studies of people's responses to dying suggest that there are five typical stages, namely denial, anger, bargaining, depression and acceptance. As further indicated by Bayly, not all persons experience all of them in that order. Seeing the casket, participating in a funeral service and standing at the graveside are part of the healing, grieving process of most people. It should be understood, however, that a funeral, as some pastors and most families worldwide including the Agikuyu and other African Christians seem to portray, is not a time to glorify the dead, to impress the community or to make amends for past failures. These as indicated by Decker (2007:9) are mistakes that a grieving family may easily make.

Recommendation Towards Formulating A Model For Agikuyu Christians' and other African Ethnic Communities Funeral Rites That Integrates Relevant Cultural, Scriptural and Practical Norms

The Recommended New Model For The Agikuyu and Other African Christians' Funeral Rites and For Comparative Purposes Funeral Practices Of The Contemporary Agikuyu

(For comparative purposes, the Agikuyu Traditional Practices, Biblical and Patristic Traditions are as shown in the table in Chapter 7 of this book, pages 196–201)

EVENT	CONTEMPORARY AGIKUYU PRACTICES	RECOMMENDED MODEL
1. How the idea of burial arose	From practices of numerous other cultures, religions and their own ingenuity.	This study might provide new methods to the Agikuyu and other African ethnic communities for coping with death.
2. Actions performed before death	The Roman Catholics anointing the sick; administering viaticum. Other denominations prayers and solace to the dying.	The Roman Catholics to be accorded appropriate rites including anointing of the sick and administering Viaticum. Other denominations prayers and solace to the dying. For the sick to be encouraged to confess their sins and repent. Where possible obtain the wishes of the dying including where they would wish to be buried and who should inherit what they own.
3. Actions performed soon after death	Alerting the immediate family and neighbors; body wrapped in sheets or bedcovers; taking the body to mortuary; advising the relevant government officials.	Those involved in the funeral to remain in control of things to prevent falling into the many difficulties involved in funerals due to poor planning and other exaggerated demands. To establish whether the deceased left a will or whether he indicated where and how he wished to be buried. Decide what type of funeral he will be accorded. These indicators will guide how and where the body will be preserved, as well as how the funeral will be planned. To ensure that the body is appropriately preserved during the whole procedure of the funeral process. To advise the relevant government agency (agencies).

EVENT	CONTEMPORARY AGIKUYU PRACTICES	RECOMMENDED MODEL
4. Clothing of the dead	On the day of burial, body dressed either in their church uniforms (e.g. Woman's Guild) or in the clothes they wore during life. Occasionally some dressed in new clothes and shoes.	The body should be clothed in a dignified manner. In other words, in dignified attire without going to excess. Clothes worn during life, and where appropriate, uniforms of the guild to which the deceased was affiliated in his or her church would be most suitable. Those to be cremated to be wrapped in sheets, bed covers, blankets, or in clothes worn during life. Avoid extravagance such as purchasing new clothes or shoes.
5. Crowning the dead	The dead are not crowned.	Under no circumstances are the dead to be crowned.
6. The wake held over the dead	No wake per se is held. Largely because the body is at the mortuary from death to burial.	Wake is a practice that is foreign to the Agikuyu. To them a wake as such should not be held. However, prayers and gathering of friends and relatives at the residence of the deceased from date of death to the night before burial is encouraged, as often it brings healing to the family.
7. Mourning	Not mourning "unduly".	In accordance with the practice of our ancestors, early Christians and that of the contemporary Agikuyu Christians, we should desist from mourning "unduly".
8. Funeral procession	Very complex; body accompanied by a convoy of many vehicles, even at times headed by motorcycle outriders.	The current trend should be simplified and the numbers of those forming the procession trimmed down. On the day of the funeral, should the body be at the mortuary (funeral home) the procession to comprise only the hearse, a few vehicles carrying the nuclear family and close family members and friends. The rest of the mourners to wait at the church, graveside, residence or at the place where the funeral service will take place. Motor cycle outriders should be discouraged, as they are just for showing off.

EVENT	CONTEMPO-RARY AGIKUYU PRACTICES	RECOMMENDED MODEL
9. Time of burial	On the average, one week after death, but often many weeks or months after death.	Where and when possible to revert to the same day as death burial as was done by our ancestors, biblical times and by the early Christians. Should this not be possible then as soon as possible. It is worthy of note that our patriarchs were accorded private funerals. I strongly advocate immediate private family graveside service and funeral. As a show of love to the deceased, such burial, handling of the body and so on, to be done by relatives and friends of the deceased as was done traditionally, during biblical times and early Christianity. Where possible avoid using the services of funeral homes and other intermediaries. An immediate private burial is recommended followed at a later date if deemed necessary by a public memorial service in the church or residence. To facilitate an immediate funeral, the funeral can be officiated and concluded by other recognised church officials, other than an ordained minister in circumstances where the latter is not available for an immediate funeral. To remove the numerous "customary" funeral requirements of modern creation which are not necessary such as the funeral announcements, taking the body to the mortuary, taking the body to church, and so on. If it is "a must" then the announcement to be short and to the point. Names of too many relatives, where they are domiciled (e.g. USA), where they work and similar should be left out. To avoid heading the advertisement "CELEBRATING THE LIFE OF XYZ" as celebrating a life is the belief and practice of the non-Christian religious sect known as HUMANISTS who do not believe in the resurrection, and during whose funerals all Christian symbols must be removed or covered. We should have nothing to do with humanists nor encourage them.

EVENT	CONTEMPORARY AGIKUYU PRACTICES	RECOMMENDED MODEL
10. Interment	Follows the Liturgy of the Church; body borne in a coffin; flowers placed on the grave after burial and a cross inserted on the grave. Recently in accordance with their wishes a few cremated.	To try as much as possible to minimise the cost of funerals. To follow the liturgy of the denomination to which the deceased was affiliated. The body to be placed in a simple but dignified coffin. Very few flowers to be placed on the coffin or on the grave. Instead of flowers, mourners to be encouraged to donate to the bereaved family or to charity. A simple but dignified cross to be inserted on the grave. Desist from taking too many photographs and videos which soon after the funeral serve no meaningful purpose. Not to feed mourners, but where possible provide snacks for those who have travelled from far. Desist from producing funeral programmes whose purpose is doubtful. They are an unnecessary drain on the bereaved family's resources. Additionally, they are a means of showing off. Most of them are discarded immediately after the burial. Mourners instead to be encouraged to carry hymn books to funerals. Desist from taking the body to church during funeral service, as there is no known theological reason for doing so. To always remember that funerals are for the living not for the dead. At the funeral collect alms for the poor as was done by the early Christians.

EVENT	CONTEMPORARY AGIKUYU PRACTICES	RECOMMENDED MODEL
11. Place of burial	Graves dug on family ancestral land; public cemeteries, and so on. Recently a few who die overseas are buried where they die.	For those who die far away to be buried where they die e.g. those in the diaspora to be buried there. I strongly recommend that those Africans residents far from their country of origin (diaspora) form their own burial societies to bury their own there, and desist from ferrying bodies back to their homeland. For others, depending on the size of the family land-holding, to be buried either in the family's land or in a public cemetery. Due to the acute shortage of burial space in Kikuyu District, and other parts of Africa, I encourage families to accept and adopt cremation or to donate their bodies to medical schools. I would strongly advocate to those families without adequate land, but who wish to give their dead an earth burial in the ancestral land for them to adopt the practice of "second burial" as practised in Scripture and by early Christians. For the patriarchs to be buried at a convenient place in the family land, if the family has sufficient land. He should not be buried at the "*thome*" (homestead entrance) as this is not cultural. Patriarchs were buried in the "*kiaraini*" (rubbish midden) and not at the gate (*thome*). To desist from constructing expensive tombstones which serve no purpose. They are a way of showing off and they look hideous a few generations later. To always remember that the dead have no legal rights. Additionally, to remember that the land is for the living not for the dead.

EVENT	CONTEMPO-RARY AGIKUYU PRACTICES	RECOMMENDED MODEL
12. Rituals performed after burial	One week after burial, an announcement placed in newspapers thanking all who participated in the funeral; one year after a ceremony of "unveiling" the cross and gathering of family and friends for prayers and remembrance of the deceased.	To desist from placing announcements in the newspapers a week or so after the funeral thanking all who attended the burial and all those who participated in any way in the funeral process. Such announcements are neither cultural nor scriptural. To desist from holding ceremonies of "unveiling" the cross, as there are no theological reasons for doing so. The practice is neither cultural nor scriptural. However, the family and friends can meet at the deceased's residence or at the church one year or so after death to pray for the family and for the soul of the deceased. In accordance with our culture and as indicated in Scripture, for a responsible male or female (in these days of gender equality) to be identified (such appointment to be acceptable to the widow) to assist the widow in dealing with various issues that arise after the death of the husband. Where possible for friends and extended family of the deceased to contribute to settling any debt left behind by the deceased. Alternatively, to recover any money owed to the deceased.
13. Life after death	They believe that if you are righteous, on death one will go to heaven, the sinful to hell; believe in the resurrection of the body and of the life everlasting.	To continue upholding their current conviction and belief that should one be righteous, on death one will go to heaven while the sinful will go to hell. To continue believing as most do in the resurrection of the body and of the life everlasting.
14. Economy of burial grounds and spaces	Not yet established. This book might furnish the solution to this issue.	For the Agikuyu and other Africans to adopt new methods of disposing of their dead including reuse of graves, cremation; to desist from the practice of burial in perpetuity but instead introduce the practice of "second burial". Also for them to consider donating bodies to medical schools.

Range of Recommendations

Of importance and worthy of note is that as expressed in this study the liturgy of the church does not fall within the scope of this study nor of the following recommendations.

The recommendations given below touch on the issues that a grieving family has to deal with, but do not include those issues on funerals that are within the competency of the church and the clergy. It should also be noted that the recommendations given below are based on what has been presented in this study, on my own thoughts and observations together with views expressed by other scholars including those whose works bear some similarity to this study, plus the views of a considerable number of contemporary Agikuyu Christian laity and pastors. Additionaly from views of a considerable number of persons from other races and African communities.

Legal Aspect

This study does not purport to offer legal advice on any topic covered or give any other specific legal advice, although on occasion it will point out the areas where legal advice needs to be considered and obtained.

Acts to be performed before death including leaving a will, and similar

As presented in chapter 2, when a Mugikuyu elder realised that he was about to die, he ensured that he left a verbal will. So did a number of patriarchs in the Old Testament as presented in chapters 4 and 7. This is a practice I would recommend the Agikuyu and other Africans to adopt. In this modern era, I would urge them to draw written wills long before death, as in the event of their death this would prevent those entitled to inherit their assets from engaging in often lengthy, costly and bitter court battles. Currently in the Kenya Law Courts there are numerous court cases going on which would have been avoided if only the deceased had left a will. The will should preferably be written, but if this is not the case or possible, then an oral will in front of creditable elders or witnesses should serve. Better still is to have a *recorded* oral will. Also where possible, the dying should bless their people as was done traditionally and also as was done in scripture. What is indicated above, that traditionally and biblically the patriarchs left oral wills should be sufficient to convince the Agikuyu and other African Christians that there is no taboo, or anything known relevant to their faith and tradition that would prevent them leaving a will.

As presented in Chapter 7, the Agikuyu and other African Christians where possible and practicable should give solace, comfort, and prayers to the dying, and assist them to confess and repent of their sins, and for them also to register the last words and wishes of the dying person.

Indicating how and where one wishes to be buried

Traditionally elders often marked with a peg where they wished to be buried. This might be the exact spot in the *kiaraini* (rubbish midden) or in any other place within the elders' clan (*mbari*) landholding. Likewise, a number of patriarchs in the Bible used to indicate where they would be buried, or alternatively it was understood where they would be buried. A good example of this is the burial of early biblical patriarchs and matriarchs including Sarah and Abraham at the cave of Mechpalah. Others are the burial of the kings such as David in the tomb of kings at Zion (Jerusalem).

I would recommend that the Agikuyu as well as other Africans, especially the elderly and indeed all who might be in a position to do so, to indicate in writing or verbally to family members and close friends where and how they would wish to be buried. This would eliminate the confusion that often arises when those left behind have to decide where and how to bury the deceased. Such wishes ought to be practicable, as otherwise those left behind might be unable to fulfil the intended wishes.

Fear of death

As revealed in chapter 2, the Agikuyu did not fear death. As a matter of fact, when one grew old and ailing, they would often be heard requesting the High God (*Ngai* or *Mwene Nyaga*) to hasten death. They would often be heard asking "*Kai Ngai yariganiirwo ninii tondu itaranjiira?*" (Has God forgotten me, that it is not coming for me?). Note should be made that the Agikuyu referred to God as "It" almost as if it was a creature not human. They made such prayers (requests to God) as traditionally they did not fear death, especially the sick and elderly, and indeed they looked forward to dying, as they were convinced that immediately after death they would be in the land of their ancestors, which in every respect resembled their earthly existence, if not better. Additionally, they believed that they would be warmly received by their loved ones who had gone before. Equally death was not much feared in the Bible as the patriarchs and others believed that on death they would move to Sheol (in the Old Testament) or on death the righteous in the New Testament and early Christianity would move to heaven.

Fearing death is therefore neither traditional nor biblical. Thus, we should, where humanly possible, not fear death since most Christians believe, as I do, that to die is to be with Christ and that on death we will be destined for a better place where we will be with our LORD forever. However, this applies only to the righteous. When one takes the whole portrait of New Testament eschatology seriously, then if one is in right standing with God through Christ, one need not fear death. But for the unsaved, it is a fearful thing to fall into the hands of the living God. I would therefore encourage all professed Christians to become saved.

Death however is never easy—not for the family nor for the pastor. Nonetheless, Decker (2007:21) is of the view that "it need not be feared". The Christian "need not fear death since he has the hope of God's promises" asserts Decker. Additionally the family need not fear death; though it will bring grief and loss, since they too, as indicated in the scripture, have a Christian hope that will serve to carry them through difficult days (Ibid., 21).

Respect to the Body

Currently as presented in chapter 3, the Agikuyu Christians do respect the mortal remains of their loved ones. This is the way it ought to be, and my recommendation is that they continue affording respect to the bodies of the dead and handling such bodies with care. This attitude is unlike the Agikuyu traditional practice of not taking a lot of care nor respecting the bodies of the dead apart from a very few selected elders and matriarchs. The bodies of all the others were left in the bush to be devoured by wild beasts. In scripture we note on the other hand that biblical characters showed great care and respect to the bodies of their deceased loved ones. As indicated by Jones (2010:340) "the Jewish practice of preparing a body with perfumes and spices, such as was done to King Asa (2 Chr 16:14) and Jesus (Luke 24:1; John 19:39-40) was an expression of care, not an attempt at embalming or mummification". Likewise, early Christians were taught by their leaders to respect the human body and handle it with care. St Paul in 1 Corinthians 6:20 advices that "we should honour God with (our) body". Though this according to Decker (2007:9) refers to the living body, yet he (Decker) feels that upon death, a body ought to be honoured. Numerous early church fathers, among them Origen, Tertullian and others impressed on their followers that they respect the body. Origen in his treatise, *Against Celsus VIII*, 30 expresses the view that "For it is not right that the dwelling place (i.e. the body) of the rational soul should be cast aside anywhere without honor". Likewise St Augustine in his treatise, *The City of God* 1, 13 indicates "the bodies of the dead are not on this account to be despised and cast aside, least of all the bodies of the just and faithful". It is worth noting that, as presented in chapter 6, death does not end one's existence. It is also worth noting that the specifics of what happens to the corpse do not affect the existence of the soul. Death must, however, be viewed from a holistic perspective, that is, one which has both material and non-material effects on the person (Ibid., 4). Therefore, as Scott (2006:436) asserts "Christians should treat the human body, with its strange and idiosyncratic design, with special respect; why? because this is the form in which God became flesh". "We should view both the physical body and soul/spirit" advices Jones (2010:344-5) which he feels "are separated at death, to be equally dignified". Indeed, just as the soul/spirit is renewed at conversion (2 Cor 5:17), so the physical body will be renewed at the end of the age (Ibid., 344-5). For these reasons he feels we ought to take care of bodies of the dead. Additionally, he advices that the body is theologically significant; thus both the act of and the imagery conveyed by the treatment of the deceased ought to be weighed carefully. As Boettner (2000:51) asserts "the body is as really and eternally part of man as his spirit" (cf. Wakeford 1890:13-24; Tsavo Media Canada 2014). I fully concur with the views of these scholars.

Acts to be performed soon after death

All the necessary steps should be taken immediately death occurs to ensure that the body will be appropriately preserved during the whole duration of the funeral process. Those involved in preparing the funeral should, where possible, remain in control of issues, as things will move quickly. Additionally, those directly involved should avoid, where possible, falling into many of the difficulties involved in funerals due to poor planning and other exaggerated demands (Aspx 2012).

Those close to the family of the deceased should assist in the funeral arrangements and give necessary guidance, as those directly affected by the death might be too emotionally affected and might not act rationally. They need to be guided to prevent them acting in a way that they might regret in future. One of the key issues to be addressed as a first step would be to obtain a copy of the deceased's will, or the views of his close family members and or confidants to find out if the departed had any special requests concerning funeral arrangements or other issues that need to be considered when planning the funeral. For minors or youth, the family need to be consulted to establish whether his family has a particular inclination or tradition regarding funerals of any of their family members. Accordingly, family members and available close friends of the deceased, after weighing the wishes of the deceased and the wishes of the family, must decide what type of funeral the deceased should be accorded. This, for the Agikuyu Christians of Kikuyu District, is the responsibility of a funeral committee which is formed almost immediately death occurs. Decisions need to be made which among other things will guide how the funeral will progress including decision(s) as to whether burial should take place on the same day as death or the next day; whether it will be delayed for a few days or weeks due to various factors; whether the deceased, if he died far from home will be buried there or whether his remains will be transported back home; whether the deceased will be cremated or accorded an earth burial; if the latter where he will be buried—public cemetery, church compound or in the ancestral land; who will bury him—the church or others; funeral service—private, public, in the church or at the graveside, and so on. These are examples of various issues that have to be decided to guide funeral planning.

Same day as death funeral or an immediate funeral

Traditionally the Agikuyu used to bury on the same day as death, which was in accordance with their then strictly adhered-to custom of "*Athikwo riua ritanathua*"—(to be buried before the sun sets). They were buried on that day or at the latest the following day. Modern Agikuyu Christians rarely bury their dead on the same day as death. As was presented in the study, the Jews and early Christians used to bury on the same day as death. A good example is that of our Lord Jesus, who was buried the very day he died. This proves beyond any doubt that WE DO HAVE A PRECEDENT. The fact that Jesus was buried on the same day as death has been shown both in the New Testament and also by numerous scholars. McCane (1990:31-43) observes 'For we know that in Jesus' day burial took place as soon as possible after death, almost always on the same day' (cf Meyers and Strange, 1981:96-7). Likewise, the early Christians were buried on the same day as death or at the latest the following day.

I would strongly urge Christians of Kikuyu District and other African communities to consider seriously adopting this attitude, as it will drastically cut numerous requirements during funerals, that to all intents and purposes are not really necessary, and are neither traditional nor scriptural. There are several issues that on the surface might seem to be obstacles to the same day burial. Those obstacles are superficial and of modern creation, and can be easily overcome as follows:

All Government permits for burial can be obtained on the same day as death. Muslims in Kikuyu District obtain such permits from the Government authorities within a day and bury their dead on the day of death or the following day. The Christians of Kikuyu District are under the same laws and government agents as the Muslims, so why can't the Christians also obtain those same permits and bury their dead on the same day of death? I have made numerous enquiries from Muslims and from Kenya Government Officials on this; the latter confirm that unless death is caused by suicide, murder, or under suspicious circumstances, a death permit can be issued by the Government (Locational Chief) and burial take place on the same day as death.

Regarding preservation of the body, if for only one day or two, it need not be taken to the mortuary for refrigeration. The body can conveniently be cooled at home using the Agikuyu tradition of cooling the body by laying it on banana tree trunks (*Miramba*) and covering it with the same. This, as traditionally proved, is an effective coolant for the body for a day or two. Should the family wish to preserve the body for a few days at home, they can have the body embalmed at home by obtaining the services of a mortuary attendant, who I am reliably informed can perform such an act at the home of the deceased for a very nominal fee. The procedure is not complicated, and the mortuary attendant will do it in his spare time.

The announcement of death through the mass media which includes radio, television, newspapers, is a modern creation that from my observation and experience serves very little purpose. This is so, as the majority of those known, related or connected with the deceased these days learn of the death and funeral arrangements very fast through modern means of communication such as cell phones, SMS messages, E-mail, Facebook, fax, and so on. There is therefore no need for those mass media advertisements, as the only beneficiaries are the owners of the radio and television stations; newspaper owners and cell phone operators. Members of the family are requested not to insist on such advertisements. This is because most do so to satisfy the pride and ego resulting from the death of their family member being advertised, and also with their names appearing in the advertisement. The issue of the death announcement is discussed as an attempt to remove the ill-conceived belief that it is necessary for the family to advertise the death before burial can take place.

Another hindrance to a sameday burial or immediate burial by the current Agikuyu Christians is the fact that most of the Christians and their families, and indeed the deceased, would wish or would have wished for his body to be taken to a particular church during the funeral service, or alternatively for the funeral service to be conducted by a pastor of a particular denomination. As presented in chapter 4 and 5 of this book, in scripture and early Christianity, the dead were not taken to church for funeral service. The practice of taking dead bodies to church was introduced late in early Christianity and the medieval church, initially for the purpose of allowing Christians to hold a wake inside the church. Later on, as presented in this study, during the Middle Ages it became a common observance for the book to be present inside the church during the funeral service. There is no known theological reason or value of having the body inside the church during the funeral service.

I have obtained the views of a number of pastors from various Christian denominations based in Kikuyu District, who confirm that there are other hierarchies of church officials who can officiate and conclude burial in the absence of an ordained minister of the church. For example, the PCEA Church (Presbyterian Church of East Africa) allows in the absence of an ordained minister an Elder of the church or Evangelist to officiate and complete a burial. In case of the Anglican Church (ACK) in the absence of an ordained minister, a Lay-Reader, Evangelist or Captain can deputise for the minister and conduct the whole funeral and burial process. In the case of the Roman Catholic Church, in the absence of a Reverend Father, a Deacon, a Seminarian, Catechist or leader of a small Christian community can bury the dead. The above is given to refute what is believed by a considerable number of Christians, that it is only ordained ministers who can bury the dead. The above is proof enough that the funeral need therefore not be delayed awaiting the availability of an ordained minister, as his role can effectively be discharged by church officials of the status indicated above. Alternatively the family can request the church to allow the family to invite an ordained minister or pastor from another parish or church to come and conduct the funeral. Based on the above, there is therefore no excuse for delaying burial simply because the diary of the local pastor was full, and hence does not allow for an immediate funeral. It is worth bearing in mind that the deceased will not be aware of who is burying him or where his funeral service is being held. None of this will alter his eternal status or fate.

Numerous other scholars hold similar views on immediate burial. A good example is Decker (2007:14) who advises "I would suggest that families ought to consider immediate burial without embalming as more honoring to the body and less expensive". In such a case, according to Decker, a private family graveside service or funeral may be in order, followed at a later time by a public memorial service. He feels as I do that "there is no necessity to have the body present at the public service, that is, at the memorial service". Decker further advices that "the primary value of its presence (i.e. of the body) for a private family service is for the immediate family being able to see the body before burial. This act assists in dealing with the reality of the death and as a symbolic farewell so that the family can begin to cope with the new situation".

Ten Tips for Saving Funeral (2/1/2013) indicates that there is no need to take the body to the mortuary. The only beneficiaries here in Kenya and elsewhere in the world, are the owners of funeral homes. *Ten Tips* points out to the American public, something which has relevance to the Agikuyu Christians. Paraphrasing to suit the Agikuyu Christians' situation as described in Chapter 3, for the large part of the last century, the Agikuyu used to handle funerals from beginning to the end at home. Funeral homes, or here in Kenya, mortuaries, should not be regarded as the only organisations which can handle and bury the dead. Should a family be in a position to do so, then why not follow what our Christian ancestors did during most of the last century? This will save a lot of unnecessary expense, and will give family members an opportunity to handle the body with love—finding the process therapeutic, and in a real sense extending the final act of love to the deceased. Alternatively, should family members and close friends find it uncomfortable to handle the body, then they can obtain the services of a funeral home (mortuary) attendant, who, in his spare time and for a nominal fee, can prepare the body for burial at the residence of the deceased.

It is most gratifying that, as was shown in chapter 3, a number of Agikuyu have adopted immediate burial at a private graveside funeral followed later, at a more convenient date, by a public memorial service, be it in a church, home or other facilities.

Planning of Burial if it will take place a few days or weeks after death.

In this case, it will be necessary for the family to take the body to a mortuary of their choice. The date that the funeral will take place will be decided by the family. Additionally, from my own observation, the date of the funeral will often be guided by when the ordained pastor of their faith is available to conduct the funeral. However, as indicated above, this problem can be overcome, for example, by having other mandated church officials conduct the funeral should the date the family wish to hold the funeral not fit their pastor's diary, particularly where such a date for the burial cannot be altered.

The funeral committee should deal with issues that are a necessity and refrain from raising various issues that have become "customary", but which, as revealed in this study, are neither absolutely necessary, traditional nor scriptural. The so-called "customary" issues that should be ignored as they are time-consuming, a drain on the family resources and serve no meaningful purpose, include drafting funeral announcements and placing such announcements in the mass media; drafting the deceased's life history—the one that forms the larger part of the funeral programme, and which often contains numerous photographs of the deceased with family and friends as well as a written eulogy- and other matters like these. It is worthy of note that in my view, such written eulogies do not sound genuine. They appear artificial, as a genuine eulogy should be spontaneous, namely, from the heart; it should reflect the feeling of the one giving the eulogy, and should dwell on a few positive and negative characteristics of the deceased. Currently, almost all written eulogies are extremely monotonous, and indeed one wonders whether they serve any purpose. The issue of funeral programme will be discussed later.

When those two factors are removed, that is, drafting the funeral announcements and funeral programme, the funeral committee is then left to decide on the mode of burial, the date, where and how the grave will be made, the purchase of the casket (coffin), the settlement of any medical bills outstanding as well as settling the mortuary fee. Additionally, the funeral committee should address an issue that is often ignored; the issue that, as much as humanly possible for the larger family and friends of the deceased, to be invited to contribute, towards raising sufficient sums to settle any debts the deceased might owe. Should it not be possible to settle all the debts in full, then the creditors should be requested to give the family sufficient time to settle the debts. This would prevent auctioneers harassing the bereaved family soon after the funeral. It is worth of note that, as observed in chapter 2 of this book, various tribes such as the Kisii of Kenya have a similar custom, attending to debts owed to and by the deceased.

An issue that traditionally was observed and effected, but which has been totally neglected or forgotten, is for the clan immediately after the funeral to decide who among the male relatives should look after the affairs of the "widow" and the children of the deceased. This is an issue that I would recommend should be revisited by the Agikuyu as well as by other Africans, and the tradition be reinstated. It must be noted that I am in no way suggesting anything remotely resembling wife inheritance. Definitely not! What I am proposing is that the clan (family) should nominate, with the widow giving her consent, who among the deceased's relatives she should be consulting on issues that customarily require a male, for example, boys' circumcision, the marriage of the deceased's children, the family inheritance of the deceased, assisting the widow in claiming any inheritance from the clan due to her husband; assisting the widow in apportioning among her children assets left by her husband; handling the burial of her children, and any other matters of this sort. This was an Agikuyu and numerous other African tribes tradition; also very similar to the scriptural practice among the Jews. In my own case, after my father died in 1976, one of my paternal uncles (*baba munyinyi*) was appointed to that position. He fulfilled his responsibilities remarkably well until his death in 2001, which was followed soon thereafter by the death of my mother in 2002. The Agikuyu practice, however, as indicated earlier was in many respects different from that of the Jews. As revealed in chapter 2 of this study it was also a common practice among numerous African tribes. I have observed that currently numerous widows are caused suffering by the clan as well as by the children of the deceased due to lack of such a trustee. I am persuaded that a responsible male or female in these days of gender equality could be identified. I am equally inclined to believe that such an appointee, recognised by the clan, might be of great benefit and use to both the widow and the children left behind by the deceased. As a precautionary measure, and to prevent the likelihood of the appointee abusing his position, the clan (family), at the request of the widow or her children, should unconditionally terminate the nomination, and should the widow so desire, someone else of her choice be nominated. The widow should also have the right to not have anyone nominated as the trustee, and for her to be recognised as the sole or joint administrator of her husband's estate.

Planning for the burial of those who die far from home, especially outside the country

As presented in chapter 2, traditionally for the Agikuyu, when a person died far from home, the body was left where it was to be devoured by wild beasts. Where possible however, and if the distance was reasonable, the body of a respected elder or matriarch was carried that very day on a bier by their sons or nephews, and brought home for burial. It should be noted that this was done for extremely few persons. In scripture there were only two patriarchs whose bodies were transported over long distances, namely that of Joseph and that of Jacob. The bones of King Saul and his sons were transported, but not over long distances, and it was not their bodies as such which were transported but their cremated bones. These scriptural instances were exceptional, and the practice was not normative.

The practice of transporting dead bodies over long distances is therefore foreign to our tradition and religion. As such, it should be done away with. It is worth noting that traditionally among the Agikuyu there were no taboos that would cause the family harm if the deceased was buried far from their ancestral land. However, for those determined to be buried in their ancestral land, their wish could be fulfilled as indicated by Leakey (1977:974), where he tells of an incident where a Mugikuyu elder wished to be buried after his death in the Ngong Hills, which was in the Maasai country. At the time of his death, there was tension between the Maasai and the Agikuyu. There was therefore no way that his body could be carried safely to be buried in the Ngong Hills. To get round this, some warriors were sent by the elders at night to obtain a handful of soil from the Ngong Hills. Luckily, all went well. They did this, and returned home safely before daybreak. The elder was buried in Kikuyuland (his ancestral land) surrounded, as it were, by soil from the Ngong Hills, which was sprinkled in the grave before his body was lowered, and some more sprinkled on his body before the grave was filled with Kikuyuland soil. To all intents and purposes he was, therefore, literally buried in Ngong Hills! From this historical incident, although as proved several times in this study that it was not cultural for the majority of the Agikuyu to be buried, and so the question of being buried in the ancestral land did not arise for a large proportion of them, yet for those inclined to be buried or to bury their loved ones in their ancestral land, then I would recommend that those who might migrate to places far from their ancestral homeland, or those who travel to seek medical treatment abroad, or those who travel overseas to bury their loved ones, for them to carry a handful of soil from their ancestral land, so that in the event of dying in those foreign lands, they will be buried there surrounded, as it were, by their ancestral soil, which will be sprinkled on their body before the coffin (casket) is closed.

However, a word of caution is in order here. When transporting soil from one country to another, it has to be established from the authorities whether this is legal. Otherwise, persons doing this might find themselves in very serious trouble, and for what, one might ask? For something which is neither cultural nor scriptural. The whole thing borders on witchcraft and superstition. As was revealed in the study, early Christians were not concerned whether they were buried in their ancestral lands or their place of birth, or buried with their close relatives. A good example, of this is St Augustine's mother St. Monica, who at the end of her life, shared with Augustine the mystical experience recorded in Augustine's *Confessions* (9:10). Of great relevance, and worth being noted and adopted by Agikuyu Christians and Christians worldwide, is the fact that St Monica died and was buried at Ostia in Italy, and that she no longer insisted on burial with her husband, as she was confident of resurrection. Additionally, Augustine in his confession indicates that St. Monica did not desire to be buried in her own land, nor have an elaborate funeral with spices, embalmment, or choice monument and other trappings. According to Augustine she did not recommend these things to us (*Confessions* 9). Christians should take heed of this.

Should the family and the funeral committee opt not to bring the body home, but for it to be buried in those foreign lands, then only one relative, or just a few need travel there to bury their kin. In extreme cases when it is not possible for anyone to travel due to various reasons such as lack of finances, lack of travel documents, or similar problems, then the family can be represented by an official of their embassy, or by a member of their country's diaspora resident there. Should this be adopted, then the cost of the whole funeral process is minimised. Videos can be made covering the entire funeral and brought back home to be viewed by the family and friends of the deceased. In this modern era of advanced technology, the whole funeral can even be broadcast in real time using simple technologies.

Regarding the above, and as indicated in Chapter 7 of this book, members of the Kenya and African diaspora in countries and continents far from their ancestral homeland are hereby urged to form burial societies as done by the Jews. In the event of the death of one of them or one of their own there, they can be buried or bury their own in those places they have migrated to, instead of the dead having to be brought all the way back to their ancestral homeland in Africa.

Simplifying Funeral Procedures, Reducing Costs and Adopting Alternative Funeral Practices

Based on what has been presented in this study, as well as from my own observations, and the views of numerous Agikuyu and other African Christian pastors, and laity, as well as views obtained from other researchers whose studies and works have close similarity to this study, albeit on other races and covering other continents such as Europe and America, I would recommend in addition to what has been indicated earlier for the Agikuyu and other Africans to adopt new methods of simplifying funerals, reducing costs and adopting alternative funeral practices. Additionally, they should adopt where necessary fresh and different attitudes and manners of coping with death.

Simplicity

As shown in chapters 4 and 5 of this study, it was the norm during biblical and early Christianity periods, as well as for many centuries thereafter, that funeral practices reflected nothing but the utmost simplicity. It should also be noted that during those periods, the majority of the deceased were carried in a winding sheet and placed upon a bier (no coffin) (cf. Wakeford 1890:16). As observed in the study, the Agikuyu Christians, and indeed almost all Christians worldwide have over the last one hundred years or so moved in the opposite direction, from simple burials, or none at all, to extremely complex and expensive ones. In my view, a lot that is incorporated in the contemporary Agikuyu and other African Christians' funeral practices is neither scriptural, traditional or practical, and ought to be done away with, or modified as soon as possible, in the manner recommended above and also in the following sections.

Mortuary

Taking the body to the mortuary or funeral homes, as most of the Agikuyu and other African Christians believe they should do, is not mandatory, traditional, necessary or scriptural. It is absolutely not necessary to take the body to the mortuary if burial is immediate (same day of death or the following day), followed by a memorial service a few days, weeks or months later. It is worthy of note that the major beneficiaries of taking the body to the mortuary (funeral home) are the funeral home (mortuary) operators, and the transport industry, rather than the family of the deceased or the deceased himself.

The purpose and usage of funeral homes (mortuaries) in regard to funerals, as well as the contention indicated above and elsewhere in this study that funerals have been commercialized is supported by Steck (2001:367) who is of the view, which I support, that " . . . in modern western world (and this can as well apply to the contemporary African Christians funeral rites) . . . there are many symptoms of the repression of death. These become constitutive elements in the funeral ritual . . . they go hand in hand with the commercializing of the funeral to meet the supposed needs of mourners" (and in the African case 'the bereaved'). Steck goes on to indicate that "A funeral creates an illusion of death that is the counterpart of an illusory life". Steck notes "with the help of embalming and the use of the dead person's clothing, the corpse is made to seem asleep rather than dead". "The funeral parlor" Steck further advises becomes a "slumber room and the coffin a showcase".

Delaying Burial

This is neither scriptural nor traditional. I recommend, as indicated earlier, an immediate burial (on the same day as death or at the latest the following day) in a private funeral, followed later if found necessary by a public memorial service. Our pre-colonial ancestors did this, and our Lord and Saviour Jesus Christ was buried the very day he died. Though the manner of burial of Jesus was not normative, Christians, however, should where possible emulate Jesus in life and death. The early Christians did this. We would be well advised to follow suit.

Announcements

These are neither scriptural nor traditional. With modern communication facilities, all concerned with a particular death, can be reached within twenty-four hours or thereabouts via fax, e-mail, telephones, cell phones, Facebook, word of mouth and the like. Additionally, expensive advertisements placed in the local media (newspapers) thanking those who participated in the funeral as well as advertisements for the anniversary and "unveiling" of the cross should not be encouraged. They have no theological value, and it is worthy of note that as far as has been ascertained the dead cannot read these advertisements. Additionally, such advertisements serve no purpose, they are a foreign modern creation whose beneficiaries are the owners of such facilities, and not the deceased nor his family.

One African scholar who captures most of the odd things that form part of the funeral-related advertisements referred to above is Kwame (1994:307-322) in his article on *The Economics of Akan Funerals*. He portrays issues applied by the Akans of Ghana in their funeral announcements that are very similar to the ones of the Agikuyu Christians. One is left to wonder who borrowed from whom—the Akans from the Agikuyu or vice versa. Kwame's paragraph on funeral announcements reads:

> "All funeral rites today have similar features that also constitute items of expenditure. These include announcements on the radio and in the press, detailing all the deceased's relations and, in certain cases, friends concerned in the rites. The details emphasise their "station in life" and their places of sojourn,

including—indeed emphasising—the major foreign cities, such as Berlin, Bonn, London, Paris, New York and Washington. It matters not whether those mentioned can attend the funeral. The details serve a dual purpose. They emphasise the social status of the deceased, as demonstrated in the number, occupations and locations of his maternal relations and his children, and they inform the sundry friends and relatives of the deceased of the programme of the funeral rites."

Except for very few differences between the Akan and the Agikuyu, the former being a matriarchal society and the later being patriarchal, one might think that Kwame was describing an Agikuyu funeral announcement. It is obvious that the Akan or the Agikuyu funeral announcements for that matter are not meant so much to inform others of the death, but rather they are a means of showing off.

There is little need for the announcements, but if produced, then names, locations and status of the relatives, friends, doctors treating the deceased, clergy who buried the deceased, dignitaries who attended the funeral, and all such details, should be left out. The announcement, if found necessary, should be limited to the name of the deceased, date, time and place of burial and of the location, time and date of the memorial service.

It should be realised, as indicated above, that the deceased wherever he is will not read or appreciate such announcements. Theologically, he is beyond such earthly human emotions and sentiments, and is completely out of this world with all that entails.

I would strongly urge the Agikuyu and other Christians when placing funeral announcements in newspapers to desist from heading them "CELEBRATING THE LIFE OF XYZ". The reason for this suggestion is that the non-Christian religion or group called "Humanists" as discussed in Chapter 2 of this book do not believe in life after death, and when burying one of their own all religious symbols have to be removed. They believe among other things that the funeral ceremony is intended to "celebrate" the life that has been lived and properly honor that person's life. It is evident that this is a non-Christian religion, and by our placing advertisements of that nature, we are promoting its religion and ideologies.

Clothing the dead

The dead should be clothed in moderation, preferably in the best clothes they wore during life, or in the uniforms they wore when they were serving specific guilds of the church, and the like. Whatever clothes a person is buried in, it should be realised that the clothes will decay along with the body, and that when the soul goes to heaven, or at the resurrection, our bodies will have new garments given by the Almighty, which will have no similarity to the ones we wore in the world, or the ones in which we were buried. The justification for being moderate in how we clothe the dead, is found in the fact that in scripture, the dead were clothed simply. Most were only wrapped in sheets. Early Christians also were clothed in the garments they wore during life. As revealed in this book, the early church fathers condemned clothing the dead with rich attire, and urged the Christians to clothe their dead with moderation, preferably in the clothes they wore during life. The Agikuyu traditionally also were buried in the skin garments they wore during life. So, their descendants, namely the current Agikuyu Christians, should be clothed similarly, but certainly not in the traditional skin garments, rather in the modern clothing they wore in life. There should definitely not be any purchasing of new expensive garments, and at times even new shoes, for that purpose, as some families have been known to do.

Those being cremated should preferably be wrapped in a sheet or dressed in the clothes they wore during life.

Funeral procession

Should it be necessary for the body to be taken to the mortuary, then on the day of burial, only the vehicle transporting the body and a few vehicles carrying very close relatives and family friends should go to the funeral home and form part of the procession. The rest of the mourners can wait at the church, graveside or residence. It should be noted that having a large entourage of vehicles, and more recently hiring motor cycle outriders to head the procession, serves no social or religious purpose. It is one more example of showing off. It is a modern habit of the Agikuyu and probably of other African communities that should be discouraged and trimmed down to size.

Funeral photographs and Videos

A tendency has arisen to take numerous photographs and videos at every stage of the funeral, of various groups involved with the funeral. For example, those of the widow or widower, children, parents, siblings, in-laws, extended family, close friends, and guild members. Such photographs and videos serve no purpose, as, from my own experience, a few months after the funeral hardly anyone ever views those photographs or videos. The only valuable use of the videos having been taken, is if they will be sent to relatives and friends far from the scene of burial, who cannot therefore attend the funeral. However, from my own experience and observation, large numbers of such videos are rarely sent to such persons, and neither are those videos requested in large numbers by such persons.

My recommendation is that if taking photographs and videos forms part of the healing process for the widow and her children, then they should be taken. They should, however, not be taken just because it has become a custom. Whose custom, one may ask. If they are to be taken, then the number and the cost of doing so should be kept to a minimum. From my own experience, having buried both of my parents, a couple of brothers and sisters, as well as numerous close relatives and friends, I can vouch that no one takes any interest in those photographs and videos a few months after the funeral. So why take them at all? The other irony is that the videos are used after the funeral by some bereaved families and funeral committee to "investigate" or see who attended the funeral. Why do so? My guess is that those who attended will be regarded highly by the family, but in future the bereaved family might reciprocate by also not being too kind or warm to those who did not attend. Tit for tat—not a Christian attitude, if I may say so.

Taking the body to church

There is no scriptural account, example or reason given for taking the body to church for the funeral service. Taking the body to church, as presented in this study, commenced during the late early Christian era, the era of the medieval church and during the Middle Ages. The purpose was to enable Christians and the bereaved family to hold a wake in the church. Agikuyu, as discussed in the study, do not hold a wake for the dead. This is demonstrated by there not being a single night that they stay in the same room with the body keeping watch. Gathering at the home of the deceased, singing Christian songs there, conducting prayers and comforting the bereaved family cannot be equated to a wake. Even if what they do might be confused with a "wake", for all intents and purposes, there is no justifiable reason, neither any known theological reason for taking or having the body inside the church during the funeral service (cf. Mitford 1963:246).

It is worthy of note that even if burial has not taken place, there is no reason to take the body inside the church; the body can remain at the funeral home (mortuary) or in the hearse while the funeral service is going on. Another recent reason for the body being taken inside the church during the funeral service is for the pastor to invite the family members to gather around the casket (coffin) for family prayers. This is a good gesture, presumably with healing intention towards the bereaved family, but has no theological significance. The soul of the deceased, as has been expressed by many theologians, is not in the casket, and neither does the soul hover over the body for three days after death, as once believed by the Jews and even today believed by Muslims. As indicated earlier, this thought by the Jews which was linked with the eschatological belief that the soul hovered near the body for three days after death did not, it should be noted, carry over into Christianity.

My recommendation is that the Agikuyu and other Africans do away with the current practices which they have adopted for no known theological or cultural reasons. As much as practicable, they should refrain from taking the body to church. They should instead opt for an immediate burial as recommended earlier, followed at a more convenient time by a memorial service. In such a case, there will be no corpse present, as the body will have been buried a while previously.

Cost

A funeral can be one of the largest expenses a family ever has, and is likely to be one of the larger unplanned or unscheduled expenses in life (Decker, 2007:11). It should be noted, however, that whereas one family might consider Ksh. Xxx,xxx as inconsequential, to another family it might be more than that family's yearly income. So, the expression "largest" expense is relative to the particular family's fortunes and income. This point is important, as it has became a tendency for both the Agikuyu poor, middle income and the rich to "overdo" and spend when it comes to funeral, as has been repeatedly pointed out in this book. It is worth bearing in mind that the masses follow blindly the methods used by their betters, at whatever cost (Wakeford 1890:32). "When the wealthy bury theirs in a certain way", asserts Wakeford, "the poorer folks attempt to copy them although not as glamorous". I would draw the attention of the Agikuyu Christians to two of our famous proverbs that say "*Ndiakagwo na ya Wakini*" and "*Gūtirī ūinaga na mūthīgī wa Wakini*" which means "no one is forced to build his hut by the pattern of his age-mate" and "one does not dance with his age-mate's dancing stick" respectively. The English have proverbs that convey similar sentiments, two of which are: "everyone to his own taste" and the more appropriate one "keeping up with the Joneses". According to Quirk (1980:573), the latter means "to compete with one's neighbors socially, especially buying the same expensive new things that they buy".

Wakeford (1890:32) further observes, there is nothing people are so willing to spend their money upon as the funerals and related matters—the mourning, the funeral, the coffin, the grave, and the tombstone. I agree with Wakeford when he states that the motives that prompt the expenditure might be often, though by no means always, very good. Whatever the motives, however, certainly no good purpose is served by it. This should not be construed to mean, however, that the dead should not be accorded a befitting burial, but among the changes that need to be made are ways and means of simplifying the manner in which we bury the dead. The financial consideration discussed here, as advised by Decker (2007:12), has nothing to do with the person who has died, as not only is that dead person beyond any further benefit from such actions (anything relating to funerals), but as far as is known from the biblical record, he will be totally unaware of what is done in terms of his corpse or funeral. The Agikuyu and other African Christians need to realise that the considerations concerning the funeral relate directly to the family that is left behind. As can be expected, death complicates life for the living, whether as observed by Decker it is a young widow with children to raise alone, an older widow without her spouse as companion, a widower who must now learn to prepare his own meals and do his own laundry. There will be numerous financial needs for those close relatives left behind, and any finances that can be saved should be of great help and assistance to the immediate family of the deceased.

A Christian should be concerned to be a good steward even in death. This according to Decker (2006:39) should be a priority both for those with limited resources as well as those with greater means. Impressing others with extravagance is not a Christian virtue, and as revealed in chapter 5, was condemned by the early Christian fathers. As indicated earlier, funerals can be made far less expensive by foregoing many of the "customary" pratices (to me this refers to the funeral habits that the Agikuyu have adopted over the last one hundred years or so), and the professional procedures carried out during funerals. It is worth noting, as advised by Wakeford (1890:24), that when the poorer are imitating the rich, they are straining their resources, with the false idea that they are showing respect for their dead. As indicated above, the dead person will be totally unaware of what is done in terms of his corpse or funeral. The following, which appears in Decker (2007:17), should be considered very carefully by the Agikuyu and other African Christians and preferably adopted in their funeral practices; "funerals are for the living and they do nothing to the deceased" (cf. Wakeford 1890:26). As shown in Chapter 5 of this book a similar view was expressed by St Augustine in a treatise, where he indicated ". . .wherefore, all these last offices and ceremonies that concern the dead, the careful funeral arrangements, and the equipment of the tomb, and the pomp of obsequies, are rather the solace of the living than the comfort of the dead" (St Augustine *The City of God* 1.12).

Additionally Decker (2007:18) also feels that a simple funeral is no reflection of the family's valuation of their loved one. As indicated by early Christian fathers and so obvious, not only the corpse will decay, but also the clothes he is buried in as well as the coffin. There is no theological or cultural reason for delaying the decaying of the corpse. As indicated in the Bible the body should revert to "ashes to ashes and dust to dust". So why delay this inevitability? My recommendation is for the Christians to use the simplest coffin possible, made of material that can decay quickly. This suggestion was proposed by Wakeford (1890:46) who advocates the "adoption of perishable wooded coffins or better still, the pulp coffins". He feels that interment ought to be simple "without any attempt at arresting or rather protracting decay". One is left to wonder what is the sense or rationale of making expensive, indestructible, airtight coffins that hinder and delay the natural order, which is the decay of the corpse. Such coffins are for show and bring no benefit to the deceased. The only beneficiary is the industry that makes the coffins. To improve a simple coffin the family can during the funeral cover it with a cloth that can be removed just before interment. Wrapping the body with sheets and burying it without a coffin, as was done in Bible times and early Christianity is another option that should be considered very seriously. After all, what really is the use or purpose of a coffin, something that will decay along with the body, or something that will delay such decay? Another alternative worth considering is to hire an expensive coffin to hold the body from the funeral home and during the funeral service. Just before the actual burial, the body could be removed, and it would then be buried wrapped in sheets or in the clothes worn during life, or transferred and buried in a simpler, cheaper coffin. The hired coffin is then returned for future hire by other families. This might sound strange, but numerous young Agikuyu girls, because they cannot afford to purchase new wedding gowns, are hiring them only for that occasion. So what is the difference? Alternatively, a clan (*mbari*) or an extended family can buy one expensive (impressive) coffin for regular use by its members. Such coffin would contain the body from funeral home, during the funeral service and transport to the grave. Just before burial, the body would be removed and relocated and buried in a cheaper coffin (casket) or wrapped in sheets or simply in the clothes they wore during life. It is worthy of note that a few religions, especially the Muslim faith as revealed in this book, to circumvent the laws of countries that mandate corpses to be transported to the grave in coffins (caskets) do transport the bodies of their dead in coffins. However, since their faith advocates or prefers bodies to be buried wrapped in clothes only, they remove such bodies and bury them without the coffin. The coffin is then returned to a safe place for future use by other members of their faith. My recommendation is not based on the practices of such other religions. No. Only that such practices are worth adopting.

It is worthy of note that in some religious faiths such as Islam all are accorded similar simple burials regardless of their status. In Christianity a few socially very high ranking persons have opted for a simple funeral. A good example is that of the late former President of France, General Charles de Gaulle, who at his request was buried with utmost simplicity in the small cemetery of Colombey-les-Deux-Eglises in a plain wooden coffin made by the village carpenter and with only his family and his neighbors in attendance (*The New Encyclopedia Britannica* 1986:649, Vol 2). As indicated elsewhere in this study, here in Kenya, there has been a number of high-ranking Kenyans, who although they could have been accorded funerals full of all manner of pomp and colour, yet they opted for simple funerals. One such instance was the cremation of the ACK Archbishop Manasses Kuria and of his wife. The two separate cremations were proceeded by simple funeral services. Also the cremation after a simple funeral service of the famous Nobel Peace Laureate Professor Wangari Maathai. She had been granted by the Kenya Government a state funeral but in her will she had opted for a simple funeral.

Graves

The Agikuyu ancestors did not have the modern tools such as hoes and shovels for digging graves and the like. The traditional digging tools comprised of sharpened sticks (*Mīnyago* or *Mĩĩro*). The soil had to be scooped with bare hands. This might be the main reason as to why they used to dig relatively shallow and narrow graves two feet by two feet by six feet and oval in shape. On reflection, and based on my own assumption, this might be the main reason why the respected elders' grave was dug in the *kiaraini* (rubbish midden) as this was the softest spot near the homestead to dig a grave using the traditional digging tools. After laying the body in the grave, they filled it with soil and stones. The sons used to lay branches of Acacia trees on top of the grave. In Biblical times and early Christianity, as presented in chapters 4 and 5, most were buried in caves, tombs, graves, or catacombs. As shown in this book, over the last one hundred years the Agikuyu moved from simple earthen graves to indestructible graves constructed with dressed stone—floor, walls and the lid made of a concrete slab. More recently they have

RECOMMENDATIONS, CONCLUSION, AREAS OF FURTHER RESEARCH

reverted to earthen graves of three feet by six feet by six feet. The graves are then filled with earth and stones laid on top.

It is my view that alternative means of burying the dead should be adopted for the majority of Africans and in this case of the Kikuyu District Christians, as a large proportion of them simply do not have sufficient land to bury the dead. For example the current generation of those aged twenty to forty years in Kikuyu District hope to inherit a family plot that on the average measures only one quarter of an acre. Such a tiny plot is to be inherited by up to five sons and a few unmarried daughters. It goes without question that such families will not have sufficient space to farm, or build their dwellings, let alone have any space to bury any relative. A situation is approaching where even the graves of their parents and grandparents will have to give way for the current generation to use especially for their residences. My recommendation for the Agikuyu and other Africans with similar problems is to adopt the practice of (1) cremation, (2) donating their bodies for use by medical schools, (3) burying the dead in deep pits which can accommodate the bodies of many corpses. This can be achieved by making the pit, say, twenty feet deep when initially dug to bury the first corpse. The second corpse can be buried two feet above the first corpse, namely, at the depth of eighteen feet, the next corpse at the depth of sixteen feet and so forth, (4) the Agikuyu can adopt the Jewish methods of "second burial". This means burying a corpse, and giving it a period of about five years for the flesh to decay. It can then be exhumed, and all the bones of previous and future generations buried in one grave thus creating burial spaces for further burials. This, as presented in the study is what in the Bible is referred to as being buried with "one's fathers". The only obstacle to this practice being adopted is that for example here in Kenya the Law requires that to exhume a body, one must obtain a Court order. I am sure that if this suggestion is worth adopting, our Parliament and County Assemblies can legislate suitable laws that would make exhuming bodies easier.

As argued in chapter 3 of this study, burying the parents at the *thome* of the family's homestead should be discontinued forthwith, as it is misplaced—the *thome* traditionally is not where the elder was buried. He was buried in the *kiaraini*, that is, the rubbish midden which was located outside the *thome*. Currently the location of the *kiaraini* of the modern Kikuyu rural homestead is at the rear of the homestead, not at the front or entrance to the homestead. This, then, if the family wishes to bury the elder traditionally, is where he ought to be buried: in the *kiaraini*—rubbish midden at the rear of the homestead. This way, the most prime area of the homestead, which is on either side of the gate or homestead entrance, will be left available for development by those left behind, and will be passed on for use by the future generations.

The Agikuyu Christians and Christians the world over should re-examine the issue of their fatherland. They should bear in mind that this world is not our fatherland. Where and how they are buried in this world should not matter, as they should aim at death to move to their true fatherland, which is heaven. This contention is supported by Grelot (1977:168), who is of the view that "...heaven is the true fatherland...We have no permanent dwelling place here and we seek what is to come (Heb 13, 14)...All men must do as they did (i.e the patriarchs) and see beyond the corner of earth where they have taken root with their families, see the new fatherland where they will live with them forever".

Tombstones

The Agikuyu and other African Christians should appreciate that graves lose meaning with time. One need only to visit the graves of those that one used to know, or those who were related to them a number of years ago to appreciate that the feelings and emotions one had for that individual are often diminished and almost gone completely. Wakeford (1890:33) feels as I do that Christians should desist from constructing hideous tombstones, which after a few generations often look unattractive and become an impediment on the ground. As Wakeford further observes, an impartial visitor to some of our older cemeteries (he refers to those in the United Kingdom, but in this case it could refer to the ones in Kenya or in any other African country), will agree that most of the monuments of a generation ago now look out of place. The family to whom the buried one was dear has passed away; their children, in many cases, have forgotten the place of burial, or take no further interest in it. This is true of the Agikuyu Christians, who a few years after burial take no interest whatsoever in the grave. Suffice to indicate that expensive tombstones, and ones that will hinder the future generation making use of the land should not be encouraged. As so well pointed out by Wakeford (1894:35), the dead have no rights from a legal point of view—a piece of ground should not be given to a dead body for ever. Additionally, such construction violates the rights of the living. The land is for the living, not for the dead.

Flowers

Placing flowers on the grave has no biblical or traditional basis. The placing of flowers on Christian graves commenced during the Middle Ages. The use of flowers during funerals should be reduced to the basic minimum. Those who wish to purchase flowers other than the immediate family should be encouraged to donate to the bereaved family, to the poor or to a charitable organisation. It is worthy of note that the use of flowers during funerals did not feature in scripture nor in Agikuyu tradition. It has no theological significance. The only beneficiary to purchasing flowers during funerals are the florists. The deceased will not be aware of such flowers nor be in a position to appreciate them or those giving them. The Agikuyu should note that traditionally the only ones who placed any sort of plants (not flowers) were the sons of the deceased, who placed branches of the *Mūgaa* (Acacia Thorn Tree) on their father's grave.

Feeding mourners

This, if overdone, can strain the bereaved family's resources. Feeding guests should be discouraged, and if found necessary, limited only to snacks for those mourners who have travelled from far away.

Giving to the poor

During the period of early Christianity and the Middle Ages it was the church practice for bowls for the poor to be placed at the place of burial. My recommendation is that during funerals such a practice be reintroduced. Helping the poor is obeying our Lord's instructions to help the poor at all times. Currently, a lot of Christians do not do so.

Cremation

This is an option for disposing of the dead which I would strongly recommend the Agikuyu and other Africans to adopt. This method has gained great momentum in most countries of the world as one of the major ways of disposing of the dead. Statistics are available that support this contention. For example, Decker (2006:4-6) gives valuable data and statistics to this effect:

"The 20th century saw in the USA increased interest in cremation. The 1% boundary was crossed in the early 1920s, 2% in the 1930s, and 3% in the 1940s. By contrast, Great Britain's rate, though initially much slower, rapidly overtook the US rate, exceeding it in the 1950s. By 1967 Britain was cremating more than half of those who died, though the US cremation rate was still only about 4%. The cremation rates in the west have continued to increase, and most recently at a much faster pace than in the first half of the 20th century. Since 1963 when the cremation rate was about 4% in the United States, it increased to 25% in 1999 and 29% by 2004. There are now nearly fourteen hundred crematories in the US which incinerate more than half a million corpses annually. American figures are still relatively low in comparison with some other western countries. As of 1999 Australia's cremation rate was over 50%; in Scandinavia, over 60% and in Britain 70%. These figures contrast with Catholic countries such as Spain and Italy where it is still less than 10% or in Greece where the practice has been illegal until two weeks ago. The figures also contrast with the east where cremation is the norm. The rate in Japan, for example, is 98%. It is quite likely that the American rate will increase significantly in the next few decades. A survey in 1995 indicated that 43% of those surveyed would "likely" choose cremation for themselves. So that is where we stand at the beginning of a new century. A funeral practice that was practically unknown 100 years ago has become mainstream and appears to be growing quite rapidly."

The above will no doubt convince the Agikuyu Christians and other Africans that cremation is a practice that most Christian and non-Christian countries have adopted to dispose of their dead.

It is gratifying that cremation is also an option for disposing of the dead that is slowly being adopted by the Agikuyu. Among the notable Agikuyu (as revealed in Chapter 3 of this book) who have been cremated recently are the late ACK Archbishop Manasses Kuria and his wife. Also the late Nobel Peace Laureate Professor Wangari Maathai.

Jones (2010:337) gives valuable insight as to whether burial by cremation is a Christian act, and if so, then what does it communicate. While referring to the works of the first century writer Tacitus, Jones states that Jews prefer to bury and not to burn. He goes on to say that early Christians in their faith carried over a general disdain for the act of cremation and buried their dead, unlike the Romans who burned theirs. The practice of cremation, he observes, has been officially approved by the Roman Catholic Church. As presented in the study, the practice has also been approved by the Anglican Church, the PCEA church and most of the protestant churches. As given above and below, I would urge the Kikuyu District Christians and all African communities to embrace cremation as a way of disposing of the dead, as this will reduce funeral costs, and all the more because most families lack adequate places and resources to give their dead an earth burial.

Cremation has advantages for a number of reasons. *Funeral Programme 101* (Tsavo Media Canada 2014) gives these as follows: (1) it entails a cheaper funeral, especially if there is no coffin, embalming or viewing (2) it saves on interment burial expenses and can eliminate the need for a casket (coffin) and some of the more ostentatious aspects of a conventional funeral (3) it is faster and more convenient (4) it is more environmentally friendly in terms of land usage and immediacy of "return to nature". It is worth noting that in various countries such as in the USA numerous laws on cremation do not stipulate embalming before cremation, nor does the practice require the use of a casket. Additionally, it has been observed that when cremation choices are properly made, and which are best suited to the particular situation, it will lead to a reduction in the costs of funerals. In an Agikuyu case when cremation is the funeral option, the funeral committee will decide whether the corpse will be taken to the mortuary, whether to use a low cost casket (coffin) or wrap the body in sheets, then transport the body to the most appropriate crematorium. When cremation is chosen as the option, I suggest that a memorial service follow a suitable time after cremation, either in a church or another convenient place.

After cremation, the family and the funeral committee will have to decide what to do with the ashes—to purchase the "urn" for holding the ashes and then where to "bury" or keep the urn. This can conveniently be buried on the ancestral land or in other places preferred by the family. Some urns have even been kept in the wardrobe of the deceased's master bedroom! Very weird!

Unveiling the Cross

This is one funeral rite that should be discouraged, as it has no theological basis and serves no purpose. When burying the deceased the pastor inserts a cross at the head of the grave "in the name of the Father, the Son and the Holy Spirit". One is bound to ask what more blessing can be rendered to the grave or to the cross?

It is worthy of note that other countries and people have similar rites of "unveiling the cross". This contention is supported by Van't Spijker (2005:173) who indicates, "The Episcopal Church (Anglican) uses for this purpose the liturgical texts of the service in commemoration of the dead, and uses also a text of the South African Prayer Book entitled Dedication and Unveiling the Tombstone, for gatherings at the place of burial or in the church". As presented in Chapter 2 of this book, another religion that practises "unveiling" the gravestone (not the cross) one year after burial is Judaism. The Agikuyu Christian practice was most probably not adopted from Judaism.

Some of the Kenyan churches including the Anglican Church (ACK) and the PCEA (Presbyterian Church of East Africa) have similar rites. However, it is very doubtful whether the Agikuyu Christians realise that by doing so, they are commemorating the dead or at worst idolizing the grave and tombstones.

Instead, as so well indicated in the ACK Diocese of Mount Kenya South Supplementary Prayer Book, this rite, if the family really feels that they should hold it a suitable period after burial, should be "*Mahoya ma Kiririkano kia Mutigairi*" meaning "Prayers in remembrance of the late XYZ". This way, it will be family and friends remembering and praying for the soul of the deceased, but it will not remotely resemble "blessing" the grave, cross or tombstone.

I would, however, urge Christians to do away with this rite, as it has no traditional, scriptural or early Christian basis.

Conclusion

This research, for the first time, has conducted a serious study aimed towards formulating a new model of how the contemporary Agikuyu Christians ought to cope with death. The study presented numerous insights into who the Agikuyu are, how they migrated to their present ancestral land of central Kenya; how they traditionally coped with death; how the contemporary Agikuyu cope with death; the handling of death in scripture and early Christianity, and the issue of resurrection and the resurrected body, as well as how some selected tribes and races and religions cope with death; additionally, how some cities and countries are addressing the issue of limited burial space.

> "The study has achieved its main objective which is, to formulate a model for Agikuyu Christian funeral rites that would integrate relevant cultural, scriptural and practical norms."

By achieving the above, it is hoped the study will be of great benefit to the Agikuyu Christians of Kikuyu District and to all the Agikuyu Christians, and indeed to all Christians in Africa and the rest of the world. It is hoped that it will also be of benefit to theologians, scholars, researchers, seminaries, universities, theological colleges, schools, pastors, the general public and Christians the world over.

It is also hoped that the study will be of help and use to other scholars and theologians, as it fills the gap that has been there regarding how any African tribe can reform its funeral practice.

Areas of Further Research

In the course of this study, I came across a number of intriguing issues that I feel could be of interest to researchers of differing disciplines, such as theologians, anthropologists, historians, among others, or for anyone seeking an area for serious research.

Similarity between the Wa Sukuma of Tanzania and the Agikuyu of Kenya

In Chapter 2 of this study, while analyzing how the Wa Sukuma of Tanzania cope with death, I was impressed by the similarity between how traditionally the Wa Sukuma of Tanzania and the Agikuyu of Kenya coped with death. In particular, and of great interest, is the similarity between the ceremonial sex act(s) carried out by the Wa Sukuma in a ceremony that Brown (1980) feels is a form of sacrifice, and the *"kuhukura"* ceremony performed by the Agikuyu discussed in depth in Chapter 2 of this book. One is left to wonder whether there is not more to this similarity than meets the eye. Would the Wa Sukuma be a distant relative of the Agikuyu left behind during the Bantu migration discussed in Chapter 2 of this study? Additionally considering and bearing in mind that in the Nyeri County of Kenya, there is an area called "Thunguma". Could this be the Kikuyu equivalent of "Sukuma"?

The issue of widows succumbing to tradition

Again with reference to the traditional ceremonial sex act of the Wa Sukuma of Tanzania, which was discussed extensively in Chapter 2 of this study, and indeed to the rites of numerous tribes of the African continent, a mystery that needs to be addressed by theologians, missionaries and the Christian church at large was raised by Brown (1980), which I fully endorse. The weighty issue is for theologians and other men of God to ponder before condemning the African Christian who at times succumbs to African rituals of death. Theologians should, as indicated by Brown (1980), come up with an answer to what a widow is supposed to do when she alone is the only believer (Christian) in her family. How is she going to prevent her brother-in-law from insisting that she fulfill the ritual acts, intended to take away the pollution of death? If she refuses to comply, how will she respond to the family's accusation that her failure was the cause of subsequent deaths? Since the widow's children now belong to the brother-in-law, will she ever see them again if she refuses?

Brown (1980) feels that missionaries and pastors might object to the widow succumbing to "tradition." He states, and I agree with him, that it's all very well for the armchair missionaries to suggest from a distance that the acts and other cultural expressions can and should be used to communicate the gospel. He feels as I do that we have to live with the complexities and the consequences. All the facts must be considered. New options of dealing with such complex religious, cultural and social situations must be courageously addressed by listening carefully to each other in the evaluation and solutions being sought. I fully concur with Brown.

Before the current High God (Ngai or Mwene Nyagah) of the Agikuyu which was their Deity?

Judging from numerous archaic Agikuyu traditional cultural rites, some of which were presented in Chapter 2 of this study, it is apparent that most were sacrifices to a deity or to some deities. Such rites include the "*kuhukura*" performed during funerals and the "*Gutinia Kiande*" (cutting the shoulder joint of a sheep) symbolising the last stage of paying for the bridewealth, after which the wife can never be claimed by her relatives, as she is now completely "bought" (married). The latter is even practiced these days by the contemporary Agikuyu Christians and others who might be aethists, traditionalists or belonging to other faiths. A study or studies should be undertaken to establish the nature of these sacrifices and who the deity or deities was or were to whom the Agikuyu were sacrificing.

Jointly with the above, or as a separate study, research should be undertaken to find out the period in which the Agikuyu made contact with the Maasai, and additionally, to establish which of the two tribes borrowed from the other the concept of naming their High God *Ngai* (Kikuyu) and *Enkai* (Maasai). Who did the Agikuyu regard as High God before they embraced *Ngai*, and who did the Maasai worship as their High God before embracing *Enkai*?

Also, the research should compare and contrast whether the traditional manner of worshipping *Enkai* and sacrificing to Him by the Maasai has any similarity to how the Agikuyu traditionally worshipped and sacrificed to their High God (*Ngai*).

Resurgence of diseases from entombed corpses.

The medical profession as well as other relevant and interested professions should as a matter of urgency embark on research (es) towards establishing whether diseases that were in the body at the time of burial are likely to resurge many years or centuries after burial should the body be exhumed by man or nature. Additionally to establish whether such harmful organisms from the corpse could find their way back to harm those living on earth including human, animals, fish and plants or find their way and pollute our water and even the air we breath. Should the findings prove positive then this will be a very strong tool of convincing all and sundry the necessity of cremation as opposed to being accorded an earth burial.

How This Study Contributes to the Field of Practical Theology

The findings and recommendations in this book have clear implications for both Agikuyu and other African Christians the world over, the Church, theologians and other scholars in the area of Practical Theology.

Should this study be implemented in part or in whole, it will have great impact on how the Agikuyu and other Christian communities in Africa as well as those in the rest of the world, view the manner in which they should cope with death. It is hoped that the various changes they might adopt will lead to their coping with death in a faster, simpler, less expensive and more dignified manner that would be environmentally friendly, would be decent enough for the dead, would take care of those left behind and will glorify Jesus Christ our LORD and Saviour.

APPENDIX I

Saturday Nation—National News: October 10, 2009, Page 9

Villagers Force Family to Bury Man in Coffin

By SATURDAY NATION Correspondent

A FAMILY'S BID TO bury an octogenarian in a low cost ceremony was thwarted after villagers demanded that the deceased be accorded a "decent burial."

Police were called into the home of Dedan Gichuki at Ichagiru village in Tetu District to stop the burial after a dispute arose between family members and village elders.

One of the sons, identified only as Kiragu, said the family chose to conduct a humble burial to cut costs. He said the family had met all conditions after acquiring a burial permit and wondered why the neighbors were blocking the burial.

"Conducting what these people consider a proper burial is quite costly. As we are struggling to raise the funds, they will have attended the burial and returned to their homes without giving a penny (a cent, a dime etc)" the son said.

Raise the Funds

Following the dispute, the family was compelled to hire a vehicle and transport the body to the mortuary and invite outsiders to the burial.

Initially, three sons of the deceased had arranged a private burial for their father who had died of diabetes complications in his house.

They decided to cut the costs and bury the 88-year-old man without a coffin.

However, neighbors objected to their plans and reported the matter to the police. A neighbor who requested not be named said villagers were incensed when they discovered the family's intentions to bury the elderly man in a sack instead of a decent coffin.

They were also angered by the sons' decision to keep their six sisters and other relatives in the dark about the old man's death and the planned burial.

In the end, the family members agreed to conduct a proper ceremony.

One of the sons who spoke to the Nation but declined to give his names said the family would have gone ahead with the burial but feared reprisals from their neighbors.

APPENDIX II

Respondents Interviewed Regarding the Kikuyu Culture, Tradition, Religion and Traditional Funeral Rites

ELDERS

THE FOLLOWING IS A list of those elders whom I interviewed to confirm literature on Agikuyu traditional religion, culture and their traditional methods of coping with death. All the elders interviewed gave information that in every respect resembles what was written by Kenyatta 1938, M.N Kabetu 1947, L.S.K Leakey 1977 among other authors and scholars on the Agikuyu culture and tradition. The elders interviewed included both men and women. All of them were over 75 years old. They confirmed that during their youth they witnessed the information they gave. Six of those interviewed and the rest were either grandchildren of the elders interviewed by L.S.K Leakey 1977 and separately by M.N Kabetu 1947 (referred to in their books) or grandchildren of their neighbors or age-mates. I personally interviewed them orally in Kikuyu Language (all of them were either illiterate or semi-illiterate). While most had very poor eyesight, they had excellent memory. The oral interviews took place at their homes, individually, not as a group during the months of October and November 2011 on the dates indicated below.

NO	DATE	NAMES AND AFFILIATED CHURCH	AGE	RESIDENCE	REMARKS
1	10.10.2011	James Mbugua Wangige Gachuhi (ACK Ndunyu)	101	Wangige	Extremely well informed elder on the Agikuyu culture and traditions
2	11.10.2011	James Mungai Wainaina (ACK Ndunyu)	92	Muthumu	–ditto–
3	13.10.2011	Josephine Njeri Mwangi (ACK Cura)	90	Gakinduri-Cura	–ditto–

NO	DATE	NAMES AND AFFILIATED CHURCH	AGE	RESIDENCE	REMARKS
4	15.10.2011	Grace Wamucii Ngaruiya (ACK Cura)	100	Gakinduri-Cura	–ditto–
5	17.10.2011	Edmund Nyamu wa Ndugu-ini (ACK Cura)	99	Gakinduri-Cura	–ditto–
6	19.10.2011	Margaret Wambui Kimani PCEA Kahuho	89	Kahuho	Narrated in a clear and detailed manner on the Agikuyu culture and traditional religion and traditional funeral rites
7	21.10.2011	Eliud Wambu Ndugu-ini PCEA Kahuho	98	Gakinduri Village Cura	Narrated in a very clear and detailed manner on the Agikuyu culture, traditional religion and traditional funeral rites
8	24.10.2011	David Nganga Thairu Roman Catholic Church Karura	80	Karura Ka Nyungu	–ditto–
9	26.10.2011	Stephen Kinyua Muiru ACK Mukui	82	Karura ka Nyungu	–ditto–
10	28.10 2011	Tabitha Mumbi Chege PCEA Ringuti	78	Kamangu	–ditto–
11	28.10.2011	Chege Njoroge Mathanu PCEA Ringuti	86	Kamangu	– ditto –
12	31.10.2011	Peter Kimani Kanyuke Kikuyu Traditional Religion	84	Kamangu	–ditto–
13	1.11.2011	Njoroge Kamau Mwithiga Orthodox Church Kamangu	94	Kamangu	–ditto–
14	3.11.2011	Benson Githuku Nganga PCEA Ringuti	91	Kamangu	–ditto–
15	5.11.2011	Edith Nyambura Mutune (Mrs) ACK Kanyariri	83	Kanyariri	–ditto–

APPENDIX II

NO	DATE	NAMES AND AFFILIATED CHURCH	AGE	RESIDENCE	REMARKS
16	7.11.2011	Henry Kariuki Muite ACK Kanyariri	84	Kanyariri	–ditto–
17	9.11 2011	Grace Watiri Gatimu wa Kamanu Orthodox Church Kanjeru	102	Gitaru	–ditto–
18	11.11.2011	Samuel Kimani Gitau ACK Ngure	76	Gitaru	–ditto–
19	15.11.2011	Kamangu Kaberi ACK Ngure	81	Gitaru	–ditto–
20	18.11.2011	Samuel Kibue Ndegwa ACK St Paul's Kabete	89	Wabuga Lower Kabete	–ditto–
21	22.11.2011	Gideon Mungai Gachathi ACK St Paul's Kabete	90	Kanyongo Lower Kabete	–ditto–
22	25.11.2011	Antony Ngugi wa Gitungo ACK Kibichiku	81	Kibichiku	–ditto–

WORKS CITED

ACK 1994. *Supplementary Prayerbook: ACK Diocese of Mount Kenya South.* Self Published: Kijabe Printing.

———. 2001. *A Century of God's Household in the ACK Diocese of Mount Kenya South: 1900-2000.* Self Published.

Adams B N and E Mburugu 1994. 'Kikuyu Bridewealth and Polygyny Today.' *Journal of Comparative Family Studies*, 25(2), 159-166. Retrieved from EBSCO host.

Anderson W B 1977. *The Church in East Africa: 1840-1974.* Tanzania: Central Tanganyika.

Austin B R 1983. *Austin's Topical History of Christianity.* Wheaton, Illinois: Tyndale.

Augustine Retractationes (CSEL 36, P. Knöll), P Knöll, Vienna, 1902.

Badham P 1976. *Christian Beliefs about Life after Death.* New York: Harper and Row.

Bailey K E 1993. Burial Customs. In B M Metzger & M D Coogan (eds.), *The Oxford Companion to the Bible.* New York & London: Oxford University Press.

Baillie J et al. 1970. *Early Christian Fathers.* New York: MacMillan.

Barabas S 1982. Abraham. In M C Tenney and S Barabas (eds), *The Zondervan Pictorial Encyclopedia of the Bible.* Grand Rapids, Michigan: Zondervan.

Barr J 1979. *The Concept of Biblical Theology. An Old Testament Perspective.* Minneapolis: Fortress.

———. 1999. Biblical Theology. In E Fahlbusch et al. (eds), *The Encyclopedia of Christianity. Vol. 1.* Grand Rapids, Michigan,: William B. Eerdmans.

———. 2004. Biblical Theology. In B C Ollenburger (ed.), *Old Testament Theology: Flowering and Future.* Winnona Lake, Indiana: Fisenbrauns.

Barra G 1939. *1000 Kikuyu Proverbs.* Nairobi: East African Literature Bureau.

Beckwith R T 2000. The Canon of Scripture. In T D Alexander (ed.), *New Dictionary Of Biblical Theology.* Downer's Grove, Illinois: Inter-Varsity.

Beidelman T O 1982. *Colonial Evangelism.* Bloomington: Indiana University Press.

Bender A P 1894. Beliefs, Customs of the Jews Connected with Death, Burial and Mourning. The Jewish Quarterly Review, Vol. 6, No. 2 (Jan., 1894) pp. 317-347. University of Pennsylvania Press. Accessed 13-09-2011, http://jstor.org/stable/1450143.

Bercot D W (ed) 1998. *A Dictionary of Early Christian Beliefs.* Peabody, Massachusetts: Hendrickson.

Berkhof L 1981. *Systematic Theology.* Grand Rapids, Michigan: Wm B Eerdman's.

Bewes F F C 1953. *The Work of the Christian Church among the Kikuyu.* London: Royal Institute of International Affairs.

Blakely T D, Walter E A and Thomson D L (eds) 1994. *Religion in Africa: Experience and Expression.* London: Heinemann.

Bloch-Smith E 1992. Burials, Israelite. In D N Freedman (ed.), *The Anchor Bible Dictionary Vol. 1.* New York. Double Day.

———. *Judahite Burial Practices and Beliefs About the Dead*. Journal for the Study of Old Testament Supplement series 123. Sheffield Academic. JSOT/ASOR Monograph Series 7.

Blum E A 1983. Exposition of St. John's gospel – The great sigh at Bethany (Jn 11;1-44). In J F Walvoord & R B Zuck (eds.), *The Bible Knowledge Commentary – New Testament Edition*. Colorado Springs: Chariot Victor.

Blundell M 1994. *A Love Affair with the Sun*. Nairobi: Kenway.

Boadt L. 1996. Suicide. In C Stuhlmueller (ed.), *The Collegeville Pastoral Dictionary of Biblical Theology*. Collegeville, Minnesota:Liturgical.

Boer H R 1976. *A Short History of the Early Church*. Grand Rapids, Michigan: William B. Eerdmans.

Boettner L 2000.The Intermediate State. In E F Harrison (ed.), *Baker's Dictionary of Theology*. Grand Rapids: Baker Books.

Bottignole S 1984. *Kikuyu Traditional Culture and Christianity*. Nairobi: Heinemann Educational Books.

Boyd J O 1939. Abraham. In J Orr (ed.), *The International Standard Bible Encyclopaedia*. Vol. 1. Grand Rapids, Michigan: W M B Eerdmans.

Bozman E F (ed) 1958. *Everyman's Encyclopaedia*. Fourth Edition. Vol.7. London: J M Dent & Sons Ltd.

Brigham F 1979. Burial – Ancient Christians. In P K Meagher et al. (eds), *Encyclopedic Dictionary of Religion*. Washington DC: Corpus.

Bromiley G W 1960. Biblical Theology. In E F Harrison (ed.), *Baker's Dictionary of Theology*. Grand Rapids, Michigan: Baker Book House.

Brown P 1981. *The Cult of the Saints - Its Rise and Function in Latin Christianity*. Chicago: University of Chicago Press.

Brown D 1980. *Unpublished Tanzania Field Notes*. Africa Inland Mission. http://www.ifm-org/PDFs/2-3%Brown%20funeral%fixed2-pdf, accessed 3-11-2011.

Brown W A 1983. 'Concepts of God in Africa.' *Journal of Religious Thought*, 39(2), 5-16. Retrieved from EBSCO host.

Browning W R F 2009. *Oxford Dictionary of the Bible*. Oxford: Oxford University Press.

Buddhist Funerals 2014. *Commemorating Death in Staffordshire*. Located at http://www.staffspasttrack.org.uk/exhibit/ilm/Mourning%20and%20Remembrance/Types%20of%20funerals/Buddhist%20Funerals.htm, 16-06-2014.

Burdick D W and J Rea 1975. Burial. In C F Pfeiffer et al. (eds.), *Wycliffe Bible Encyclopedia*. Vol. 1. Chicago: Moody.

Byron M 2006. Burial. In K D Sakenfeld (ed.), *The New Interpreter's Dictionary of the Bible*. Vol. 1. Nashville: Abingdon.

Byrum R R 1982. *Christian Theology - A Systematic Statement of Christian Doctrine for the use of Theological students*. Anderson, Indiana: Warner.

Cagnolo C Fr. 2006. *The Agikuyu: Their Customs, Traditions and Folklore*. 2nd Edition by Fr. H. Wambugu. Torino, Italy: Instituto Missioni Consolata.

Caspari W 1911. Burial. In S M Jackson (ed.) *The New Schaff-Herzog Encyclopedia of Religious Knowledge, Vol IX*. New York: Funk & Wagnalls Company.

Childers J W 1997. Funeral Practices. In E Ferguson (ed.), *Encyclopedia of Early Christianity*, 2nd edition. New York: Garland.

Childs B S 1986. *Old Testament Theology in a Canonical Context*. Philadelphia: Fortress.

———. 2004. Biblical Theology. In B C Ollenburger (ed.), *Old Testament Theology: Flowering and future*. Winnona Lake, Indiana: Fisenbrauns.

Cole R D 2000. BURIAL. In D N Freedman (ed.), *Eerdmans Dictionary of the Bible*. Grand Rapids, Michigan: Wm.B. Eerdmans.

Collins R O (ed) 1970. *Problems in the History of Colonial Africa: 1860-1960*. Engelwood Cliffs: Prentice-Hall.

Coogan M D 1993. Hebron. In B C Metzger and M D Coogan (eds.), *The Oxford Companion to the Bible*. Oxford: Oxford University Press.

Cowan M A 2000. *The LIM Model for Theological Research: Guidelines for Doing Research in Practical Theology*. Located at http://www.satsonline.org. Accessed 2011-08-23.

———. Introduction to Practical Theology, accessed 21 January 2012, http://www.loyno.edu~mcowan/PracticalTheology.html.

Cremation or Burial? Topical Sermons. Accessed from, http://executableoutlines.com/top/cremate.htm, 30-12-2012.

Cremation or Burial? A Biblical Perspective/Timothy J Hammons. Accessed from http://timothyjhammons.com/2011/07/14/cremation-or-burial-a-biblical-perspective/, 30-12-2012.

Cross F L (ed) 1988. *The Oxford Dictionary of the Christian Church*. London: Oxford University Press.

Cruden A 1949. *Cruden's Complete Concordance to the Old and New Testaments*. Grand Rapids, Michigan: Zondervan.

Daily Nation Newspaper 2009. Nairobi: Kenya. 10th October, 2009 (page 9).

———. 2010. Nairobi: Kenya. Pages 2-3 [DN2]. 11-10-2010. Article by Cecil, Morella-Agence, France-Presse.

Daniels A 2005. *Mau Mau Revisited*. New Criterion, 23 (10), 21-26. EBSCO host.

Davidson B 1964. *The African Past: Chronicles from Antiquity to Modern Times*. London: Penguin African Library.

Davies J 1999. *Death, Burial and Rebirth in the Religions of Antiquity*. London: Routledge.

Davis J J 1985. Burial. In P J Achtemeir (ed.), *Harper's Bible Dictionary*. San Francisco: Harper & Row.

Dayton W T 1983. Death of Christ. In R S Taylor (ed), *Beacon Dictionary of Theology*. Kansas City, Missouri: Beacon Hill.

Decker R J 2006. *Is it Better to Bury or to Burn? A Biblical Perspective on Cremation and Christianity in Western Culture* – The William Rice Lectures, Detroit Baptist Theological Seminary, March 15, 2006. Accessed from http://www.dbts.edu/pdf/rls/Decker-Cremation.pdf, 22-03-2013.

———. 2007. *Is it Better to Bury or to Burn? A Biblical Perspective on Cremation and Christianity in Western Culture. Part 1*. The Journal Of Ministry of Theology. Spring 2007, 24-48. Accessed from http://www.dbts.edu/pdf/rls/Decker-cremation.pdf, 22-03-2013.

———. 2007. *Is it Better to Bury or to Burn? A Biblical Perspective on Cremation and Christianity in Western Culture*. Post Lecture Corrections and Revisions. Accessed from http://www.dbts.edu/pdf/rls/Decker-cremation.pdf, 22-03-2013.

———. 2007. *A Christian View of Death, Dying and Funerals*. Baptist Bible Seminary. Faculty Forum. March 12, 2007. Accessed from http://Intresources.com/blog/documents/DeathDyingFuneralsWeb.pdf,22-03-2013.

———. 2007. *If you meet the Undertaker Before you meet the 'Uppertaker'. A Christian View of Death, Dying and Funerals*. Baptist Bible Seminary. Faculty

Forum. March 12, 2007. Located at http://ntresources.com /blog/documents/ DeathDyingFuneralWeb.pdf. Accessed 22-3-2013.

Deroche 1989. 'Delphes: La Christianisation d'un Sanctuaire Paien', in ACTES of the 11th International Congress of Christian Archaeology, 1986. Rome; Pontifical Institute of Christian Archaeology. Pp 2713-26.

Dickson A K 1984. *Theology in Africa*. London: Longman and Todd.

Dirksen A H 1959. *Elementary Patrology: The Writings of the Fathers of the Church*. London: Herder & Herder.

Donohue J 2001. Funeral-Early Church & Middle Ages. In E Fahlbusch et al (eds.), *The Encyclopedia of Christianity, Vol. 2*. Grand Rapids, Michigan: William B. Eerdmans.

Droge A J 1992. Suicide. In D N Freedman (ed.), *The Anchor Bible Dictionary, Vol. 6*. New York: Doubleday.

Droz Y 2011. Transformation of Death Among the Kikuyu of Kenya: From Hyenas to Tombs. In M Jindra & J Noret (eds.) *Funerals in Africa: Explorations of a Social Phenomenon*. New York: Berghahn.

Dyer C H 1985. Ezekiel. The Nation Restored (Chapter 37). In J F Walvoord & R B Zuck (eds.), *The Bible Knowledge Commentary – An exposition of the Scriptures*. Colorado Springs, Colorado: Chariot Victor.

Eager Geo B 1939. Burial. In J Orr (ed.), *The International Standard Bible Encyclopedia Vol. 1*. Grand Rapids, Michigan: Wm. B. Eerdmans.

Eiselen F C et al 1929. *The Abingdon-Cokesbury Bible Commentary*. Nashville: New York: Abingdon.

Ellison J W 1972. *Nelson Complete Concordance of the Revised Standard Version Bible*. Second Edition. Nashville: Thomas Nelson.

Encyclopedia of Death and Dying. Immortality- rituals, world, burial, body, life, history, beliefs, time, person, human, T.... Accessed http://www.deathreference.com/Ho - Ka/ Immortality.html, 26-9-2011.

Encyclopedia of Death and Dying. Christian Death Rites, History of – rituals world, burial, body, funeral, life, time, pers....... Accessed http://www.deathreference.com / Ce – Da/ Christian.- Death – Rites – History- of.html. 7-8-2012.

Erickson M J 1989. *Concise Dictionary of Christian Theology*. Grand Rapids, Michigan: Baker.

Erickson M J 2005. *Christian Theology*. Grand Rapids, Michigan: Baker.

Evans – Pritchard E E 1965. *Theories of Primitive Religion*. Oxford: Clarendon.

Fay R 1999. Kenya, Kenyatta, Kikuyu, etc. In K A Appiah & H L Gates, Jr., (eds.), *Africana: The Encylopaedia of the African and African-American*. New York: Basic Civitas.

Ferguson E 1997. Preface. In E Ferguson (ed), *Encyclopedia of Early Christianity. (2nd Edition)*. New York: Garland.

Ferrua A 1991. *The Unknown Catacomb: A Unique Discovery of Early Christian Art*. trans. I Inglis. New Lamark: Geddes & Grosset.

Fontaine 1989. 'Discussion' in ACTES of the 11th International Congress of Christian Archeology 1986. Rome: Pontifical Institute of Christian Archeology; Pp. 1, 152-213.

Freedman D N 1982. Deuteronomic History. In K Crim (ed.), *The Interpreter's Dictionary of the Bible: Supplementary Volume*. Nashville: Abingdon.

Frost R 1978. *Race against Time: Human Relations and Politics in Kenya Before Independence*. London: Transafrica.

Funeral Consumers Alliance 2007. *Don't Get Buried in Debt*. Accessed from http://www.funerals.org/frequently-asked-questions/62-benefitsmembership, 26-11-2007.

Furedi F 1990. *The Mau Mau War In Perspective*. Nairobi: Heinemann.

Gamble H Y 1997. Apologetics. In E Ferguson (ed.), *Encyclopedia of Early Christianity*, 2nd edition. Vol. 1. New York: Garland.

Ganusah R Y 2001. *Pouring Libation to Spirit Powers – The Ewe-Dome*. In G O West & M W Dube (eds.), *The Bible in Africa*. Boston, Leiden: Brill Academic.

Gathigira S K 1933. *Miikarire ya Agiikuyu*. Karatina Nyeri: Scholars Publication.

Gathogo J 2008. 'Missionaries and Colonial Authorities in Kenya: A Review of the Suppression of African Religious Discourses, 1887-1963.' *Swedish Missiological Themes*, 96(1).

Gatu G J 2006. *Joyfully Christian, Truly African*. Nairobi: Acton.

Gehman J R 1989. *African Traditional Religion in Biblical Perspective*. Nairobi: East African Educational.

Gehman H S (ed) 1970. *The New Westminister Dictionary of the Bible*. Philadelphia: Westminster.

Githiga G J 1981. Doctor of Ministry Thesis 1981; *Irua and a Christian Theology of Pastoral Care*. Submitted to the Faculty of the School of Theology of the University of the South: Tennessee.

González J L 1984. *The Story of Christianity; Vol 1. The Early Church to the Dawn of the Reformation*. San Francisco: HarperSanFrancisco.

Granville R (ed) 1954. *The Mau Mau in Kenya*. London: Hutchinson.

Grelot P 1977. Fatherland. In Xavier Léon-Dufour (ed.), Translated by R C O'Connor. *Dictionary of Biblical Theology (2nd edition, revised and enlarged)*. New York: A Cross Road Book –Seabury.

Habenstein R W and Lamers W M 1963. *Funeral Customs the World Over*. Milwaukee, U.S.A: Bulfin.

Hachlili R 1992. Burials Ancient Jewish. In D N Freedman (ed.), *The Anchor Bible Dictionary, Vol 1*. New York: Doubleday.

Hallett R 1974. *Africa Since 1875*. London: Heinemann.

Hammond D 1974. *A History of the Kikuyu 1500-1900* (Book). Ethnohistory, 21(2), 176-178. Retrieved from EBSCOhost.

Hammons T J 2011. *Cremation or Burial: A Biblical Perspective*. Accessed from http:timothyjhammons.com, 30-12-2012.

Harran M J 1989. Suicide. In L E Sullivan (ed.), *Death, After life, and the Soul*. New York: Macmillan.

Harris M J 1988. Resurection, General. In S B Ferguson & D F Wright (eds.), *New Dictionary of Theology*. Downers Grove, Illinois: Intervasity.

Hartdegen O F M 1977. *Nelson's Complete Concordance of the New American Bible*. Collegeville, Minnesota: Liturgical.

Hindu Funerals 2014. *Commemorating Death in Staffordshire*. Located at http://www.staffspasttrack.org.uk/exhibit/ilm/Mourning%20and%20Remembrance/Types%20of%20funerals/Hindu%20Funerals.htm, 16-06-2014.

Hirsch F E 1939. Brother's wife. In J Orr (ed.), *The International Standard Bible Encyclopedia*, 1-526. Grand Rapids: Wm B Eerdmans.

Hobley C W 1967. *Bantu Beliefs and Magic*. New York: Barmes and Noble.
Holmes C F 1976. 'A History of the Kikuyu, 1500-1900'. *American Historical Review*, 81(4), 926. Retrieved from EBSCOhost.
Hornby A S 1992. *Oxford Advanced Learner's Dictionary*. Oxford: Oxford University Press.
House P R 1998. *Old Testament Theology*. Illinois: Downers Group.
Humanist Funerals 2014. *Commemorating Death in Staffordshire*. Located at http://www.staffspasttrack.org.uk/exhibit/ilm/Mourning%20and%20Remembrance/Types%20of%20funerals/Humanist%20Funerals.htm, 16-06-2014.
Hunter R J (ed) 1990. *Dictionary of Pastoral Care and Counseling*. Nashville: Abingdon.
Idowu E B 1973. *African Traditional Religion: A Definition*. London: SCM.
Irion P E 1968. *Cremation*. Philadelphia: Fortress.
Isichei E 1995. *A History of Chrisianity in Africa: from Antiquity to the Present*. London: Society for Promoting Christian Knowledge.
Islamic (Muslim) Funerals 2014. *Commemorating Death in Staffordshire*. Located at http://www.staffspasttrack.org.uk/exhibit/ilm/Mourning%20and%20Remembrance/Types%20of%20funerals/Islamic%20Funerals.htm, 16-06-2014.
Itote W 1967. *'Mau Mau' General*. Nairobi: East African.
Jewish Funerals 2014. *Commemorating Death in Staffordshire*. Located at http://www.staffspasttrack.org.uk/exhibit/ilm/Mourning%20and%20Remembrance/Types%20of%20funerals/Jewish%20Funerals.htm, 16-06-2014.
Johnston P S 2000. Death and resurrection. In T D Alexander & B R Rosner (eds.) *New Dictionary of Biblical Theology*.Downers Grove, Illinois: Inter-Varsity.
Jones D W 2010.*To Bury or Burn? Towards an Ethic of Cremation*. JETS 53/2 (June 2010) 335-47.
Kabetu M N 1947. *Kirira gia Ugikuyu*. Nairobi: Kenya Literature Bureau.
Kamau A K 2009. MDiv Thesis - *A Study of Kisii Burial Rites-Kisii Central District. Nairobi, Kenya*. Nairobi *Evangelical Graduate School of Theology (NEGST)*.
Kamuyu-wa-Kangethe 1988. 'African Response to Christianity: A Case Study of the Agikuyu of Central Kenya'; *Missiology*, 16(1, 23-44), Retrieved from EBSCOhost.
Kanogo T 1987. *Squatters and the Roots of Mau Mau*. Nairobi: East African Educational.
Karanja J K 1999. *Founding an African Faith*: Kikuyu Anglican Christianity 1900-1945. Nairobi: Uzima.
Kariuki O 1985. *A Bishop Facing Mount Kenya*. Nairobi: Uzima.
Kenyatta J 1938. *Facing Mount Kenya*. Nairobi: Heinemann.
———. 1968.*Suffering Without Bitterness: The Founding of the Kenya Nation*. Nairobi: East African.
Kershaw G 1997. *Mau Mau from Below*. Nairobi: East African Educational.
Kibicho S G 1972. *The Kikuyu Conception of God, Its Continuity into the Christian era and the Questions it Raises for the Christian idea of Revelation*. PhD Dissertation. Graduate School of Vanderbilt University, Nashville, Tennessee.
Killen R A 1970. Resurrection of the Body. In C F Pfeiffer et al. (eds.), *Wycliffe Bible Encyclopedia*. Vol. 2. K-Z. Chicago: Moody.
——— 1975. Levirate Marriage. In CF Pfeiffer (ed.), *Wycliffe Bible Encyclopedia*. Chicago: Moody.
Kimani V N 2004. 'Human Sexuality: Meaning and Purpose in Selected Communities in Contemporary Kenya.' *Ecumenical Review*, 56(4), 404-421. Retrieved from EBSCOhost.

King N Q 1970. *Religions of Africa: A Pilgrimage into Traditional Religions*. New York: Harper & Row.

Kingoina N and Nyangara N K 1999. *The making of man and woman under Gusii customary Law*. Kisii, Kenya: Dal-rich.

Kirwen M C (ed) 2008, *African Cultural Domains*, Book 1, *Life Cycle of an Individual*. Nairobi-Kenya: MIAS Books.

Kitchen K A 1962. Burial and Mourning in the Old Testament. In J D Douglas (ed.), *The New Bible Dictionary*. Leicester, England: Inter-Varsity.

Klassen W 1992. War in the New Testament. In D N Freedman (ed.), *The Anchor Bible Dictionary*. Vol 6. New York: Double Day.

Klausner J 1925. *Jesus of Nazareth, His Life, Times and Teaching*. New York: Macmillan.

Kohlenberger III J R 1991. *The NRSV Concordance*. Unabridged. Grand Rapids. Michigan: Zondervan.

———. 2000. *The Analytical Concordance to the New Revised Standard Version of the New Testament*. Grand Rapids: Oxford University Press.

Kunhiyop S W 2008. *African Christian Ethics*. Nairobi: Word Alive.

Kwame A 1994. 'The Economic Implications of Transformations in Akan Funeral Rites'. *The Journal of the International African Institute*, Vol. 64, No.3 (1994). Pp. 307-322. Cambridge University Press. Retrieved from JSTOR.

Lake K 1907. *The Historical Evidence for the Resurrection of Jesus Christ*. New York: G P Putnam's Sons.

Langley M and Kiggins T 1974. *A Serving People*. Nairobi: Oxford University Press.

Leakey L S B 1977. *The Southern Kikuyu Before 1903: Vols 1, 2 & 3*. London: Academic.

Lewis G R & Demarest B A 1996. *Integrative Theology*. Grand Rapids. Michigan: Zondervan.

Londsdale J 1999. 'Kikuyu Christianities'. *Journal of Religion in Africa*, 29(2), 206.

Long T G 2009. *Accompany Them with Singing – The Christian Funeral*. Louisville, Kentucky: Westminster John Knox.

Louis – Vincent T 1989. Funeral Rites. In L E Sullivan (ed.), Translated from French by Kristine Anderson. *Death, After life, and the soul*. New York: Macmillan.

M'Clintock J and J Strong (eds.) 1894. *Cyclopaedia of Biblical, Theological and Ecclesiastical Literature*. New York: Harper & Brothers.

MacCulloch D 2009. *A History of Christianity, the first Three Thousand Years*. London: Penguin Books.

Macpherson R 1970. *The Presbyterian Church in Kenya*. Nairobi: PCEA.

Maloba W O 1994. *Mau Mau and Kenya: An Analysis of a Peasant Revolt*. Nairobi: East African Educational.

Mare W H 1982. Burial. In M C Tenney (ed.), *The Zondervan Pictorial Encyclopedia of the Bible; Vol 1*. Grand Rapids, Michigan : Zondervan.

Mazrui A and Michael T 1984. *Nationalism and New States in Africa*. Nairobi: Heinemann.

Mazrui Ali A (ed) 1999. *General History of Africa: VIII - Africa Since 1935*. Paris: United Nations Educational, Scientific and Cultural Organization.

Mbiti J S 1969. *African Religion and Philosophy*. Nairobi: Heinemann.

Mbugua J N 2011. MTh Thesis – *Agikuyu Christian Martyrs: An Exploratory Study of the Faith of Selected Agikuyu Christian Martyrs During the Mau Mau Period in Kenya (1952-1960)*. Nairobi, Kenya: South African Theological Seminary (SATS).

McCane B R 1990. 'Let the Dead Bury Their own Dead'. Secondary Burial and Matt 8:21-22. *The Harvard Theological Review*, Vol 83 No. 1 (Jan 1990) pp 31-43. Cambridge University Press on behalf of the Harvard Divinity School. JSTOR.

Merriam- Webster's Collegiate Dictionary, located at http://www.merriam-webster.com

Metzger B M & M D Coogan 1993. *The Oxford Companion to The Bible*. New York & Oxford: Oxford University Press.

Meyers E M & J F Strange 1981. *Archeology, The Rabbis & Early Christianity*. Nashville. Abingdon.

Middleton J 1953. *Part V, East Central Africa: The Central Tribes of the North-Eastern Bantu*. London: International African Institute.

Miles M R 1990. Monica. In E Ferguson (ed.), *Encyclopedia of Early Christianity*. New York: Garland.

Millar J 1993. *The Roman Near East - 31 B.C to 337 A.D*. Cambridge: M.A. Harvard University Press.

Miller M S & Miller J L 1961.*Harpers Bible Dictionary*. New York: Harper & Brothers.

Milligan G 1926. Burial. In J Hastings (ed.), *Dictionary of the Apostolic Church: Vol II*. Edinburgh : T & T Clark.

Mitchiner J H 2011. *Cremation vs Burial – A Christian Perspective*. Accessed from je.mitchener@mitchinerlaw.com

Mitford J 1963. *The American Way of Death*. New York: Simon and Schuster.

———. 1978. *The American Way of Death Revisited*. New York: Albert A Knopf/Random House. Reprint, New York: Vintage Books/Random House, 1998.

Morella C 2010. 'Where the Poor Live with the Dead'. *Daily Nation*, Nairobi, DN 2 Magazine, 2-3 dated October 11, 2010.

Morris L L 1962. Resurrection. In J D Douglas (ed.), *The New Bible Dictionary*. Leicester, England: Inter-Varsity.

Muchiri K 2009 (13 Dec). 'Kenya: Villagers Want Mau Mau Veterans to Apologise for Brutal Killings'. http://allafrica.com/stories/200912140698.html accessed on 27th February, 2010.

Muchiri, M N 2004.*Saved Through Fire*. Ontario: Guardian.

Mugo E 1975. *Africa Response to Western Religion*. Nairobi: East Africa Literature Bureau.

Muller R A 1988. Resurrection. In G W Bromiley (ed.), *The International Standard Bible Encyclopedia*. Volume Four O-Z. Grand Rapids, Michigan: Wm. B. Eerdmans.

Muriuki G 1974. *History of the Kikuyu 1500-1900*. Nairobi: Oxford University Press.

———. 1976. The Kikuyu in the Pre-Colonial Period. In B A Ogot (ed), *Kenya Before 1900*. Nairobi: East African Publishing House.

Needham N R 1997. *2000 Years of Christ's Power, Part One*. London: Grace.

Ngugi wa Thiong'o 1964. *Weep Not, Child*. Nairobi: Heinemann.

———. 1976. *The Trial of Dedan Kimathi*. Nairobi: East African Educational.

Nicol T 1898. Burial. In J Hastings (ed.), *A Dictionary of the Bible*; Vol 1. New York: Charles Scribner's Sons.

Norden E 1898. *Die Antike Kunstprosa, Vol II, 516*. Liepzing. Cited in A C Rush (1941:266), *Death and Burial in Christian Antiquity*. Washington: The Catholic University of America Press.

Nowack W & L B Paton 1936. *Burial and Burial Customs*. In M W Jacobus (ed.), Funk and Wagnalls. *A New Standard Bible Dictionary*. New York: Garden City.

O'Collins G and E G Farrugia 2000. *A Concise Dictionary of Theology*, revised and expanded edition. Edinburgh: T & T Clark.
Odak O 1995. *Kemeticism: The World Religion for Black Peoples*. New York: Dr. Jack Felder.
Odhiambo E S and J Lonsdale (eds.) 2003. *Mau Mau and Nationhood*. Nairobi: Oxford University Press. (Revised edition published by Madoa Cultural Services Limited, Nairobi).
Ogot B A (ed) 1972. *Politics and Nationalism in Colonial Kenya*. Nairobi. East African.
―――. 1976. *Kenya Before 1900*. Nairobi: East African Publishing House.
Ogot B A and W R Ochieng (eds) 1995. *Decolonisation and Independence in Kenya*. Nairobi: East African Educational Publishers.
Oliver R and Atmore A 1967. *Africa since 1800*. Cambridge: Cambridge University Press.
Ollenburger B C 2004. *Old Testament Theology: Flowering and Future*. Winnona Lake, Indiana: Eisenbrauns.
Olupona J K 1991. *African Traditional Religions in Contemporary Society*. St Paul, Minnesota: Paragon.
Painter K S 1989. 'Recent Discoveries in Britain in ACTES of the 11th International Congress of Christian Archeology. 1986. *Rome: Pontifical Institute of Christian Archeology*. Pp. 1031-72.
Payne J B 1979. Burial. In G W Bromiley (ed.), *The International Standard Bible Encyclopedia*. Grand Rapids, Michigan: William B. Eerdmans.
Payne D F 1962. Burial and Mourning in the New Testament. In J D Douglas (ed.), *The New Bible Dictionary*. Leicester, England : Inter-Varsity.
Pentecost D 1985. Daniel 12:1-3, Israel delivered. In J F Walvoord & R B Zuck (eds.), *The Bible Commentary – Old Testament*. Colorado Springs, Colorado: Chariot Victor.
Perkins P 1997. Resurrection. In E Ferguson (ed.), *Encyclopedia of Early Christianity 2nd edition*. New York & London: Garland.
Peterson D 2000. *Journal of African History: Vols 2 No. 3*. Cambridge: Cambridge University Press.
Peterson D R 2004. "Be Like Firm Soldiers to Develop the Country": Political Imagination and the Geography of Gikuyuland. *International Journal of African Historical Studies*, 37(1), 71-101. Retrieved from EBSCOhost.
Peterson R A 2001. Burial, Christian. In W A Elwell (ed.), *Evangelical Dictionary of Theology*, 2nd edition. Grand Rapids, Michigan: Baker Academic.
Pfeiffer C F 1978. Genesis. In C F Pfeiffer and E F Harrison (eds.), *The Wycliffe Bible Commentary*. Chicago: Moody.
Polson C J et al. 1953. *The Disposal of the Dead*. New York: Philosophical Library.
Popovic M. *Traditions and Customs from all Over the World – African Death Rites*. Accessed http://traditionscustoms.com/death-rites/African-death-rites, 12-9-2011.
Pretzel P W 1990. Suicide. In R J Hunter (ed.), *Dictionary of Pastoral Care and Counseling*. Nashville: Abingdon.
Purkiser W T 1983. Resurrection of Christ. In R S Taylor (ed.), *Beacon Dictionary of Theology*. Kansas City, Missouri: Beacon.
Quasten J 1950. *Patrology*. Maryland: Newman.
Quirk R 1989. *Longman's Dictionary of Contemporary English*. London: Longman.

Ray B C 2000. *African Religions: Symbol, Ritual and Community*. 2nd Edition. Upper Saddle River, New Jersey: Prentice Hall.

Reed W L 1962. Burial. In G A Buttrick (ed.), *The Interpreter's Dictionary of the Bible*. Nashville: Abingdon.

Reimers E 2011. *Encyclopedia of Death and Dying: Cemeteries and Cemetry Reform*. (http://www.deathreference.com/Bl-Ce/Cemeteries-and-Cemetery-Reform.html).

Rennings H 1968. Preface. In J Wagner (ed.) Translated by T L Westow *Reforming The Rites of Death Liturgy Volume 32*. New York: Paulist.

Root J 2001. Resurrection of Jesus. In M J Anthony (ed.), *Evangelical Dictionary of Christian Education*. Grand Rapids, Michigan: Baker.

Rosberg C G and J Nottingham 1966. *The Myth of "Mau Mau": Nationalism in Kenya*. Nairobi: Transafrica.

Rosner B S 2000. Biblical Theology. In T D Alexander (ed), *New Dictionary of Biblical Theology*. Downer's Grove, Illinois: Inter-Varsity.

Rowell G 1977. *The Liturgy of Christian Burial: An introductory Survey of the Historical Development of Christian Burial Rites*. London: Alcuin Club/SPCK.

Rush A C 1941. *Death and Burial in Christian Antiquity*. A Doctoral Dissertation submitted to the School of Sacred Theology of the Catholic University of America. Washington DC: The Catholic University of America Press.

Rutgers L V 1995. *The Jews in Late Ancient Rome: Evidence of Cultural Interaction in the Roman Diaspora*. Leiden: E.J. Brill.

Rutherford R 1990. *The Death of a Christian - The Order of Christian Funerals*. Collegeville, Minnesota: Liturgical.

Sailhamer J H 1995. *Introduction to Old Testament Theology – a Canonical Approach*. Grand Rapids, Michigan: Zondervan.

Sandgren D P 1976. The Kikuyu, Christianity and the Africa Inland Mission. *A thesis for PhD at the University of Wisconsin – Madison*. Ann Arbor, Michigan: University Microfilms International (UMI) A Bell & Howell Information Company.

Sawyer J 1973. Hebrew Words for the Resurrection of the Dead Vitus Testamentum 23:218-34.

Schilling O 1970. Resurrection. In J B Bauer (ed.), *Bauer Encyclopedia of Biblical Theology*. London: Sheed and Ward.

Schmid J 1975. Resurrection In K Rahner (ed.), Encyclopedia of Theology: The Concise Sacramentum Mundi. New York: A Cross Book, Sea bury.

Schnabel E J 2000. Scripture. In T D Alexander (ed.), *New Dictionary of Biblical Theology*. Downer's Grove, Illinois: Inter-Varsity.

Scott J 2006. Issues Facing Christians Today (4th Ed). Grand Rapids: Zondervan.

Seely D R 2000. Resurrection. In D N Freedom (ed.), *Eerdmans Dictionary of the Bible*. Grand Rapids, Michigan: Wm. B. Eerdmans

Segal A 1997. *The Other Judaisms of Late Antiquity, Brown Judaic Studies*. Atlanta: Scholars.

———. 2009. Resurrection. In K D Sakenfeld (ed.), *The New Interpreters Dictionary of the Bible. Vol 4; Me – R*. Nashville: Abingdon.

Shakespeare W 1995.*Julius Caesar*. In *William Shakespeare – The Complete Works*. London: Leopard Books.

Shaw B D 1996. Seasons of Death: Aspects of Mortality in Imperial Rome. *Journal of Roman Studies* 86:100-38. Retrieved from EBSCOhost.

Shenk D W 1980. *Peace and Reconciliation in Africa*. Nairobi: Uzima.
Shillington K 1995. *History of Africa*. London: Macmillan.
Smick E B 1975. Abraham. In C F Pfeiffer (ed.), *Wycliffe Bible Encyclopedia*. Chicago: Moody.
Smith W and Cheetham S 1875. *A Dictionary of Christian Antiquities. Comprising the History, Institutions and Antiquities of the Christian Church, from the Time of the Apostles to the Age of Charlemagne*. London: John Murray.
Smith W M 1975. Resurrection. In E F Harrison (ed.), *Baker's Dictionary of Theology*. Grand Rapids, Michigan: Baker.
Spence H D M and Exell J S (eds.) 1950. *The Pulpit Commentary Vol. 1 (Genesis & Exodus)*. Grand Rapids, Michigan: Wm. B. Eerdmans.
Stager L E and S R Wolf 1984. *Child Sacrifice at Carthage – Religious Rite or Population Control?* BA Rev 10/1:30-51.
Steck W 2001. Funerals – Modern Times. In E Fahlbusch et al (eds), *The Encyclopaedia of Christianity, Vol 2*. Grand Rapids, Michigan: William B Eerdmans.
Strauss D F 1879. *The Life of Jesus for the People*. London: Williams.
Strong J 2007. *Strong's Exhaustive Concordance of The Bible*. Peabody, Massachusetts: Hendrickson.
Tenney M C 1973. Burial. In C F H Henry (ed.), *Baker's Dictionary of Christian Ethics*. Grand Rapids, Michigan: Baker.
The New Encyclopedia Britannica 1986, Vol 2, Micropaedia. Chicago: Encyclopedia Britannica, Inc.
Thompson W 1921. *The People of Mexico*. New York: Harper & Brothers.
Toynbee J M C 1971. *Death and Burial in the Roman World*. London: Thames & Hudson.
Tsavo Media Canada 2014. *Funeral Arrangement Planning*. Accessed from http://www.funeralplanning101.com/arrangement-planning, 31-05-2014.
Tucker R 2014. Practical Theology. In W R Domeris & K G Smith (eds), *A Student's A-Z of Theology: Evangelical Theology in Outline*. Rivonia, Johannesburg: South African Theological Seminary (SATS).
Turaki Y 2006. *Foundations of African Traditional Religion and Worldview*. Nairobi: Word Alive.
Unger F M (ed) 1988. *New Unger's Bible Dictionary*. Chicago: Moody.
Upshall M (ed) 1990. *The Hutchinson Popular Encyclopaedia*. London: Hutchinson
Vanhoozer K J 2005. *The Drama of Doctrine – A Canonical-Linguistic Approach to Christian Theology*. Louisville, Kentucky: Westminster.
Van der Horst P W 1991. *Ancient Jewish Epitaphs: An Introductory Survey of a Millenium of Jewish Funerary Epigraphy (300 BCE – 700CE)*. Kampen: Kok Pharos.
Van't Spijker G 2005. *The Role of Social Anthropology in the Debate on Funeral Rites in Africa*. Exchange 34 (3): 156-176.
Wakeford W 1890. *Modes of Burial: Which is Right?* LSE Library: JSTOR Archive.
Wanjau G 1988. *Mau Mau Author in Detention*.Trans. Paul Ngigi Njoroge. Nairobi: Heinemann.
Were S G and Wilson D A 1968. *East Africa through a Thousand Years*. Nairobi: Evans Brothers.
Wheaton D H 1975. Burial. In E F Harrison (ed.), *Baker's Dictionary of Theology*. Grand Rapids, Michigan: Baker.
Whitaker R E 1988. *The Eerdmans Analytical Concordance to the Revised Standard Version of The Bible*. Grand Rapids, Michigan: William B. Eerdmans.

White L M 1990. Burial. In E Ferguson (ed.), *Encyclopedia of Early Christianity*. New York: Garland.
———. 1997. Burial. In E Ferguson (ed.). *Encyclopedia of Early Christianity, 2nd Edition*. New York: Garland.
Willmington H L 1987. *Willmington's Guide to the Bible*. Wheaton, Illinois: Tyndale.
Wilson R E 1983. Resurrection of the Body. In R S Taylor (ed.), *Beacon Dictionary of Theology*. Kansas City, Missouri: Beacon.
Wiseman E M 1958. *Kikuyu Martyrs*. London: Highway.
Yarbrough R W 2000. Biblical Theology. In W A Elwell (ed.), *Baker Theological Dictionary of the Bible*. Grand Rapids: Baker.
Yarnold G D 1959. *Risen Indeed*. New York: Oxford University Press.
Young D G 1984(ed). *Young's Compact Bible Dictionary*. Wheaton, Illinois: Tyndale.

www.ingramcontent.com/pod-product-compliance
Lightning Source LLC
Chambersburg PA
CBHW070233230426
43664CB00014B/2290